The Indian Diaspora
Hindus and Sikhs in Australia

The Indian Diaspora
Hindus and Sikhs in Australia

Edited by

Purushottama Bilimoria
Jayant Bhalchandra Bapat
Philip Hughes

PRINTWORLD
Publishers of Indian Traditions

Cataloging in Publication Data — DK

[Courtesy: D.K. Agencies (P) Ltd. <docinfo@dkagencies.com>]

The Indian diaspora : Hindus and Sikhs in Australia /
edited by Purushottama Bilimoria, Jayant Bhalchandra Bapat, Philip Hughes.
pages cm
Includes bibliographical references (pages) and index.
ISBN 13: 9788124608128

1. Hindus — Australia — History. 2. Sikhs — Australia — History. 3. Hindus — Religious life — Australia — History. 4. Sikhs — Religious life — Australia — History. 5. Australia — Emigration and immigration — History. 6. India — Emigration and immigration — History. 7. East Indians — Australia — History. 8. Fiji — Emigration and immigration — History. I. Bilimoria, Purusottama, editor. II. Bapat, Jayant Bhalchandra, 1938-, editor. III. Hughes, Philip, 1959-, editor.

DDC 294.50994 23

ISBN 13: 978-81-246-0812-8
First published in India, 2015

Printed and published by:
D.K. Printworld (P) Ltd.
Regd. office : *'Vedaśrī,'* F-395, Sudarshan Park
(Metro Station: Ramesh Nagar)
New Delhi - 110 015
Phones : (011) 2545 3975, 2546 6019; *Fax* : (011) 2546 5926
E-mail : indology@dkprintworld.com
Web : www.dkprintworld.com

Dedication

GUNGA Singh's grave lies unattended in a far corner of the cemetery at Hamilton in western Victoria. His only neighbour is a Chinese who was probably a labourer at the nearby gold mine. The two lonely graves are well away from the Christian section; no one ever visits, let alone puts an occasional flower on them. Even in death, they cannot escape the humiliation of being treated as unequal. As a Sikh (as with a Hindu also), Gunga Singh's body should have been cremated. This however was out of question in Australia of his time. Cremations were forbidden and the body had to be buried, well away from the neat rows of the denominationally organised Christian graves. It would have been his wish for his ashes after cremation to be sprinkled in a sacred river in India, such as the Ganges, but this was not to be. Gunga Singh's close friend Ali Buc (Bux, a Muslim hawker) lies in another unattended grave 23 kilometers away at Dunkeld cemetery.

We salute Gunga Singh, Ali Buc and hundreds of Indians like them whose graves are strewn all over Australia. They were some of the Indian[1] hawkers who came here in search for a better life. Money they did earn but the price they paid was very high. Their's was a lonely life thousands of miles away from their home. They slept either in the open or in their old carts. Each day, they would travel hundreds of miles, hoping to make a few pounds. They would eat a meagre ration of bread and hot pickles. The monies they saved would all go to ageing parents and families back home.

We dedicate this book first to these Indians, pioneers in their own right. They arrived more than 100 years ago as hawkers, endured incredible

---

1 Any person of brown skin in 19th century India and also in Australia to the early decades of the 20th century was called a 'Hindoo' irrespective of religious identity. This included Sikhs, Pathans, Baluchis and South Asian Muslims.

Gunga Singh's grave, Hamilton Cemetery
(photo: Jayant Bhalchandra Bapat)

Ali Buc's grave, Dunkeld Cemetery
(photo: Jayant Bhalchandra Bapat)

hardships and racial intolerance and, with persistence, some of them made Australia home.

We also dedicate this work to another kind of pioneer: the late Srimati Pramila Datar, the first of an early generation of Indians who stood steadfastly for the rights and concerns of women in the second half of the twentieth century. Srimati Datar was recruited by the Springvale Library to computerise its catalogue, something highly unusual for an Indian woman, even more so because she was herself not trained in the field of Information Technology.[2]

Editors

---

2 Jayant Bhalchandra Bapat, 'Obituary, Pramila (Akka) Datar, Librarian, Feminist and Philanthropist', *The Age*, 30 January 2002. Pramila Datar, known fondly as Akka, and a mother figure in the Indian community, especially among Maharashtrians in Victoria, died of cancer at her home in Springvale. She was 79.

Indian hawker taking refreshment outside a house
(photo: Gabriel Knight. Obtained from the State Library of Victoria)

Contents

The Sikh Community in Australia

General Reflections on the Indian Diaspora in Australia (Comparative Case Studies: Women and Students' Identities)

Indian hawkers and van with customers inspecting their wares
(photo: Gabriel Knight. Obtained from the State Library of Victoria)

Acknowledgement

AT the very outset, acknowledgement is due to the original inhabitants of Australia, the Aboriginal people, who are believed to have inhabited the land for some 30,000–50,000 years before the arrival of the European settlers in 1788. The Aborigines may even have been the original migrants from India.

This ambitious project started over six years ago. A very large number of people have helped us during these years and we are deeply indebted to them. Rashmi Desai, the resident *guru* to many Indian academics, has given us useful suggestions from the very start of the project and continues to do so. We are indebted to Hazel Hughes and Sunanda Bapat for their encouragement and moral support. Marika Vicziany read the first version of the manuscript, as did the anonymous readers for publishers, and gave valuable suggestions for improvement of the volume. We are grateful to Gurdarshan Singh Gill and Nadia Ghafoor for reading the chapters on Sikhs and offering many useful suggestions and updates. We thank Preeti Talwai (of Berkeley, California) and John Harris for the superb drawings they each produced for the chapter on temple architecture. Leesa Davis, Amy Rayner and Navina Bilimoria helped with editing and certain technical needs at various stages of the development of the manuscript to its present state. Special thanks are due to Mrs Terry Nicholson of Mountjup near Dunkeld who helped one of us (JBB) with much information about hawkers in Victoria.

We wish to take this opportunity to express deep gratitude to the contributing authors (besides the editors) for their diligent work on their respective chapters: Carmen Voigt-Graf, Heather Foster, Salim Lakha, Michael Stevenson, Surjeet Dhanji, Manpreet Kaur Singh, Selena Costa-Pinto, Margaret Kumar, the late Ninian Smart, and Richard Forster. Their immense patience with the length of time it has taken to revise and update this volume (until after the 2011 census data was released) is also appreciated.

We thank Kate Brittlebank for her meticulous editing of the entire manuscript and important suggestions.

Blackwell Publishing is to be thanked for permission to reproduce modified articles from *Religion Compass* by P. Bilimoria, and Heather Foster (chapters 1 and 5, respectively); *Journal of Intercultural Studies* for reproducing a revised version of an article originally published by Salim Lakha and Michael Stevenson (Chapter 11) and Libuksha Smart for permission to reproduce an article by Ninian Smart (Appendix A). Some sections of the book were previously published in earlier forms in the CD-ROM *Australia's Religious Communities: A Multimedia Exploration*. We thank the Christian Research Association for permission to use these sections.

Last but not least, we are grateful to Vinay Lal and Balbinder Singh Bhogal for sharing their informative works on the Hindu and Sikh diasporas in the United States. And a hearty *dhanyavaad* also to John Hinnells, Martin Baumann, Gavin Flood, Knut Jacobsen, T.S. Rukmani, Pratap P. Kumar, Ajoy Sahoo, Gopal Darveesh, Arjun Appadurai, Gayatri Chakravorty Spivak, Dipesh Chakrabarti, the late Ramubhai Gandhi, Laurie Patton, Vasudha Narayan, Triloki Pandey, Ellen Goldberg, Christopher Chapple, Pashaura Singh, S.N. Sridhar, the late Max Charlesworth, the late Renuka Sharma, Serena O'Meley, Megan Flautt, Una Murphy, Jane Wiesner, Savitaben Jivanji (Baa), Umaben Chauhan, Harshila Mistry, Parizad Doctor, Sally Percival Wood, Sudesh Mishra, Una Murphy, Kim Knott and Fethi Mansouri, among others, for their valuable input, each in their own unique way, and especially for the ongoing conversation on the global Indian diaspora.

Finally, we thank the members of the executive committee of the Hindu Society of Victoria, Sri Venkateswara Temple Association, Inc. (Sydney, NSW), Hindu Council of Australia (Sydney), Swaminarayan Sanstha (BAPS, Australia), the Hare Krishna (ISKCON) network, and the Blackburn Sikh Gurdwara (Melbourne) and El Sobrante Gurdwara (N. California) — for lending their unstinted support and co-operation on our specific research needs. Last but not least our gratitude to Shri Susheel Mittal (of D.K. Printworld) and his diligent staff for undertaking the arduous task of seeing this work through the press.

Namaskar!

Editors

Foreword

In Europe and the US, current debate about religions and religious communities of immigrants strongly focuses on Islam and Muslims. For some two decades, mainstream media as well as academic research have focused on this religion and its various sub-traditions. In particular, the terrorist Islamic attacks in the US in September 2001 and following attacks in Madrid (2004) and London (2005) channelled journalists' attention and social awareness towards Islam and Muslims. In contrast, Hindus and Hindu communities, for example, seem almost non-existent in public discourse, as the Hindu chaplain at Princeton University told me in a conversation in the Fall of 2011; and likewise in respect of the Sikh community. The focus of discourse and public attention on Muslims and Islam has become almost an obsession. Other non-Christian religions, in contrast, seem to generate no public interest and remain unrecognised. Unfortunately, with a few exceptions, academic research and studies on immigrant religious communities strongly mirror this biased public picture. To some extent this focus appears understandable. These days, it is much easier to obtain a grant, financial support and public recognition for studying Muslims due to the perception of potential 'social menace' than for research into putatively 'exotic' and 'tolerant' Hindu, Buddhist and Sikh immigrants and their communities in the North American, European and Australian diasporas.

The current book edited and in large part written by Purushottama Bilimoria, Jayant Bhalchandra Bapat and Philip Hughes provides a welcome exception to the obsessive focus on Islam and Muslims in Western migration research. It highlights that Hindus and Sikhs in Australia have experienced over a century-long diaspora. It emphasises that religious belonging and religious identity have proven to be vital to the immigrants as they construct their new homes-away-from-home in Australia. 'The religious world-view', as Bilimoria stresses in the first chapter, 'brings with it a cultural imaginary of difference (however vague its self-articulation) and reinforces a sense of worth of the otherwise marooned or alienated individual that one becomes in this transnational migration process' (p. 15). The process, paradoxically, also strongly helps to generate and retain a sense of self-esteem and dignity, and it finds material expression for these in the construction of their magnificent Hindu temples and Sikh gurdwaras. In addition, socially 'the *mandir* and *gurdwara* make the Hindu and Sikh identity publicly visible' (p. 16) and thus a noticeable part of current multi-faith Australia.

Certainly this volume is not the first of its kind on Indian people in Australia, but it is the most encompassing, detailed and timely. Earlier accounts by the same authors date back some 15-20 years. Following the pioneer study by Marie de Lepervanche on *Indians in White Australia* (Allen & Unwin, 1984), Purushottama Bilimoria published his book on *Hinduism in Australia: Mandala for the Gods* (Spectrum Publications with Deakin University Press, 1989). This was followed a few years later by the co-authored study with Philip Hughes, *Hindus and Sikhs in Australia* (Bureau of Immigration, Multicultural, and Population Research, 1996) and the well-known multi-author volume edited by Gary Bouma, *Many Religions, All Australian* (Christian Research Association, 1996). Though these books provide solid and insightful accounts with much information, data and discerning analyses, there is an urgent need for a fresh and timely publication.

In the quarter century since the first major studies on Indian people in Australia were published, the Indian diasporic presence in the sixth continent has increased tremendously: from some 40,000 settled Indian immigrants in 1981 to almost 300,000 Indian-born people in Australia in 2011 (see in detail Chapter 6). And the second and third generation is growing with more than 50,000 children of Sikh and Hindu families born in Australia according to the latest census (2011). Taking a longer perspective, it is apparent that Hinduism and Sikhism in Australia, despite much smaller numbers (around 4,500 Indians in 1900), have seen major developments, particularly as Australia moved from its early restrictive 'White Australia' policy to a more open, multicultural and multi-faith nation state with new policies of immigration since the 1970s. It is, then, indeed propitiously timely for a major up-date to the earlier books that will certainly further our understanding of Hindus and Sikhs, and their religious practices, ideas and traditions in Australia. In fact, informed descriptions and explanations of the religious traditions form an important part of the volume.

The well-documented 150-year narrative from the mid-19th century arrival of Afghan and Indian camel drivers, hawkers and colonial indentured labourers to *terra australis* to the early 21st century arrival of Indian engineers, surgeons, doctors and academics in contemporary Australia is not without its own theory and multivariate analyses. As the title of the volume highlights, one theoretical angle with which to contextualise the developments and adaptations of these two immigrant peoples is that of *diaspora* studies — despite the editors' misgivings about the term 'diaspora' itself (pp. 2-4). Though studies on immigrant groups and settlement in foreign countries have a long tradition, the usage of the term 'diaspora' is comparatively recent. It was once exclusively used in a context-bound way, in relation to Jewish history and the plight of Jewish people being dispersed 'among the nations'. In the late 20th century the folk term became generalised on a grand scale, starting with the classic paper by George Shepperson who suggested the concept of the 'African diaspora' (1966). Analogous to the expulsion of Jews in early times, the dispersion of sub-Saharan Africans through the colonial slave trade was described as an enforced expatriation, accompanied by a longing to return to the homeland. Since the 1980s, diaspora was increasingly used to denote almost every population living far away from their ancestral or former homeland (Baumann 2000). The generalised usage of the trope 'diaspora' became, so to speak, institutionalised with the launching of the high-quality journal *Diaspora* in 1991. Editor Khachig Tölölyan declared:

> We use 'diaspora' provisionally to indicate our belief that the term that once described Jewish, Greek, and Armenian dispersion now shares meanings with a larger semantic domain that includes words like immigrant, expatriate, refugee, guestworker, exile community, overseas community, ethnic community.
>
> — Tölölyan 1991: 4

As scholars in African studies, political science, anthropology and linguistics increasingly made use of the newly-discovered term, the study of religions was a latecomer. The first to highlight the 'Importance of

Diaspora' was the late historian of religions Ninian Smart with his seminal, though somewhat hidden, published article in 1987. Rightfully, the editors of this volume express their debt to Smart and his early insights by reprinting the paper in the Appendix A. A decade later, British scholar John Hinnells compellingly took up the notion of diaspora, systematising ten factors in a diaspora religion's change and continuity, and differentiating seven areas of research (Hinnells 1997). Chapter 5 of this volume likewise makes use of Hinnells's insights. It emphasises the strategies used by Hindu communities to both socially adapt and religious-culturally maintain themselves in the new surroundings.

As an analytical concept, the term 'diaspora' has the potential of being employed for transcultural, comparative purposes. Indeed, the academic discipline of the study of religions is based fundamentally on comparative insights and the establishing of meta-terms to capture similar structures, dynamics, and continuities. Studying the Hindus and Sikhs in Australian society is thus not only of value for the people of Australia and various scholars interested in the cultural history of that continent; rather, as numerous chapters in the volume highlight, studying the processes of the Indian people settling in this formerly racially exclusivist White society brings to the fore typical processes and changes similarly observable among other immigrant people, be it in the Americas or Europe. Amongst other features, the immigrants' feeling of loss and dislocation from their former homeland gradually gives way to a cultural and religious reorganisation of their lives in the new country. Provisional places of religious worship are founded and, with increasing visitors and financial opportunities, these are transformed to grand purpose-built constructions in typical Indian architectural style — as evidenced by the new Hindu temples (Chapter 4) and Sikh gurdwaras (Chapter 9) on the Australian soil. Also, at times these diasporic communal places of worship may acquire a heightened importance in relation to the country of origin. These places serve as both an emotional guarantee and psychological self-assurance for immigrants and their offspring, not forgetting the religious and cultural heritage, and keeping the memory of (former) origin alive. Moreover, these self-defined spaces of religious and cultural identity may serve as safe haven from where to embark to face the challenges in the new, at times discriminatory, environment. Rather than constituting places of distinction and withdrawal, the temples and *gurdwaras* often serve integrative functions for immigrants as they provide refuge, respectability and resources to ease and facilitate processes of social incorporation (Hirschman 2004).

Furthermore, employing the term 'diaspora' importantly emphasises the delineation of the triangular relationship of a diaspora group, country of present residence and (former) ancestral homeland. In this regard the authors of this volume, in underscoring the relationship between Indian immigrants and Australian society, have stated elsewhere in this volume that any diasporic experience produces major changes both in the receiving culture and the incoming culture of the diasporic group. A lot of accommodation is required on both sides. Australia has seen her fair share of racial and cultural intolerance since the white settlement 150 years ago and it needs to be avoided at all costs (pp. 334-37).

The history of Hindu and Sikh diasporas in Australia provides ample evidence of this relation, too often fraught with suspicion and discrimination. However, as White dominance and sense of superiority gave way to a more tolerant and culturally mixed society, another important diasporic feature came to the fore. Typically, a diaspora group's retention of religious difference does not impede its socio-economic integration and a sense of national identification. So far, this insight appears to be confirmed primarily by data of Indian-born people in the educational and economic sectors of society (see Chapters 6 & 10). However, will the second and third generation offspring of the 1980s, 1990s and 2000s Indian immigrants also lean towards a strong identification with Australia, at the same time staying firm in their religious convictions and ritual practices? If so, this development will take on important bearings for political discourses about plural and multicultural societies in order to underscore the possibility of well-functioning, multi-faith, modern societies.

In addition, venturing to take a look into the future, anticipated identity developments of a diaspora group from its incipient first immigrant generation to later second, third, fourth and following generations strongly raises the question of belonging *vis-à-vis* dislocation, and where exactly is the 'homeland'? Will the Indian sub-continent for the grandchildren and great-grandchildren in Australia still be the homeland or will Australia be the place of identification and feeling at home? Future processes will provide evidence of possible shifts of belonging. Existent comparative developments, however, argue for an increasingly strong identification with the land of residence and solely nostalgic remembrance of the former country of origin. In this regard, for instance, century-long established Japanese Shin Buddhists in the US (Tanaka 1997) and Indian Hindus in Trinidad (Baumann 2004) have shifted their identity towards the US and Trinidad respectively and away from Japan and India. Ironically, such shifts and dynamics make it increasingly problematic to speak of a diasporic group at all. American Japanese Buddhists and Trinidadian Hindus have become fully recognised citizens and have advanced on the socio-economic ladder. They no longer share the feelings of first generation immigrants of 'dislocation, disruption, distance from the "homeland" and the limits of hybridisation' (p. 4). However, it is too early to speculate about such forthcoming developments. The Hindu and Sikh diasporas in Australia, though dating back to the 19th century, exist no earlier in an uninterrupted generational line and are only present in sufficient numbers since the 1980s.

Despite this brief length of time, the authors point to changes with regard to attitudes among this first generation of Hindus and Sikhs. Signs of a 'Protestantisation' (p. 77) within the Hindu Australian community have become evident, stressing a more individualised faith and distancing themselves from ritual temple worship and the priest as intermediary (p. 229 & p. 339). Will such trends possibly lead to tendencies of secularisation or to a newly-interpreted understanding of Hindu faith and practice, possibly stressing pan-Hindu ecumenical features in the subsequent generations, as author Heather Forster notes (p. 150)? Or will the pattern of Sikhs in Woolgoogla, New South Wales, with their social distance from the Anglo-Australian majority and their strong sense of community be the preferred method to preserve culture and faith, warding off secularisation tendencies within the second generation, as Carmen Voigt-Graf analyses (p. 228)?

The rich collection of data, images and narratives provide ample opportunities to learn more about the Hindu and Sikh communities in contemporary Australia. It invites comparison of these insights and findings with other Hindu and Sikh communities and different religious diasporas in other nation states.

Martin Baumann
Universität Luzern, Switzerland

Preface

EVER since the lifting of the 'White Australia' policy in the early 1970s — and even before that — immigration has been steadily transforming the profile of religious diversity in Australia, as it has in a number of Western nations. Up to the 1950s and 1960s, historical accounts of Australian religiosity focused primarily on variants of the religion brought over by the settlers and later missionaries, namely, Christianity, and occasionally on the apparently receding culture of the indigenous people. Not unlike in North America, today the new immigrants and their locally born descendants follow an array of the world's religions — Islam, Judaism, Buddhism, Hinduism, Sikhism, Shinto, Confucianism and Daoism.

There are two ways of looking at this new phenomenon, which may be summarised in the form of questions:

1. How is a basically 'Christian' nation — the secular constitutional separation of church and state notwithstanding — dealing with the challenge of incorporating religious people whose beliefs are not necessarily commensurate with Christianity?[1]
2. Is Australia on the brink of a radical transformation, whereby new socio-theological categories wait to be framed in order to reflect the ensemble of diversely religious lifestyles, or spiritualities if you like? In what ways is the diversity of religions actually changing the nature of religion in the Australian context? Is it simply providing Australians with a 'supermarket' of religions, or are deeper and more profound changes occurring?

---

1 We take this from a study of the American context by the Princeton sociologist Robert Wuthnow, in his recent study, *America and the Challenge of Religious Diversity*, Princeton: Princeton University Press, 2005; the question as cited is posed in a review of the same in *Journal of the American Academy of Religion*, 2006, 74/4, p. 1020.

Our present undertaking, however, which will contribute to these larger issues, is to consider the place, the *topos*, of two minority 'new-comers'[2] among the immigrant religions in the backdrop of the dominant cultural framework. Where do the religions of the immigrant Hindus and Sikhs fit into and belong in the broader canvas of Australian life, in respect of both the secular and the religious contours of the nation? We may also ask in respect of the post-secular — i.e. the return or the infusion of the religious or spiritual back into the secular — which is the form of secularism followed in India, how are these religions being changed by the Australian context and how are they contributing to the changes in the Australian context?

Our task, as we note above, cannot be accomplished without first documenting in as thorough a fashion as possible the whole history of the immigrants in the 'lucky country', from the early post-slavery indenture recruitment experiences, through the lean days of immigration restrictions, to the recent relatively large-scale influx of professionalised modern Hindus and their Sikh counterparts, as well as students of the same background from the subcontinent and elsewhere. This is a presence no Australian is likely to miss in almost any metropolitan and suburban region across the country, whether boarding a tram or bus, hailing a cab, looking for 'Asian tucker', stopping for fuel at a petrol station, making a quick purchase at the corner 7-11 store, or arriving back home at an airport terminal.

Unlike standard histories of immigrants and their demographic profile, ours is the history of *religious* beliefs, customs and practices as lived by the communities of immigrants in question. For that, we must provide the background to their traditions or spiritualities of the people, for otherwise the reader will be at a loss to contextualise the perceptions and experiences of the groups, nor be able to make much sense of the qualitative and quantitative analyses that follow in the later chapters of the study. The current work brings together experts and informants from the world of scholarship, as well from within the two traditional immigrant communities, in order to provide balance between the fault lines of 'insider' and 'outsider' perspectives. Having been trained in philosophy

2 Although one could argue — and we certainly do in our historical chapters — that their faint presence was etched here since the time of the settlers.

and social sciences we have been particularly sensitive to this methodological thrust.

What is being offered in these pages, then, while not pretending to be a comprehensive account by any stretch of imagination, is what could be called 'the middle point account of the theology, history, socio-anthropology and demographic life-profile of Hindu and Sikh immigrant communities in Australia'. Our intention throughout in bringing together these essays, although academic in structure and scholarly in their discursive engagements, has been to make the text accessible to both lay readers and students in schools, who in many instances work on projects relating to Hindu and Sikh members of their community.[3] Australian historical and literary productions have turned a new page since the early phobias and alienations aroused by the tyranny of distances; ours is a small contribution to these developments, as well as to South Asian studies, inasmuch as the transnational diasporic (*bharatiya pravasi*) experience is an inexorable part of the identity of the 'new Indian' (in the making).

Themes and Summary of Essays in the Book

THEME

While the book is primarily descriptive of the history of the diaspora of Hindus and Sikhs, and of their beliefs and practices, there are some significant themes that run through the work:

1. The shape of the diaspora community has been determined to a significant extent by Australian government policies of immigration. These have produced today a diaspora that is distinct from the Indian population in terms of education, occupation, age and other factors. (We believe that this needs to be stated alongside the reality of an increasingly globalised world in which millions of people are on the move.)
2. The shape of the belief and practice of the diaspora community is determined by the ways in which the community relates to the

[3] See 'Educational Lending Rights' and 'Public Lending Rights' reports, a Government of Australia reporting scheme for books checked out on loan from educational and public libraries across the nation.

receiving community. Belief and practice are not simply copied from the homeland but are re-shaped by the new circumstances. Among the factors which shape them are:

- the size (and wealth) of the diaspora community, which means some compromises must be made in terms of building temples and holding festivals for each regional section of the diaspora community; and
- the way that individuals negotiate their identity in their new cultural environment, sometimes leading to a heightened awareness and deepened practice of their homeland religion as they seek to maintain their old identity, but sometimes leading to compromises with the new cultural environment, as people seek to be accepted within it. (This process can be seen to change over the generations.)

The way the community is received determines, at least to some extent, the dialogue that develops between the receiving culture and the diaspora community. Part of this dialogue is taking place in the context of interfaith committees, councils, conferences and events, and the particular demands made by, and expectations of, the receiving culture. For example, there has been a demand within the Australian culture for Hindu 'chaplains' at hospitals. The interfaith context raises questions about how Hindu belief in the gods relate to the beliefs of other religions in their God or gods. The development of interfaith rituals is another part of this, both at a civic level, such as in times of crisis, like the Bali bombings, and at the personal level, in terms of interfaith marriages.

SUMMARY OF ESSAYS

The book comprises a set of closely-knitted essays written by different individuals. While they make for an overall thematic discussion as noted above (and in Chapter 1), each essay also stands as a compact exposition and analysis from the standpoint of the author's own research into one aspect or another of the diasporic experience among Sikhs and Hindus, as well as Indians more generally. Hence, there is not the flow and movement towards a single argument as one would find in a single-authored work. The editors feel strongly, in bringing together these essays and Appendix items, that the readers stand to benefit from vignettes and gaining a deeper understanding of aspects of the two communities covered in this project. Indeed some readers may choose to selectively engage with themes and aspects that interest them most. Some may be in search of knowledge merely of the beliefs of the Hindus or Sikhs, for example, others their practices, and yet other readers may have an interest in the socio-demographic profile and interactive contribution of the communities to the host society (and the receptive response of the latter). As they say, there are horses for courses. A single author may not have been able to accomplish such a broad-ranging discursive task and provide a diversity of material, resources and analyses as will be found in a multi-authored anthology as this. The following provides a brief summary of each essay.

Chapter 1 serves as the Introduction. It walks the reader through some of the theoretical discussions that have been taking place internationally in the areas of South Asian diaspora studies in the broader context of religious and post-colonial studies and transglobalism. It engages with Arjun Appadurai's thesis of the tension and transition from the global to the local (glocal), and critiques it from the viewpoint of the Australian experience, while also demonstrating its applicability in areas such as that of the itinerant IT professionals who travel between Australia and Silicon Valley, California. The chapter also sets out the basic questions the book intends to raise and explore, and presents highlights from some of the later chapters (in respect of demographic profiles).

Chapter 2 presents an outline of Hinduism (as in theory and practice), from early history to the present day. It then moves on to a discussion of local observances, such as auspicious days in the Hindu almanac and the rites that accompany their observance, how the major festivals are celebrated, and so on. This may seem somewhat prosaic in a 'social sciences' type of study. However, our experience has been that many people — students, teachers and lay readers — have gone to the authors' previous books on Hinduism/Hindus and Sikhs in Australia to learn about Hinduism and Sikhism, because this information in a reliable form is rather sparse in the Oceanic context.

Chapter 3 explains Hindu and Sikh religious practices in India and in Australia and comments on how these practices have changed in the country of adoption. This chapter examines the shifts and changes over the last 100 years since the arrival of Hindus and Sikhs with almost no place to worship at, to the emergence of a large number of temples and community organisations across the country. With the broader range of such migrants in the recent phase (farm-hand workers, merchants, IT-professional, students, family reunion, Sri Lankan Tamil refugees, Indo-Fiji Hindus, etc.), the performative expressions and social involvements have also grown.

Chapter 4 discusses religious architecture and its symbolism — the Hindu *mandir* or temple. It examines the classical textual Agama and Vastu Shastra prescriptions for the location and structure of a typical Hindu temple as represented in south India, as well as the transplantation of this art and craft to the local Australian context, the rituals involved in consecration and instalment, and the 'awakening' of iconic deities.

Chapter 5 is a case study of what gives sense to a Hindu community and its sustaining cultural pursuits. It looks at the strategies the migrant community has adopted to establish itself in its new surroundings. The chapter is situated in the framework of the study of diasporic Hindu communities undertaken by Raymond B. Williams, John Hinnells and Purushottama Bilimoria, and for its example draws on devotional practices and social engagement in the larger society of a group of followers of the late mega-*guru*, Sathya Sai Baba.

Chapter 6 presents a statistical overview of the Hindu community in Australia. It draws on the previous chapters and charts the changes in cultural and demographic profiles of Hindus to the present day, taking into account rolling census data from 1911 to the present day.

Chapter 7, in a similar way to the history and profile of Hindus in Australia, begins with a study of Sikh history and migration, and continues with a discussion of the beliefs and practices of the Sikhs. It is followed by a more detailed discussion of the migration of Sikhs to Australia and the development of the Sikh community in Australia.

Chapter 8 presents a historical account of recent 'finds': the two graves of early Sikh hawkers in Victoria and how the interred remains of one were returned to his former homeland.

Chapter 9 is an account of Sikh practices and life in rural Australia, followed by a section on the diverse Sikh communities in Australian cities, and the cultural and economic transnationalism of Australian Sikhs. There is also appended to this chapter an outline of the design of the Sikh temple or *gurdwara*, and the religious and social functions the *gurdwara* plays in the community, as well as in the national ethnospace. The discussion ends with a brief history of the earliest Sikh *gurdwaras* in Australia.

Chapter 10 discusses Sikh immigration and social profile over the last century and charts the changes in cultural and demographic profiles of Sikhs, such as birthplace, age, geographic distribution, marital practices and related issues. The copious data and ensuing analyses draw on census statistics since 1911 to the current statistical releases from the Australian Bureau of Statistics.

Chapter 11 begins with a set of general reflections on the Indian diaspora in Australia and brings together the two religious communities under a common identity (with some reference also to Muslims) under the rubric of 'Indian', and argues for a closer homogeneous nationalist sentiment between the two major Indian diasporic communities than exists on the subcontinent. The chapter also goes beyond religious practices to other cultural involvements and preoccupations, mostly to do with food (cuisine and restaurants), language, public life and so on.

Chapter 12 considers how the process of migration generates a sense of alienation and/or dislocation, and how this 'anomie' impacts on Indian women in their diasporic daily lives. Drawing on survey data and narrative evidence, the writer argues that this response is based on two sets of factors. The first is their religious nurturing in India and the second is the level of displacement experienced in Australia, the host country. Analysis, based on patterns of religious behaviours such as rituals, temple attendance, and customs involving prayer, food and dress, indicates that Indian women draw on their pre-migration experiences to evolve coping strategies for everyday living that are both traditional and contemporary.

Chapter 13 explores the experiences of Indian students (basically Hindus and Sikhs) who account for a sudden increase in the South Asian migrant presence in Australia. There have been some awkward episodes and even violent attacks on Indian students by members of the host society, which this chapter attempts to contextualise, as well as discussing other ramifications of the 'Indian student phenomenon'.

Chapter 14 notes how the attitudes of Australians of European heritage have changed towards people of various religions since the 19th century. Using survey data gathered in 2009, it describes attitudes towards Hindus in the Australian culture and suggests various factors significant in those attitudes.

Chapter 15 summarises the preceding chapters and explores implications of the South Asian transnational presence and involvement in Australia. The chapter discusses possible trajectories for future developments of Australian multicultural hybridity and pluralist religious society (given the declining regenerative statistics of Anglo-Celtic-European population). This is explored in the context of the Asia-Pacific rim extending to the shores of California; the Australian nation's own ambivalent relations with its former sovereign, Great Britain; and until recently its larger trading partners in the first-world powers, the United States and Japan (now increasingly replaced by China and India).

We are fortunate to have been able to include in the Appendix a chapter on 'diaspora' by the late Ninian Smart, who was a pioneer in the field of secular religious studies and who was responsible for raising its status as an academic discipline. Although written in the early 1990s, his observations are every bit as relevant today, as interest in diasporic religious communities grows. An additional Appendix, written by Richard Forster, describes one of the earliest groups of Indians to come to Australia: the cameleers who worked across the untamed outback in the 19th century.

1

Transglobalism of Hindus and Sikhs in Australia

Purushottama Bilimoria

Tyranny of Distances[1]

THE South Asian religious diaspora is now a global phenomenon, from the early immigrant experience of the colonial indentured labourers, through to the transnational movement of professional Indians to all corners of the globe. Australia has increasingly become the land of new opportunities, attracting Hindu and Sikh professionals and workers of all descriptions. It is widely reported in the media that Indians, especially Punjabi-speaking Sikhs along with Hindus, have become the largest source of permanent migrants to Australia, comprising over 15.7% of the intake under the country's migration programme in 2011-12 (a topic re-visited in detail in later chapters). However, a much longer history, albeit an uneasy one, with discontinuous moments and phases, precedes this current attraction to the sixth continent. In this book, as noted above, we present a history and extensive analysis of the Hindu and Sikh diaspora experiences in Australia from the early days of the colonies to the present day, with some reference to North America for comparison. This introductory chapter contextualises the study of the particular diasporic experience in Australia, by placing it within the broader theoretical thinking on transnational migration, globalisation and heterogeneity. We also consider changing perspectives within the receiving culture. Another concern is to understand how distinctive the religious diasporic experience of Hindus and Sikhs in Australia is from those of the international South Asian diaspora. Much literature on South Asians in the West neglects the

---

[1] With apologies to Geoffrey Blainey.

implicativeness of religion, while recent studies reveal the considerable prominence of religion in various migrant South Asian communities, 'especially in comparison with the secularising tendencies typical of many white societies' (Hinnells 1998: 819-20).

A word on the term 'diaspora' in this context is apposite. 'Diaspora' is one of the 'buzzwords of the post-modern age' sibilantly exotic and wave-breaking as it rolls off the tongue or to other shores (Baumann 2000: 325-26). While we have followed the growing trend and speak of 'the Hindu and Sikh diaspora' in the course of our study, we do have some misgivings about the term itself. An epistemic issue arises about the widespread use of the term 'diaspora' and its application to religions outside their homeland on the objection by Robin Cohen (1997: 189) that religions span more than one ethnic group (Christianity and Islam come to mind here), and that unlike ethnic groups, religions do not aspire to return to their homeland. In his studies of the global Hindu diaspora, Steven Vertovec (2000; 2004) argues that apart from the case of Jewish and Sikh groups, defined more by their religion than by their respective 'ethnicities', Hinduism outside India represents a special case of diasporic community. This is because Hindus maintain a particular reference point to India, as a people of caste-knit Indian origin with a sacred belonging that harks back to the homeland where Hinduism is the dominant tradition or orthodoxy.

The term or trope 'diaspora', with its etymology in the Greek *diaspeirein*, 'to distribute or disperse', has political roots, namely, the goal of reconstructing and defending Jewish identity as Jews waited for a time when a return to the promised homeland could become a reality and not just a passing dream or unrequited longing (Baumann 2000). The adoption of this descriptor has not always been successful, but it has been made to work or taken as a universal given for all people who have been dislocated from their real or imagined homeland base, and who may in any case be several generations away from their 'homeland'. James Clifford has tried to iron out the ambiguity in the use of this term by restricting it to displaced peoples.[2] Often the conditions and context of the dislocation

[2] James Clifford cites Khachig Tölölyan: 'Diasporas are the exemplary communities of transnational moment', and 'the term that once described Jewish, Greek, and Armenian dispersion now shares meanings with a →

and the reasons for looking back, or forward, to the virtual homeland might be so different as to render any supposed parallels almost incomparable if not incommensurable (cf. Stanley Tambiah 2000: 169). In any case, all migration involves some degree of displacement, even if it is undertaken voluntarily and a community moves quickly to establish its own 'borderland' zones, such as the Vietnamese and Chinese 'Towns' in major Western cities, and the Indians with their 'Little India' and 'Sikh Halls' in other parts. Gayatri Chakravorty Spivak (2000) finds the rubric of 'diaspora' somewhat rubbery and is content instead to substitute it simply with 'expatriate'. In a way, Spivak is right, the majority of the people of Indian origin settled in 'other worlds' are expatriates, i.e. first generation ethnic Indians, followed by 'twice-migrated' people of Indian origin from former colonies or India's neighbourhood, and after that the second or third generations — not-born-of-the-homeland-soil — who only marginally retain their 'diasporic' identity, at least for some time. For this last group, their social, economic and political networks now cross not only nation states but span the globe (Vertovec 1997: 277). So it is inappropriate to ascribe a discursive space to such a group, as though their homeland is somewhere messianically in the future. Perhaps not surprisingly, the ambiguous nature of the term 'diaspora' escaped the scholars who turned their gaze on the dispersed communities of South Asian origins in various parts of the world. Some earlier writers on South Asian communities abroad, such as Jayawardena and Hugh Tinker, made no reference to the concept of 'diaspora' in their work on subcontinental migrants, focusing instead, on the colonial context.

Sudesh Mishra (2006: 17-18), following Vijay Mishra, identifies three phases in the making of a diaspora individual: 'dual territoriality', 'situational laterality' and 'archival specificity'. In the first phase, the diasporic subject has a sense of dislocated identity between the stable host country and the former homeland, which is marked by 'living without belonging in one, belonging without living in the other'. In the second, the boundaries are transcended and there is a more fluid identity

← larger semantic domain that includes words like immigrant, expatriate, refugee, guest-worker, exile community, overseas community, ethnic community'. 'Diasporas', *Cultural Anthropology*, **9**(11), 1994: 303; see also, Cohen 1997; Baumann 2000; Vertovec 2004.

formation, with the diasporic citizen ambivalent about returning to the former land. In the third, the subject moves away from the preceding phases and questions the history and identity written as it were on his or her migrated body, sometimes even turning to wider moral and religious reconfigurations to form a specific identity distinct from that found in the first two phases. The ensuing chapters in their own ways both present a critique of and at the same time demonstrate within limits the merits of Mishra's theoretical insights, in respect of the different phases undergone by the South Asian diasporic subject in Australia, which are not that dissimilar to the South Asian diasporic experience in North America, as summarised recently by Vinay Lal (2008).

Nonetheless, the peculiar origins of the term 'diaspora', in the homeless re-identification of the Jewish people, still raises two issues that mitigate against its widespread adoption in the study of transnational migration and settlement among Hindus and Sikhs, namely:

1. Most of the Hindus and Sikhs in the so-called diaspora are in actual fact *expatriates*, who, 'chose to leave' and continue to have more concrete than virtual ties with the 'home-land', which is real and not just a messianically imagined territory.
2. The descriptor, 'diaspora' fails to capture the process of re-location and the concomitant psycho-social anomie of dislocation and displacement, along with the variables within the Hindu immigrant experience, even among long-settled second or later generations, which are characterised by linguistic, ethnic, cultural and regional diversity. We therefore refer to this process as *disporia*: the *aporia* of dislocation, disruption, distance and the limits of hybridisation as also of distanciation. Thus our analysis draws on this latter nuance, even though we stay with the terms 'diaspora' and 'expatriate' and use them interchangeably to define the migrant communities under review.

There is a certain anomie that is experienced by the migrant as the gaze turns towards the promising but unknown horizon: promising in terms of what it might deliver, unknown in terms of what it might take away from one's personal and social identity. Robert Cohen has summarised the contours of the diasporic angst rather succinctly. Upon arrival in the new territorial frontier, among the elements that become a capital for exchange, in identity negotiations between the host society and others of the same ethnic and/or religious group, are the following (Cohen 1997: 26):

1. a collective myth and memory about the homeland, including its location, history and achievements;
2. an idealisation of the putative ancestral home, and a collective commitment to maintenance, restoration, safety and prosperity, even to its creation;
3. the development of a return movement which gains collective approbation; and
4. a strong ethnic group consciousness sustained over a long time and based on a sense of distinctiveness, common history, and the belief of a common fate.

An expression was once used in Australia to describe the angst of the settler culture that lived out its life as if marooned or cast off at a great distance from the centre of the world (the Northern hemisphere, with the particular reference point being Britain), namely, 'the tyranny of distance' (Blainey 1993). But there has been a shift in Australia's own self-perception, in respect of three strategic developments. Briefly:

1. while the nation has not freed itself entirely from the erstwhile imperial connections with Britain (as someone said, 'once a penal colony always a colony'), it has nevertheless entered the neo-liberal market economy and the politically driven force of globalisation;
2. by espousing the universalist globalisation movement, Australia can resist pressures for it to Asianise, i.e. see itself, with some ambivalence and historical trepidation, less rather than more integrated with the Asia-Pacific neighbourhood (Goldsworthy 2001; Walker 1999; D'Cruz and Steele 2003), as well as, of course, with the indigenous Aboriginal culture; and hence,
3. not continue to worry about its distance from Europe, or the most powerful Western nation, the United States. This move curiously has ramifications for the lucrative options available to South Asians

eager to join the migration train: *where there is economic capital there is likely to be cultural capital as well,* at least in the eyes of post-colonial, modernising hi-tech Hindus. This is a key point in our critique.

Before moving on, though, a Cook's tour of the history of migration of Indians to the southern continent is required.

Four Phases of Hindu and Sikh Migration to Australia

PHASE I: TRANSNATIONAL BANISHMENT

The detailed history of each of the two religious communities under inquiry is presented in later chapters. What we wish to do here is to set the context for the theoretical ruminations begun above, so as to move the discussion on to the discourse and context of globalisation.

The earliest Indian migrants to the Australian continent came from the Punjab and North-West Frontier regions soon after white settlement during late 18th century, when trade between the Australian colonies and British India also commenced (from 1792 onwards), and with the opening up of the outback in the early 19th century (the country was not federated into a single nation state until 1901). The first people from the subcontinent classed as 'Hindoos' to arrive in Australia were Baluchi-Pathans, who were mostly Muslims. In 1858, George Landell, who exported horses to India was commissioned to buy camels and recruit camel drivers.[3] Twenty-four camels and three drivers, two of whom were Muslims, arrived in Melbourne in 1860. By 1901 there were between 2,000 and 4,000 cameleers in Australia. Although there were many instances of tensions between these Afghans and white labourers, the general consensus was that without the former, many of the towns would have simply ceased to exist. Along with the camel men came the Indian hawkers and merchants. They travelled the Australian countryside and offered their goods for sale to remote settlers.[4] While most settlers were grateful

---

[3] A fascinating history of such early connections between India and Australia is recorded in the recent publication by Joyce Westrip and Peggy Holroyde, *Colonial Cousins: A Surprising History of Connections Between India and Australia*, Adelaide: Wakefield Press, 2010. This history, as well as the contribution of Holroyde, is discussed in Forster's chapter in the Appendix B.

[4] http://uncommonlives.naa.gov/muslim-journeys/stories/cameleers-and-hawkers.aspx. Accessed on 22 April 2011.

for their services, there were those who objected to this 'invasion' by the 'coloured race' of their white homeland. A printed notice of a motion dated 9 February 1893, issued by Avon Shire in Gippsland country, and addressed to the mayor of the town of Northcote in Melbourne, protested strongly about the nuisance of the Indian hawkers and urged the council to put a stop to this increasing source of terror – "*this dangerous and menacing evil*" – to females and children while their men were away going about their duties.[5]

There was also a handful of lower-caste Hindus who came from the Chota Nagpur region in eastern India, brought out as agricultural labourers to work on banana and sugar cane plantations, mostly along the East Coast of Australia, where they settled with their male family members who came to join them later. Regardless of their religion or ethnicity, they were all classed as 'Hindoos'. They came without wives or women, so many of them saved up money and returned to the subcontinent. This pool of imported Indian labour became available across the British empire, including South and East Africa, the West Indies, Fiji and Malaysia. This was driven by the abolition of slavery, and, more significantly, changes in land tenure instigated by the imperial British regime creating a surplus of labour among the disenfranchised, landless class, especially in the rich agrarian regions of the Punjab. An indentured labour system replaced the barbaric slave-labour migration, which effectively continued with an apparently humanitarian face. This movement of people from the subcontinent to imperial outposts and colonies was managed by the Europeans. The treatment of the immigrants, from the moment they boarded the ships on which they were to travel, was not the most humane by any standard. South Asians from poorer regions and caste groupings were driven off to the labour-intensive fields of the colonies and Australia vied for its share.

Fig. 1.1 is a telling example of the conditions these hawkers and labourers faced. They led a lonely life of total isolation, without their families and kin, and endured sub-human treatment by their white masters, in living conditions often unfit for human beings.

There were political trade-offs and agreements between the respective

[5] http://museumvictoria.com.au/collections/items/717941/notice-re-the-indian-hawker. Accessed on 22 April 2011.

fig. 1.1: Hawkers in Melbourne. Source: *Illustrated Australian News*, 1893

colonial governments and the British Imperial Office that facilitated the translation of an economic imperative (need of labour power) into the actual movement of people (most often voluntary, but occasionally with deceptive allurement). This situation created a model that can best be described as one of 'transnational banishment', or 'coolie transnationalism'.

In Australia, there were anti-Asiatic tirades and open protests by local workers against the threatening competition from coloured labour and the ensuing lowering of wage scales. The official response (on both sides, including the Indian government) was to enact a series of prohibitions on the Indian coolie labour influx, particularly to Natal in southern Africa, except for the occasional itinerant visitor. In Australia this proscription culminated in the infamous 1901 Immigration Restriction Act that heralded the so-called the 'White Australia' policy.[6] These were early signs of public reaction to the presence of 'Hindoos' around the 1890s, and it set the stage for certain stereotypes in the White Australian psyche, such as the 'heathen and niggardly' characteristics of the immigrants (*Australian News*, 1 May 1893; Bilimoria 1989a, 1996a). The restricted passage of South Asians to Australia remained in force throughout the two world wars, with only a trickle of migration, particularly of camel drivers (mostly Afghans routed via the British India Office), hawkers, pedlars, merchants, students and commercial visitors. The resident Indians continued to agitate for their rights, and after a memorable visit in 1922 of Rt. Hon. V.S. Srinivasa Sastri, the eminent Indian delegate to the Imperial Conference held in London in 1921, Indians were given entitlement to own property and to license their own businesses. They also gained access to the aged-pension and were granted limited voting franchise (ahead of other migrant groups, such as Chinese and Jews), because they were British subjects of sorts (Tinker 1977: 3-5; Bilimoria & O' Meley 2015) (See Chapter 2, p. 67, note 8).

PHASE II: HOMOGENISING TRANSNATIONALISM

A more decisive form of transnationalism in the diaspora context emerged with the second phase of Indian migration that followed in the wake of the abolition of the racially exclusivist 'White Australia' policy in the 1970s. The imperatives for opening up the doors of immigration were again economic and to some extent political. 'Populate or perish' was a common motto at the end of Second World War and the start of the 'Cold War' era. However, this opening-up was not to be sacrificed at the cost of homogenisation. So an assimilationist policy was devised which made a subtle demand on the incoming diverse religious, cultural and class or caste groupings that required them to culturally assimilate into what was broadly conceived as 'Royal Britannia' Australia. Even so, potential non-

---

6 See for example, a Presbyterian minister's defence in 1901 of 'the noble ideal of a White Australia — snow-white Australia if you will' (Bilimoria 1989a: 33) and Allan Walker, *Plan for a Christian Australia* (Melbourne: Methodist Church of Australia, 1955). The latter outlines the history of this movement and its persistence in the church, especially amongst the Methodists.

white immigrants were still viewed with suspicion and therefore kept at bay. However, in the face of mounting international (including vociferous official Asian) criticism, the adoption of multiracial migration policies by other English-speaking Western countries, and the dire shortage of a skilled labour force in Australia, forced the country to open its doors to Asian immigrants within certain restrictive categories, Indians included. With the adoption of the official 'multicultural' mandate the rhetoric changed from the erstwhile assimilationist policy to one of integration. Here the host-nation can be seen to loosen its own identity so that certain characteristics of the immigrants' homeland culture are absorbed into the new social formation, so as to ease the psychological anomie engendered by the alienating dislocative experience of migration. The stratagem of integration, however, tends toward a 'melting-pot' mentality, and it does not take long for political expediency, in times of trouble and uncertainty, and the riff of national boundary tensions, to push the rhetoric back toward the assimilationist, in some version or other, such as the universal requirement of English-language proficiency and literacy.

Migration therefore remained by and large an issue of the preservation of national homogeneity through appropriate selection of migrants, a way to expand and develop the nation along the lines of racial and cultural purity (Humphrey 1998: 5). This attitude is reminiscent of the notorious remark made in 1947 by the then Labour Minister for Immigration, Arthur Calwell, that 'Two Wongs don't make a white!' Homogenisation is a form of maintaining control by hegemonic forces. Culture and race, then, during this phase, remained as markers of social differentiation, if not discrimination. For both, as Michael Humphrey comments,

> are indicators of social position and cultural capital, while the individual act of migration itself, from the perspective of the host society, is still interpreted as a tacit acknowledgement of the superiority of the new over the old society and ways. A recent national inquiry into Australian immigration policy revealed how little the underlying premises of social and political integration had changed. An official report, entitled 'Immigration: A Commitment to Australia,' suggested that far too many migrants demonstrated their lack of allegiance to Australia by failing to take out citizenship . . . Immigration policy sought permanent

> settlers who would express their gratitude for selection by quickly becoming naturalised Australians and by learning English. Becoming part of the same linguistic community was seen as essential for social membership in the Australian national community.
> — Humphrey 1998: 7

Not all cultural capital is easily convertible, especially the deficiency in English language, overseas qualifications and education, social knowledge, and religious and moral predilections, which are re-configured as 'ethnic'. This becomes a problem for pluralism. The construction of ethnicity under the multicultural banner is as problematic as the notion of an authentic voice speaking for others, as Spivak reminds us (2000: 245-69). Caught in this tension, some migrant groups set about the task of reinterpreting and re-evaluating their own tradition, or look back to the 'homeland' for cultural authenticity as for a means of asserting their identity and control over their future. A few opt for a more transient and middle position, leaving open the possibility of return migration or shifting to another destination, so as to maintain access to parallel social worlds in other ethnospaces.

PHASE III: POST-COLONIAL PROFESSIONAL INDIANS

In the 1950s, the migrant community from the subcontinent was just too sporadic and scattered for a sense of ethnic–religious identity to grow. The 1954 Census recorded a mere 2,647 Indians in this vast nation. With the end of Second World War and subcontinental Independence, immigration to Australia was open only for those with over 50% 'European' heritage. The late 1950s saw a slight increase in the number of Hindus opting for Australia rather than for England, the United States and Canada. What attracted most were certainly not the promises of an open environment where religious aspirations could be freely pursued. Instead, for many modern secular Hindus, the sixth continent appealed as a safe refuge from the religious orthodoxies and caste-ridden life back home. When packing their tin-chests, the emigrants asked: 'What can we leave behind?' It might occur to them later that they had left behind some important ingredients of their identity. Re-tracing their steps along the transnational conduit traversed, therefore, later becomes an important signification of rootedness.

After the early 1970s, when the 'White Australia' policy was officially dropped, the reception of immigrants changed, although reservations about admitting people with different standards of living, tradition and culture did persist. The overall image of Australia too had changed dramatically from an open rural land to an industrialising, developing nation with professional opportunities. Thus while the 1961 Census recorded a total of 4,047 Indians, by 1971 there were 22,930. The number nearly doubled in the 1980s, reaching 41,730 by 1981, and by 1996 close to 100,000, which does not include another 10,000-15,000 Indian students on study visas. The 2011 Census indicated that there were 295,362 Indian-born people living in Australia. The figures of course include people of a wider religious orientation than merely Hindus and Sikhs and also those of European descent born in India. Just under half (47.3%) of India-born Australians were Hindus, 19% were Sikhs, 24% were Christians, 3% were Muslims, while the remainder registered an assortment of faiths or no faith (see page 156 in Chapter 6). Sikhs born in India made up 77% of the Australian Sikh community in 2011 (see page 237 in Chapter 11). Increasing numbers in both communities are now children born in Australia of immigrant parents.

The transnational conduit we refer to, however, is not confined exclusively to the bilateral *yatra* (pilgrimage) between India and Australia; it extends to other countries besides India. Professional Hindus have also been drawn from Sri Lanka, with an increasing number arriving from other parts of the world, whom diaspora scholars have called 'twice migrants', and even 'thrice' in some cases, where the immigrant has moved from one country to another, usually over a period of two to three generations. An example of the latter would be East African Indians fleeing to Britain during the Idi Amin coup, and later moving to Canada, the United States, Australia and New Zealand. Hindus living in other former colonies began to migrate to Australia as well: from Malaysia and Singapore, Fiji, Mauritius, British Guyana, the United Kingdom, New Zealand, the southern and eastern African states, and most recently Hong Kong. Two Fijian-led military coups in the late 1980s, involving the ousting of an Indian-led government, and political upheavals in Sri Lanka and some African states, increased the number of Hindus seeking to leave their adopted homes, and many looked to Australia. In New Zealand, for instance, Indian Fijians (the majority of whom are Hindus and Sikhs) constitute the largest single group of ethnic South Asians in that (former) dominion and, exploiting the trans-Tasman arrangement that exists between the two countries, they periodically visit and at times simply relocate to Australia as bona-fide Australian residents (without having to suffer the long delays in processing visa applications to Australia as experienced by their subcontinental Indian and African counterparts) (Bilimoria 2013b). In 2011, there were some 57,000 people living in Australia who were born in Fiji, of whom 37,500 described themselves as having Indian or South Asian ancestry.

The educational profile of Hindu and Sikh immigrants is considerably and visibly higher than their Australians counterparts. In 2011, 43% of all Hindus had university qualifications, including 19% who had postgraduate degrees (see Table 6.9 in Chapter 6). Thirty per cent of all Sikhs in Australia also have university qualifications (see Table 11.9 in Chapter 11). Indian-born immigrants have amongst the highest levels of post-secondary education of all immigrant groups. Hindus and Sikhs at one time did badly in skilled vocational qualifications, largely because of their concentration in academic and professional sectors, but all that has changed in recent years with the labour demands in Australia and the lucrative billion-dollar education and trade-training industry. They exhibit high levels of motivation, much due to the post-colonial legacy to 'succeed where the master once had ruled', backed by a heritage of traditional learning. The second- or third-generation Hindus and Sikhs go on to universities, but do not necessarily or in large proportions opt to become doctors, psychiatrists, surgeons, academics and engineers with the same earnestness as their parents did. Perhaps this is a sign of the *post*-post-colonial reversal.

The subcontinental Hindus, or India-direct migrants, arrive with their cultural, linguistic and religious links with India or Sri Lanka still intact. Of the Hindu community in 2011,

- 177,500 were born in South Asia,
- 43,000 were born in Australia — mostly of Indian and Fijian parents, and
- 26,000 were born in Fiji (see Tables 6.2 and 6.4 in Chapter 6).

Among the Sikhs,

- 55,000 were born in South Asia,
- 11,000 were born in Australia, mostly of parents born in India, and
- 2,500 from Malaysia and other parts of South-East Asia.

In both cases, small groups have come from the United Kingdom, Africa and New Zealand.

These disparate Hindus and Sikhs, like earlier South Asian immigrants, have utilised the educational system for training in skills and achieving social and economic mobility. Many came with money too, and quickly found themselves in well-salaried positions, choosing to live in select manicured suburbs or housing colonies, although some have struggled to find employment consonant with their qualifications, as has happened in other parts of the world (Lessinger 1999). The contribution of Hindus from these regions toward forging a distinctive religious identity in Australia cannot be overlooked. We observe a special kind of inward-looking transnationalism at work in this particular 'twice-thrice' migrant group.

Chain and Educational Migration

Since the immigration policies favoured and restricted migration of skilled and professionally accomplished or promising persons only, in response to labour market and economic factors, unskilled persons, including spouses, children and relatives of the settled residents, had to rely on the slow success of family reunification (or reunion) and sponsorship provisions. Over twenty or thirty years, this has led to a phenomenon characterised as 'chain migration', which has brought in lesser skilled, as well as unskilled and dependent relatives, plus hordes of temporary stayers, students and casual workers, the majority of whom will be vying for PR (permanent residence) status. Even if some of these new arrivals have skills and training, such as higher degrees in a number of cases, their qualifications are often not recognised in Australia or they may fail to obtain gainful employment in their fields. Thus a prominent taxi rank in a suburb of Sydney is known as the 'PhD Taxi Rank' (Voigt-Graf 2000; see also p. 203). This is because many of these cab-drivers are community-sponsored academics from an agricultural university in the Punjab on extended leave, who were at one time in great demand in the Australia labour force, but whose qualifications have not earned them equivalent jobs in Australia, and they are waiting to become full Australian residents.

International students are a financial cornerstone of the Australian education industry. Most such students, though, carefully select Australia with a view to gaining residency status after graduating and finding gainful employment in the industry sector in which they are qualified, usually in the hi-tech field. However as discussed in Chapter 13, some are not successful, as they chalk up huge debts in their parents' bank accounts or in loans and find themselves working long hours (viz. at 7-11 stores or fuelling stations, and driving or owning cabs) to make a meagre livelihood while trying to study and survive (Bass 2006b: 14).

This kind of transnational migration, then, reduces both the careers and self-worth or dignity of the migrant who arrives in good faith. But it also creates a movement of temporary visitors and casual or short-term workers, alongside the number of students from India, in both directions. Some see themselves as temporary residents only and have their gaze fixed on moving to the United States, where the occupational and earning prospects are perceived to be higher. This involves them in a secondary transnational movement. The restrictive skilled, professional migration policy and the reunion provisions that set up chain migration, abetted by temporary and student residents, are directly linked with the national economic motivations of the day. Transnational migration is indeed an effective Trojan horse for de-proletarisation of the labour force. It introduces an element of competition (or, as some would say, cheapening of labour power) and diffuses the sense of working-class identity and solidarity, for the migrant worker does not see himself or herself as being rooted in the conventional working-class ethos, but aims rather to move up the ladder, and to outer gentrified suburbs from inner city areas, as quickly as he or she has 'made a few good bucks'.

It is here that the re-configured religious identity provides an escape route from a particular kind of alienation in mainstream culture, especially at the early settling-in stages of the migration experience. The religious world-view brings with it a cultural imaginary of difference (however vague its self-articulation) and reinforces a sense of worth for the otherwise marooned or alienated — 'atomistic' — individual that one becomes in this transnational migration process. Religion and transnationalism go hand-in-hand to build a portmanteau identity, a sense of being both here and there, from which comes the idea of hybridity that modern expatriate Indian writers like Salman Rushdie and Homi Bhabha have exploited in their writings.

In a short span of time, both Hindus and Sikhs have successfully organised themselves. By drawing on their own professional skills, bureaucratic contacts and business dealings, they have been able to move towards building spectacular temples to their gods or *guru*s in various parts of Australia. But again, the emulation is transnational in two directions: of the United States for the initial inspiration and model; of India for the resources, template, *shilpi* (masonry) skills, shipment of the stone-cast gods and the ritual process of installation and sanctification of the divine spaces within the walls of *mandir* or *gurdwara*. It is significant to note that after a period of gestation, the amorphous community perceives the need for a firm Hindu and Sikh cultural base and temples. Imagining the temple presents a pre-text for the coming together of Hindus and Sikhs in the diaspora. As a signifier for prescribed ritual and interiorised practices, the temple enables greater confidence in these practices. As a permanent presence, *mandir* and *gurdwara* make the Hindu and Sikh identity publicly visible. It also provides a matrix for ironing out differences and tensions between the different sectarian and regional groups, or alternatively to bolster the political interests of their respective home-based movements. Internal divisions however remain, and fractured groups shift to other sites, adding yet another temple.

Let us now move on to look at some contemporary political engagements of Hindus and Sikhs, a topic that is developed further in the following chapters and appendices.

New Found Hinduism

To recap, much of 20th-century, continuing into 21st century Hindu migration elicits different perceptions and responses to those that people faced in the 19th century and early 20th century. Internal and external factors contributed to both change and continuity, paving the way for a distinctive religio-ethnic identity to emerge. The diversity of regional, linguistic and historical backgrounds of Hindus, of course, adds to the complexity of the baggage each group carries with it to a distant shore. The migrants from India and of South Asian descent, who at home would more likely call themselves Vaishnavas, Shaivas, Shaktas, Lingayats, *bhaktas*, or Vedantins, readily identify themselves as 'Hindus'.[7] These 'Hindu' migrants in recent years have borne the burden of preserving their respective traditions. They have participated in debates on multiculturalism and attended inter-faith meetings, but they are usually unaware of the subtle process of 'authentication by ethnicity', which 'whitewashes' or marginalises their real political status and treatment as citizens of a civil society.

Unlike Western religion, Hinduism is generally regarded as having no fixed doctrines, tight-knit structures, hierarchical governance, and rigid organisational bases with ecclesiastical control. However, its presence in a foreign land has led to the development of loosely bound societies and organisations which can serve them in a predominantly Christian environment. In this context, there are certain sentiments that can be more readily exploited. For instance, some members of the Hindu community are anxious that the larger temple complexes have become routinely ritualistic and impersonal, neglectful of diasporic needs, in particular education in vernacular languages and transmission of values, Hindu mores and customs to the younger generation. One must add that this is not true of all local Hindu temples. Within the diasporic communities, there are a variety of religious beliefs and political ideas that compete for the attention of the migrants. Some right-wing organisations such as the VHP (Vishwa Hindu Parishad, or Universal Hindu Organisation) and the RSS (Rastriya Svayamsevak Sangh, or National Volunteer Group), which is known in Australia as VHS (Vishwa Hindu Sangha, or Universal Hindu Group) have established themselves here but have had insignificant influence upon the larger Hindu community. And there are moderate Hindu *sansthas* (sectarian organisations), such as the growing presence of the two Shree Swaminarayan (BAPS & Temple Mandir) groups, with their hugely decorative and architecturally opulent temples in the major cities. It is also heartening to know that the organisers of such bodies here are wary of bringing extremist views to the tolerant land that they have adopted. This transformation is particularly visible in the teachings of the VSS in Australia. The so-called 'Satsang Parivar' (company of the truth group) is based in Melbourne and has suspected links with the right-

7 The British colonialists transformed to 'Hindu' the Persian appellation for people beyond the Sindhu (Indus) River, who may have been known as 'Sindhus'.

wing Sangh Parivar in India and the Hindutva movement in the diaspora. However, any sway towards the Hindu Right is highly unlikely to bring Hinduism into a confrontational stance with the larger host society or its more liberal platforms.

On the other hand, in some of the discussions the authors of this volume have had with many Hindu migrants to Australia, most of whom are highly educated, middle-class professionals, there seems to be a distinct opinion among many that most Muslims are fundamentalists. This view resonates with the Hindu Right's picture in India of the minority Muslims. The Bali incident brought these same fears one step closer to the adopted home of these Hindus. They feel less safe now than when they had watched closely on their televisions the plethora of terrorist activities in the Middle East, in Jammu & Kashmir, in the United States, or even in Godhra, Gujarat. Terrorism — echoing a carefully chosen phrase by the then Prime Minister of Australia, John Howard — 'was now on our doorstep'. The Bali bombing which inflicted death and injury on a large number of Australians and Balinese, as well as other nationalities, accentuated the growing angst and resentment towards the identity known as 'Muslim', compounded by media images of Muslim-led terrorism by such groups as Al-Qaeda, the Taliban and most recent ISIS.

In the aftermath of 9/11, the Hindu immigrant community, feeling threatened, began to identify strongly with the ideological values of the settler community (Bilimoria 2006). They, along with Christians, Buddhists and others, felt uncomfortable and destabilised in the presence of Muslims: not just Muslims making their passage to Australia but also Islam as an international presence in many parts of the world. Regardless of what particular ethnic origin or regional location Muslims might belong to or come from, modern Hindus and Sikhs have unsettling memories of the centuries of apparent tension and occasional bloodshed between their own kind and Muslims in the subcontinent. During the British *raj* and the nationalist freedom struggle, this communal divide increased and led to the partitioning of India. Thankfully, such feelings of unease and tension do not seem to be present in members of the younger, second generation in Australia. The events of 9/11, it seems, have accentuated suspicion of Muslims among many Hindus and Sikhs, both residing in India and in the larger diaspora; indeed, the Hindu Right, led by the Bharatiya Janata

Party, capitalised on the convergence of the threat of Islamism to external security and the internal threat to the purity of India (Appadurai 2006: 105-10).

PHASE IV: GLOBALISED HINDUS/SIKHS

The last phase of transnationalism, unlike the previous phases, directly involves globalisation and only a trace of localisation. Globalisation has many faces, but the part of the process that is relevant to this phase concerns the even more rapid mobility of personal and social space made possible by the new technologies of travel, time traversing, long-distance communications, mass media and the deregulation of the market that leads to the expansion of TNCs (transnational corporations), and interconnected 'flows of capital, information and people' (Tambiah 2000). The view is that the world has become but a 'village', or a homogenised 'open door' that enables states to stake claims in trade relations, the free-market economy, financial structures and even the governance of smaller, poorer nations and their inhabitants. Agents of globalisation are able to both pull and push information or data and choices across the globe.

> The data transferred is stripped of its local cultural significance and the circumstances, both personal and social, of its creation are discounted. —Jordan 2000: 7

Religion too can be de-sacralised or secularised and stripped of its cultural specificity or local signification and application, even as it is universalised in the name of God. A different kind of labour flow emerges as well, as transnational forces locate and shift the sites of their technological and capital-intensive activities. Today it is Hong Kong, tomorrow it could be Sydney, and another day Atlanta, Georgia, or Toronto, Canada. Arguably, the United States appears to be at the helm of this system, driving as it does the unfettered forces of high-velocity capitalism, media control, open market economy, trade monopoly, long-distant credit and multilateral sanctions, leaving disadvantaged communities feeling fractured, economically disenfranchised, nationally dislocated and facing ethnic extinction (Appadurai 2006: 22-25; Harvey 1973 and 2005).

The most recent group to become transnational migrants under this global trend has been the computer professionals from the Indian state of Karnataka. Bangalore took the lead in transforming itself into a major infotech city, teaming up with TNCs, software and IT industries in Silicon Valley and other parts of North America, gradually saturating some sectors of this industry in the global arena, and increasingly adding call centres to the industrial outsourcing. Software and IT specialists from this region (and lately from Hyderabad, Maharashtra and Gujarat) have been in much demand outside India. Collectively they own and operate almost the second largest conglomerate, in terms of dollar and stock market value, of IT industries in the United States, and they boast the highest number of 'start-ups'. Australia too was not to be left behind in this global race and since the late 1980s has permitted a slow but steady stream of IT graduates and professionals to service its own needs, although Indian companies have not been attracted to establish their 'start-ups' and sister operations here, unless they come via the United States, other than call centres and certain outsourced satellite outposts. All the major cities in Australia have up to or over 2,000 Kannadigas gainfully employed in this sector of the industry, which still only equals the number of professionals arriving in the United States in any single year (Voigt-Graf 2000). This is a close-knit, cohesive group and they frequent the Hindu temples in larger numbers than do their north Indian counterparts with comparable educational and urban background. Clearly, social networks are also important for maintaining a sense of belonging and identity in the local context. Certainly globalisation has led to a diversification of the migration pattern, but diversification without the mark of difference.

Unlike the earlier Indian migrants and in stark contrast to the Indian Fijians, however, the Kannadigas (there are many Marathis in this boat as well) are not the typical 'glocal' residents, for they maintain strong links with their home city and the parent companies they originally worked for, and they visit India more frequently than other Indian settlers do, reinforcing the close links and obligations across the Indian Ocean (Voigt-Graf 2000). Some work hard and save up earnestly so that they can return and live more comfortably in their favourite home city. In addition, they have close connections with the professional diaspora in the United States, where most of their contemporaries or cyber-cousins have relocated, and where they themselves would prefer to be, given that the vocational returns and earning capacities there are deemed to be much higher than in Australia, the lower cost of living and a slower pace of life in Australia notwithstanding. Some succeed in transferring across the United States after gaining added credentials in a 'Western' setting. Work assignments may take them for short periods to adjacent Asian countries as well, or to the rapidly developing Four Dragons. These are transnational cyber-settlers in transit, equipped with tri-band cellular phones and internet-on-the-run, subjecting themselves to more frequent relocation than was the case even with the twice migrated groups. Theirs is not an experience of diasporic dislocation, as they are already well-trained global or multi-transnational citizens, the products and harbingers of 'ISD-globacity', who have already achieved the identity status of being RNI (resident non-Indian), while finishing college or landing their first apprenticeship in one of India's urban centres.

Curiously, both the transnational groups (i.e. of the last three phases we have discussed) have had a peculiar re-enculturative impact on secondary Indian migrants, particularly the Fijian Indians. Since Fijian Indians, with their business and local trading skills, have set up large numbers of Indian spice, clothing, jewellery and video outlet shops, their social contact with India-direct migrants and temporary residents (IT workers, students and visitors) have increased, with the consequence that the faded memory of the forebears' homeland of India becomes a more accessible, imagined home country. They are also drawn into the religious, social and cultural activities of the transnational Indians whose sole endeavour seems to be to bring India little by little in all its facets to this country. Fijian Hindus and Sikhs never managed to construct such grandiose temples as have appeared in the Australian landscape, complete with the elaborate ritual practices enacted by sectarian priests brought out from India (another important transnational import). In Fiji the concern was with retaining the *political* identity of an ethnically distinct Indian group, which is more under threat than ever before, but in Australia the same group is exposed to a different kind of post-colonial discourse, where cultural capital, the morality of *dharma* and religious identity are at a premium as vehicles for retaining Indian-ness. They further seek out their own kindred in terms of regional, linguistic and caste groupings, which was comparatively less diverse and sophisticated in Fiji, the Gujaratis or 'Bombayites' being the only Indians who seemed closely connected with India (being much later émigrés).[8] Last but not least, Fijian Hindus in Australia are also drawn into *sangha*s (religious congregations) in their worship of various popular gods and *guru*s, the most prominent of the latter being the late Sri Sathya Sai Baba, the enigmatic local preceptor known for his miracles and significant social reform activities, but whose globalising skills from a remote *ashram* location in Andhra Pradesh and intermittently in the outskirts of Bangalore, have been underestimated. More to the point, Fijian Hindus find themselves travelling to India more frequently as a result of this exposure than might otherwise have been the case. Whenever one lands in Bangalore airport, one is always intrigued to find a fresh large group of jetlagged Indians from New Zealand and Australia on their way to Puttaparthi, the location of the *ashram* and mega-hospital of Sathya Sai Baba. Upon closer look a good number of them turn out to be of Fijian Indian origin. Twice-over transnationalism can also take the form of return to the long discarded imagined homeland, in a metonymic, spiritual sense.

'The Global Production of Locality' and the Promises of Disjunctured Globalisation: Small Numbers at Large

What is the identity of those we described under Phase IV (and even, perhaps, Phase III)? Arjun Appadurai argues that the primary identity is diasporic since the immigrants in question wanted to leave India anyway and merge their identity not as a 'resident alien' but as a hyphenated, transnation/post-nation American (he is writing in America about the Indian American), who only catches glimpses of her or his life in the dissimulating mirror held up by the 'rustic tribes' that flood his neighbourhood or workplace and claim him as their very own. This scenario creates ambivalence in the diasporic citizen of the new world. But Indians are a heterogeneous people, and as we have been at pains to show, their own pattern of migration and settlement, location, dislocation and relocation has been varied, and more so in the Australian context than in the North American. Appadurai's revised thesis captures the heterogeneity, dislocation and variation in the experience in question (2006). He thus observes:

> In the United States and in the ten or so most wealthy countries of the world, globalisation is certainly a positive buzzword for

[8] The Bombayites in Fiji are called "passenger Indians" by native Fijians.

> corporate elites and their political allies. But for migrants, people of colour, and other marginals (the so-called South in the North, it is a source of worry about inclusion, jobs, and deeper marginalization. — ibid.: 35

On the positive side of globalisation — which is not measured by the welcome gestures of the dominant, or 'vertebrate', nation states — Appadurai's thesis argues for radical disjunctions in the process, especially against the views of Wallerstein (1974a, b), Robertson (1994), and Weber (1946: 342) (cf. Bilimoria 2009a), who align contemporary globalisation to the spread of the nation form, dictated by the concurrent spread of colonialism and print capitalism — i.e. the stress remains on nationalism and the nation state, de-emphasising the global journeys of capitalist modes of thought and organisation. Against this, Appadurai wants to tie in the global with the local and post-national, deterritorialisation, the unboundedness or porousness of territory and cultural productions following decolonisation, particularly in the emergence of immigrant, diasporic and transnational movement or experience (1996: 188). All of this makes for an argument for the production of locality, as he construes this trope. Appadurai argues that globalisation is 'itself a deeply historical, uneven, and even *localizing* process' (ibid.: 17). He welcomes heterogeneity that does not any longer demand strict adherence to the liberal, social contract of the modern West; rather there is a greater role to be played by *culturism* (modern ethnic movements) and imagination, even in a world of schizoid rootlessness and alienation. For him, post-industrial cultural productions have entered a post-nostalgic phase and, furthermore, it is terms like the 'image, the imagined, the imaginary' that 'direct us to something critical and new in global cultural processes: the imagination as a social practice' (ibid.: 31). Appadurai captures his thesis most succinctly in the following passage:

> The many displaced, deterritorialized, and transient populations that constitute today's ethnoscapes are engaged in the construction of locality, as a structure of feeling, often in the face of the erosion, dispersal, and implosion of neighbourhoods as coherent social formations. This disjuncture between neighbourhoods as social formations and locality as a property of social life is not without historical precedent, given that long-distance trace, forced

> migrations, and political exits are very widespread in the historical record. What is new is the disjuncture between these processes and the mass-mediated discourses and practices (including those of economic liberalisation, multiculturalism, human rights, and refugee claims) that now surround the nation-state. — ibid.: 199

> Modernization has made all this possible as an affect and after-effect (hence 'modernity at large'). Its own creation of diverse spaces and mechanisms (for communication, relocations, mobilization of people, distinctions all intended for homogenization and disciplinary-control), also unwittingly ensues in informal techniques for subversion, evasion, and resistance, sometimes scatological, sometimes ironic, sometimes covert, sometimes spontaneous, etc. — ibid.: 191

If Appadurai is right, and the race is on to join the modern in 'self-exile', one must still ask how systematically (and not just systemically) organised, consciously planned and productive is the race in terms of culturalist and re-localisation trace movements? How conscious are the 'self-exiled' of their historical identity, culture and genealogies or heritage that are not already tied to commercial consumption and monetary mobilisation? It remains to be seen whether the suffering, identity crisis, gender-based abuse and discrimination they experience are taken seriously, dealt with through cultural and political institutions constructed by the groups themselves.

Granted, the globalisation of culture involves the use of a variety of instruments of homogenisation: armament, advertising campaigns, language hegemonies and clothing styles. Yet these can also be instruments of cannibalisation and false reproductions. Nevertheless, Appadurai has explanatory devices to circumvent such counter-examples and has confidence in the dynamics of benign global cultural flow, even within the optic-fibrous corridors of narrow specialisation in single-state hi-tech and financial sectors that may profoundly determine 'the shape that ethnoscapes, ideoscapes, and mediascapes may take' (ibid.: 47).

Deterritorialisation Revisited

We have found some of the salient insights in Appadurai's thesis, particularly his *Fear of Small Numbers: An Essay on the Geography of Anger* (2006), helpful in our study of Indian communities both in Australia and in the South-east United States. Appadurai believes that the old order of things and settled ways of life, on the part of the immigrant groups, are increasingly hard to find. He is correct when he observes that

> The United States, always in its self-perception a land of immigrants, finds itself awash with global diasporas, no longer a closed space for the melting pot to work its magic, but yet another diasporic switching point. People come here to seek their fortunes, but they are no longer content to leave their homelands behind ... most groups that wish to renegotiate their links to their diasporic identities from their American vantage points are now free to do so ... thus ... Indian doctors from Michigan set up eye clinic in New Delhi. — 1996: 172

Ruefully he notes,

> The formula of hyphenation (... as Asian-Americans, and African-Americans) is reaching the point of saturation, and the right hand-side of the hyphen can barely contain the unruliness of the left-hand side. — ibid.

From Gokulam to Glocalum

Indeed, there is no gainsaying that Hindus and Sikhs in the diaspora — in their hyphenated identity, as Indian-Americans first, and Hindus and Sikhs second — have learned (with their left hand) to organise themselves as religious bodies and raise funds (with tax-free breaks for their own kind), erect as many large temples as possible as part of the sacralising act of 'recreating' their erstwhile Indian or imagined religious site, culture and ecology, and they dot these shrines across the landscape of the United States and Australia. They have further understood what it is to be aggressive and assertive about their rights and culture, as the transnational Hindu fronts such as VHP, BJP, and the platoon of *gurus*, *swamis*, cults, *sampradayas*, etc. with their gaze set on the West, expects of them, and which is their form of 'diasporic nationalism', underscoring the *politics* of accommodation, integration and assimilation (Tambiah 2000: 175), and, most importantly, success. They have also created voluntary support and start-up networks for professional aspirants in their community (expatriate and second-generation), with some gestures toward the needy, the homeless and the battered. They also send large sums of money and resources back 'home', where they believe they have an interest or a cause to support, for, as they often say, 'we must be giving back something to our mother-country, no?' At times, though, the motivation may be simply to provide local jobs, earnings and dividends for the excess relatives left behind, for space is also limited and exorbitantly costly in their new land. Hindus and Sikhs have probably not engaged in such transnational-cross-border and long-distance exchange, interrelations and politics since their cultural conquest of South-East Asia and the Malay–Indonesian archipelago back in the sixth to 9th century CE. Globalisation has indeed made all this possible, perhaps, again. The limit of the new modernity is the limit of imagination: new worlds are on the horizon.

However, as Rustom Bharucha has rightly observed, such 'virtual struggle . . . is an illusion, an abdication of direct confrontation', describing it as

> the voyeuristic site of a privileged global intelligentsia, who can afford to surf the possibilities of resistance through mediated discourses, transmitted from the trouble spots of Third World into the padded cells of first world intellectual production.
>
> — Bharucha 1998: 171, 178

They certainly do not reflect 'the power of mass literacy' in any linguistically or philosophically significant sense, nor do they augur for 'large-scale productions of ethnic affinity', no more than it happens in the land of hyphernates or disunited states of 'Amrika', or for that matter in Australia, or the among the increasingly cosmopolitanised RNIs in the urban locales of the subcontinent (see Lal 2008).

So while the productions of localities are happening all around us, these are not matched in proportion by radical disjuncture between territory, subjectivity, politics and collective social movement, or for that matter by the steady erosion, principally due to the force and form of electronic mediation, of the relationship between spatial and virtual neighbourhoods, and much less by the slow demise of the nation state breaking up into neighbourhoods of self-defined allegiances and affiliations. As David Ludden argues in the context of the modern global development regime that controls the so-called free-market economy, '[imperial] empires form spatially expanding and contracting — hence essentially mobile — systems of territorial order' (Ludden 2006: 28). In other words, where historically-mapped boundaries fracture, as nations disintegrate or are pushed to disintegration — through famines, war, regime changes and so on — the imperial forms of power infiltrate and take control of the emptied spaces, and filling it up with their own national modernity dressed as a universal, saving 'gift'.

At the same time, and this is a paradox to which Appadurai alludes, there is the unprecedented implosion of 'other subjectivities, caste mobilisations and new ethnicities' or 'ethnic affinities', the empowered imaginary of the marginalised. There are also experiences of extreme oppression and containment under mobile national economic policies.

These are the realities, then, that in the virtualisation of history, culture, religion and politics are driven to the borderlines of 'otherness' as a consequence of the normative and aesthetic abdication of modernity from these troubled locations; the ambiguous interplay of the two modernities (Eastern and Western) here leaves much to be desired, or is submerged in the persistent traces and desires of post-modernity.

Yet another problem that has escaped even the best theoreticians is that concerning the relation between religion and transnationalism, alongside the phenomenon of hybridity, in the broad sweep of globalisation, both in theory and in concrete modalities. Where this is noticed as a problem it is quickly subsumed under the analytic of culture, cultural formations and productions or reproductions as processual localities, ethnic and migrant identities refashioned, resistant indigenous sensibilities concerned about the loss of tradition and so forth, all of which in the longer trajectory make for a melange of a kind of chaotic implosion of 'ex-colony', 'de-compressed', 'deterritorialised', 'delocalised trans/ post-nation' and 'post-colony communities' bound together by a loose collective of inchoate 'ethnoscapes, mediascapes, linguoscapes', thereby contributing to the hybrid-heterogeneity of world culture, whose representative metaphor is the infusion of world-music — regge-bangra, multicultural-Bharatnatyam, Bombay-Duck and Hindustani-Bollywood films/songs/dance and so on.

But, again, what of religion? As Peter Beyer has correctly observed, religious systems are not able to claim for themselves an autonomous authoritative space or 'real assets' and are for that reason less coherent and less powerful than comparable political systems (*pace* Parsons 1961; Beyer 1998: 69-70). Nevertheless, being part of the particular cultures that are relativised in the wake of globalisation, religions do not disappear, nor do their identities become reductively assimilated into the secularised, de-sacralised civil space of the 'melting-pot' or the national culture (cf. Stephen Warner 1998). Rather, religions also undergo transformation and are reproduced in differentiated formations and local identities that also, with some groups at least, manifest global pretensions; i.e. they seek to break out of the 'windowless monadic' seclusion. In the case of migrated religions, or religions in the diaspora, the identity re-formation may well be overtly or covertly tied to territory, more likely positioned elsewhere (the imaginary of the 'home-land').

Organisationally, religion will likely utilise all the available instruments of institutionalised authority: elegant edifices, media and other transmissive communications, training programmes for the youth, missionary activities, even evangelical showcasing and, most importantly for its survivability and influence, alliances with powerful political systems. Religion is not necessarily swallowed up in the torrents of globalisation but itself becomes either a platform for resistance to the liberalising ethos of modernity (one way of usurping power), or a simulation or simulacrum of the globalising process itself, with its own ambiguities and local differentiations, as well as presenting itself as the focus of universalist aspirations. On the other hand, one has to be careful about the kind of conception and theory on which religion is based in this equation. While the systems-theory approach (based on belief systems and Luhmannian communication account) works in one respect, namely, at the 'macro' level, it also glosses over the more opaque dimensions of ritual and practice at the 'micro' level, and, let us say, within marginalised indigenous sensibilities. Liberal systems work with a very differently nuanced notion of religion, one that fits better its secular, civil systems, and one that is close to a 'civil religion', an ideology in which globalisation also has a vested interest (Padget 1999; Jordan 2000: 8; Maddox 1998).

Appadurai is aware that localities are fragile, even transient. In North America it is more evident that the size of temple congregations is declining, with the conspicuous absence of large numbers of second-generation Indians in the temples, although they are there for traditional dances and no-holds-barred celebrations and excesses allowed at festivals such as Holi, but this is part of fun and cultural festivities. It becomes a challenge to continue the robust priestly functions that require highly oral-based recitational training in classical Sanskrit or the southern vernaculars. In Australia the trend is almost reversed. Larger number of devotees and worshippers are attending temple rituals, including among second and third generation Hindus. This trend can only continue and increase with a constant flow of diasporic believers and transcontinental seekers. The inflow could cease as soon as the labour demand is exhausted, or the 'masked' protestors outside the WTO-WEF meetings in Seattle or in Melbourne win their right to organise global labour collectives and check the expansionist strategies of TNCs in complicity with the governments of the day, but that doesn't seem to be likely or anywhere in sight, at least in Australia.[9]

Religion as a Cultural Resource

While large numbers of devotees may be attending temple rituals in the diaspora community in Australia, some scholars have argued that the nature of religious faith has changed, partly as a result of the globalisation of religion. The prominent scholar of religion, James Beckford, for example, has argued that in the Western world, religion is more readily viewed as a cultural resource rather than as a social institution. His thinking has been enlarged and developed by many other scholars (Beckford 2007; Scheifinger 2010). Part of the reason for this change in the nature of religion is that religious rituals have become disembedded from their original localities and contexts. In the Western world, this has often been accompanied by a decline in the confidence that people have in religious institutions. It also reflects the fact that much of life is now lived in the Western world without reference to religious symbols or actions. Religious symbols and actions are, for most Westerners, additional sources of meaning or additional community activities in which people engage as or when they wish, rather than being an integral part of their whole way of life.

---

[9] Since 2003, a north-west council of Melbourne, the City of Darebin, has been actively involved in this celebration of the Ganesha Chaturthi. It is noteworthy that this celebration involved the local tram company and the State Electricity Service (SES) as well. The money placed in front of the god by the devotees is donated to the SES.

There has been some debate among scholars as to whether or to what extent Hinduism in diaspora communities in the Western world has taken on such forms. It has been noted that Hinduism does not have a unified institutional base that can be rejected in the way many Western Christians have rejected their institutions. It has also been argued that Hinduism has never made the distinction between the religious and secular domains of life that have dominated Western thinking about religion since the enlightenment. To that extent, Hinduism cannot be clearly separated from other spheres of life (Scheifinger 2010: 329-30).

On the other hand, for many diaspora Hindus, Hinduism is a series of symbols, rituals, even festivities, in which they participate as they wish. Hindu rituals are not omnipresent in diaspora communities such as Australia in ways that dominate every aspect of life. Hindus often attend temple rituals as they personally feel is appropriate or helpful. They engage in a *puja* at home to the extent they wish to do that. They may or may not choose to decorate their homes with pictures of Hindu images and symbols.

One particular example of this disembodied Hinduism is the placing of Hindu images on the Internet. A number of Indian temples have placed images of their deities on their websites. In a few cases, they have actually established webcams so that there is a continuing video feed from within the inner-sanctum of some of their temples. It has been claimed that this has allowed the practice of *darshan*, the gazing by the deities into the eyes of the devotees in order to receive their blessings, to occur over the Internet. In this way, Hindu *puja* is entirely separated from the physical temple and from the Hindu community that would normally gather at a temple (ibid.: 333). Indeed, some of the temples that are using the Internet in this way, such as the Jagannatha Temple in Puri, Orissa, would not allow non-ethnic Indians from entering the inner sanctums of their temples. Hence, they are providing ways in which non-ethnic Indians may access their deities while maintaining the restrictions on access at the physical site (ibid.: 338).

It is not known to what extent Australian Hindus or other interested Australians are accessing such sites. However, it is evident that there is a process of globalising Hinduism, as is also occurring in Sikhism and Buddhism. To some extent, the use of the Internet is contributing to this trend. At the same time, the process of disembedding Hinduism from its original locations, and the context of communities in which Hinduism was part of their whole way of life, may be changing its nature. To some extent, within the diaspora communities, as Hindu practices become options, Hinduism moves in the direction of being a 'cultural resource'.

Conclusion

Some of the issues for an analysis of transnational diaspora that we have examined include the following:

1. How is a tradition like Hinduism or Sikhism with its own unique cultural practices, and moral beliefs 'transplanted/translated/trans-created' in new, transnational, settings?
2. How in turn is the local host country — its geography, cultural landscape, economic character and symbols — transformed by an ethnic-religious group's need for and negotiated acquisition of social, ritual and cultural (perhaps even political) space?
3. How do each religion's adherents cope with, survive and stake or strengthen, further claims in the imaginary?
4. What is the impact of new religions on the new environments in which they are planted? How do people who have very different heritages respond to these beliefs and practices, which may appear very strange to them?

We have shown that Indian immigration was a mixture of 'coolie' recruits, domestic servants, farmhands and plantation labourers, camel drivers and hawkers, who were primarily Hindus and Sikhs. Estranged from their families, a good few eventually returned to their homeland. The ethnic-religious identity also came to prevail among the few remaining Indians. Thus, a Hindu merchant by the name of Pamamull, who came from the Sind region as an opal polisher, gradually built a family opal trade that has prosperously continued with his third- to fourth-generation descendants, who too remain devout Hindus, contributing generously to Hindu-Indian causes. The 20th-century Hindu migrant displayed different perceptions and response to the challenges they faced. Both internal and external factors have contributed to change and continuity, paving the way for a distinctive religio-ethnic identity to emerge. The closing decades of the 20th century, continuing into the 21st century, witnessed a more globalised and globalising pattern in the Hindu and Sikh diasporic experience. Here the local and global seem to be in tension, although some theorists are sanguine about the symbiosis of the two spatial directions, or in their dialectic of disjunctures, ruptures and emergence of new localities, hybrid and hyphenated identities and post-nation, ex-colony communities. This reinforces our analysis in regard to the distinctive identities that become constructed in the sense of general Indian-ness as well as specific ethnic identity. In the context of transnationalism and globalisation, religious communities, through their various religious institutions have, more often than not, also entrenched narrower ethnic identities. A good example is the Swaminarayan communities in the United Kingdom and the United States, where they have perpetuated as a result of their institutional approach to Gujarati linguistic or ethnic identity. Another example is evident in the experience of the Sikh community, which illustrates how religious communities entrench ethnic identities within the context of globalisation through their transnational networks, which run along ethnic lines rather than along broader national lines. It is not sufficient, therefore, to approach transnational identities through broad categories of nationalities, but rather one should also look at transnational networks along ethnic lines (Pratap Kumar 2011: 1).

While there is greater freedom of movement and mobility, and ease of transnational or transcontinental communication or connectivity, there are threats to the stability of the migrant communities' long-term presence and identity. Any number of globalising forces vie for control and a stake in their high-profile achievements, from TNCs eager to poach the high achievers, to extreme religious forces, Hindu, Tamil or Sikh, operating in the diaspora and eager to enlist their own kind in long-distance struggles in and fights for the homeland. But this much is politics.

As many a scholar of diasporas generally, and of the Hindu–Sikh diaspora in particular, have pointed out, religion has played a key role in creating or challenging modern identities.

> In doing so, religious communities recreate not only their conventional identity that they bring to the host society, but also produce new identities through assimilation and adaptations.
>
> —ibid.

The beginnings may be ever so humble, indentured labourers gathering in a humble shed to recite Tulsidas *Ramayana* or prepare for the festivity of Ramalila, but over time their grand edifices begin to compete with the Christian cathedrals or Mughal *mahals*.

> Beyond the religious myth-symbol complexes that informed the nostalgia for an 'ancestral homeland' among emigrants, historical records show that in many, if not most locations where stable South Asian diasporas developed, the archetypal institutions directly produced through the agency of these emigrants were typically religious. In the case of the 'old' diaspora born out of colonial capital, the initial structures of these places of worship may have been unassuming — a banyan tree housing a Hindu diety, or simple thatched huts with a corrugated iron roof [serving as a *gurdwara* or a mosque], but that not in itself limit their role as important building blocks for organising and mobilising incipient diasporan communities. — Rai and Sankaran 2011: 7

At the same time, the nature of identity and the part that religion plays in that identity for the Australian population has changed. Particularly in the major cities, most Australians are well aware that the Australian identity is often one part of a transnational or global identity. There are Chinese-Australians, Indian-Australians, Greek-Australians and Italian-Australians. For others that identity has become primarily a global identity. There is a sense of being human beings, first, who happen to be born in Australia (Batrouney and Goldlust 2005). Few Australians now see their identity as Australians as linked to a particular religious heritage. Religion has become a personal choice, part of a biography that the individual creates. As such, there is an openness to, sometimes a fascination with, religions from various cultures around the world.

Here we cannot help but echo the sentiments of Tambiah who we believe put it in perspective:

> . . . today there are multiple modernities that are evolving, and . . . such complex processes cannot be grasped by a general theory of modernity at large or encompassed by blanket terms such as hybridisation, eclecticism, creolisation, deterritorialisation, and so on. Such terms tell us something but not enough.
>
> — Tambiah 2000: 189

No less so in the broader Australian society. Here too the Hindu temple, along with the smoke from the Arya Samaji fire-oblation, and the chants of the *Granth-Sahib* in the Sikh *gurdwara*, symbolises the struggles within a multicultural and ethnically pluralising society. Religious diversity is a reality that Australia can no longer ignore, despite the anxiety to preserve the homogenising hegemony of Anglo-Celtic identity against the challenges of transnational pluralism, and especially of globalisation, that threatens to bring about radical change in a much shorter span of time than piecemeal social engineering accomplished over a century or two.

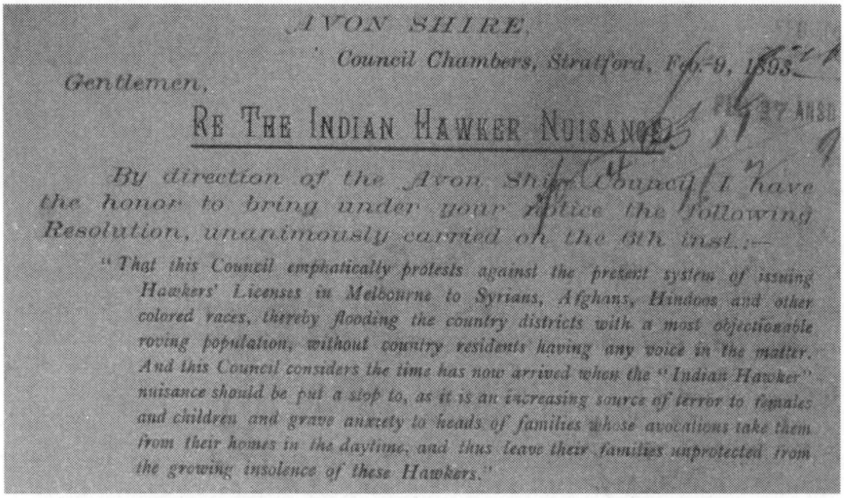

AVON SHIRE.

Council Chambers, Stratford, Feb. 9, 1893.

Gentlemen,

RE THE INDIAN HAWKER NUISANCE.

By direction of the Avon Shire Council I have the honor to bring under your notice the following Resolution, unanimously carried on the 6th inst.:—

"That this Council emphatically protests against the present system of issuing Hawkers' Licenses in Melbourne to Syrians, Afghans, Hindoos and other colored races, thereby flooding the country districts with a most objectionable roving population, without country residents having any voice in the matter. And this Council considers the time has now arrived when the "Indian Hawker" nuisance should be put a stop to, as it is an increasing source of terror to females and children and grave anxiety to heads of families whose avocations take them from their homes in the daytime, and thus leave their families unprotected from the growing insolence of these Hawkers."

fig. 1.2: The "Indian hawker nuisance", Avon Shire, Stratford, Victoria, 9 Feb. 1893 (source: Museum Victoria)

fig. 1.3: Sikh taxi drivers in Australia (source: flickr.com/public domain)

The Hindu Diaspora

2

Hinduism and the Historical Roots of Hindus in Australia

Purushottama Bilimoria and *Jayant Bhalchandra Bapat*

The Origin of the Religious Community and Its Development

A BRIEF HISTORY OF HINDUISM (Purushottama Bilimoria)

HINDUISM is a religious philosophy and a social system or way of living within society. It is associated predominantly with the Indian subcontinent or Greater India (*Bharatavarsha* in Sanskrit). The word 'Hindu' did not originally denote a member of a class or a community; it was merely a geographical designation. Nevertheless, the religion signified by this name predates the idea of 'India' as a country, and certainly any idea of a nation state. Indians were perceived, by foreign visitors and invaders alike, from the Ancient Greeks through the Muslims to the British and other Europeans, as being a particularly religiously-oriented people. The word 'India' comes from *sindhu*, the Ionian Greek name for the great Indus River in the north-west of the subcontinent. The name was later appropriated by Muslim groups, who intonated it as *Hinduh* and it came to refer to the people (Hindus, or Hindustanis) who occupied the land-mass on the far side of that river. Hence the region came to be called 'Hindustan'. 'Hindustan' as a geographical term included the whole of northern India and its inhabitants, whatever be their religion.

The term 'Hinduism' as such was used for the first time around the 1830s by the British, to provide a convenient description of the many sects among those adherents identified as Hindus. Furthermore, under this new homogenising category many more people, tribes and non-caste groups, including followers of the religion of Mahavira Jina, known as

Jains, as well as Sikhs, came to be included in official records, particularly the census, which the British introduced and used for purposes of governance. As we will see in Chapter 3, the British used an overarching term 'Hindoo' for all people of all extant religions and ethnic groups of the subcontinent. But it was a misnomer, and even offensive to people, especially Muslims and Sikhs, who are religiously distinct from the dominant Hindus. To this day, whole clusters of tribal groups and aboriginal peoples in India are counted among the Hindus, even though they may not see themselves as such. One could also speak of 'Hinduisms' — as the scholar of the world's religious philosophies, Ninian Smart used to say — as the people we call Hindus never saw themselves as a homogeneous group, following one monolithic tradition that did not acknowledge and tolerate internal diversity. In the history of religions, though, it has become commonplace to speak of 'Hinduism' as heuristic marker.

Hinduism is amongst the oldest of the living religions in the world today and one that shows no signs of abating despite, or perhaps in the face of, the three centuries of philosophies which have defined reality in terms of what can and cannot be logically and empirically investigated. Today Hinduism boasts over 1 billion adherents (15% of the world's population);[1] 95% of Hindus live in India. A few million Hindus live as minority groups in various other countries, including countries that have adopted Hinduism as either their national or as a recognised religion, such as Bali, Nepal, Sri Lanka, Bhutan, and much of South-East Asia. There are pockets of Hindus in varying numbers to be found in just about every country in all corners of the world. In North America, there are 2,250,000; the Middle-East and North Africa 1,720,000; the Sub-Saharan region 1,670,000; Europe 1,290,000; Latin America-Caribbean 660,000. In addition, Hindus have a median age of 33, which means that Hindus are younger than the global population.[2]

However, as a religion, far from being a monolithic and coherent

---

1 The figure based on the 2010 calculation in the Pew Research Center report is 1,033,080,000, of which 1,025,470,000 live in Asia-Pacific regions. Pew Research Center's Forum on Religion and Public Life, *Global Religious Landscape*, December 2012.

2 Ibid.

system of beliefs and practices, Hinduism has struggled and grown through discontinuities, divisions and fractures that have given rise to the abundance of sects, orders and other groups that constitute the vast and varying tapestry of Hinduism. Ninian Smart (1989: 44) has identified five major phases, described below, in the formation of the Hindu identity, its religious ideas and practices. Again, we have to be cautious in acknowledging that the category 'Hinduism' was not available to the early adherents of forms of religious belief and ritual and spiritual practices that were prevalent in the periods and regions discussed below. Let us begin at what might almost be the beginning.[3]

PROTO-HINDUISM

Proto-Hinduism in the earliest phase possibly dates from around 3000 BCE, with the Indus Valley Civilisation. Undeciphered inscriptions and artefacts bear testimony to the worship of a form of feminine divinity and a figure that scholars have identified as a proto-ascetic god, perhaps a forerunner of the great Hindu god Shiva.

VEDISM

The Vedic phase began around 1500 BCE with the influx of warlike pastoral nomads from the central Asian steppes, who settled in north-west India before gradually moving into the Gangetic plane during the second millennium BCE. Their agrarian culture, dependent on the gods of nature, is reflected in the repertory of sacred hymns, the earliest of which are collected in the Rigveda. The Vedas, from Sanskrit *veda* (what is known), grew into a huge body of recited and memorised 'texts' that both eulogised and appeased the gods. They were used in liturgical sacrifices and elaborate rituals supported by the chanting of the sacred *mantra*s (coded formulaic syllables).

As well as fighting amongst themselves, the Vedic peoples — who called themselves *arya*s[4] — directed their antagonism towards the

---

[3] Even the foundational category of beginnings or 'origins' is something seriously contested by some schools of Hindu thought, such as the Mimamsa, who consider their particular religion based on the sacred Vedas to be eternally present or re-kindled in successive cosmic-trace recurrences or temporal cycles, called *yuga*s, without the intervention of any divine force.

[4] In Sanskrit, *arya* means 'noble one'.

preceding inhabitants of the land, who are referred to in the Vedic texts as *dasyus* (dark-coloured) people. It is possible that the reference here is to the Dravidic (later, Dravidian) people who may have been pushed southwards by the invading nomads (with their distinctive linguistic and cultural patterns that mark them off from the 'northerners' to this day). During this period, a new order of things, cosmic and social, was thus born in north India. Within this social-ethical framework was found the idea of *varna* (ordering of society by caste). The brahmana priest (Brahmin) was the highest among the 'twice-born' castes,[5] equipped to recite the sacred formulae and prepare *soma* (sacred drink of the gods). He was therefore divinely privileged to take charge of sacrificial ritual and to dispense morality in the human realm.

BRAHMANISM

In this pre-classical phase, the Vedas more or less provided the framework for the development of creative world-views, with adopted elements from the local and indigenous cultures. Different strands of Indic civilisation matured over the millennium from roughly 1000–100 BCE, with the composition of the philosophical texts known as the Upanishads (800–400 BCE), the Jaina codification of the teachings of Mahavira, and the arrival of the Buddha (*c.* 500 BCE). These strands together marked a shift from ritual life to a speculative, semi-ascetic and contemplative form of life. Some of the strands developed into other forms of spiritualities or sects. A few developed certain heterodox practices, including explorations of the unconscious and sexuality in the spiritual, which at the far end of the spectrum was collectively known as left-hand Tantra, or the tantric tradition, across both Hinduism and Buddhism.

CLASSICAL DHARMA AND THE BHAKTI MOVEMENT

The great classical period, from 200 BCE to CE 1100, continued the pattern of pre-classical religiosity, with Hinduism developing a strong moral ethos (*dharma*) and a range of rituals and practices associated with worship in temples. The classical development emphasised the dimensions of devotion (*bhakti*) and devotional worship (*puja*) directed towards a plethora of gods and goddesses. *Yoga* (practice of moral self-disciplining) and some

[5] 'Twice-born' refers to an initiation, or 'second birth', that members of these groups undergo and that confers on them the right to wear a sacred thread.

community religious activities were also in evidence. Traces or echoes of the esoteric Tantra were to be found in both *bhakti* and, particularly, in *yoga*. A great many texts were composed or compiled during this period, including personal ethical or moral manuals, as well as social and political treatises and popular Hindu poetical or lyrical lore. These included the Dharmashastras, which were treatises on codes of conduct, and the Arthashastras, which are treatises about society and ethics. The great epics, *Mahabharata* and *Ramayana*, were composed during this time. So were many other philosophical and theological works by great teachers, such as Shankara (8th century) and Ramanuja (10th century).

The Puranas, which are mythological stories told in an intertwining manner, were also composed during this time. However, unlike the earlier texts, the Puranas and the whole range of devotional literature called Smriti (the popular scriptural sources) contained religious ideas and practices that drew heavily on localized developments from below, as it were. They reflected the more general perceptions, aspirations and experiences of the common people, often in contrast to the preoccupations and ritualism of the brahmins. For example, while the Vedic gods were most often sky-gods, or prototypes of celestial beings, the gods of the Puranas took on animal and half-human forms, reflecting the culture of India of that time, which was based on agriculture.

With this new beginning, a colourful picture of a multitude of gods emerged from the all-inclusive impersonal transcendent principle found in the Upanishads. Each of the gods acquired a personal face and assumed a role in the running of the cosmos. For instance, the god Brahma was the great being (or Being) associated with 'creation' or emanation of the universe. Vishnu was seen as the preserver and sustainer of the universal forces. Shiva was the god of destruction and revitalisation, also serving as the symbol of inward contemplation and release from the nets of worldly existence. Vishnu and Shiva, in their own ways, were virtually elevated beyond the other gods. They were regarded in a way similar to the Almighty Deity in the Judaeo–Christian tradition, as responsible for the salvation of human beings.

Unlike the Judaeo–Christian tradition, however, the female personification, known as *shakti* (dynamic energy) emerged strongly in the Puranas and was manifest in different forms, such as Lakshmi, Durga,

fig. 2.1: Goddess Visalakshi with Lord Vishvanatha in the Shri Shiva–Vishnu Temple, Melbourne (photo: Shri Shiva–Vishnu Temple Management)

Sarasvati, Devi, Parvati and Ganga. Shiva's two sons, Ganesha and Murugan or Karttikeya, also came to prominence. Vishnu was appropriated in human forms, especially in the *avatar*s (divine embodiments) of Rama and Krishna.

MEDIEVAL AND MODERN HINDUISMS

From CE 1100 to the time of the arrival of the British in India, certain features from the classical period continued to evolve , but Islam, which arrived on the subcontinent from the 8th century onwards, also significantly influenced the Indian people. Muslim culture permeated Hindu households and institutions and vice versa. Buddhism went into decline and Hinduism adopted some elements from Islam, as well as later from Christianity. The latter led to revivalist and reformist movements within the Hindu polity. These movements developed partly as responses to British imperialism and partly as reactions to a stridently obstinate orthodoxy of the brahmins, which was oppressive and discriminated against women and the lower-castes. Nevertheless, the 19th century neo-Hindu or 'renaissance' movement in which leaders — mostly Bengalis and some Hindu-Punjabis and Marathis — such as Swami Dayanand Saraswati (founder of the Arya Samaj), Lala Lajpat Rai, Bal Gangadhar Tilak, and most notably Swami Vivekananda (who was inspired by the mystically-intoxicated Calcutta-based Sri Ramakrishna, and 'stole the show' with his powerful speech at the Parliament of World Religions, in Chicago, in 1893). Before these 20th century reformists, from the end of the 18th century, there had emerged thinkers, such as Rammohun Roy (1772–1833) and Keshab Chunder Sen (1838-84), both of whom played prominent roles in recasting Hinduism as a universal, more liberalised and pragmatic religion in response to the British–European denouncement of certain Hindu practices still prevalent at the time, such as *sati* (widow-burning). Other so-called 'blights' or blots on India's dominant and historically ancient but bewildering faith included the absence of an over-arching ecclesia or church; belief in casteism, astrology, reincarnation or redeaths and fatalistic *karma*; asceticism, matched by excessive ritualism and the poly-perverse eroticism of Tantra; absence of natural law doctrine; the proclivity of Hindus toward polytheistic idolatry; foeticide (especially of girls); child marriage; selective polygamy; *niyoga* (prohibition of widow remarriage); the practice of dowry ('bride-price'); and other kinds of disenfranchisements of female, caste, and under-caste groups. In a country burdened with communal, religious, linguistic and ethnic differences and tensions, as well as the negative impact of European colonialism, the reformists argued that Hinduism should be modified or reformed so that it was concerned as equally with the welfare and good of the people in the real-world as with the transcendental.

After the end of First World War, the rise of Mahatma Gandhi contributed to the strength of popular Hinduism. Through him the religious ethos was developed in such a way as to aid the patriotic freedom struggle, which gave the subcontinent its independence from two centuries of British rule. Yet, on the eve of Independence, the world also saw the rise of two bitterly opposed nations with immense internal ethnic and religious diversities, namely India and Pakistan (East and West). East Pakistan later broke away to form what is now Bangladesh. The colonial and post-Independence periods, with the opportunities they presented for travel, but also the uncertainties of life under turbulent conditions, instigated a far greater movement of Hindus from India and Sri Lanka (among its Tamil population) to regions outside the subcontinent than had ever occurred before in its history. It led to the phenomenon now widely known as the 'Indian diaspora'. Australia's links with Hinduism and the Hindu community begin here, with colonial contacts and the early 'coolie' migration.

Beliefs

TRADITIONAL SOURCES

Although not a 'Religion of the Book' as such (unlike the Abrahamic religions), Hinduism has its own body of canonical sources. The foundational scriptures, the Vedas, are regarded by Hindu philosophical systems at least, as a kind of 'authorless revelation' (*apaurusheya-shruti*), literally, 'that which was heard', since the timeless Words were simply 'heard' by contemplative seers around the beginning of the present epoch (*yuga*) (Bilimoria 1994a). The idea that there are 'authorless texts' does not mean that in practice Hindus do not believe in a 'Creator', or 'Transcendent Revealer'. Some see these texts as stemming from a demiurge, the Great Lord (*Ishvara*) (Bilimoria and Stansell 2010).

As we have seen, the broader Hindu tradition came to embrace other scriptural texts after the Vedas and the philosophical Upanishads as being significantly authoritative. Included in the list are the epics *Ramayana* and *Mahabharata*. The Dharmashastras and Puranas followed later. These texts contain prescriptions for rituals, worship and observances; philosophical or 'higher' principles to guide people through issues and problems in life; codes of law; moral and ethical teachings for self-discipline, managing emotions, social conduct and care for sentient creatures; manuals on government and social organisations; wisdom teachings on Yoga, Tantra and meditation as aids to self-realisation and liberation; vignettes on death, rebirth or life-hereafter.

fig. 2.2: Sages taking instructions on the Vedas from an *acharya* (grand-*guru*)

Classical Hindu philosophy underscores the belief in one ultimate reality known as *Brahman,* the impersonal absolute Being, that is also responsible for the blueprint of the emergence and dissolution of the universe over the vast temporal cycles called *yuga*s. A hymn in *Rigveda,* Purusha-Sukta proclaims that the entire cosmos and the gods, divinities, and all beings alike, emanate from *Brahman*, with which they all merge at the end of the Time, only to re-emerge again, possibly in a different geometric and cosmological arrangement. Hindu mythology attributes the material task of 'creation' to the first-born god, Prajapati or Brahma (not to be confused with *Brahman*). However, even the gods and holy mothers rely on the inexorable principle of *karma* ('Law of Action and Reaction') to maintain the universal order (*rita*), even as they oversee the harmonious governance (*dharma*) of the planetary, social and individual (across all species) life-worlds.

KARMA AND REINCARNATION

There are two cardinal doctrines of the Hindus which are followed assiduously and are popularly known are *karma* and reincarnation (or rebirth). *Karma* is the notion that every action creates conditions for its own reaction and retribution or reward, either immediately or later in life, or perhaps in another lifetime. Indeed, the momentum of unresolved *karma* may well necessitate a subsequent physical embodiment in which the accumulated *karma* (good and bad) can be worked through. It is not necessary, therefore, to postulate a Supreme Being or God for the process of retribution, dispensation of rewards and balancing of good against evil and the suffering in the world. In other words, merits and demerits that accrue from actions, in the form of deeds, words and thought or desires, impinge directly and inexorably on the destiny of the individual, here and hereafter. Since one lifetime may not be sufficient for the cumulative *karma* to be adequately resolved and fully exhausted, the cycle of recurrent death and birth (*samsara*) continues until the individual is able to block all *karma*-producing actions and thereby gain liberation (*moksha*) from recurring deaths. *Moksha* means that the individual has successfully cast off the shackles of *maya* (delusional nature of reality) and reached the highest truth, which is said to result in re-merging or oneness with *Brahman*, even while living.

This state of enlightenment need not await death or another birth, as both are thought to have been overcome in enlightenment. It is a state of the 'clear-light of mind'.

THE CASTE SYSTEM

Traditionally, Hindu society is divided into four hierarchical caste groupings, namely, *brahman* (priestly class), *kshatriya* (warrior and ruling class), *vaishya* (agricultural and commercial class) and *shudra* (labouring, serf class). Then there are unspecified caste groups plus 'tribes' or clusters of non-urban or economically 'backward' tribal peoples that fall outside this fourfold scheme. They are referred to variously as 'outcastes' or 'untouchables' (*achhuta*s) or, as Gandhi called them euphemistically, *harijan*s (children of God), and nowadays as *dalit*s. Officially they come under the category of 'Scheduled Tribes (ST) and Scheduled Castes (SC)'. Below the vaishya, hardly any of these caste, non-caste or tribal groups identify themselves as Hindus (the official census, however, does). The trend since Indian Independence has been for these groups to identify themselves as neo-Buddhists or materialists, or Marxists, or to see themselves as living for whatever pleasures life might offer them. Many have converted *en masse* to Islam as well, or more recently to Christianity.

Society, then, was and largely remains organised along hierarchical lines determined by caste-distinctions, with the additions of numerous sub-castes and further divisions within the sub-caste groupings, called *jati*s (*jati* means 'birth'). Each caste and sub-caste differs in respect of the distribution of rights, entitlements and privileges, and denials and disadvantages afforded to its members. Some would argue that there were advantages associated with the caste system and structuring of society: namely, maintenance of the village economy and social order, assurance of employment and framing of social networks among the kindred for mental stability and moral support. The precise caste ordering of hierarchy and inter-caste relationships may vary from region to region, between one linguistic and ethnic or religious group and another, and also between the genders.

The cosmic principle of governance (*dharma*) became in time to be identified with the duties, rules, regulations and localised laws of different castes and ethnic groupings. As well as demarcating occupations and skills, the caste divisions have tended to entrench social divisions. They have at times been exploited for political and sectarian ends. Higher castes, or groups with a slight advantage over others, oppressed the 'lower' groups.

REFORM AND EVOLUTION

It is a feature of Hinduism, as with other religions, that from time to time every aspect of Hindu social practices has been scrutinised, questioned and sometimes reformed. For example, *Bhagavad-Gita* ('Song of the Lord'), a section of *Mahabharata* and the most celebrated of Hindu scriptures, has served as a common vehicle for rethinking Hinduism from its profoundly philosophical dimensions to its crudest popular or devotional manifestations. As noted earlier, in the late 19th and early 20th centuries, culminating with the freedom struggle headed by Mahatma Gandhi, there were genuine reformist movements, which attempted to eradicate many erstwhile customs, superstitions and outworn beliefs and practices. In more recent times, a revisionist trend associated with the Hindutva movement has set in, and an aggressive if not 'fundamentalist' tendency has surfaced, mostly among urbanised Hindus in the northern Hindi-speaking belt and in mid-western states such as Maharashtra. We are yet to see whether a reaction to this initiative will develop, such as the earlier liberal-reformist movements.

THE PATHS (MARGAS)

Socially-orientated reformist movements have not been the only transforming forces within the Hindu fold. Another movement, which transformed traditional Hinduism to a great degree, and which continues to exercise enormous influence at grassroots level, was the Bhakti movement. This is a personalised path of 'loving and faithful devotion — a total surrender' to a deity or aspectual divinity of one's choice or heritage. It came to prominence and gained wide popularity around the 14th to 16th centuries CE. One notable product of the Bhakti movement was a more open form of devotional worship to the 'blue' god Krishna, an *avatar* of Vishnu, which eventually arrived in a more popular form in the West with the Hare Krishnas. The founder of Sikhism, Guru Nanak (1469–1539), who had syncretised Hinduism and Islam into a form of mysticism, was also influenced by devotees of *bhakti*. *Bhakti* led to the relaxation of the formal and elaborate modes of worship that had developed under the aegis of the Brahmins over several centuries. One could say that *bhakti* led to the democratisation of Hinduism.

Three other widespread approaches to ultimate salvation, *moksha*, should also be mentioned, namely, *yoga*, *sannyasa* and *jnana* (Hindi, *gyan*). *Yoga* involves the practice of self-discipline, through which the individual seeks physical well-being and a balanced mental and psychical constitution. Physical exercises, controlled breathing, and mental concentration and meditation culminating in deep absorption, are central to *yoga*. Its devotees believe that special postures (*asanas*), supported by repetition of *mantras* (syllabic sounds or coded invocative incantations), such as the principal sacred syllable *Om* (intonated as *A-U-M*), help one achieve the goal of deep absorption. Traditionally, *yoga* is also associated with some preliminary disciplines and observance of ethical codes, such as truthfulness, non-injury, steadfastness, equanimity, non-attachment to the pleasures of life, and continence.

Sannyasa relates to renunciation of worldly commitments, possessions, and family and social ties, as a devout Hindu retreats to a total life of contemplation. Usually, a person does not enter the *sannyasa* path until all the responsibilities of life, family and community have been fulfilled. *Bhagavad-Gita* places a different emphasis on the role of the *sannyasin* (*sadhvi* for the female mendicant), in that it teaches the individual to be detached from the fruits or rewards of action rather than to renounce action (duty) itself. Disinterested performance, therefore, of one's duty according to one's station in life was commended in its own right. Unfortunately, however, this also tended to de-emphasise action connected with service to others. Altruistic actions are also deemed to be *karma*-accruing and therefore an impediment to liberation. Not until the early part of the 20th century was this principle reinterpreted to bolster commitment to the welfare and uplift of the 'other', the downtrodden and displaced, as Gandhi underscored in his slogan, 'work is worship'. 'Duty for duty's or rather *dharma*'s sake' and 'wise action for the benefit of others [*lokasamgraha*] through detached desire [*nishkama*]' have become common adages in modern Hinduism, based on the popularity of the moral teachings of *Bhagavad-Gita* and Gandhi.

Third, there is the path of *jnana* (knowledge and wisdom). This involves years of engagement in enquiry, deconstruction of everyday reality, reflection upon the truths gleaned, deep contemplation and further learning, usually under a wise and enlightened teacher or *guru* (Bilimoria 1989b). The Upanishads and various philosophical texts, including *Bhagavad-Gita* and *Brahma-Sutra*s, are used as guides for investigation of the enigmas of life, the quest for ultimate truth and how truth itself should be conceived. *Jnana*, along with *yoga* and *bhakti*, is incorporated into the system of enquiry known as Vedanta. Vedanta is literally the teachings that constitute the 'end' or culmination of the Vedas. This path attained immense intellectual and philosophical heights under the scholar Shankara and his followers, which is rivalled only by a parallel development in Buddhist philosophy.

Finally, in the Hindu understanding of reward and retribution through the karmic cycle, there is no need to believe in heaven or hell. However, in mythology and in popular belief, heaven (*svarga*) at least plays an important role as the dwelling place of the gods, along with those creatures who, by their enormous good deeds, have earned entry into the celestial space of unsurpassable joy, peace and harmony.

THE GOALS OF HINDU LIVING (Jayant Bhalchandra Bapat)

The ideal Hindu life is organised around three major goals or *purushartha*s ('human kingdom of ends'), namely, *artha* (the rightful pursuit of livelihood and prosperity); *kama* (the joys, in moderation, of the good things in life including the enjoyment of sexual pleasures); and *dharma* (the regulative pursuit of worthy conduct, rightful existence and moral stature). *Dharma* provides the framework for ethical social life and a personal ethic as well, which may cross into concerns for, or perhaps even duties toward, other sentient creatures. Virtues such as temperance, non-injury, equanimity, tolerance, self-control, gentleness and wonderment are emphasised.

The common adherence to the principle of non-injury, for instance, in Jainism, Buddhism and Hinduism, when applied to animals, is probably one of the earliest forms of animal liberation recorded in human history. Gandhi later successfully developed non-injury (*ahimsa*), into a positive law of non-violence, which he attempted to exemplify in his own political and social struggles. His approach became an exemplary strategy for bringing about justice and has been followed in other parts of the world.

Hindu *dharma* has spawned other virtues and attitudes that have attracted the attention of moral thinkers, bioethicists, environmentalists and common people alike, in search of a global ethics for humanity. This is not to say that the field of *dharma* is immune from its own paradoxes and dilemmas, which a Hindu might experience, especially in a modern and secular world. The problems are enhanced among immigrants living in countries that present very different sets of choices, pressures, restrictions and possibly even conceptions of ethics, from those in India.

Furthermore, what is deemed right (*dharma*) for one individual may not be *dharma* for another individual, given their personal differences as well as their place and responsibility in the larger social whole. *Bhagavad-Gita* seems to suggest that 'conscience' (*buddhi*) could be relied upon as the final arbiter of one's *dharma* (*svadharma*) where all other sources have been exhausted or come under doubt or suspicion. Modern Hindus look to gurus or revered teachers to enlighten them about their respective *dharma* in a world that does not have the traditional structures in which *dharma* evolved.

The notions of *dharma* and *karma* are intertwined. In other words, *dharma* implies that one's way of life has to be governed by certain codes of conduct that ensure that *karma* is minimised and individual obligations and social responsibilities are maximised. Thus *dharma* entails a social and an ethical system of ordering things in which the individual participates, and in terms of which life is organised. As for the ways people live, most Hindus see *dharma* as recommending an inward spiritual life, commitment to family and community, a disciplined lifestyle, and often vegetarianism and temperance. However, in the cause of preserving or revivifying *dharma*, many violations or exceptions to these ideals have been justified. How one resolves such conflicts and tensions, and negotiates the consequences of the resolutions, are of equal importance from the Hindu moral standpoint. In the last analysis, the responsibility rests firmly with the individual, and not with any outside force or authority.

Hindu Practices and Worship

Given the complexity of Hinduism, a vast assemblage of customs, taboos and expectations prevail among Hindus. The Hindu year abounds with observances, mandated rites and festivals. Hindus believe that the movements of the sun, moon and the various planets or stars have a special spiritual significance for life on earth. Their lunar calendar lists days that are auspicious or propitious, for such things as weddings, certain personal activities or for new business transactions. Hindus in Bali and Java in Indonesia are also beholden to this 'gods' eye' syndrome so much so that Sukarno and Suharto with their distant Hindu backgrounds would consult local astrologers before staging their planned military coups against each other.

Hinduism is a strictly personal religion, and does not entail any weekly congregation. Most Hindu homes have a mini-altar or a small wooden shrine in an alcove set aside for offering devotional worship (*puja*) to their chosen gods or *guru*, followed by *mantra* recitation and meditation. In previous times, the daily worship was performed by the man of the house; nowadays, women seem to have taken over the role. Before performing the *puja*, the family member bathes to purify herself and puts on simple, clean clothing. The concept of purity is all-important to Hindus. The deities are then symbolically washed, dressed and decorated with flowers and perfumes. Waving of incense and of light (*deep*, *deeya*) and sounding of bells are followed by prayers, and specially prepared delectables (*prasad*) such as sweets, coconut, water and milk are offered. Finally, the gods are requested to return to their abode in the skies

fig. 2.3: A goddess shrine in the Vinayagar (Ganesha) Hindu temple in Melbourne (Photo: Philip Hughes)

(*antariksha*) and to return again to bless the family when invoked the next day. The consecrated offerings are then distributed and consumed. On special occasions, an invited priest performs the rituals in greater detail. He is then fed, given clothing and money and his blessings are taken.

Temple worship is more elaborate. The Hindu temple consists of a central portion called *garbhagriha* (womb-shrine), where the main deity resides. Temple deities are installed through the performance of highly elaborate sets of prescribed rituals called *pranapratishtha* ('installing life in the icon or image') in especially dedicated shrines (see Chapter 4). In front of the main shrine or shrines is a large hall where devotees gather and pray and attend special worship services. Only the priest is allowed into the *sanctum sanctorum*, where he performs rituals that involve the awakening, bathing, dressing and feeding of the deity in the form of a highly-embellished icon. After this, incense, ghee or oil lamp, lit camphor and fruits are offered (*aarati*). During *aarati* worshippers stand facing the deity, while the priest waives the lamps around the deity and rings a bell to symbolise the warding off of harmful spirits, in a gesture that signifies the end of the ritual. The devotees may join in the singing of special incantations and hymns.

Hindu Rites of Passage (Samskaras) (Jayant Bhalchandra Bapat)

There are in all sixteen rites of passage (*samskara*s) associated with the major events in Hindu life, from the moment of conception to death. Most of these take place at home, which signifies the importance to the community of home and family life. The four most important rites are as follows.

***Birth*:** Special care is taken with the horoscope for the newborn infant, as it also suggests suitable syllables for the child's naming process. Many families perform a special act of worship (*namakarana*), which has its parallel in the baptism service among Christians.

***Initiation or Threading Ceremony* (*Munj* or *Maunjibandhan*):** In India this is of great importance for the brahmin boys in particular, as it indicates their readiness for religious education, much like *bar mitzvah* in the Jewish tradition. A festival for the attainment of puberty is also celebrated. The candidate bows to his parents and later the relatives to receive their blessing before sitting on a special seat to receive gifts before an elaborate feast. The most sacred *Gayatri mantra* is given to the candidate by his father during this ceremony. The priest then gives the sacred thread to the candidate.

***Marriage* (*Vivaha*):** Marriage in Hinduism is not a contract as such but rather a sacrament and a pledge-making event that is witnessed by the gods and the community. (In modern India, Hindu marriage is accorded legal status. Within a month after the ceremony, the wedding must be registered at the registrar's office. An official certificate is then issued.) The time and place of the wedding are determined according to the religious calendar. In the past, the ceremony itself used to take three to

fig. 2.4: Hindu bride dressed for wedding

fig. 2.5: Hindu bride and groom seated before the sacred fire
(photos 2.4-2.7: Jayant Bhalchandra Bapat)

fig. 2.6: Hindu priest conducting a wedding

seven days to complete; however, these days it lasts for about two hours.

As with any ceremony, the elephant-headed god Ganesha is invoked first. This is followed by the worship by the bride of Shiva and Gauri, Ganesha's parents, who are also considered to be the father and mother of the world. Lakshmi, the goddess of welfare and prosperity and Indrani, the wife Indra are also worshipped. The bride seeks a long and happy married life from these goddesses. Next come the rituals of welcoming the groom (*madhuparka*), exchanging of garlands, giving away the bride (*kanyadana*) and the tying by the husband of the sacred necklace (*mangalasutra*) for the wife. Offerings are made to Agni, the god of fire, in

fig. 2.7: A Hindu–Christian wedding

a central fire-altar, around which the bride and bridegroom go four times and pledge important binding oaths. They then take seven steps together (*saptapadi*) on seven heaps of rice, taking new vows each time. These vows signify pledges to share food, strength, wealth, fortune, auspicious seasons and everlasting friendship. The groom takes a vow to follow the codes of conduct as decreed by his own *dharma* and observe the sanctity of the marriage by following religious duties, earning a decent living and thereby looking after the family and enjoying sexual pleasures within wedlock. The couple also pray to the gods to be blessed with healthy offspring. Prayers for the presiding deities in the respective family homes of the newly weds are also offered, followed by a sumptuous feast and gifts from the guests.

***Last Rites* (*antyeshti*):** Hindus believe that the deceased should be cremated, not buried. The two exceptions to this rule are holy men (*sannyasins*) who have renounced the material world and are therefore outside the pale of social norms, and still-born foetuses and infants who have not yet been initiated. In both of these instances the bodies are buried. Cremation signifies the offering of the body to the gods as the ultimate sacrifice after the completion of the present lifetime, through the medium of fire and smoke. In India, traditional rituals involve placing

fig. 2.8: Final rites ceremony at the time of dispersing ashes (south India) (photo: P. Bilimoria)

fig. 2.9: Cremation, Bagmati River, Kathmandu (photo: Philip Hughes)

the cleansed body wrapped in cloth on a wooden pyre, and smearing with *ghee* (clarified butter) while the eldest son ignites the pyre to the accompaniment of Vedic *mantra*s and aligned chants from sacred texts. In Australia, a lighted incense stick is placed on the coffin by the closest relative as a symbolic gesture of lighting the pyre. The entire *antyeshti* ritual is believed to facilitate a smooth journey for the departing soul (*atman*) onwards to the celestial regions. On or after the third day of the cremation rite, the ashes are scattered in one of the holy rivers. The fourteenth day is a time of celebration, when the soul of the deceased is thought to have been freed entirely from all earthly bonds and suffering, or pleasures. To be cremated on the banks of the Ganges in Banaras is an ideal that is shared by many Hindus.

FESTIVALS

Besides these significant rites, Hindus observe many festivals. Festive days and important astronomical constellations, particularly the four phases of the moon (new, full and tenth day after each, called *ekadashi*), are observed assiduously in most Hindu households. Hindu communities have begun to distribute computer-generated *panchang* (almanacs) that register agreeable or propitious timings for novel or risk-bearing tasks, as well as the precise significance of the day in the lunar monthly cycle. This 'time-tuning' helps the family earmark days appropriate for observing certain rites, as well as fasting and maintaining purity in the household, which usually entails refraining from placing meat or alcoholic drinks on the dining table. Girls and women during their menstruation periods are generally discouraged from participating in *pujas*, observances or visiting temples.

Major festivals such as Dussera, Diwali (festival of lights), new year's day (according to variant Indian calendars), Sankranti, Pongal (among south Indian Hindus), birthdays of Rama and Krishna, birth and death anniversaries of the Buddha, and days dedicated to Ganesha, Shiva, Karttikeya, the goddesses Durga, Lakshmi and Sarasvati are celebrated with much panache. The celebrations variously consist of *puja*s, preparation of sweets and other delicacies, inviting family and friends to the home, exchange of greetings and gifts, prolonged chanting and musical enraptures, enacting and joining in a stylised fertility folk-dance (*garba*), and so forth. It can be an occasion for 'one big holy partying'.

fig. 2.10: Bengali Durga Puja celebration in Melbourne
(photo: Jayant Bhalchandra Bapat)

The major festivals are (with approximate dates from the Common Calendar):

Makara Sankranti (January): A festival of goodwill and celebration.

Vasanta Panchami (January): Related to Sarasvati, the goddess of learning.

Holi (March): A popular festival related to harvest, celebrated with joy, play with colours, bonfires and feasts.

Ramanavami (March-April): The festival commemorating Lord Rama's ascendancy to the sovereign throne, with readings from the epic *Ramayana*.

Guru Purnima (July): Annually on the mid-cycle full moon (usually the biggest in northern hemisphere), is dedicated to the worship of one's personal or clan *guru*, whether living or dead. The *guru* among planets, Jupiter, is also worshipped with much pomp on this special night.

Raksha-bandhan or *Rakhi-Purnima* (July-August): A renewal of the sacred thread for brothers by sisters and giving of gifts to sisters by brothers.

Krishna-janmashtami (July-August): Celebration of the birth of Lord Krishna.

Ganesha-caturthi (August-September): A ten-day period of worship dedicated to Ganesha, the remover of obstacles.

Vijaya-dashami or *Dussera* (September-October): The tenth and concluding day of the Nava-ratri or Nine Nights ceremony, with each day dedicated to an aspect of the Great Goddess (or Feminine Divinity), including Durga, a form of the terrifying Kali.

Dipavali or *Diwali* (October-November): For four days, rows of oil-lit lamps decorate towns particularly all over India, during the so-called festival of lights, marking the triumph of Rama over the demon Ravana.

Nava-varsha (New Year): The different ethnic and regional areas have their own new year. In northern India, it usually occurs the day following Diwali, while in south India it could be in January, or in April. The southern equivalent of Sankranti is Pongal, when homage is payed to the sun-god (Surya), which also marks the fresh harvest. There is also the Ugadi festival in the south, which is equivalent to Diwali and New Year and falls around Easter time in the Christian calendar.

Origins of the Community in Australia (Purushottama Bilimoria)

In this part of the chapter we map the religious contours of the South Asian diaspora in the Australian context, and highlight some specific features of this experience and its socio-history. This profile however cannot be understood without reference to the collective South Asian experience during the colonial period over the previous century and a half. And so we begin with a brief historical tour (some of which has already been touched on in the Introduction).

There are stories, now legendary, of Indian traders leaving the trading ports of Java and Sumatra and reaching the northern tip of a great southern continent in the last millennium. South Asian merchants had settled in small numbers in Malacca, from where Indian goods were shipped to islands as remote as the Moluccas and Timor. Hindus had long speculated about a vast inhabited landmass farther to the south of the archipelago islands (now known as Indonesia) 'beyond the moving sea'. However, fear of the formidable abyss of *Pausengi* (a mythical daemonic tree) prevented contact with this 'barbaric' world (Clarke 1971; Bilimoria 1989a: 16-17).

Another story, which is less credible, suggests that Tamil Hindus had sailed far southwards on double-rigger boats, making commercial and cultural links with inhabitants of islands in Melanesia and Polynesia. According to this account, the boomerang, the didgeridoo and totemism found their way to south India, along with some Australian Aborigines, identified as the Nishadas (Proto-Australoids) of tribal India. To add to the mystification, the previous Shankaracharya, or head, of Kanchi Koti Math, apparently advised a touring religious group from south India, *en route* to Australia, to seek out the 'lost tribe of Tamil Shaivas' who were said to be the vestiges of the indigenous community in *Austaalya-desam* ('the country of Australia)!

The Australian anthropologist A.P. Elkin suggested that connections may be discerned between the tantric-yogic practices of Tibet and India and the psychic practices of 'Aboriginal men of high degree' (Croucher 1989). Curiously, the Australian Aborigines seem disposed to this linkage with their own ancestry. Many Aboriginal stories refer to the coming of 'our people' from India long back in antiquity, contrasting it with the more recent invasion of the 'white men'. On the other hand, the Aborigines are known to have inhabited the continent for some 40,000, and perhaps even 60,000, years. Clearly such stories are wanting in historical corroboration, but they have become part of the multicultural narrative, and several volumes have appeared in India that attempt to re-construct these ancient imaginary links between the subcontinent and the last (or 'lost') continent.[6]

THE 'COOLIE' DIASPORA

The first concrete evidence of Asians arriving in Australia is dated around the early years of the 19th century.

However, since Hindus in Australia are part of the larger South Asian diaspora, we shall discuss their arrival in this broader context. A handful of people from the subcontinent reached the Great South Land soon after the early Europeans began to settle in the penal colony, around 1787. In an array of fleets (most built in the sea-ports of India, at the instance of British East India Company), that brought white settlers and convicts from Britain to *terra australis*, from 1787–1868, there was also a sizeable number of prisoners and dissidents from India, China and Africa (Menon 2011: 33). Trading ships leaving the Bay of Bengal and Colombo had Indian and Ceylonese (Sri Lankan) crews, along with other South Asians

---

6 On the possible relationship between the Aboriginals and South Indians, see Westrip and Holroyde (2010: Preface).

in the service of their British masters on board (Jayaraman 1988: 542). Since 1779 there had been attempts to import cheap labourers from India, to work on land in the emerging colonies. The British administration in India desired to send convicts held in that country to Australia and many were transported. Before beer took hold across the colony, Bengal rum had made quite a salubrious impression on the settlers. One Tamil-speaking Ceylonese, known locally as 'Black Jim', fled the docks and wandered the country extensively as a fugitive and ruffian, with a police price on his head. It appears he took refuge in the Aboriginal outback and was never sighted near the town pubs again.

Another fifty years were to pass before Indians were permitted to arrive somewhat freely or as *bona fide* labourers and merchants to Australia. As the hinterland opened up, renewed demands for recruitments of Indian labourers arose, and by 1837 about forty Indians were successfully indentured by a British planter from India to work in plantations in New South Wales. They were Dhangar (shepherds) tribal people from Chota Nagpur region who maintained quite different habits and practices from Hindus and Muslims. More men arrived in the next ten years and some dispersed into the neighbouring colonies. One shipload is said to have brought women and children as well, but this has not been confirmed.

This period marked the phase we dubbed 'transnational banishment' in Chapter 1. Heather Foster, from her research into the South Australian situation, adds the following observation:

> Two groups of indentured labourers were brought to South Australia in the late 1830s. The fates of these young men, both Hindus and Muslims, were tied to the fortunes of two settlers, Joseph Bruce and E.B. Gleeson to whom they were indentured. Bruce's suicide in 1838 (*SAGCR* 1838, Sept. 8, p. 6) and Gleeson's bankruptcy a short time later . . . resulted in just over forty indentured labourers without return passage to India. Their unfortunate lives can best be uncovered through the newspaper of the time and the South Australian state records. Stories of mistreatment, death in custody, and abandonment, paint a dismal picture of their lives (Foster 1994, 2002) and although two of the men married [local women] (one producing children) . . . no Indian or Hindu community developed from this group. There is, however, evidence to suggest that these indentured labourers

> retained their cultural and religious practices during their life time.
> — Foster 2010: 224

As we saw in Chapter 1, there was official apprehension across the colonies that the Indian practices of 'idolatry' and other moral 'evils', along with the threat of competition with white labour, might evoke violent reaction from European settlers. This led to the submissions to the Indian government to restrict emigration of Indian indentured labour. The Indian Emigration Act, 1839 came into force, although the government favoured a sponsorship scheme that assured return passage for young married couples with up to two children. A few Indians took advantage of this scheme and migrated as itinerant merchants, with 200 Anglo-Indians joining the printing industry, followed by Ceylonese Burghers. The 1857 Victorian census recorded 277 persons of Indian or 'Hindoo race'.[7] Hindus outnumbered Muslims and Sikhs from the Punjab region, and there was even a Parsi recorded in the 1881 census (Bilimoria and Ganguly-Scrase 1988a).

The latter half of the 19th century saw the arrival of 'Ghans' (short for Afghans). They were mostly Pathans from the Punjab, Sind, North-Western Frontier Province of Baluchistan and Afghanistan. Officially classed as Indian nationals, they were also racially identified as 'Hindoos', or even as 'Syrians'. Some indeed were Hindus and Sikhs, but the majority comprised Punjabi-Muslims, who spoke Pashto, Baluchi, Farsi, or a mix of Urdu-Punjabi. Their arrival in good numbers was the result of a decision to import camels to explore the formidable interior of the continent. In time, they provided ready transportation between the ports and colonial outposts. Since the solo camel that was shipped from Canary Islands in 1846 to Adelaide was put to death for having caused injury to its unexperienced white rider, an ex-British army officer from India, George Landell, travelled to Peshawar and Afghanistan in 1858 to buy camels and recruit handlers (Rangan and Kull 2010: 56). Twenty-four camels and three cameelers arrived in Melbourne, 'well in time for the Victorian expedition to traverse the interior to the Gulf of Carpentaria in 1860, the famously ill-fated Burke and Wills expedition' (ibid. See also, Chapter 5 and Appendix B).

---

7 'Race' was a common classification used in this period to register colour and religious roots.

fig. 2.11: Itinerant Indian merchant and his cart, early 20th century (photo provided by: Philip Hughes)

Thereafter, confidence in using camels did not abate and more camels were imported and more recruits arrived from the subcontinent. They worked, again, as camel drivers and handlers and helped local explorers cross the arid deserts westwards. Later, some ventured to gold mines in Victoria. A few enlisted as pastoral workers, while others set up camel-breeding stations or caravanserais. As women from the subcontinent were not allowed to join them, the men married local white or Aboriginal women. They built makeshift mosques in order to offer *namaz* (Muslim prayers).

Hindu and Muslim Pathans became hawkers and pedlars in small rural outposts. Liberalised licensing provisions in Victoria by the 1890s drew Asiatic hawkers in large numbers to obtain or renew hawkers' licences. The Indian hawker was a common sight with his bundle of silk and utensils and other wares, which he sold from door to door. When a Hindu or a Sikh died, he would usually be cremated in the open on a pyre made from eucalyptus logs. Most Afghans returned to the subcontinent to retire; some older men continued their small business or lived on casual earnings.

The first signs of public reaction to the presence of South Asians are recorded during this period. Notably, a news magazine report in 1893 repeated some of the stereotypes, especially about Muslims, already prevalent in the colonies (*Illustrated Weekly News*, 1 May 1893). The columnist chided the 'niggardliness' of Hindus and Mahometans [Muslim Pathans], who hoard money to take back to their own country. While they beg for tea and tobacco, they are less frugal with drinks, under whose influence they seem either horribly dangerous or irredeemably nasty'. Hindus, it was observed, were more liberal minded than the Muslims, allowing themselves 'more drink, better meals and clothes', but Hindus would not take food from a Muslim as a matter of religious principle.

Queensland moved to introduce Asian labourers on cotton and sugar cane plantations and passed the Indian Coolie Act, 1862, followed by a similar enactment in 1882. These moves were violently resisted by those opposed to imported labour and the Acts were repealed in 1886. This did not prevent free immigrants, including 500 Singhalese Buddhists, from landing to work in the banana plantations. In 1892 hysteria against imported coloured labour surfaced again. In 1895 there were magazine items in New South Wales that made derogatory references to the presence of 'black and turbaned heathens' (Jayaraman 1988: 542-45).

In sum, the pattern of South Asian immigration went through a mixture of indentured or 'coolie' recruits, working variously as domestic servants, shepherds and farmhands, later as sugar or banana plantation labourers, and camel drivers and handlers, hawkers and pedlars. Estranged from their families, many immigrants travelled back and forth and a good number eventually left for their original homeland. The merchant instinct also came to prevail among the Indian immigrants. A firm of Hyderabad merchants had branches in Melbourne by 1896 and thirty Sindh merchants settled there two years later.

This group included one Mr Pamamull from the Sindh region, who began his career here by polishing opals and later went on to establish a prosperous opal trading enterprise, which is continued to this day by his third- and fourth-generation descendants. They remain as devoutly Hindu as was their grandsire.

WHITE AUSTRALIA POLICY

The number of Indians rose from some 300 in 1857 to 2,000 in 1871 (58 of whom were recorded as 'Ceylon-born'), with a steady rise to 3,000 by the end of 1880. By the turn of the century there were approximately 4500 ethnic South Asians in Australia. Though not significant, the numbers were sufficient to fuel apprehension among the dominant white inhabitants, as there were also disturbances in other Crown colonies, and a near diplomatic impasse between India and Australia. Legislatures in the colonies introduced various restrictions on importation of Indian labour. Consequently, Australia never developed a unilateral non-discriminatory policy to allow free entry of South Asian migrants, and only a handful risked entry under private sponsorships for ill-paid, often short-term, employment provisions.

The official position further hardened against continued immigration of South Asians, indeed of all Asians. This anti-Asian attitude culminated in the Immigration Restriction Act, 1901 which effectively heralded what became known as the 'White Australia' policy. Racial exclusiveness was one way of asserting the superiority of the 'white race' and of its presumed supporting religious base, namely Christianity, and was repeated by many leaders in Australia over several decades.

The enactment of this bill effectively stopped migration from Asia. The introduction of a language test in which potential immigrants had to take dictation in a European language and various restrictive criteria made it almost impossible for anyone from Asia, other than a handful of students, travellers and merchants with British passports to obtain temporary permits to enter Australia. An average of five visitors a year came to Australia from South Asia under this arrangement between 1905 and 1923. The new restrictions virtually prevented the arrival of intending spouses, women family members and dependents from the subcontinent, some of whom were deported upon failing the language test.

The 1911 population census counted 3,698 'Hindoos', i.e. Indian nationals (Hindus, Sikhs and Muslims), including their offspring born in Australia, usually of mixed parentage. Employment became increasingly hard to obtain as the federated states introduced acts restricting participation of coloured labour in the fields. Despite protests and some easing of restrictions for British subjects, which most Indians were, the attitude of the society denied equal status to the coloured immigrants. The hawker-pedlar, who found it more difficult to renew his trading licence, found it even harder to settle down to farming or grazing. It was virtually impossible for him to acquire land or a leasing permit. Eventually, the railway and motor vehicle displaced his wagon.

Hindu-Indians, like all other South Asians, could barely survive in the so-called 'lucky country' under these circumstances. That they did survive is a testimony to their cultural endurance. In 1914 an ardent Hindu activist, Totaram Sanadhya, who had been living in Fiji, visited Australia only to receive the proverbial welcome with which Indians in Australia were all too familiar. He was greeted with the rhetorical phrase: 'All black; have you got no soap?' Sanadhya commented on the absence of any sense of community cohesion or religious identity among the Indians scattered in different parts of Australia. Most Indians appeared to survive by intermarrying and assimilating with the host society, as was expected of them (Sanadhya 1919, 1973: 72).

It was only the intervention in 1922 of the Indian diplomat and Hindu leader, Rt. Hon. V.S. Srinivasa Sastri (see Chapter 1, p. 9), that won the Indian residents certain rights and privileges, most significantly electoral franchise. Nevertheless, stereotypical and well-entrenched prejudice in the Australian psyche about the religious characteristics of the Indian continued to be printed. Wild and weird rites which Gandhi and the Hindus of his community allegedly practised were recounted in local papers. Even the cremation rite witnessed by many in the outback aroused allusions to 'Suttee' (*sati*, 'widow-immolation') (Bilimoria 1989a). This attitude was not helped by the liberal Sastri, who railed against Gandhi, the great hero and symbol of the Indian diaspora, and poured scorn on the 'philosophic anarchy' of the fervent fellow believer now lost to an extremist Hindu cause. The image Sastri painted of Gandhi as the 'plucky little bloke in a loincloth', continued to be printed.[8]

THE POST-INDEPENDENT HINDU SETTLEMENT

The Indian population in Australia continued to decline. In the 1950s, when one or two Indian academics arrived to take up visiting academic

---

8 *The Argus*, 2, 27 and 30 June 1922; a more detailed account of Sastri's visit to Australia, his accomplishments, and his relations with Gokhale, Gandhi, Annie Besant, Smuts, and The Servants of India, as well as with Prime Minister Billy Hughes, the Australian government, media, politicians, and resident Indians, will be presented in P. Bilimoria & S. O'Meley, 2015.

appointments, the number of Indians in any major Australian city could be 'counted on the fingers of one hand'. The 1954 census recorded 2,647 Indians in the country (Palfreeman 1965). In the post-war years the only group to experience any improvement in their condition were those with 50% European heritage. Many British and Australian nationals living on the subcontinent migrated to Australia along with their dependents, as did Anglo-Indians and Eurasians (Burghers) from Ceylon (Sri Lanka). In other words, before 1948, the trickle of migrants who arrived from the subcontinent was small, sporadic and far too scattered for a sense of ethnic or religious identity to evolve.

During this period South Asians arrived with different intentions and differing religious backgrounds. They worked hard, some travelled, a few studied, a large number returned to their extended families in the subcontinent. Those who remained usually intermarried with local white or Aboriginal women, and felt alienated from both the mother-country they had left and the uncertain surroundings in which they attempted to settle.

There are stories from within the Aboriginal community, or re-traced memories, that suggest that there were moments of amicable relationship between 'Hindoos' (from wherever, possibly the Indo-Malay archipelago as well) and the indigenous people, especially in eastern and northern parts of the country.[9] For example, Bundjalung people of the Brisbane–Grafton region remember three men named 'Mamoon', 'Ya Birrein' and 'Birrung', who had arrived with their grandma 'Gaminya' ('fast walker'). They came from Ngareenbeil. 'Negara', could be a local pronunciation of *nagara* (town), but more likely, as our informant pointed out, is a term for the state systems of Malaysia and Bali, and of brahmin ceremonial traditions. In Bundjalung, *ngrara* means 'ritual'. 'Coombadjha' (Kampuchea?) is a sacred site where the Dahn Dahra stream flows swiftly from the mountain (as in Dehra Dun in north India). Persian 'Vahu [Varu] Manu' means 'a learned man', could also be a name for Brahma, and Baiame is the creator in Bundjalung, along with Mahhji. Mahaji is a form

9 John Welch of Armidale, NSW, in personal correspondence (6 October 2008), cites local sources and typescripts prepared in the University of New England, and refers us to the website of the Australian Institute of Aboriginal and Torres Strait Islander Studies.

of Shiva in Thai-Hindu mythology. Indooroopilly, 'running water' (Tamil *palli*, 'well'), is a suburb today on the Brisbane River. Likewise, the narrative goes on, Gurre/Kgari, resonating with 'Gauri' (Shiva's white consort), is the shining white sky-spirit woman who formed what in white-fellow's cartography is renamed Fraser Island, off the Queensland coast, which has pure rainwater lakes that reflect the sky.

We discussed in the Introduction some of the consequences of transnationalism and globalisation for immigration ('open door') policies and the relatively freer movement of people in regard to labour needs, tradesmanship and requisite professional expertise. We return to this discussion in Chapter 3 where we look closely and in some detail at the statistics for the post-1970s.

Concluding Remarks

We now offer some concluding observations as we draw this section on Hindu migratory patterns to a close.

Some important factors contributing to the social and institutional development of a migrant community are said to be: resettlement after a period of uncertainty following migration and the tyranny of geographical isolation; competition for employment, resources and education for the young; confronting socio-political marginalisation; efforts to maintain cultural tradition in an alien environment; establishing ties, networks and associations to foster religious practices, spiritual and cultural events;

fig. 2.12: Swami Ranganathanada, who visited Australia

reassessing links with the 'home country'; and the ability to think through traditional institutions and adaptively cultivate a new way of living (Clarke, Peach and Vertovec 1990).

Such factors have played a considerable part in the development of the Hindu community as of the South Asian diaspora generally in Australia over the past century and a half. As with all people who leave their homelands for distant promises, Hindus in Australia have endured many hardships, persevered despite social and cultural alienation, and encountered racial prejudice and disempowerment as a result of their colour or religious background. Only in recent times has the community been able to resist the pressures of an assimilationist ideology that all but erased their earlier distinctive presence in the vast Australian landscape. This was exacerbated by numerically small and tightly controlled immigration with specific inbuilt biases, such as gender preference and skill-base.

The Hindu community in Australia has been slow in asserting and celebrating its ethnic identity or developing a heritage of values and customs which it could pass on to the next generation. Recently, such a dream has provided a focus for the community. The hope has been that the aspirations are not lost on the new arrivals, or the second generation. There are always tensions for immigrants between their hopes and aspirations and the reality of settling into their new country, and finding meaning amidst the pressures of a new existence.

One of the first visible signs of institutional development of Hindu religion in Australia was the arrival of Hindu *guru*s and *swami*s in the early 1960s. Several of them set up retreat centres (*ashram*s), along with organisational networks to propagate their teachings, recruit 'devotees' or converts, and offer classes. Since then, there has been a gradual shift in focus towards temples and more communal-centred worship amongst immigrant Hindus. This is one of the themes that we examine in some detail in the next two chapters.

3

Hindu Practices and Hindu Organisations in Australia

Purushottama Bilimoria and *Jayant Bhalchandra Bapat*

Rituals and Practices

GENERALLY speaking, Hindus in Australia aspire to continue and perpetuate the entire range of Hindu beliefs and practices. However, due to obvious constraints and limitations that are faced in a predominantly Western, secular environment, in the diaspora a more modified approach to traditional rites often results. For instance, elaborate Vedic–Agamic rituals, which require a large contingent of priests and other paraphernalia, have been performed only on the rare occasion of temple consecration ceremonies in the major urban centres. To a lesser extent, some elaborate rituals might be performed during the most auspicious days in the Hindu almanac, marking historic legends such as: Mahashivaratri (Great Night of Lord Shiva), Ramanavami (the birth of Lord Rama), Krishna-janmashtami (the birth of Lord Krishna) and Lakshmipujan (the worship of the Goddess Lakshmi at Diwali).

Rituals involving large-scale sacrificial offerings (*yajna*s) would not be contemplated. A mixture of Vedic and Puranic rites still comprises the bulk of traditional Hindu wedding ceremonies, although these are almost invariably performed in a shorter time, followed immediately by a secular reception. A Hindu marriage celebrant from Fiji may recite the invocations in a middle Hindi dialect, rather than in Sanskrit, as his counterpart from India may be better equipped to do. To avoid this 'short-circuiting', the more ardent Hindus take their marriageable children to India, to benefit from a ceremony performed in full regalia and with attention to details in customary practice.

Here, a word on attitudes towards caste identities in the diaspora may be appropriate. Among the earlier migrants, up to the 1960s, it was not uncommon to be identified in terms of one's village or town of origin and caste. Forty years on, caste is almost never discussed openly and much less does it determine the make-up of social and religious gatherings. Because of the secular climate of the adopted country, some local Hindus happily invite Muslim and Christian friends to *pujas* and allied functions. However, when it comes to the issue of marriage, caste considerations may play a significant role. Arranged marriages continue to constitute the majority of Hindu marriages and the suitable boy or girl is often selected along equivalent caste lines (although not always sub-caste or *jati*, or linguistic lines any longer). Preferences are stated, even in local and internationally circulated matrimonial columns of Indian newspapers, for particular caste background; although a compromise may be reached if the level of education and social-economic standing of the prospective partner is attractive enough. A Hindu family in Australia will happily have their daughter marry a boy of comparable (or even lesser) stature residing in North America or the United Kingdom, rather than enter into wearisome negotiations on dowry and immigration sponsorships for an identical caste suitor in India. Overall, caste preferences are staked not in deference so much to orthodox strictures but rather as an antidote to the perceived relaxed moral and sexual attitudes in Western society. However, despite such apprehension and the apparent failure of a few mixed-caste marriages, some Hindu families leave the matter entirely to the choice of the young adults in finding their prospective partners. In India, priests who perform funerary rites are not permitted to perform other rites, including marriage rites, on grounds of 'pollution' associated with death. However, in Australia priests have had to attend to funerals as a matter of social urgency; while the north Indian priests have risen to the call, their south Indian counterparts prefer not to do so.

With the sharp increase in the population of Hindus over the past ten to fifteen years, the demand for and the frequency of public and private ritual performances have dramatically increased. This has created an urgent need for professional priests (*purohitas*) who can attend to such community needs. Apart from funerals which are becoming increasingly frequent, the most commonly performed rituals in the two major cities have been weekly fire sacrifices (*havans*) by the Aryasamajis and the Satyanarayan Puja by most members of the community. The latter is performed either to seek material gains from Satyanarayana (Vishnu) or to thank him for something auspicious that has already taken place in the household. Another major ritual that often takes place in Hindu households is the blessing of the new abode by a priest (*vastu-shanti*). As most Hindus in Australia are professionals, they earn good salaries and are buying or building new houses in the better suburbs. It is not uncommon to see over 200 or 300 people at the house-blessing ceremonies held in such large abodes.

Funerary rites (*antyeshti*, see Chapter 2 p. 56) reflect an even greater change, in order to adhere to local health regulations. In the early days

fig. 3.1: Chandra, Tara, Renuka Sharma epitaph, Necropolis, Melbourne
(photo: P. Bilimoria)

cremation was neither popular nor encouraged in Australia. The first recorded cremation in Australia did however take place in 1895, when a Mrs Henniker of Richmond, a suburb of Melbourne, was cremated on a beach in the outskirts of the city in the month of March of that year. In the same year, some months later, a Hindu cremation followed. Chalmers perspicuously reports that it was 'bad enough when Europeans turned bayside beach into crematoria, but when Hindus followed their ancestral customs on a nearby beach later that year, mayhem was unleashed' (Chalmers 2001: 79). Only very gradually did the urban necropolises introduce, with the support of government regulations, proper facilities for cremation by those who had made a prior choice to be so disposed. In the early stages the cremation facilities used wood pyres, and it was not until 1936 when the first modern (furnace-style) crematorium appeared in Springvale, Victoria. There is a class of Hindus who have traditionally buried their dead. A case in point is that of Chandra Pratap Sharma, who, according to his ancestral custom, preferred burial.

In contrast, his daughter, according to her wish, was cremated and some of the ashes were interred in the same tomb as her father's while the rest were scattered in the sacred Ganges in India.

Hindu scriptures prohibit cremation of infants and *sannyasins* (monks). These days however cremation is increasingly availed and the practice is becoming common among non-Hindus as well (*fig*. 3.1).

If death has occurred away from home, the body of the deceased is generally not taken back home, unless special arrangements have been made with the funeral directors engaged. The local authorities do not permit the usual Indian practice of the eldest son torching the funeral pyre. As noted in the previous chapter, the family has to be satisfied with placing an incense stick atop the coffin lid as it is lowered into the high-voltage furnace. The ashes are returned to the family for scattering in holy rivers, such as the Ganges, Kaveri or Tungabhadra, or local rivers, or in the nearby Indian Ocean. These days, upon special request, family members are allowed to witness the actual cremation through a glass window.

Another observation to be made, in the context of those priests who are available, is that they are not necessarily as well-versed in the life-cycle and almanac rites as priests in India might be expected to be. The main reason for this is that the priests in Australia (except temple priests) have other occupations or vocations and conduct such community rituals on a voluntary basis. Nevertheless, it is often the case that the dedication of the key participants and sponsors (*yajamana*) of such rites is quite strong, and the task is carried through with a sense of duty and respect for the tradition. Almost all of the priests give away the honoraria (*dakshina*) they receive to charities in Australia and abroad.

The Arya Samaj is a major reformist sect within Hinduism, and its members, known as Aryasamajis, account for approximately 30% of Hindus in Australia. They tend to be more socially organised than other Hindus and regularly congregate in homes to perform Vedic *homa* (sacrificial offerings) to Vedic gods through Agni, the Fire-god. The Hindu majority, called Sanatanis, popularly congregate to offer *archana* and *aarati* (light-devotion), and perform amongst other rites, Satyanarayan and Ganesha *pujas*. There are a large number of devout Hindus, including Anglo-Australian followers, who form small community groups and meet regularly to chant *kirtans* or *bhajans* (devotional songs) to their *guru*, such as Sai Baba, Sathya Sai Baba, Ramakrishna or another godman, or Ammaji (The Mother), whose large colourful poster-images adorn the petalled-*mandap* (make-shift altar) and the walls of their homes.

fig. 3.2: Puja at home (photo: Jayant Bhalchandra Bapat)

Festive days and important astronomical constellations, particularly the four phases of the moon (new, full, and tenth day after each, called *ekadashi*), are observed assiduously in many Hindu households. Hindu communities have begun to distribute computer-generated almanac (*panchang*) that registers agreeable or propitious timings for new or risk-bearing tasks as well as the precise significance of the day in the lunar monthly cycle. This time-tuning helps the family earmark days appropriate for observing certain rites, as well as fasting and maintaining purity in the household, which usually entails refraining from placing meat or alcoholic drinks on the dinning table. Girls and women during their menstruation periods are generally discouraged from participating in *puja*s (observances or visiting temples).

Major festivals such as Dussera and Diwali (festival of lights), the first days of the two new years (Shalivahana, Shaka — CE 78, and Vikram Samvat – 56 BCE), Sankranti and Pongal (among south Indian Hindus), birthdays of Rama, Krishna, birth and death anniversaries of the Buddha, and days dedicated to Ganesha, Shiva, Karttikeya, the Goddesses Durga, Lakshmi and Sarasvati, are celebrated with much panaché. The celebrations variously consist of *puja*s, preparation of sweets and other delicacies, inviting family and friends to the home, exchange of greetings and gifts, prolonged chanting and musical enraptures, enacting and joining in stylised fertility folk-dance (*garba*), and so forth. It can be an occasion for 'one big holy partying'.

Most Hindu homes will have a mini-altar set aside in a corner of the house for the purposes of worshipful prayer, *puja* (meditation) by the members of the household, individually or collectively. In terms of doctrinal emphasis, neither *Bhagavad-Gita* nor Gandhi plays a significant role. The emphasis, if there is any, is usually associated with a mixture of popular Hinduism, *bhakti*, with a smattering of Vedanta teachings, and some reference to *karma* and rebirth, but with little of the moral tone of the classical teachings. Most Hindus are educated in the Western systems and motivated towards achievement, which seems counter to the apparently fatalistic presuppositions of *karma* and rebirth. Usually, there is little interest by adults in seeking explanations for beliefs and practices, or different forms of worship. However, in the last fifteen years or so, the population of the young has increased substantially and their generation often seeks explanations of the rituals. On the other hand, adults will happily sit through extended 'discourses' on *dharma* and the more subtle practices of Vedanta by visiting *swamis* and *gurus* of some eminence. These *pravachans* (discourses) are reproduced in the respective society's newsletters.

There are also signs of what might be termed 'Protestantisation' evident in the Hindu diaspora in Australia. The first factor in this configuration is the environmental constraint. The Western context with its decided materialistic and secular ambience makes even the most devout Hindu somewhat circumspect about the extent to which traditional and orthodox beliefs and practices can be maintained without attracting attention to one's 'otherness', despite multiculturalism. The second factor is related to the aspirations, career motives, educational aspirations (for the younger generation) and the desire to get on with life and all its demands, or to integrate more effectively with the host society. This is not to say that the phenomenon of the 'recovery of tradition' does not happen with the Hindu migrants. Once they settle into the cultural milieu of their adopted country, buy a home and raise a family, they strive hard to maintain contacts with the culture and traditions they left behind and often discover religion anew.

The third factor has to do with changes in religious orientation being experienced in the subcontinent in the broader context of nationalist and communal tensions, where an element of politicisation, if not militancy, in expression of primordial allegiances has entered into the fabric of everyday Hindu life. Hindus in the diaspora, from Mahatma Gandhi's 'home-rule' struggle to the present turbulent times, which have witnessed a greater emphasis towards a Hinduised polity, have not been spared this fervour. Indeed, some observers claim that the ferment on the subcontinent in this matter is largely fuelled or funded through resources, instigators and sympathisers from within the diaspora.

There is a growing and strong transnational link between Hindus in North America, the United Kingdom, Africa and Australia. The diasporic agenda is marked by a zeal for reforms in India that allegedly would help preserve the heritage of Hindu civilisation, as well as certain fundamental rights of the Hindu as a *bona fide* citizen of India, against the alleged encouragement of partisan communal, religious, or caste-based claims by other groups within the vast Indian landscape.

Similar sentiments appear to guide the organisation and activities of Tamil-Hindus from Sri Lanka, who have forged closer working relations with Hindus from other regions of southern India. There have also been numerous reports of Tamil migrants being approached for donations to support the erstwhile Tamil liberation fight in Sri Lanka in the heyday of the LTTE (Liberation Tigers of Tamil Eelam) struggle for a separate state. A major cause of schism and eventual split within the first broad-based Hindu temple association in Victoria was attributed to the different allegiances of moderate and extremist elements among the Tamil community representatives. Similar patterns have been noted in the other states also, particularly in New South Wales.

These factors tend to de-emphasis the mystical or the esoteric aspects and internal diversity of the faith, in the urge to universalise and present a more unified and accessible creedal front than the tradition has hitherto afforded. Second, the operational threads of community affairs assume a more centralised structure and defined authority, as in a political party structure. Third, there is emphasis towards shifting the focus from home worship to the temple or community centres, where patrons are encouraged to 'sponsor' special or regular *puja*s, such as bathing of the gods (*abhisheka*s), fire sacrifices (*havans*), food offerings (*prasadam*), in return for public recognition. The level of afforded donation becomes, perhaps curiously, a measure of one's dedication to the religious community.

Leadership and Language

There are ramifications in what we have just discussed for the kinds of leadership made possible within the community. Community priests are called upon to conduct *puja*s and certain life-cycle rites; temple priests likewise are revered as functionaries keeping alive a tradition. Beyond this, on matters relating to values, disputes, official family or community affairs, and representation in the larger social formations and so on, the priests have no status or significant voice in the community. All such matters are negotiated with leaders derived from within the ranks of the local temple association or in the community at large. Indeed, the leadership issue can be contentious and lead to many fractious divisions.

Eminent community members and secular leaders, including consulate representatives of the Indian government, have played an active part in giving cultural and even spiritual direction to the community. They have brought together diverse and fragmented groups within the community and have promoted cultural events, such as the arts, traditional dance, and gatherings of Sanskrit, Hindi and Tamil scholars. The work and dedication of these non-aligned leaders, who attempt to preserve the honour of their office, are not always reciprocated by faction-ridden Indian or Hindu organisations. The importance of transmitting cultural values and the traditional background of the culture, for which language and classical learning are indispensable vehicles, is not widely recognised in the community. Nor is it matched by action and organisation beyond the usual annual 'gala Indian cultural festival' organised by one association and boycotted by another.

A number of other social issues may arise in the Australian context for people of Hindu background, such as when confronted with certain medical procedures. Hindu women are not as averse to receiving medical attention or submitting to clinical examination by a specialist, unlike some Muslim women. Some of the Jains may not agree to surgery as this involves killing micro-organisms in the body. However, traditional Hindu and Sikh women are likely to find forthright questions by male doctors on contraception and gynaecological issues somewhat intrusive. Generally though, the medical attention and care for the whole family that an Indian immigrant is able to procure in Australia is recognised by Indian migrants to be far better in quality than in India and for this reason she or he would grow to appreciate the system. Of late, however, due to the availability of excellent medical facilities in India for those prepared to pay the top rupee, many Indians choose to go home for specialised surgery or dental procedures. It is still cheaper to pay the airfare, and do this in India as compared to getting it done in Australia.

LEADERSHIP TRAINING

Hindu religious leaders are not locally trained, as there are no existing seminaries, universities or institutions of learning offering training in ancient and classical recitations, the chanting of Sanskrit and Agamic scriptural texts and the rituals of worship. Even in India, it is only in the last twenty or so years that structured training has started for community priests (*purohitas*). It is heartening to see that women are now taking an active role in such activities and in places such as Pune, in the state of

Maharashtra, there are several institutions that train women exclusively to become community priests. On the other hand, training for temple priests continues mainly in south India, reflecting an age-old tradition.

In Australia, a handful of community priests, who learned the modicum of rituals and rites necessary for social ceremonies, such as marriage, continue to serve the community. Some have become official Hindu marriage celebrants. They have learned these rituals from their brahmin forebears or other traditionally-trained priests, as in the case of Fiji-Hindu priests. Other kinds of leadership training are more random, as community leaders emerge out of their own educated background to ascend ranks within community groups or associations. It is an 'on-the-spot' training for most of them. Some guidance may come from the communities themselves or the consuls-general. Some aspiring leaders may have had a background as school prefects, or officials within the local Jaycee or Lions Club or Chamber of Commerce bodies. There are a few cases where north Indian communities have persuaded retired academics to take up religious leadership to conduct Aryasamaji fire offerings (*havan*s) for their groups.

As for language, three or four universities in Australia teach in the specialist areas of Sanskrit and three in Hindi. Distance education material has been produced and is being used in these universities. While there is much discussion about the need to support and promote teaching of Indian religions, languages and philosophies in schools and universities, negligible effort is forthcoming from the community itself. However, the Bengali community in 1994 succeeded in gaining accreditation for Bengali as a non-English language option in high school curricula. Otherwise, it is left to temple organisations and Hindu missions to organise language classes or study groups in Sanskrit, Hindi, Gujarati and Tamil and classical dance classes (Bilimoria 1994b). One of the success stories is La Trobe University, which has developed a very successful 'Learn Hindi' programme in distance education; and this is now being continued at the Australian National University.

Video replays of lectures by *swami*s, often delivered in North America or the United Kingdom, are used for doctrinal teachings, although the younger generation shows little interest. Nevertheless, the thriving Indian video industry has captured the imagination of Australian Hindus. Family members with guests will gather around the home VCR to enjoy a

'Bollywood' Hindustani fantasy, or serialised episodes of the epics *Ramayana* and *Mahabharata*, or *Chanakya*.

Organisation of Hindu Communities

STRUCTURES OF AUTHORITY

We now turn to how Hindus in Australia have set about organising and giving structure to their religious and social activities. Western religions tend to rest on fixed doctrines, tight-knit structures, hierarchical governance and a rigid organisational base, capped by the 'holy see' or ecclesiastical control over all sacred matters right down to the moral behaviour of its adherents. Such a situation is conspicuous by its absence in Hinduism. It was only with the advent of European, especially British, educational and Christian missionary activities from the 18th century, that a commonly identified religious identity emerged across the vastly different and disparate lineages or branches of major orders (*sampradaya*s), devotional (*bhakti*) followings, temple establishments, secular-atheistic groupings and so on. In addition, the model provided by the church and semitic (Judeo–Christian–Islamic) monotheism, at once suggestive of a monolithic identity and mechanics of organisation, has certainly captured the imagination of 20th-century Hindu leaders. This has helped them make political gains out of their zeal for this self-acclaimed mission. These leaders or their proxies elsewhere have indeed had a profound impact in the Hindu diaspora, from which they derive a substantial amount of support, both moral and material. In Australia, however, the impact of such a thrust has been fairly recent, and it does not belie or overwrite the humble beginnings of the attempt towards creating a more organised, egalitarian and communitarian base for Hindu practice and culture in Australia. This history is itself a fascinating one, which we shall now briefly discuss.

As Hinduism did not have a rigid structure of organisation or authority, there has been a tendency for it to be unwieldy and subject to a number of interpretations of the spoken and written word (*shruti*s and *smriti*s) by religious and political leaders. This openness has often resulted in movements that have attracted popular patronage. The same openness has also been responsible at times for bitter struggles between factions for internal control and against foreign political and cultural invasions. Perhaps as a direct result of this unique situation, Hinduism has come to be grouped around *sampradaya*s along sectarian or *guru* lines led by an *acharya* (a leader) with supreme authority over the sect. These *sampradaya*s have been divided initially into three main groups: worshippers of Shiva, Vishnu and Devi. Added to this are multitudes of *sampradaya*s that owe their allegiance to various *guru*s.

The worshippers of Shiva, Vishnu and Devi have a number of sub-*sampradaya*s within their fold. Although many an *acharya* will lay claim to the overarching leadership of all the splinter orders and groups, his authority may not be so recognised outside his own particular sect. A case in point is the seat of the Shankaracharya. In the 8th century, the Adi (first) Shankaracharya established four religious seats in the four corners of India (Shringeri, Dwarka, Puri and Jyotirmath) to guide Hindus in religious matters. Each of these Shankaracharyas is elected to the office and is responsible for the upkeep of religion in the area under his control. His opinion is sought and also highly respected. However, the Shankaracharyas being celibate *sannyasin*s, are strictly speaking beyond the pale of Hinduism, and hence their advice, although sought, is not always followed. Also, the Shankaracharyas are Shaivite monks and hence their authority is not recognised by the followers of Vishnu.

In the 13th century, the state of Karnataka experienced a major religious upheaval when Lingayatism (also called Virashaivism) replaced Sanatana Dharma solely as a result of the teachings of its founder, Bhasavanna. The Lingayats are staunch worshippers of Shiva and they established their *matha*s and their equivalent of the Shankaracharya in the same places where the Shankaracharya's seats existed. These Lingayat *acharya*s are called Shivacharyas. The substantial Lingayat community in Karnataka, Maharashtra and Andhra Pradesh owe their allegiance to the Shivacharyas. Australia has a large population of the Lingayats and their Shivacharyas pay regular visits to Australian Lingayat homes.

Most Hindu organisations are self-governed by a *kendra* (*de facto* committee) formed from among the members and patrons, with an elected executive. Some temple associations seek affiliation or close liaison with individual temples (*devasthanam*) in South Asia, or with bodies such as the Hindu Charitable and Endowment Department of the Tamil Nadu government in south India or a major Hindu Trust, such as the Hindu Heritage Foundation, in north India. In the case of living teachers and *acharya*s, a trust is organised around each one's establishment to look after the day-to-day affairs of the organisation. Some teachers have moved their trust headquarters to the West. Others remain firmly in South Asia. The devotees of the representative teacher (*guru*) form a local chapter or group-association and seek recognition and spiritual assistance from the trust. There is, however, in either case, no overarching Church that can legitimately claim jurisdiction over the religious affairs of the diverse number of Hindu and neo-Hindu organisations.

The involvement of religion in the affairs of the state was not unknown in traditional times in India. However, since the days of the British Raj, there have been attempts to keep religion and matters of the state at arm's length, except in personal law concerning marriage, property, kinship and inheritance entitlements. The official government policy of secularism meant that religion was not to play an active role in the affairs of the state, in the judiciary, in the legislature, in public educational institutions or in the public sphere at large. Recent trends and movements, however, have challenged this exclusion on the grounds that tradition did not exclude religion from the social and political spheres of life. While there is much truth in this assertion, the way in which current party politics appropriates this traditional position goes completely against traditional wisdom. Often religion has been used politically to stir up communal tension and isolationism, and even to perpetrate violence on the weaker minority groups.

THE GURUS' TOUCH

In Australia, organisational structures developed not so much in service of the immigrant Hindu community but in response to the growing appeal of Hinduism, *yoga* and meditation among the youth in the larger community. In the early decades of this century, theosophists and spiritualists had organised themselves into 'Lodges' around illustrious teachers of Indian wisdom, such as Annie Besant and C.W. Leadbeater, both of whom had visited Australia in the 1920s.

The first significant Hindu *guru* to visit Australia was J. Krishnamurti — then associated with the Order of the East or the Theosophical Society in Madras — in 1925. But it was in the 1960s and 1970s that *guru*s and their movements with a neo-Hindu, universalist outlook, began to arrive in large numbers. An assortment of *gurus*, *yogis*, *bhogis*, *babas*, *swamis*, tantric advocates, self-made goddesses, spiritual mothers, harbingers of universal brotherhood and 'moral armament', began to traverse the last spiritual frontier seeking converts, mostly among the disenchanted youth, as they moved from city to city, or settled down in a comfortable inner city *ashrams*, supported by their middle- and upper-class followers. It was during this period of the widening quest for 'alternative' spiritualities and therapies that the phenomenon, or the cult, of 'the *guru*' came to prominence in Australia. The influential teachings spilled into New Age movements, from upbeat *yoga*, meditation and astrology to down-to-earth ecology. Esoteric bookshops flourished in major cities, and to this day Theosophical Society bookstores remain the largest outlet for literature of the Hindu variety.

Notable among the spiritual visitors was the late Swami Ranganathananda of the Ramakrishna-Vivekananda Mission, who came in 1964 and several times after that (see p. 69). His visit helped to found the Vedanta Society of NSW, which ran a spiritual bookshop for a while. Maharshi Mahesh Yogi of the TM (Transcendental Meditation) fame and one-time *guru* of the Beach Boys and the Beatles, gained a wide and popular following. TM also made inroads into professional circles as well. In 1969 came the Hare Krishna movement, officially known as the International Society for Krishna Consciousness (ISKCON), first founded in New York's East Village (Soho) as a centre in 1966 — and a year later registered as ISKCON in San Francisco — by Bhaktivedanta Srila Prabhupada, fresh off a boat from India; he visited Australia on several occasions from the 1970s to the 1990s.

Equally popular is the Siddha Yoga syndicate, brought to Australia in 1970 by Baba Muktananda, a highly colourful *guru* who made his debut in the United States in the late 1960s. His followers considered him to be an adept meditation master possessing mystical powers (*siddhi*) that he could transmit spiritually (*shaktipat*) to his disciples. His proclaimed successor, Gurumayi Chidvilasananda, has now taken control of the multi-million dollar Siddha Yoga empire, which stretches between Catskill in up-State New York, upper Mumbai and Melbourne's North Fitzroy. There is another group that also claims to be in the lineage of Muktananda led by Swami Shankarananda, which has a large *ashram* in Mt Eliza in Victoria and commands a sizeable following.

Also in the 1960s came Guru Maharaj-ji, then a teen-age boy, who claimed to be privy to the 'ineffable knowledge' which he would transmit to his disciples in devotional–meditational sessions managed by his Divine Light Mission. Although philosopher turned mystic Rajneesh, of Osho (Orange-clad) fame, never visited Australia, he gained a sizeable following alongside a wide range of Indian *guru*s who sent emissaries, recorded teachings, and goodwill to the West. Among these *guru*s were Swami Shivananda of the Divine Life Mission based in Rishikesh, three of whose brother-disciples made their presence felt in Australia, namely, Swami Saccidananda (dubbed the 'Woodstock Rock Guru'), Swami Venkatesananda, who established a farm-*ashram* near Perth, and Swami Satyananda Saraswati who operated out of an *ashram* near Mangrove Mountain in New South Wales. Their ecumenism and 'Integral' approach was not unlike that of the late Dom Bede Griffiths (1906-93), a Benedictine *sannyasi* (monk) who lived in India from the mid-1950s and experimented with melding aspects of Hindu practices and Christian spirituality. Dom Bede visited Australia twice, in 1985 and 1992.

The most widely read Indian or Hindu *guru* in Australia, as in the rest of the world, is Yogananda Paramahansa, through his popular *Autobiography of a Yogi*. He was the first of the California-based *guru*s who exploited the American (or Western) thirst for spiritual 'know-how' of a numinous kind. Yogananda Paramahansa is followed by Paul Brunton, an enigmatic European *yoga* advocate who travelled widely in India, claiming to have been initiated by the *jnani*-mystic Ramana Maharshi, who also has followers in Australia. Another influential *guru* was Swami Chinmayananda who founded the Chinmaya Mission. From his flamboyant erudition of traditional scriptural teachings during his several visits to Australia in the 1980s and 1990s, he later switched to emphasising the political instability of Hinduism, and publicly endorsed Hindu extremism.

In 1987 a temple dedicated to the worship of Sri Shirdi Saibaba (a spectacular popular *sant* (saint) who lived around the turn of the 19th century and early 20th century) was established in the outskirts of Sydney, in Stratfield. The congregation has grown considerably in the years since, and a dispute has also arisen over lease agreements with a rather recalcitrant landlady who happens to be an expatriate Indian doctor. The managing organisation is therefore planning on building a bigger temple structure for which a sizeable piece of land has been bought nearby from the large amount of funds that has been accumulated through devotees' and visitors' offerings in the temple *hundi* (coffers).

Perhaps the guru and spiritual figurehead who is most popular among local Hindus today is Sri Sathya Sai Baba (historically unrelated to Shirdi Sai Baba, autobiographical claims aside) who died at age 86 in March 2011 in his home-town *ashram* of Prashanti Nilayam in Puttaparthi, Andhra Pradesh. Not without his own controversies and allegations that marked his life in India, Sri Sathya Sai Baba managed to summon considerable popularity through his devotional teachings, educational activities, building of huge free-to-public hospitals, as well as the supposed powers to perform miracles that produced material items said to heal diseases and so on. His afro-style hair, slim posture, simple though unusual attire, and his ecumenical leanings with profound commitments toward social transformation and human values, endeared him to many around the world. Sri Sathya Sai Baba groups in Australia co-ordinate service and educational activities as well, especially for the aged and the younger members of the community. In this respect, Hindus, and their sympathisers or fellow devotees drawn from the larger Anglo-multicultural community, dedicate a portion of their time and energy towards social and community services. Although they might lack institutional structures and support for long-term programmes, such gestures are to be applauded. It is only through such incentives that the Hindu community has begun to give thought to establishing its own nursing homes for the aged and infirm. A wealthy Hindu family establishment might offer, as they have in Melbourne, to lend a large warehouse or building to be used by the community as a hall and meeting house, with facilities to set up welfare and counselling services in the precinct. Such activities are often organised through one or other of the major Indian associations.

OTHER DEVELOPMENTS

The Hindus who arrived in Australia from the late 1970s have managed to keep their customs, traditions and beliefs alive and, in spite of their small number, they seem to have made their mark on the Australian landscape. This is especially so in the fields of public celebrations of Hindu festivals and propagation of the already established *guru* cults, etc. not to mention Indian cuisine. Major Australian cities now boast hundreds of Indian restaurants and even small country towns have Indian take-aways. Institutions such as the Ramakrishna Mission, the Chinmaya Mission, Shirdi Saibaba and Sathya Sai Baba centres are now firmly established in all the major cities. Ramkrishna and Chinmaya missions in Melbourne and Sydney have been able to attract a substantial following amongst expatriate Indians and their children, as well as amongst local Australians. Thanks to some generous devotees, both have managed to acquire large properties. Retreats are regularly held at these places and under their auspices in country Australia. Sri Sathya Sai Baba is very popular with many white Australians as well. In addition, Australia now has over forty-six Hindu temples. As one would expect, Sydney and Melbourne have the largest number of them. While the main deities in most places are either Shiva or Vishnu or both, there are now special temples dedicated to Ganesha, Murugan (Karttikeya), Durga, Shirdi Saibaba and Sri Sathya Sai Baba as well.

The Shiva–Vishnu Temple in Melbourne and the Venkateshwara (a southern form of Vishnu) Temple in Helensburgh just outside the Sydney metropolis comprise large shrines situated on several hectares of land. Such temples host a number of community activities associated with calendric religious festivals. The largest Hindu temple in Australia is the one in Helensburgh. It initially began as an idea floated at a meeting in the home of an academic, B. Bhaskara Rao, which eventually led to the establishment of the Sri Venkateshwara Temple Association, Inc. (SVTA). SVTA enlisted a renown *sthapati*, V. Janakiramana from Chennai, to design the temple in the Dravidian style, with a large loan received from the Tirupathi Tirumala Devasthanam (TTD) in Andhra Pradesh, the largest pilgrimage temple in India. The temple layout, sketched according to Agamic traditional specifications, was transformed by a company of Sydney architects and engineers into structural plans conforming to the local town-planning requirements (see Chapter 4). A grand temple arose on the hills between Sydney and Wollongong, and was inaugurated in a grand Mahakumbhabhisheka ceremony in June 1985. So as to cater for the heterogeneous Hindu adherents who worship gods and goddesses other than Sri Venkateshwara, and who had been ardently patronising and providing support to the temple, an additional Sri Shiva Temple complex was added and completed in 1994. This latter comprises large shrines housing icons of 'Sri Shiva Lingam, Sri Thiripurasundari [*sic.*], Sri Subramaniaswamy, Sri Durga Devi, Sri Rama, Sri Anjanneyar and Sri Navagraha Moorthys'.[1] It is not usual, at least in India, for the shrines (and worshippers of) Shiva and Vishnu to be in such close proximity; here, none the less, the spirit of diasporic ecumenism and unity-in-heterogeneity — not always a sanguine mark of Hindu sectarian communities anywhere — appears to have prevailed.

Festivals such as Ganesha Chaturthi, Holi and the birthdays of Rama and Krishna are celebrated with great gusto at all these temples. Holi, which recreates Krishna's frolics amongst young *gopi*s (female cowherds) of Vrindavan, is very popular amongst the young where they get a chance to sprinkle friends and especially members of the opposite sex with coloured water and some licentious behaviour is tolerated.

On the day of the Ganesha Chaturthi, Ganesha's clay image is ceremoniously installed at the temple. Devotees come to pay homage at the time of the evening *aarati* everyday. The image is subsequently taken through the streets to the nearest river, bay or lake and ceremoniously immersed (*visarjana*) amongst loud chants of *ganapati bappa moraya* (Hail Lord Ganesha). It is not uncommon for over a thousand devotees to take part in such processions. Ganesha is a particularly favourite god in Maharashtra in India and the Marathi communities in Melbourne and Sydney have been celebrating this festival for the past twenty years. The Gokhale family in Mentone, a suburb of Melbourne, started this celebration on a private scale some thirty years ago. It has now become a major event, mainly for the Marathi and Gujarati communities of Melbourne. Close to a thousand people attend the *visarjana* ceremony at Mentone beach. Large numbers of women volunteers cook *prasad*, which is served at the completion of the ceremony. The observance of this particular calendric festivity is now widespread amongst all the various groups and sects, whether north or south, of Hindus, including the large number of students now present, across the country. It is is likely that, after Diwali and Holi,

---

1 Sri Venkateswara Temple Association, Inc. Mahakumbhabhishekam, Sri Shiva Temple Complex, 23 January 1994, Souvenir Publication (Helensburgh: SVTA, Inc.).

Ganesha Chaturthi will be the third great Hindu celebration that will be recognised nationally in the multicultural 'betwixt and between'.

Sri Ganesha cuts a popular image globally, and is a favourite among the young ones as well. As we saw earlier, the Darebin City Council in Melbourne actively supports the annual observance of the Ganesha festival, and Ken Evans, a local sculptor, creates the eco-friendly image out of pure clay. At the time of the *visarjana*, SES volunteers escort the procession of devotees and sympathetic local residents that parades the newly-awakened urban Ganesha through the streets of Preston (an adjacent suburb) to the tram depot where a Yarra Tram awaits the arrival of Lord Ganesha. The image is taken on-board the tram for a fair ride to Bundoora Park where it is ceremoniously immersed in its large pond, with great aplomb.

fig. 3.3: The Ganesha sculpture for the Ganesha-Chaturthi celebration at Darebin Town Hall, Melbourne with sculptor Ken Evans
(photo: Jayant Bhalchandra Bapat)

fig. 3.4: Annual Ganesha Puja (photo: Jayant Bhalchandra Bapat)

fig. 3.5: Ganesha-Chaturthi celebrations, Darebin Town Hall
(photo: Jayant Bhalchandra Bapat)

fig. 3.6: Ganesha Chaturthi procession (photo: Jayant Bhalchandra Bapat)

fig. 3.7: Ganesha Chaturthi celebrations (immersion of Ganesha idol) (photo: Jayant Bhalchandra Bapat)

Many Marathi families now install Ganesha, together with 'Standing Gauri' images, according to the tradition of the Deshastha brahmins of Maharashtra. Once again, people flock to *darshan* and partake of *prasad*.

For the past few years, Diwali (Deepavali), the festival of lights has been celebrated on a grand scale by cultural programmes in the Federation Square and fireworks on the Yarra in Melbourne and fireworks at the Harbour Bridge in Sydney. The Gujarati community in all the major cities celebrates the Navaratri festival, with *garba* dances for nine nights. Such events, held in public halls, attract huge crowds and are often an important venue for matrimonial matchmaking. Thus, while the Indian community is a long way from being politically active through a presence on ethnic community councils and by fielding candidates at elections, it has started to make its distinctive cultural presence felt within the Australian community.

Another South Asian religious community that is closely connected with the Hindu is the Jain community. Jainism has its roots in the Shramanic tradition, which is connected with a form of ascetic *yoga* and predates Hinduism. It is widely known for its strict adherence to non-injury and consequently vegetarianism, although it has not gained a public profile in Australia. The reason for this is that there has never been more than a sprinkling of Jains on the continent, compared even to the Parsis, the followers of Zoroastrianism, who also came from India. Some Jains arrived from Africa and, like many Jains who emigrated during the colonial period, they are Gujarati-speaking entrepreneurs and teachers who have adjusted to living outside the subcontinent. Although few Jain families have come directly from India, they have been concerned about adjusting to a Western-Christian environment. It is estimated that only a few hundred Jain families have settled in Australia since early 1994. They conduct their worship and religious rites mostly at homes and occasionally visit Hindu temples. As a rule they marry only amongst their own community.

TEMPLE ORGANISATIONS

In each of the major cities in Australia, particularly Sydney, Melbourne and Canberra, Hindus have organised themselves into Hindu societies and erected temples. Curiously, the initial impetus for organisation and temple planning almost invariably arises among the north Indian Hindus. However, to the south Indian Hindus, especially Tamils, the religious purview and practices of this latter group appear to be limited in scope and in some ways compromised by the pressures of modern life. There is also a perception among some of them that, due to the influence of Islam, north Indian Hinduism is not as authentic as south Indian forms. Whatever the reason, there is no doubt that south Indians as a whole are very devout and tend to attend temple services much more frequently than others. In Sydney, Melbourne and Perth, Tamil groups have often assumed responsibility for organising temple services. They believe that their attendant rites are more traditional and grounded in Sanskrit scriptures of the Agama tradition. The temple priests in most temples come from south India (or Sri Lanka) as well.

The co-operative spirit and the tensions that can mark the Hindu communities are illustrated in the building of the four Hindu temples in Sydney and Melbourne, and many others that are being planned or are in the process of being built (see next Chapter on Hindu temples). As already noted, before the mid-1970s, there was an absence of spiritual fellowship among the Hindus, apart from the swamis who provided the odd occasion for participation in a spiritual discourse. Solemnising marriage through proper Vedic rites was even more difficult — the accoutrements and personnel were simply not there. However, a few incidents helped alert the community to these needs. The story of one of the editors, at the start of this volume, is one example. Another is the case of the spouse of a visiting Sri Lankan Tamil Hindu, who had collapsed and died while shopping in Sydney in the early 1980s, who enquired after a traditional funeral rite but without success. A concerned community member then initiated a drive to establish a venue for religious and cultural practices. This led to the purchase of a decrepit old church building that functioned, with the help of a voluntary 'priest', as a regular locus for city Hindus. Prayers were offered on a daily basis and special ceremonies were conducted on days auspicious in the Hindu almanac. The gods worshipped there were those invoked in urban north Indian temples, namely Krishna and Rama, with their consorts.

Differences and factionalism did emerge, however, not the least between the diverse north Indian groups, each of which took successive control of the temple organisation. Through a series of protracted internal discussions and disputes, a consensus arose that a more traditional style temple, fulfilling all the canonical strictures of temple worship, ought to be planned, which led to the establishment of the Helensburgh temple. The old church building continues to serve the needs of the majority of north Indian Hindus. However, another group of north Indians, mostly upper-caste Gujaratis and predominantly Shiva worshippers, have organised themselves under the aegis of the Indian Heritage Research Foundation to build the world's first 'Underground Hindu Temple' in Minto, a suburb outside the city of Sydney. The motivation to go underground did not arise from any religious necessity or vision. It was simply a strategy to avoid the intransigence of the local council, which had earlier rejected the temple plans on the grounds that the project entailed interference with the natural surroundings. No part of the temple would be visible above the ground level, except a flower garden descending towards the main entrance facing the pastures. The major deity chosen to be housed was Sri Vishvanatha (Shiva, 'Lord of the World'), after the famed Vishvanatha Temple in Banares. Even so, there was still heated debate within the council chambers where local residents voiced opposition. The temple project later ran aground in late 1993, when the key engineer-builder, who had devised the 'underground' plan, was charged by the temple committee for repeated violations of the terms of the contract and inadequate structural progress. This led to counter-charges. The legal deadlock brought the project to an embarrassing halt, leaving a large hole in the ground. By 1995 the building project had resumed, after intervention by the founder of the Heritage Foundation. The temple was completed in 2000.

Meanwhile, a third temple, dedicated to the god Murugan, has been erected in the Sydney metropolitan region. This has been organised predominantly by south Indian worshippers of Shiva, of Tamil and Telugu background, who have migrated from Malaysia and regions other than the subcontinent. A Murugan Temple has also been built in Melbourne. In fact, one can say that a temple, whether on a small or large scale is added in the Sydney and Melbourne metropolitan and outlying areas every three to six years.

In Melbourne, HSV (Hindu Society of Victoria) was incorporated in the late 1970s. A major temple project, incorporating adjacent shrines to Vishnu, Shiva and Devi (the goddess) under one massive canopy, was planned to cost an estimated one million dollars. Again, help came from TTD in India. The foundation stone for the temple was laid in June 1988. However, contentious meetings and splits within the Hindu community led, first to the exit of the north Indian Hindus who had been at the helm of the conception, and then of Hindus from Malaysia and other regions. The latter renegade group withdrew some of its pledged funds, formed the Melbourne Vinayagar Hindu Sangam, and directed its efforts towards the building an alternative Ganesha (Vakrathunda Vinayagar or Vijneshwara) Temple in the outer suburbs, at The Basin, near Boronia. The Mahakumbhabhisheka (grand temple dedication ceremony) of this Ganesha Vinayagar Temple, designed in a quasi-traditional style, was held in October 1992, with further ceremonies in 1993. Regular prayers and celebrations take place in the temple, conducted mostly in Tamil. The temple was partly damaged by fire in 2005 but has since been refurbished and is fully operational.

The HSV later combined its energies with Sri Lankan Tamil Hindus, taking firm control of the affairs, and completed constructing the adjacent Shiva–Vishnu Temple by mid-1994. Traditional craftsmen (*shilpis*) completed the stylistic embellishments and fine aesthetics that the temple design embraces. The grand dedication ceremony of this temple and the

fig. 3.8: Swaminarayan BAPS Temple, Melbourne (construction 2014)
(photo: Yagnesh Brahmbhatt, BAPS, Melbourne)

colourfully adorned granite icons of Shiva, Vishnu and Devi, now housed in their individual shrines as originally planned, took place in May 1994. The temple also houses many other gods and godlings around the two main deities, Shiva and Vishnu. In addition to the regular daily *puja*s and special *puja*s on the important days for Vishnu, Shiva and the other deities housed in the temple, the temple also celebrates important religious days in the Hindu calendar, such as Holi and Makara Sankranti. (See Section 'History of the Hindu Society of Victoria' below for a more detailed history of HSV.)

In 2002, Melbourne witnessed another temple dedicated to 'Shree Durga Mata' or the Goddess (a form of Parvati, the consort of Shiva, widely worshipped in north-eastern India). This was designed by a temple architect, Subhash Rao, for erection in Rock Banks in the northern region of outer Melbourne for the Shri Durga Bhajan Mandli (Inc.), which was established two decades ago (see *fig*. 3.8). A number of other popular gods are also installed in dedicated shrines inside the complex, which also boasts a large *sabha* (hall) for religious and cultural functions.

In the nation's capital territory, Canberra, there are three different Hindu collectives, namely, the Sri Mandir Society of Australia, the Hindu Temple and Cultural Centre of the Australian Capital Territory and the Shaiva community. The first two societies declare allegiance to Vedanta and the Bhakti tradition, and each group is constructing its own Hindu temple on the outskirts of the city. The Sri Mandir and Hindu Temple and Cultural Centre temple in Canberra was inaugurated ahead of the arrival of its three stone images from India, in April 1992 at its foundation laying ceremony. The Hindu Temple and Cultural Centre is unaggressive in promoting its cause, and devotes a good deal of its efforts and energy towards educational activities, running classes in Sanskrit and taking *havan-puja* offerings to people's home on a rotating basis. The temple work commenced in March 1993, then in August 1995 the temple consecrated its Ganapati shrine and the construction work was completed shortly afterwards. The deities installed are: Radha–Krishna, Rama–Lakshamana–Sita–Hanuman, Shiva–Parvati–Ganapati–Murugan and Durga. It is clear that funds are raised among its members in the form of sponsorship for each stage of the project, including the purchase of particular images and their installation (*sthapana*).

There are now several temples in the capitals of other states, namely South Australia, Queensland and Western Australia, although the state of Tasmania has yet to build a fully-fledged Hindu temple (apart from a fledgling Hindu prayer centre). Melbourne, Perth and Sydney each have a temple associated with Swaminarayan sects, with the one in Perth modelled to some extent on the sect's grandiose temple outside London.

The last organisation worthy of note is the Melbourne Community of Hindu TRAC (Tradition, Religion, Aspiration, Culture), which regularly organises conferences for 'dynamic local Hindu youth leaders', as well as cultural events on calendric days.

THE POLITICAL HINDU

Unlike Sydney and Melbourne, the division in the Canberra Hindu community is not clearly defined along the north and south Indian divide, reflecting instead personal and ideological differences. A third group of more orthodox Shaiva south Indians have recently begun work on their temple in the capital. North Indian Hindus in Australia, as elsewhere in the diaspora, have growing links with the Vishwa Hindu Parishad and the Bharatiya Janata Party, and occasionally with the Rasthriya Svayam-sevak Sangh (RSS) as well. This connection with the right-wing Hindu movement is a cause of tension and split among the north Indian Hindus. In addition, anti-Muslim sentiments exist among some of the Hindus and are often expressed publicly when Indian Muslims and Pakistanis are not invited to *puja*s, ceremonies and inaugural gatherings. Thus, for example, in June 1997 the Sri Mandir in Canberra was officially and publicly consecrated in the presence of the chief guest, the Prime Minister of Australia, John Howard. While the Mandir leaders saw this as a sign of the open-arm embrace by the Australian people of Hindu values and their presence in Australia, critics have read the semiotics differently. They expressed concern about the underhanded 'unholy' alliances such a gesture portends. It transpired that one of the son's of the Mandir high officers is closely connected with a counterpart in the Howard family. It may all be innocent and coincidental, but there are reasons to suppose that the event was more than a mutual gesture of 'a gift to the entire Australian community'.

A LASTING HINDU SYMBOL

The 20th-century Hindu immigration as we have seen — and as entered the 21st century — involves a radically different set of challenges and responses to those faced by the 19th century immigrants.

What is, however, more significant to note in these events is that after a period of gestation the amorphous collective coincided with the perceived need for Hindu temple structures. It would be appropriate to say that the symbol of the temple more than anything else provides the context and pretext for the coming together of Hindus in the diaspora as an organised group. The temple has both a private and a public frame. As a symbol for prescribed ritual and interiorised practices, the temple makes it possible for Australian Hindus to continue with greater confidence their respective practices. As an edifice, the temple signifies a permanent fixture and a powerful presence which makes the Hindu identity publicly visible. The Hindu temple in Australia also provides a matrix for ironing out differences and tensions amongst the different sectarian and regional groups, occasionally leading to the formation of a new group.

As noted by the scholar of Sanskrit and the Canadian Hindu diaspora, T.S. Rukmani (2005), after the initial pangs of re-locating in a new space are overcome, groups identify themselves as homogeneous units through religion, region, culture of other factors that mould them together as a community. They observe the strength of the weekly congregation gatherings in churches and synagogues that contribute to the preservation of identity of those groups. The spiritual life of Hindus is not based on similar congregational worship; their approach is clearly more holistic. Nevertheless, they learn that building temples is a sure way of marking their religious identity, and providing at the same time a powerful symbol for the transmission of their values and cultural practices to the next generation. While men take the lead in the architectural and ritual structuring of the temple complex, women join in to fulfil other tasks.

> A temple, also being (or has adjuncted to it) a cultural centre, many activities like music and dance classes, *yoga* classes, teaching of languages, etc. take place within it, in which women generally play a main role.
>
> — Ibid.

In the broader context of mainstream Australian society, the Hindu temple symbolises a multicultural and ethnically plural ethos. The resulting interaction of cultures, and fusion of discordant horizons, promises to produce a society that is more tolerant, more enlightened, more artistic and more democratic — or so the nation's leaders hope. Religious diversity is a reality that Australia is no longer prepared to ignore, despite the occasional ruffle in parts of society anxious to preserve the dominant Anglo-Celtic-Christian identity against the challenges of pluralism. But it has taken some 200 years to reach this more sanguine state of affairs, in which the contributions of the diasporic Hindus, along with Jains, Sikhs, Parsis, Muslims and Buddhists from South Asia, have been significantly marked and recognised.

History of HSV (Hindu Society of Victoria)[2]

HSV reached an important milestone in 2012, which marked twenty-five years since its original vision of erecting a Hindu temple. Known as the Shiva–Vishnu Temple, the shrine is a major landmark in Melbourne and is a testimony to the proud achievement of the visionaries amongst the Hindus in Victoria. Hindu communities have always been deeply influenced by a core traditional adage, namely, 'a town without a temple is not worthy of living in'. For centuries, temples have been places dedicated not only to worship but also to religious education. In addition, they have been centres for the practice of fine arts, such as dance, music and drama. At the centre of temple building is the belief that the outer manifestation of the temple and the images (*vigraha*) are none other than the divinity that lies within the souls of all individuals and the community (see Chapter 4 on architectural homologies). Ultimately, temples are seen as a way of turning the lives of communities toward the Supreme Presence. It was a remarkable feat of inspired devotion for the 200 Hindu families living in Victoria in the early 1980s to take the initiative that today has resulted in the sprawling temple complex at Carrum Downs.

---

[2] We have included this section for two reasons. First, it records the historical development, from very modest beginnings, of one of the largest Hindu temple-cum-cultural complexes in the southern hemisphere. Second, it is a telling example of what a small community can achieve with determination and effort in a short span of time. It draws on an article by C. Kathirgamanathan and G. Srikanthan, abridged and modified by Jayant Bhalchandra Bapat and Purushottama Bilimoria.

The spark that energised the initial discussions on building a temple came from a member of the Sri Lankan Parliament who visited Melbourne after attending an international conference in New Zealand. While in Melbourne he met with several Tamil Sri Lankan expatriates and talked about their lives in the country of their adoption. He enquired as to what opportunities existed for Hindus living in Melbourne to practise their religion. This question seems to have ignited the latent yearning to give substance and form to a place of worship for Hindus. Shortly after, active members of the fledgling Hindu community from India and Sri Lanka, as well as a handful of Indian academics, agreed that the time was ripe to bring the Hindu community of Victoria under one banner. At the initiative of certain convening members, HSV was officially launched on the Sarasvati Puja day in 1982.

The newly-elected management committee began arranging prayer meetings on the last Saturday evening of each month in the city, beginning in November 1982. The congregation sang *bhajan*s followed by *puja* and *aarati*, and ending with a short religious discourse. Initially, volunteers took turns to perform the *puja*, until a regular priest was appointed. In June 1984, HSV was incorporated as a charitable body. The principal objective stated in the HSV's constitution was 'to build a traditional Hindu Temple in Victoria'. It was decided to name the temple, 'Shri Shiva–Vishnu Temple'. This was a sensible move since it assured the support of two major sectarian groups within Hinduism, the Shaivites and Vaishnavites, and the inclusiveness augured well for the future direction of the temple.

Building a temple was more a reflection of the passion within the community than a decision to be conditioned by realities on the ground. To think of building a temple in that situation was, as the saying goes, 'building castles in the air'. To many it had seemed that the project was unfeasible both in terms of funding the construction as well as its maintenance and long-term survival, given the meagre support base. Notwithstanding the hurdles, and convinced that building a temple was the best option for the Hindu community in Victoria to preserve their religious traditions, HSV resolved to embark on the project.

HSV searched for a suitable site for the new temple, and a plot of land of 14.35 acres at Carrum Downs was selected. It was purchased at auction for Au$ 72,300, with the 10% deposit advanced by an individual member of the Society, who also put up his own house as a bank guarantee. A local architect drew the first plan for the temple, consisting of a main hall in front and a pentagonal area at the back for shrines.

At an urgent meeting of the management committee the issue of raising the required funds before the settlement (closure) date was pondered. A twofold strategy was adopted: first, to raise interest-free loans and seek donations from Hindus and, second, to secure a bank loan. A loan of Au$ 45,000 was secured from the State Bank of Victoria and the balance was raised as interest-free loans, to be repaid over a period of ten years. By now the Hindu population in Victoria had grown to about 250 families. With the generosity of the members and well-wishers, the loan was repaid within eighteen months. Once the land transaction was completed, work on clearing and levelling the temple site commenced. The first issue of the official newsletter of HSV, aimed primarily at disseminating information about the temple building project and forthcoming religious events, was released in August 1985. It was named *Panchamurti* ('Five Gods'), subsequently changed to *Panchavati* (five banyan trees; a religious site in Maharashtra).

Sub-committees to oversee planning and technical matters were formed, and another set of building plans were drawn up. A *sthapati* (classical temple architect) from south India was recruited to refine the plans. It was decided to have major shrines for five main deities, namely the gods Shiva, Vishnu, Ganesha and Subramaniam, and the Goddess Parvati, along with enclaves for twenty-seven other deities. The drawings and plans were sent to the Shankaracharya of Kanchipuram and to TTD for their clearance, after which they were submitted to the City Council of Springvale for approval. A planning permit was obtained on 5 January 1988. The Mayor and staff of the Springvale Council extended their co-operation toward facilitating the building project.

Foundation stones (*pancha-shila*) were cut in India and blessed by the chief priests of some of the prominent temples in India. Upon arrival in Melbourne, daily *puja*s were conducted on the stones until the 'foundation stone-laying' ceremony. This took place in June 1988. The Minister for Ethnic Affairs in the Government of Victoria unveiled a plaque to commemorate the occasion. Before the building operations commenced, in keeping with traditional practice, images of Bhairava and Ganesha and a few other deities were installed at the temple grounds.

fig. 3.9: A renowned Indian classical dance maestro, Dr Chandrabhanu of Melbourne (photo: Devika Bilimoria)

The temple site became a hive of activity, with volunteers clearing the temple site and planting trees. Of the many issues confronting the Society, the hardest was raising funds for the construction. In the interim, a temporary temple was erected at the site. The first of the bi-weekly *puja*s was commenced in May 1990, replacing a bi-weekly gathering at Preston. Although collections from *puja*s were high, the problem of raising funds, for a project of the size and scale of the proposed temple, remained a major challenge. A wide range of fund-raising activities was launched, including door-to-door collections, vegetarian dinners, raffles, music concerts, etc. Students from leading dance schools in Melbourne conducted performances, proceeds from which were donated toward the project. The advanced stages of the project needed further large funds. Between the years 1992 and 1996, the peak construction period, volunteers succeeded in raising funds in excess of a million dollars. By this time the Hindu population in Victoria had significantly increased. The Ladies' Auxiliary was another group that was in the forefront of the fund-raising activities. The largest cash donations came from two Hindu families. During this time, the Society also successfully negotiated an interest-free loan of Indian Rs. 1,000,000 from TTD.

The final building permit was secured in January 1990. The project was divided into five stages, the last of which, under the first phase, was the construction of the *rajagopurams* (main spires). In October 1990, after procuring connection of all essential services to the site, excavation work commenced. The Society secured from State Bank of Victoria a loan of Au$ 150,000 and an overdraft facility of Au$ 60,000. In November 1992, the *sthapati* and his team of eight artisans arrived from India and started work on the shrines. The Shiva shrine was the first to be completed followed by the shrine for Vishnu. A contingent of six additional artisans arrived from India in January 1994 to accelerate the pace of construction. By May an exquisite temple stood tall on the virgin soil of Carrum Downs, fulfilling the deep spiritual yearnings of the community.

The auspicious date for the *mahakumbhabhishekam* (holy consecration) was fixed in consultation with an astrologer for the morning of 22 May 1994. More than 5,000 devotees and visitors participated in a grand ceremony conducted by Hindu priests from India, Sri Lanka and Australia, amidst chanting of *mantra*s to the accompaniment of *nadasvaram* music and *om namah shivaya, hari om*. The hall and corridors of the temple overflowed with people who arrived for a glimpse of the moving ceremony, for many their first. This day saw the decade-long dream come to fruition.

The next major construction challenge was the completion of the two *rajagopurams*, each 13.5 m tall, at the entrance. The task of installing 45 massive granite images in their ornate shrines in record time and meeting the massive costs was demanding enough. It would have been tempting for the Society to call for a pause to the activities before undertaking any further construction work. However, a sudden cessation of such activity might have resulted in inertia (if not also amnesia), which could have proved too difficult to overcome, as was demonstrated in the case of the Srirangam temple in south India. The Nayaka kings left the *rajagopuram* unfinished at the pedestal level after completing the magnificent temple complex. It took 800 years before sufficient momentum could be mustered in the devotees to complete the *gopuram* in the 1980s! With the decision to press ahead, the crew of Indian artisans under the guidance of the *sthapathi* proceeded with the construction of the two *rajagopuram*s. The construction of the two majestic *rajagopuram*s was completed as planned, with myriad intricate images of divine forms. On the morning of Sunday 25 May 1997, the *kumbhabhishekam* of the *gopuram*s took place. Cranes were used to reach the pinnacle-domes atop the spires. It marked a historic moment for the community, as it witnessed the actualisation of a dream project conceived some thirteen years earlier.

Diverse groups from both north and south of the subcontinent make the temple their home for regional (Diwali) festivals and celebrations. The grand Hindu festivals of Holi, Deepavali and Pongal attract large groups of Hindus. New Year's day, 1 January, though not a Hindu festival, is strategically included in the temple festival calendar, and attracts a large flock of local people mingling with regular temple patrons eager to make a propitious start to the year. Such a social intermingling is indeed a rare sight, seldom seen on other festive occasions. Thus, despite its location to a far side of the city, it appears that the temple has become a major centre of the cultural and social life of the community. There are now, of course, other Hindu temples and cultural centres that have come up in and around the metropolis, serving similar functions. Over the years, many developments have taken place to cope with the ever-increasing numbers of people visiting the Sri Shiva–Vishnu Temple. Expansion of the catering services, asphalting and lighting the outer courtyard (*veli veedi*) and car park, building of the priests' quarters and the temple kitchen (*madapali*) are a few of the ongoing developments.

The constantly growing congregation created an urgent need for some structural modifications. In a well-established temple, repairs and extensions are a challenge, as the sanctity of the place is to be preserved at all times, and the daily, six-time *puja*s must go on regardless, as no impairment to the spirituality of the temple is permissible. The ideal opportunity to address the problems came in 2007, when it was time to conduct the *punarudharana kumbhabhisheka* (restorative consecration). The Hindu Agamas prescribe such a consecration rite to be performed every twelve or so years, so as to re-energise the deities in the temple, in the belief that their powers wane with time. The *punarudharana kumbhabhishekam* was arranged and major structural works were carried out during 2006-7, comprising relocation of the nine planetary deities and Hanuman, the Monkey-god, as well as new shrine for Alvars (Vaishnava saints), the modified *vasanta mandapam* (special celebratory niche) and embellishment of the *Dwara Ganapati* shrine (Ganesha at the entrance). The gala occasion of the *punarudharana kumbhabhishekam* took place on 29 April 2007, much to the joy and delight of thousands of patrons.

Constructing an extensive Cultural and Heritage Centre has been a significant part of the original plan for the Shiva–Vishnu Temple complex. Initiated in 2004, costing Au$ 8.4 million (funded through donations and a generous Victorian government grant), the Centre was finally inaugurated in 2012 in the presence of the Victorian Minister for Cultural Affairs and Citizenship. The Centre offers several facilities for community functions and cultural events. It has a multimedia library that provides information on Hindu culture and philosophy. A museum will be added at a later date.

The vision, dedication, sacrifice, courage and indomitable spirit of the members of HSV have yielded a priceless and lasting legacy in the form of a magnificent temple on the Australian landscape. HSV has, by and large, lived up to the expectations of its founders and continues effectively to serve the Hindu community of Victoria. The many volunteers continue to provide valuable service and resource. A sound structure and space for the practice of the ancestral culture has been bequeathed for future generations of Victorian Hindus as well. Overall, whether as an act toward preserving their culture, or expressing their spirituality, the Hindu community continues to add colour, succour and vibrancy to the multicultural tapestry of Australian society.

fig. 3.10: Shiva–Vishnu Temple (HSV) Carrum Downs, Victoria (photo: Jayant Bhalchandra Bapat)

4

Temple Architecture
A Brief Overview and Its Symbolism

Purushottama Bilimoria

The Origins

THE temple, it is needless to say, is not an Indian invention, for civilisations elsewhere had temples and sacred sanctuaries erected for the purposes of worship or dedication to the deceased ones; the Greeks had their *oikos*, the Jews their roving Covenant (Hebrew *baitel*, later the 'synagogue').[1] It is likely, though, that the idea of the Indian temple was a somewhat independent development, whose origin recedes into obscurity, as several notable scholars, including Stella Kramrisch in her monumental work on Hindu temples (1946) and Ananda Coomaraswamy (1977: 3-10) have remarked. From all accounts, however, it would appear that the earliest origins of the Hindu temple go far back to the fire altar used for Vedic sacrifice (*yajna*), whereby the burned offerings were conveyed to the gods with the smoke of the fire (*agni*), sacredly or magically energised by the incantation of *mantra*s. Bricks were piled to give an ascending pathway for the fire,[2] (*figs*. 4.1-2) and this hypaethral, or open-to-the-sky, symbol

---

[1] Possibly the world's first temple, built 11,600 years ago, has been excavated at Gobkeli Tepe in Turkey. See, Charles Mann and Vincent J. Muni, 'Dawn of Civilization', *National Geographic*, June 2011, pp. 39-59.

[2] The now no longer extant and most interesting of Vedic rites, the Agnicayana, required some 10,000 bricks in sequence of five layers, resembling a falcon (signifying the body of Prajapati) with the sacrificial fire (signifying the 'spirit' intending immortality) (*fig*. 4.3) Since 1975 with the encouragement of the Indologist, the late Frits Staal, Agnicayana has been performed a few times in Kerala, south India. see: http://www.you tube.com/watch?v=Pl0lJJeHj4A&list=PLx1fJYDXjQ2FGvJppIRzFLmbuFj5 XWP5U. For a more recent performance of Athirathram Yajna (at Panjal); see http://www.youtube.com/watch?v=FISuF_kJS4A.

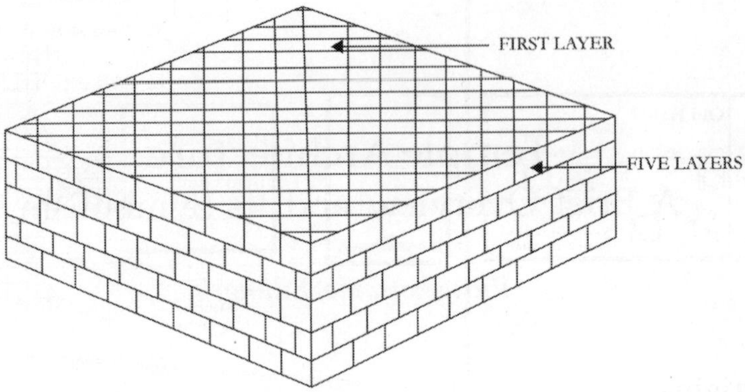

fig. 4.1: Layout of a Vedic altar, brick by brick

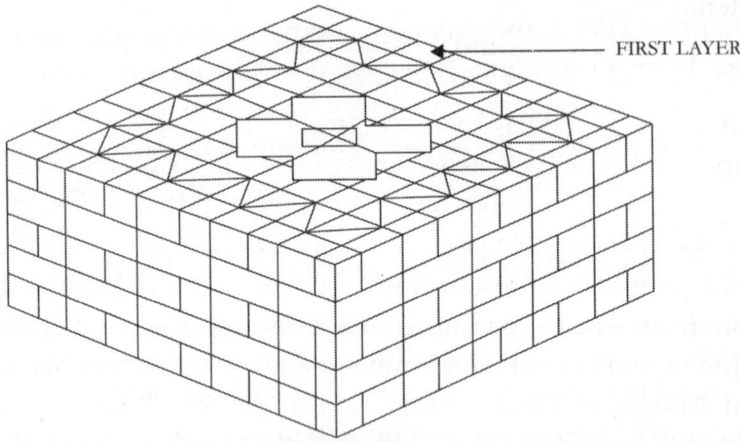

fig. 4.2: Centrepiece tending heavenwards

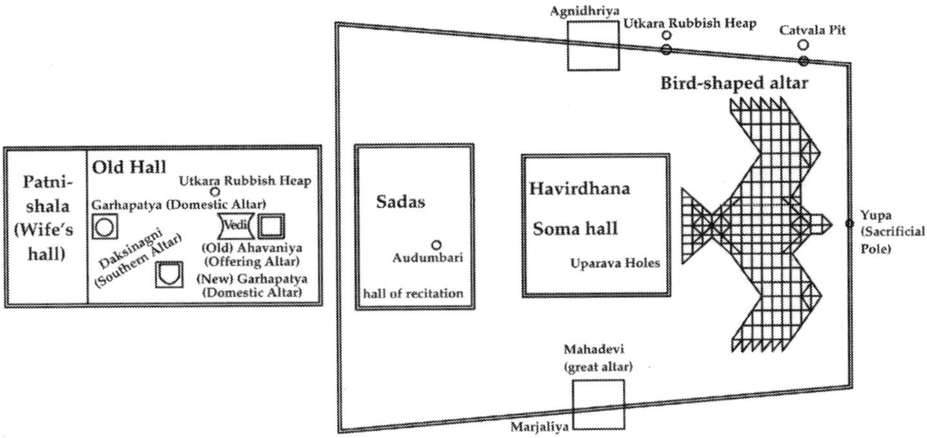

fig. 4.3: The ritual enclosure (not to scale)

became the mainstay of not only later Hindu shrines or temporary enclosures, to which the gods were expected to resort, but also of Buddhist *stupas*.

The Buddhist *stupa* was a circular tumulus of bricks or stones, or a sacred mound or memorial, commemorative of the Buddha's enlightenment (i.e. his entry to the 'gateway of liberation') (*fig*. 4.4). The Buddhists erected *stupas* and pillars on holy spots and these in the course of time were developed into magnificent structures embellished with exquisite carvings and bas-relief sculptures. The *stupa* symbolised the way to escape conditioned existence (*samsara*), and it was entered through a gateway (*torana*) of freestanding columns and pillars, often sculptured from rocks, with architraves and an abacus across its capital carrying Buddhist symbols and inscriptions. At Sanchi, in modern-day Madhya Pradesh, many *stupas*, dating from 1st century BCE, were erected from rock-cuts in Stonehenge-like arrangement (*fig*. 4.5); there were similar ones at Amaravati (2nd century BCE) in Andhra Pradesh. The *stupa* probably influenced the idea of the steeple or inverted conical finial or spire (*sikhara*) for the temple, which, again, also resembled the heaven-tending rising fire of the Vedic altar. This is attested to in Buddhist shrine structures, such as the Mahabodhi tower at Bodh-Gaya (2nd century CE) in Bihar, others later in Taxila (3rd-4th centuries, *fig*. 4.6) in the north-west and in the famous learning centre of Nalanda (5th century), also in

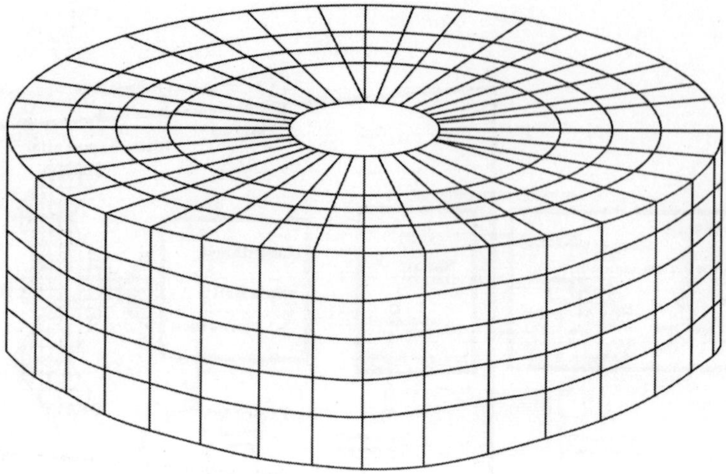

fig. 4.4: Tumuls

fig. 4.5: Stupas in Sanchi and Nepal

Bihar. The Jains followed the Buddhists and erected similar *stupas*, ruins of which are found in parts of north India. And both Buddhists and Jains fortified their places of worship with rock-cut caves and barrel-vaulted *chaitya*-halls, often carved on face-cliffs.

Image worship, which is central to an Indian temple, was absent in Vedic times, although worship of sacred relics was prominent during the Mauryan emperor Ashoka's time (*c.* 250 BCE). Buddhist influence in regard

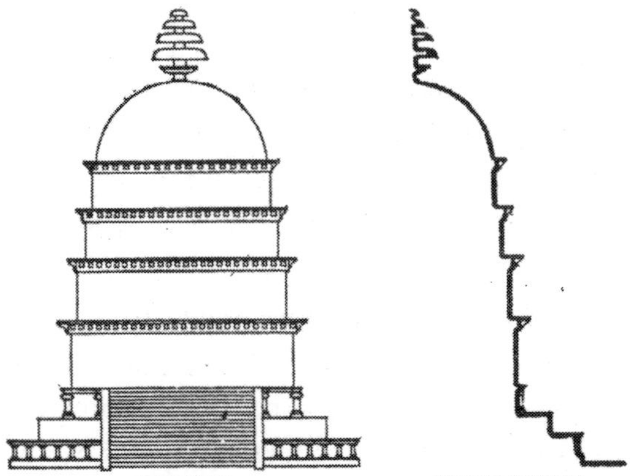

fig. 4.6: Kushan Stupa modelled on Taxila Stupa of Kunala

(Source: *Indian Architecture in India and Abroad*, P.K. Acharya, J.K. Publishing House, Bhopal, 1979, *Pl.* XVIII, p. 41)

to image worship has not been ruled out, and Brahmanical shrines dedicated to the divinity Vasudeva seem to have been in existence around 2nd century BCE. Heliodorus, a Greek convert to the cult of Vasudeva, apparently erected a pillar with an inscription mentioning a shrine dedicated to Bhagavata or Vishnu at Besnagar in Madhya Pradesh. Inscriptions and remains of structural shrines in Nagarjunakonda in Andhra Pradesh appear to suggest the early prevalence of temple-worship among Hindus. On the architectural side, elaborate popular timber architecture was in evidence by the time Megasthenes visited Chandragupta Maurya's court in north India (*c.* 300 BCE).

It was only a matter of time before image-worship and architecture would combine to create a more enduring edifice that embodied the sacredness associated with the relics, signs and images. Buddhist and Jaina monks took up habitation in *vihara*s or *sangharama* (monastic dwellings) carved into the face of rocky mountains, which were complete with halls and meditation chambers that housed smaller *stupa*s. In Gandhara (*c.* 300 BCE) in the north-west, Hellenistic art influenced representational forms, plasticity and details, which later appeared in the frescos, reliefs, friezes and figurine carvings on the walls of Buddhist *vihara*s, such as at Ajanta (*c.* CE +500) in western India.

Thus, over the centuries, from the Vedic altar, Brahmanical shrines,

Buddhist and Jaina *stupas*, as well as relic worship and rock cuts, a sophisticated groundplan for the Hindu temple emerged. The impersonal powers of nature, the fecundity associated with earth, and the lofty resourceful gods of the sky were grounded in visible, concrete and material embodiments, housed in elaborately decorated god-houses (*garbhagrihas*) (actually oil-lit chambers), and attended to as highly-honoured guests (*atithi*). After the 3rd century CE, when Hinduism heralded a new era of revivalism under the Gupta regime in the north, image-representation and construction of simple shrines and temples were undertaken with some zeal in order to promote a more popular acceptance of Hinduism and Hindu culture, hitherto eclipsed by the dominance of Buddhism on the Indian scene. These had become quite prominent by the close of the 4th century CE, as recorded in the copious notes taken by Fa-hsien, the Chinese Buddhist monk who travelled to India at that time.

By the 5th century CE, under the Chalukya dynasty, which was powerful in the south, temple structures had attained their recognisable form. Indeed, the earliest temples that survive in India date from this period. By the 6th century, stone had replaced bricks and timber, and by the 7th century, under the Pallavas (CE 600–900), temples were constructed as rock-hewn, pagoda-style monoliths, as found in the shore temples of Mamallapuram (or Mahabalipuram), just outside Chennai. The years between 6th and 8th centuries CE also saw the rise of wonderful rock architecture in north India, such as the Hindu rock-cut caves of Badari, Elephanta, and the famous Kailasa Temple in Ellora (probably a reaction to the earlier Buddhist structures in Ajanta and Ellora). The leogriff motif of the Pallava style, which dominated the south, was a type of pilaster with a prominent, moulded, lion on it surrounded by carvings and ornately fluted beams. Several temples were built in this style in Tamil Nadu, but they were located in open space rather than hidden behind the fa®ade of rocky cliff faces. The Chalukyan temples of Aihole and Mahakutesvara, and the Pallava temples of Kanchipuram and Mamallapuram, as well as the early temples of Bhubaneswar in Orissa (8th century), are monuments to this exciting era of temple architecture in India.

It was the Chola dynasty (*c.* CE 900–1150) that contributed overhanging cornices, fa®ades and, more significantly, *sikhara* over *vimana* (pyramidal tower) in a multi-tiered structure. It is said that with the Cholas the genius

fig. 4.7: The temple architecture at Halebid, Vijayanagara

of Dravidian architecture attained its profoundest expression. The Cholas were succeeded by the Pandyas (*c.* CE 1100–1350), who added further visual art and elaboration to the outer structures, particularly to enhance the fa®ades with elaborate crutches, corbels, florid ornamentation and so on. The outer surrounding grounds or patios were also landscaped and the courtyard aesthetically integrated with the temple precinct.

Last but not least came the famous Vijayanagara empire (CE 1350–1560), which greatly transformed the spirit and substance of temple architecture. Possibly due to the inspiration of the sage-philosopher Vidyaranya (after whom the founders of the empire, Harihara and Bukka, named the empire, first as Vidyanagara, then Vijayanagara, or 'City of Victory'), temple or sacerdotal art during the two centuries of the empire reached an 'extreme limit of florid magnificence', with much embellishment and flamboyancy to niches and pilasters, the inverted lotus bud (*padma*) in corbels, and the harmonizing of form and formless in single representations (Brown 1971: 47-50) (*fig.* 4.7).

The culmination of south Indian temple architecture occurred in Madurai (16th-18th century CE) where gateways and towers basically duplicate those that encompass the entire city on the outer walls. The Meenakshi Temple in the Madurai district of Tamil Nadu bears testimony to this style (*fig.* 4.8);

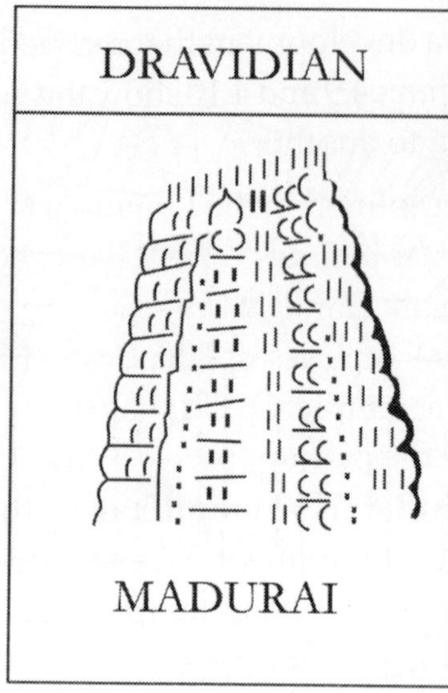

fig. 4.8: The Meenakshi Temple, Madurai

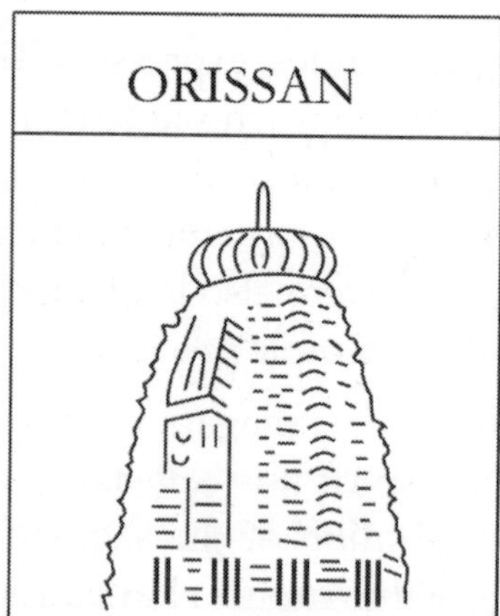

fig. 4.9: *Shikhara* of the Lingaraja Temple Bhubaneswar, Orissa

fig. 4.10: *Shikhara* of the Kandariya Mahadeva Temple, Khajuraho

another example is the Srirangam Temple (17th century) near Tiruchirappalli in Tamil Nadu, which not so long ago inaugurated what has been described as the world's tallest gateway (*gopuram*).

One of the outstanding characteristics of Hindu temples built since the 9th century is the towering height of their *shikhara*s or their heavenward (*akashaka*) elongation, a development that reached its zenith all over India in the 11th century. *Figures* 4.9 and 4.10 show the varying styles of *shikharas* from one part of India to another.

This feature is exemplified in the Lingaraja (*c.* CE 1000) and Raja-Rani temples of Bhubaneswar in Orissa, the Rajarajesvara and Brihadishvara temples of Thanjavur in Tamil Nadu, the Kandariya Mahadeva (*c.* CE 1000) and other (erotic) Temples of Khajuraho in Madhya Pradesh, and the Nilakantheshvara temple of Udayapur in Nepal. The increased elaboration of temple decoration, between the 12th and 16th centuries, especially in south India, is exemplified in the Nataraja Temple of Chidambaram and the temples of Tiruvannamalai (post-Chola), the Pampapati and Hazara Ramasvami temples of Hampi in Karnataka, the site of the city of Vijayanagara, and the stupendous Sun Temple of Konarka in Orissa. Such latter-day temples as these, in the words of Stella Kramrisch (1946: 6), teem with forms which have the urge and fullness of Indian nature in their towering shapes to the last point of their height, step by step, level by level, they lead the eye and mind of the devotee from this world to the worlds above. The temples rise from a broad base: differently built according to specific types, they have their variations in time and place and their shapes were elaborated in many schools. As they are today in southern India their high superstructures ascend in pyramidal form, while in northern India they fling their curvilinear faces towards a meeting point above the sanctuary.

Mandala of the Gods: Ritual in Temple Building

THE COSMOLOGY OF THE TEMPLE

Before we turn to the profound transcendental and at the same time arrestingly earthly aesthetic symbolism germane to Hindu temple (*oikos*) architecture, a digression is apposite. We visit the thoughts on the temple more generally (and particularly in the ancient Greek context) of the 20th-century German philosopher, Martin Heidegger, who wrote a major work on art and aesthetics. In his long essay, 'The Origin of the Work of Art' (written in 1936), Heidegger has these observations to make:

> It is the temple-work that first fits together and at the same time gathers around itself the unity of those paths and relations in which birth and death, disaster and blessing, victory and disgrace,

> endurance and decline acquire the shape of destiny for human beings. The all-governing expanse of this open relational context is the world of this historical people. . . .
>
> Standing there, the building rests on the rocky ground. This resting of the work draws up out of the rock the mystery of that rock's clumsy yet spontaneous support. Standing there, the building holds its ground against the storm raging above it and so first makes the storm itself manifest in its violence. . . . The temple's firm towering makes visible the invisible space of air.
>
> . . . we call this ground the *earth*. . . .
>
> The temple-work, standing there, opens up a world and at the same time sets this world back again on earth, which itself only thus emerges as native ground. — Heidegger 1971: 42

Explaining the symbolism alluded to by Heidegger in this short description, Jeff Malpas notes that the temple opens up a place for 'the "between" of human dwelling' by holding together the earth and world in a creative tension or what Malpas calls an 'oppositional belonging' and Heidegger the 'intimacy of striving' (Malpas 2006: 199). What this means, in the words of another scholar, is that the 'tension of their striving with one another thus "makes space for" the appearing of earth and world, and for human existence in relation to both of them' (Heidegger 1971: 45;

fig. 4.11: Ancient Greek temple (photo: Philip Hughes)

MacKinlay 2010: 505, *fig*. 4.11). Furthermore, the temple is built in order to make visible the 'world of meaning and value in which we dwell, and to make space for decision about action in that world'. And, finally, the temple itself can appear as a being, rather than as a piece of equipment. '*That* it is', which is true of all beings, only appears when a being is withdrawn from the usefulness in which beings generally disappear (Heidegger 1971: 65). Heidegger concludes that a building like the temple, that is a work of art, 'in its standing there, first gives to things their look and to men their outlook on themselves' (cited in MacKinlay 2010: 506).

Heidegger paves the way for us to now examine in more detail the imagery of the Hindu temple, which resonates with Heidegger's topology of 'temple-work', but in other ways stands out as something unique and particular to the religio-spiritual culture in which the temple has its origins. Heidegger makes no mention in his account of the space of the divine or the sacred or rather the 'transcendental' non-work peculiar to the *telos* or purpose of the Hindu *oikos* or *templum*. Thus, we may note that everything about the Hindu temple design and particularly the location — i.e. the earth on which its stands, the image of the rocky hill, the running water, the axial elevation of the superstructure that looks out into the world, and so on — signify a sacred geography that goes towards breaking down the boundaries between the human and the 'other world'. As Georg Michell puts it: 'A sacred mathematics is created, composed of a language of precise measurements, which permits a symbolic realisation of the underlying cosmic ideas' (Michell 1977: 61). This is the symbol of the *mandala* that permits, through dynamic rituals and ceremonies, the realisation of these ideas so that the Hindu temple functions as a place of transcendence, where the human may progress from the world of illusion to a universe of knowledge and truth.

The word *mandala* literally means 'circle' and in *Rigveda*, the term refers to a set of hymns that appear in sequence (hence a circle of hymns). (*Rigveda* consists of ten *mandala*s.) But *mandala* is also a mystic picture of the entire reality; a pictorial representation of the homology between microcosm and macrocosm. This representation often has geometric dimensions, and is thus known as *yantra*, which is replete with a magical efficacy (*fig*. 4.12).

fig. 4.12: Sri Yantra

Basically, as a geometric symbol, a *mandala* may be a closed polygon or square that can at the same time be converted into a triangle, a hexagon or an octagon, while retaining the basic measurement (*pramana*) for the model desired. And there can be other variations, also, such as the multiple overlays of triangles to form a tantric *yantra*, as in the well-known Sri Chakra used for the worship of the Hindu feminine deity. Again, a *mandala* can be structured so as to encapsulate the analogous relationship between the body (*sarira*, *purusha*), the groundplan, representing the microcosm, and the superstructure, as an edifice (*vastu* or *alaya*), representing the macrocosm, i.e. the universe. It is this latter signification of the *mandala* that concerns us most here.

It may be noted in passing that Buddhists have a somewhat different conception of the function of *mandala*. The geometric principles are, by and large, the same for Hindu and Buddhist *mandala*s, but more specifically the Buddhist *mandala* 'is essentially a vehicle for concentrating the mind so that it may pass beyond its usual fetters' (Arguelles and Miriam 1972: 15). In Buddhism, therefore, the function of a *mandala* is therapeutic, as it assists an individual to become aware of the levels of consciousness within, as well as the energy that unifies him or her with the environment.

Elaborate *mandalas* accompanied by ritual performances and mystic intonations are offered to the deities or to the cosmic processes.

By contrast, in the Hindu conception, a *mandala* symbolises the integration of the ontology of the universe, in which existence is represented by the *purusha* principle, the supernal or cosmic being, and the earth or terrestrial principle by *vastu*. *Vastu* in traditional literature is described as the residue of sacrifice: what has been left over. This residue, in which the gods reside (*vas*), is also the place of the germ of things to be and of the order of things. Thus we get the idea of a *vastumandala* (sacred geometric diagram) that is the microscopic configuration of the essential structure and order of the universe. This is synchronised with the supernal being (*vastu* as *purusha*). In plain terms, if we take *vastu* as signifying the site or foundation of a building, *vastumandala* as the plan for the building, and *vastupurusha* as the subtle 'body' that infuses the site (i.e. its deity) then the identification of the expansive but intangible 'body' with the spreadsheet of the plan results in the *vastupurusha-mandala* (Kramrisch 1946: 45-49).

The first function of the *vastupurusha-mandala* is to delimit the area where the temple is to be constructed: in this regard it provides a 'ritual' groundplan for the Hindu temple. In its diagramatic representation a *vastupurusha-mandala* is built up either from circles or from square spaces, the outer limits of which define the 'templum' for the overall structure. The square, more than the circle, is considered to be fundamental and sacred in Indian architectural symbolism. This square figure must be divided into 64 or 81 parts, in divisions of 8 or 9, respectively. The latter is a more common division. The divisions and the propriety of one over the other type are suffused with rather complex numerological and hierarchical symbolism and significance. The 9- better than the 8-square division accommodates the 32 divinities who settle on the 'body' of great *Purusha*. The nine squares in the inner core symbolise the terrestrial realm, with the central square corresponding to the 'womb' or navel of the cosmos. Each square is presided over by a deity or planetary divinity, and the centre is for the 'descent' of the main deity, *Purusha*, concerned with creation or regeneration (usually but not always Brahma or Prajapati). In the famous Rigvedic hymn, the Purusha-Sukta, the cosmic being is sacrificially dismembered and through this act a whole new world is issued, whereby each dismembered part represents certain essences or aspects of the world (or the many worlds (*loka*s) bearing in mind that the gods and the ancestors have, as it were, their own realms of existence). The ontological ramifications of this symbolism are enormous.

The 'creation' of a temple follows a somewhat analogous symbolism. A temple modelled on the *vastupurusha-mandala* permits an identification of the spatial and physical correspondence between the worlds of gods and of human beings. This symbolic connection (*yantra*) binds the worlds in a cosmology where earth and heaven stand unified. Now a temple regulated by the form of the *vastupurusha-mandala,* based on precise astronomical (and astrological) calculations, becomes more than a symbol for divinity: it is as though it were a structural *avatara*, an incorporation or embodiment of the divine presence in the material form (*vastu*). Ritual and architecture here combine to achieve this union of heaven and earth.

Stella Kramrisch describes this marriage of ritual and architecture:

> The drawing of the square plan, or the *vastupurusha-mandala* is imperative prior to building a temple. The knowledge of its meaning and execution is the first discipline which the architect must master . . . the actual drawing of the diagram on the ground which the temple (*prasada*) was to occupy seems to have been the rule. (*fig*. 4.13)
>
> — Ibid.: 39

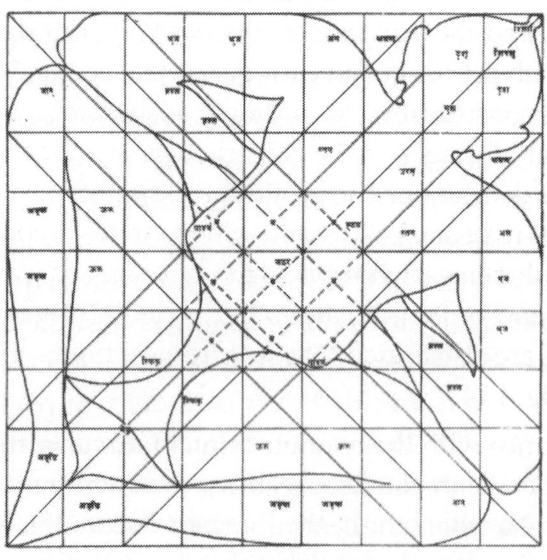

fig. 4.13: The *vastupurusha-mandala*

From the stretching of the cord, or the drawing of lines of *mandala*, everyone of the movements is a rite and sustains, in its own sphere of effectiveness, the sacred building, to the same extent as the actual foundation supports its weight. These movements, rites and meanings are not accessories, nor are they mere accompaniments, as equipment, to the building itself. They go into the making of the 'body-ontology' of the Hindu temple, its shape and proportion and that of every carved detail and every figure, each at its proper place, with rhythms and gestures appropriate to it. If the universe were to be conceived as a large 'body-corporate plan' that stretches over, in and across the spirit of the divine, then the temple is one or more condo or apartment, an individuated sanctuary for the Supreme Soul's earthly dwelling (Bilimoria and Stansell 2010).

Temple Construction and Ritual

There are various terms in Sanskrit for a temple. Coomaraswamy (1977: 4, n. 7) notes *brahmapura* (city of God) from *Atharvaveda* (X.2.30) as one of the very early terms; others more commonly used, and which invariably connote 'abode or house of god(s)' are: *devaniketa-mandala, devayatanam, devalaya, devasthanam, devagara, devagriham, devakulam, vesman, prasada, vimana* and *mandira* (a more popular term used these days). Since a temple is a 'house' (*oikos, baitel, templum*), with analogical equivalents to the human body on the one hand, and the universe on the other, its dimensions have to be worked out with precision and each part sacralised or consecrated in the process of the construction. Accordingly, elaborate and dynamic rituals are involved at all stages of the construction of a temple, from ground-breaking to its dedication. The groundbreaking ritual involves the burial of *pancha-shila*s (five stones) (usually blue granites), representing the five *devata*s (heavenly beings) who uphold the structure and ward off bad omens. Often, jewels and ornaments and other precious elements, such as gold and diamond, are also buried. The features of a typical Hindu temple are displayed in *fig*. 4.14.

In accordance with the configuration of *mandala*, the Hindu temple begins with the womb-chamber (*garbhagriha*), which is usually a darkish enclosure or cella where the central shrine (*sanctum*) is to be located. This chamber is enclosed in a towered sanctuary, crowned with a pyramidal dome or a tapering spire (*sikhara*), possibly in several tiers, and finished

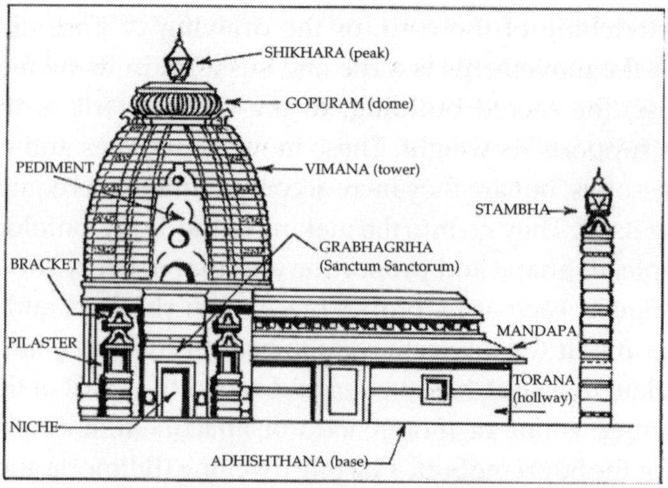

fig. 4.14: The parts and features of a Hindu temple

fig. 4.15: The gods' home: rear view with domes of Helensburg SVTA Temple (photo: Philip Hughes)

with a finial at the pinnacle. The entire sanctuary is called a *vimana*, although the term is also used to refer to the tiered, domed structure as well. The area where *vimana* is to be placed is cleared and consecrated for laying the spiritual foundation.[3]

The textual sources for these liturgical rituals are usually the Pancharatra Agamas, which comprise one of the two basic sources for ritual worship in

---

[3] *Fig.* 4.14 is the temple master plan sketched by V. Janakiramana, with stylised production by Brewster Murray, Sydney, 20 September 1983 (*courtesy:* SVTA).

most Vaishnava temples in south India. Ramanuja, the 11th-century philosopher and peripatetic scholar, whose teachings the Vaishnavas by-and-large follow, favoured and interpreted the temple ritual prescriptions of the Pancharatra Agamas. The textual prescriptions were followed with precision at the Helensburgh site in New South Wales, in the presence of the *sthapati*.

Garbhagriha is approached through a vestibule or an intermediate chamber (*antarala*), which in turn is entered from a hall (*mandapa*) that opens out to a courtyard. The whole structure is surrounded by a low-lying enclosed courtyard, which may house a further complex of shrines, perhaps beginning, close to the entrance, with an independent shrine for God Ganesha. There is also usually an archway, which may be a free-standing monolithic tympanum (*gopura*), marking the gateway to the temple complex. As noted earlier, the Pallavas seem to have initiated *gopura*, which achieved gigantic proportions, almost triangular in shape, in the late Chola period (10th-12th centuries), and especially so under the Pandya rulers of the 12th century.

The Shilpa-Shastras (also part of the more extensive Agama-Shastras) are the standard canons of sacred architecture and they provide the technical details for a temple construction. A master temple architect, however, is expected to be versed in aspects of the Vedas and various branches of the traditional corpus that deal with astronomy, measurement, carving, embedding, building and material sciences, harmony of structures, aesthetics, the history and classification of temple architecture and much else. The Agama texts ordain the use of stone slabs in the construction of temples. By the 12th century, temples in south India would have their walls built of stone, the ceiling of the inner *sanctum* in wood, and the superstructure of bricks. However, bricks alone, made from a particular mix of earth, sand and cement, may suffice for the entire structure, from the outer walls to the inner shrine housing, as indeed was the case in the construction of the Sri Venkateswara temples in Helensburgh.

CONSTRUCTION OF THE 'BIG TEMPLE' OF HELENSBURGH

Shortly after the ground-breaking ceremony, bulldozers, concrete mixers, labourers and engineers moved in to commence their part of the job. Thanks to the conservationist sense of the planners, a healthy spread of gum trees was left to stand all around the courtyard, thus blending the temple complex harmoniously with the larger surroundings. The first structure to be completed was the Ganesha shrine, located near the entrance of the temple, and facing north-east. This minuscule structure, and a shrine in its own right, was built according to the Shaiva tradition of worship. Some 5.5 m (18 ft) high, it is capped with a large dome, characteristically representing the back of an elephant and crowned by a finial on its pinnacle. Before long, the Ganesha image, until then lodged in the 'Meditation Room' on the campus of the University of New South Wales, was brought out and installed, although its dedication had to wait until the entire complex was ready for inauguration. Ganesha, also known as Sri Vigneshvara, is the first deity worshipped upon entering the temple complex, before one goes towards the main shrine.

In the meantime, on a return visit to India, the *sthapati* had organised the carving of the major images and other idols or figurines in Mahabalipuram in Tamil Nadu, a centre for temple arts. Since he was the architect for both the temple structure and the shrines, he had worked out the exact measurements, shapes and sizes of the images in proportion to the houses they would be lodged in. He then had them shipped out in time for the arrival in Sydney in November 1984 of the seven traditional craftsmen-masons (*shilpi*s). By this time the base structure had been completed. It remained for the *shilpi*s to complete the details of the sculptural ornamentations and to carve the appropriate images and symbolic decor, so that the temple achieved the grandeur and sanctity of the Dravidian temple, with all its embellishments. The *sthapati* had combined, in harmonious structural form, the three major temple architectural traditions of south India, namely the Pallava, Pandya, Chola and the elaboration achieved in the Vijayanagara arts.

Lotus-corbels, a feature of Vijayanagara style, are in prominence in the Helensburgh temple, as are *kudus*, horseshoe-shaped window frames, which are crowned with lion-heads and foliage that date back to the Chola style. The design of the niche, parapet, pavilion, pillar, pilaster, corbels, and flexured quoin combine features from one or the other, or a mixture, of the traditions. Dwarfs of fierce mien and urchins hiding struts or column brackets and other structural protrusions, are examples of such other syncretic features. While the builders prepared concrete profiles for the domical towers (*shikhara*) and smeared loose plaster over slaps and beams, pilasters and pavilion-roofs, the craftsmen set to work with a minimum of hand tools (but no geometric devices) to graft intricate decorations and ornate curvatures, corbels, niches, florals and floriated tails, as well as embossing symbolic markings, faces, arms, eyes and carving torsos of fiendish-looking dwarfs and door-keepers or guardian deities (*dvarapalas*), depicting figures and images from folk mythologies. Some of the creatures depicted may have once represented an 'evil' force or tendency in the human collective that was captured by the 'good' gods, and forever entombed in sacred architecture to perform the very minor functions of upholding a pillar, a column, a door strut, or as a gargoyle. The perpetual war between the righteous gods (*devas*) and the unrighteous gods (*asuras*), leading to the triumph of the former, is echoed in the rich and varied symbolism that shapes the exterior of the temple. The fa®ade adorning the vestibule leading into the shrine chambers (*garbhagrihas*) had also to be prepared with the same décor. A majestic structure, and in some ways a unique architectural feat, steadily arose, silhouetted against the indigenous landscape.

The Mandala Anthropomorphised

TEMPLE AS THE SIGN OF COVENANT (PRATIJNA-PATRA)

We noted earlier the cosmological configuration symbolised in *mandala*, but we also mentioned its terrestrial significance, whereby it symbolises a correspondence between the worlds of gods and of human beings. To achieve the latter identification, *mandala* is transformed into a cosmic person, arranged diagonally, and the squares become linked with some portion of the body. This cosmic figure is identified with the process of creation of the universe and its underlying structure (see *fig.* 4.13).[4]

The cosmic person is then stretched out in a horizontal incline or repose. A structural model for a temple is thereby created that at once achieves the correspondence symbolised in the image of a *mandala*. A *mandala* is anthropomorphised:

> The anthropomorphic approach imagines the cosmic man (*mahapurusha*) displaying the whole of creation on his body, providing a means of access to higher and more sacred spheres

---

4 *Fig.* 4.13 is from Michell 1977.

through his spine which is identified with the vertical axis.

— Michell 1977: 71

A temple, then, from a more grounded perspective, is basically a structure laid on an axis that resembles the repose of a reclining body so that the elevated *garbhagriha,* signifying the head, is axially aligned with the protruding feet, represented by the outer gateway (*gopura*). Each part of the temple, therefore, has to be carefully proportioned in metrical scale so that an overall harmony is achieved in the entire structure. In addition, the vertical axis is associated with a deathless trunk of a tree, supporting the universe by its roots in strategic places. The ascent along the vertical axis symbolises the door to salvation (*moksha-dvara*) and signifies progression towards enlightenment. The goal of this journey is identified with the crowning finial (*kalasha*) that marks the pinnacle of the superstructure of the temple.

Another significant feature of the temple is a large flagpole (*stambha*) erected at the pre-axial by the temple entrance. This is identified with the support of the heavens and likened to the imperious staff of royalty or, which is the same thing, kingship over the kingdom. Since most major temple establishments were patronised or endowed by royal houses, *stambha*s displayed the appropriate emblems. Traditionally, temples face east, so that the early sunlight falls on the deity's face, but the Tirupati Temple in Andhra Pradesh faces west, since Sri Venkateshwara's face is supposed to be blindingly luminous itself and his eyes are thus covered over. The main hall (*mandapa*) adjoining the shrine-chambers covers the rest of the reclining 'body', and is therefore also a sacred space, used for different forms of worship (*bhoga*), offerings (*arcana*) assembly and public celebrations. Just outside the main doorway, at the axial knee-point, is a shelter for the *vigraha* of Garuda (mythic eagle) who is Vishnu's celestial vehicle. Since the Helensburgh temple follows the Tengalai (southern Tamil) tradition as distinct from the Vadagalai (northern Tamil) tradition, the main temple in Helensburgh incorporates three *garbhagriha*s: a large one in the centre for the main deity, Vishnu-Venkateshwara, flanked on either side by two relatively smaller chambers, set slightly back, for the two feminine deities as the 'consorts' of Vishnu. On his right is Sri or Mahalakshmi or Padmavati (who is really Vishnu's inseparable *shakti* (dynamic energy)) and on his left is Andal (redeemer of the world; she is

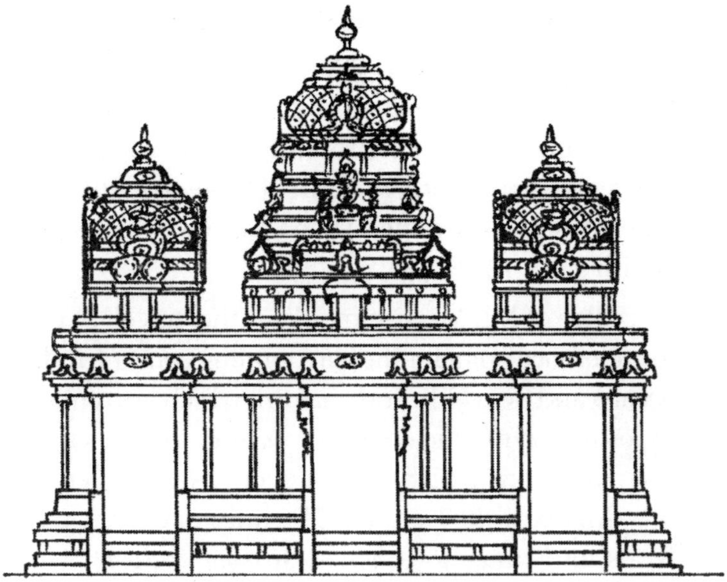

fig. 4.16: The grand *vimana* of Sri Venkateshwara Temple, Helensburgh, Australia

also known as Godadevi) or Bhudevi (goddess born of earth) who is Vishnu's terrestrial companion.

On the outer and upper side of *vimana*, atop *garbhagriha*s, stand dome-shaped towers (*shikhara*s). A *shikhara* also denotes a shape curvilinear in the vertical section, but more specifically in the case of south Indian 'high' temples, it designates only the cupola that is placed on top of the superstructure. A large two-tier *shikhara* protrudes above the Vishnu sanctum, known as Vishnugantha, and is crowned on its pinnacle by a golden *kalasha*, which symbolises the absolute and timeless principle beyond repetition and relativity. One either side, are mounted single tier *shikhara*s, projecting over *garbhagriha*s of the two feminine divinities. These are also tipped by finials. Together, the trio of domes form the grand *vimana* of the superstructure (*fig.* 4.16).

A worshipper standing in the main assembly hall, facing the vestibule, is able to have a glimpse of the domes through a glass aperture formed like a canopy on the roof. This vision (*darshan*) of *shikhara*s with their finials is itself of significance, in terms of reminding one of the transcendental goals to be achieved. Just as it is important for a Hindu to have the auspicious sight (*darshan*) of the gods in the shrines, and a fortiori be 'seen' or beheld by the gods, so is it important to have a *darshan* of the temple.

The Mandala Expanded: Mt. Meru, the Mythic Universe

The temple also represents the mythic universe of Mt. Meru (or Mt. Kailasa), which forms the *axis mundi*. As a cosmic map, the temple has four corners and four doorways representing eight directions, presided over by creatures and theriomorphic figures (*vahana*s) that embody certain mythic-psychic powers, as well as serving as conveyances for gods and goddesses (Smith 1981: 12-29, 153, n. 70).

Just as the centre of Mt. Meru symbolises the 'navel' of the universe, standing as the reference point for the surrounding concentrically arranged continents, oceans and heavenly bodies, from which also emanate world-making energies, the symbolic centre or 'womb' of the sanctuary is its most dynamic part, from which sacred energy is radiated outward in four directions (Mabbett 1983: 64-83). The lines of energy pass through secondary icons and images (*vahana*s, *apasmara*, *dvarapala*s, celestial damsels, doorkeepers and so on) and are positioned strategically in all eight quoins of the temple. The temple is the architectural facsimile of the sacred places of gods, providing for the worshipper the merit that would be his or hers through an actual visit to the sacred mountains, such as Mt. Kailasa in the Himalayas (ibid.: 69). All temporal forces, desires and drives have to be neutralised before one enters the sacred chambers or 'womb' (*garbha*) of the eternal. This occurs as one crosses the lines of energy and becomes absorbed in its radiation, moving gradually towards the centre. Older style temples are fortified by a series of outward enclosures that have to be traversed before one penetrates the increasingly sacred inner enclosures, eventually reaching the *sanctum sanctorum*. The chief axial line runs from east to west since the deities face one of these directions (usually east), although, as we noted, this is reversed in the case of Sri Venkateshwara Temple. A processional circumambulatory path (*pradakshinapatha*) is built around the temple.

A devotee, after worship, leaves by the northern doorway and circumambulates the temple (*pradakshina*) in a clockwise direction, paying respect to images and icons that introduce further aspects of the divine. Again, a gaze (*padarshan*) at *shikhara* and *kalasha* is intended to remind the pilgrim of the ultimate goal of the journey that they have been on over many lives. *Pradakshina* finishes at the Garuda *vigraha* by the western entrance. In this way, the devotee has worshipped the gods as well as the temple and participated in the 'sacred threading' of the entire 'universe', symbolised by the temple.

Clearly, the temple is not just a place of worship, but is itself an object of worship, for the whole temple precinct is, as it were, transubstantiated, through the dynamic ritual and ceremonies, into a divine cosmos, which the worshipper enters as would a *bhakta* the Body of God. The temple superstructure, very much as the deities it houses, in the course of the pilgrimage and worship gradually achieves a deeper meaning that transforms the temple from a mere symbol to a dynamic repository of numinous power to which the pilgrims find themselves transported. The inner elevation brings about the realisation of the inherent connection between 'this world' and the 'other world', or rather of their 'non-difference'. The symbol and the symbolised become one.

The Helensburgh temple stood complete, except for the gods, who, still in their pristine dormant state, slept in the crates nearby in which they had travelled the long distance from Tamil Nadu, and unwittingly crossed the 'dark waters'. However, that could not be interpreted as their 'fall', for they had not been 'ensouled' yet, for which preparations were underway. Plans went according to schedule and on 30 June 1985, the great day arrived for the ritual consecration of the temple and 'dedication' (*mahakumbhabhisheka*) which is itself a highly symbolic event.[5] It is symbolic because it is the first day of *darshan*, the revelation or sight of the body of *Purusha* and its worship. Its *raison d 'ê tre* is symbolic but at a higher level it is also metaphysical.

Mahakumbhabhisheka: The Dedication Ceremony

The dedication of a temple (*mahakumbhabhisheka*) proceeds in two stages, and the rituals involved are rather complicated. There are some twenty-five rites to this ceremony, but here we shall discuss these in the most condensed terms. The first stage of the ceremony is called *pratishtha* (sometimes *yajna*) or the installation and consecration of the hitherto inanimate idols or images symbolising the presiding deities. The second stage involves the actual dedication or sanctification (*mahakumbhabhisheka*) of the temple superstructure. This is a profoundly symbolic moment in

5 SVTA newsletters. On the ritual, see Clothey (1983: 186); see also note 6.

Hindu orthopraxy. In practice, the deities are first installed and then ritually consecrated, after which the whole temple is dedicated.

PRATISHTHA

Pratishtha literally means embodying 'images with the fullness of the divine'. This particular ceremony comprises a very important and significant set of ritual procedures aimed at sanctifying, consecrating, or blessing a building, image, or liturgical implement, thereby 'establishing' it for purposes of effective worship.

The cluster of rites observed during the *pratishtha* ceremony represents, as it were, a juncture, a transitional moment, at which a 'structure of stone or wood becomes a sacred shrine; when a piece of granite or bronze or plaster becomes the palpable presence of the divine plenum manifested before our very eyes; when the ordinary becomes extraordinary, the profane becomes venerable' (Smith 1981: 52). The process then is one of sacralising or making the ordinary sacred.

For the purposes of the *pratishtha* ritual, a special *yagashala* (Tamil, *yakacalai*), or temporary shrine, is prepared outside the temple building (near one of its side entrances, usually facing north) and this serves as a 'surrogate' *garbhagriha* or *sanctum* and a ritual universe. The *yagashala* is, what I would like to call, the chosen 'space for ritual dreaming' or, if I may be allowed to coin a neologism, a 'dreamspace' (not too far off from the ideogram of 'the Dreamtime'). In other words, the boundaries of the symbolised space to be occupied by *garbhagriha* is demarcated, purified and sacralised, so that the spirits can be invoked to empower and, through another ritual process, confer sacredness onto the icons and the supporting items to be installed in the temple proper (including the dais or pedestals on which the icons are stood). While it is reminiscent of the biblical tabernacle, it is actually closer to the Buddhist meditational praxis of concentration on *mandala* (or its Hindu equivalent of the geometric *yantra*) for the purification and enlightenment of the mind. But *mandala* itself has to be purified, sacralised and homologised before it is, as it were, absorbed into the mind, or vice versa.

Once consecrated and empowered, this whole 'sacred dreamspace' is literally transferred to the *sanctum sanctorum*, so that the designated *oikos* (home), truly becomes the sacred 'womb', patterned, as we noted earlier, on the 'navel' (Mt. Meru) of the mythic (macrocosmic) universe, and as the centremost square in the (microcosmic) *vastupurusha-mandala*.

Since the temple symbolises a human body and a universe, the *yagashala* is prepared so as to represent both of these, from their 'navels' outward. *Yagashala* is a miniature symbol but it is also a metaphor, for it inscribes all the essential signs that stand for most of the more fundamental elements of the cosmos (*fig*. 4.17). First, a large square space is demarcated to form a *mandapa*. In the centre the main raised cubical altar (*vedika*) is inscribed and set up, to represent the triune towers and to symbolise the 'navel' of the universe. Around this altar, six fire-pits (*kunda*s) are prepared, each dug into the ground and set in concrete in front of a pedestal or dais for each of the major images to be symbolically seated. Given that the 'dreamspace' is a minuscule form of the larger temple complex, surrogate representations, rather than the actual images, are placed in the determined spots, along with the more manageable images (*utsavamurti*s) used during processions and celebrations. There are pedestals for Sri Venkateshwara, Mahalakshmi, Andal, Ganesha and one also for Garuda. There are smaller altars for *ankurarpana* (rites of the seeds and their germination) and *dvarapala*s.

Ankurarpana, which obviously has agrarian or fertility overtones, is

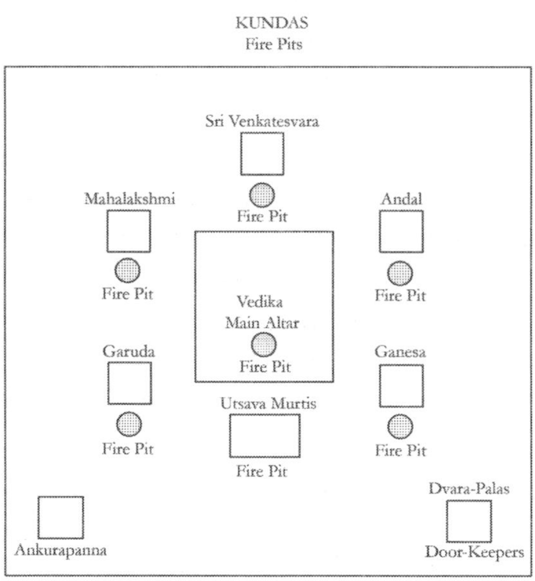

fig. 4.17: Yagashala Plan of the Helensburgh Temple

the very first step. The rite of auspicious germination is symbolic in another way in the sacerdotal arts, inasmuch as the structure of the temple that grows from the 'seed' absorbs the essence' of the earth (*bhu*) and transmutes it. Next, utensils are assembled, and the *yagashala* space is consecrated. Festooned arches (*taranas*) and flags decorate the entrances to the symbolic *mandapa*. Conical vessels, with coconuts placed over their mouths, and containing items such as germinating grains, rice, scented water (from sacred rivers), gems and jewels, betel nuts, sandalwood, and decorated with leaves, cotton threads, saffron cloth, and a special *darbha* grass, are placed on the altar and in strategic positions around the other altars in the decorated *mandapa*. The placing of the stoup-like conical vessels is called *kalashasthapana*. The significance of the vessel or pot is that it represents the body (*sharira*) of the deity: the outer casting as flesh, the water as blood, the coconut as head, the thread as veins, the gems as bones, and the grains as food. The *mantras* recited while pouring the water is thought of as giving *prana* (life-breath) to the deity. In the process, the presiding deity or spirit of the land (*vastudevata*) is also pacified and venerated in a ritual called *vastushanti*. (One informant ventured to suggest that the spirit invoked in this ceremony had to be 'native to the land', which he took to mean a spirit from the Aboriginal Dreamtime.)

After this, the (surrogate) images are cleansed and their eyes are ritually opened in a ceremony known as *akshimocana*, and the sacrificial fires are lit, into which oblations are offered. By pouring libations into the fire-altar during a sacrifice, contact is supposed to be established between earth and heaven. Heaven is, as it were, brought down to earth, so that the bounded space can be sacralised, and a whole new 'universe' is founded. By the latent potency generated by this performance, and by the speech-acts or performatives that accompany these rites, the divine presence is 'established' in *mandapa*. Again, as Fred Clothey suggests, 'according to the textual formulation known as the *vastupurusha-mandala*, this mini-cosmos is equated with the human body' (1983: 186). He explains:

> That is, the symbolism of the body as utilised in such techniques as Tantra and Yoga are homologised to the temple. The temple, the sacrifice room (*yagashala*), the human body — all are seen as microcosms in which life-changing rituals can be performed. The consecration process follows closely these symbolic manoeuvres.

And so the 'universe' and its elements (represented in the items in the conical vessels) are sacralised and homologised, as is the ambit surrounding them, and there the gods would take their respective seats on the anointed sacred pedestals. The public is invited to witness this spectacle.

An officiating priest, Shri T.V. Anantharamaseshan, who had come from India, presided as *acharya* at the Helensburgh dedication. An *acharya* serves as the chief functionary at an official gathering (*sangha*) who invites, salutes and receives guests and co-ordinates or conducts the day's performances, but he also does more than that. He plays a ritual function as well. By entering into a state of meditation (*dhyana*), and by reciting *mantras*, *acharya* consecrates and sacralises himself. In this role he is *yajamana*, the sacralised sacrificer in a Vedic rite. Then by the power of his *bhakti*, he conducts the recitation of *mantra*s, ritual offerings and symbolic sacrifices which take place over four days (or longer in more orthodox traditions). The ceremony is concluded on the last day when the temple dedication has been completed and the deities have ritually assumed their respective seats or thrones in the temple's *garbhagriha*.

As the ceremony proceeds, *acharya*, clad in surplice-like silk *dhoti*, after seeking protection from Vishnu, summons in his thought the 'all-sustaining, eternal, immeasurable, inconceivable, featureless, formless essence of all things' to become present or manifest in the water in the vessel. Vishnu is then honoured with flowers, water and other items. The other deities are treated similarly. The vessels are now fully empowered.

Meanwhile, the larger images are removed from their resting crates and set up by the *shilpi*s in their proper seats in their *garbhagriha*s or *sancta*. These have also to be purified, and their eyes gradually 'opened' through appropriate *mantra*s, and they too are ensouled or given 'life'. This is the next important phase of the *pratishtha* ritual and is known as *abhisheka*, literally, 'bathing with water'.[6] (The water in the vessels and for other rituals was said to have been brought from five sacred rivers of India.)

Amidst chanting, singing and *mantra* recitation, the festooned and water-filled vessels that had been sacralised and homologised and the *yagashala-mandapa*, are solemnly carried by a charged procession, headed by *acharya*, into the temple, into *garbhagriha* and placed beside the images.

[6] On *abhisheka* ritual details, see *Padmasamhita*, H. Daniel Smith (1978: 229).

The water, by-now charged with *shakti*, is taken from the vessels with strokes of a tuft of grass and sprinkled over the principal image to the accompaniment of *mantra*s that praise and invite the god such as, 'This is Vishnu . . . I praise Him . . . May he come.' *Acharya* next requests the god to emerge from the vessel and infuse himself into the image, so that the image may be 'ensouled' and become a living icon of the deity (*parivaradevata*). Then and only then does the granite-image become deserving of the epithet god (*deva*), not before that. From here on the image becomes a sacred sign that, as a signifier, achieves a complete harmony and identity with the signified. The 'image' is not a symbol standing for or pointing to something else: it is what is supposed to be signified. The integral co-union of the signifier and the signified, *shakti* and *deva*, the image and the god, is accomplished, affirmed even, by the stroke of this water-soaked tuft.

More water is poured over the icon as the bathing continues and appropriate *mantra*s, hymns and eulogies are recited. This procedure is repeated with each of subsidiary images in the adjacent cellas. When the bathing ceremony is completed, the water is dried off and the gods are anointed with sandal paste, oil and other sacral substances, and then dressed in resplendent garments. The gods have to be pacified and honoured with food offerings, gifts, and other delights; they are also invited or entreated to be present in their new abode thereafter. An unwritten 'covenant' (*pratijna-patra*) is made, whereby the devotees pledge unstinted allegiance (*prasamvida*) to their newly-arrived Lord and his consorts in return for their compassion and care.

The ceremony described above concludes the stage that fully empowers the granite image with divine presence; it is now no longer a granite sculpture, but a living sign that has become a fit embodiment through which the deity may manifest its transcendental, or rather earthly form. The signifier as it were appropriates the signified within its own space: the text has now been divinised, and the deity textualised. The deity is considered to be very much alive in the image, but only as long as the appropriate rituals continue to be performed and the universe it occupies is not desecrated in any way. All these various images are, in their turn, similarly consecrated on the gala day for the gods. This concludes the *pratishtha* part of the ceremony.

Bathing the Temple Vimana and the Gods

The second stage of the dedication ceremony and the consummating ritual is *mahakumbhabhisheka* in the form of the temple *vimana* itself. Large vessels containing the *shakti*-empowered water, collected from the five sacred rivers in India, are raised on a giant crane, accompanied by *acharya* and his assisting priest. The crane is positioned facing the upper end of the largest dome. The *acharya* raises the tuft of grass in his hand, and gracefully waves it towards the sky, in ritually measured movements, as though it were a magic wand. The act is intended to summon the spirits to descend on and engulf the temple *vimana*, which *acharya* then also sprinkles with water and anoints with other substances. We mentioned earlier that *vimana* with its tapering off, cockpit-like *shikhara* and antenna-like finials is compared to a vehicle that transports the gods from their heavenly abode to a safe and sacred spot on the earth. A kind of yogic-power rather than the force of mechanical propulsion is imagined as lifting the vehicle and flying it. Here, the temple superstructure, and particularly its *vimana*, is being transformed into an ethereal capsule which the gods might use for traversing from one dimension of space into another. It should be noted that the 'distance' between the boundaries of the spatial locations is merely symbolic, for the whole purpose of the homologisation ritual is to cut asunder the boundaries and, in a manner of speaking, collapse the disparate planes into a singular spatial frame. Since time, in this cosmological frame of reference, is not conceived as a dimension distinct from space, the 'traversing' or, indeed, the 'inversion' of the space can happen instantaneously (or, as someone explaining this imagery to me put it, faster than the speed of sound and light!).

From *kalasha* down to the images placed around each dome, every item is systematically consecrated in this process. It is only then that the *vigraha* (Lord's icons) are said to have been firmly 'established' and empowered. Each dome and the various images in the smaller pavilions, and *vahanas*, doorkeepers and so on, are consecrated. By this symbolic gesture, the entire temple superstructure, or the universe encompassed by the temple, is 'bathed', and thus purified and rendered sacred. In Clothey's words: 'The highlight of the ritual is the settling of golden domes (*kalashas*) on top of the temple's major towers and anointing them, an act which signifies that the temple itself is set aside as sacred space'.

Again, Clothey tells us that *mahakumbhabhisheka* incorporates (and extends) 'the symbolism of the *pratishtha* rituals so that . . . the temple itself, and especially the temple tower, is 'set up' or installed as an embodiment of the divine presence' (ibid.: 184-85).

The procedures that we have described above culminate in the sacralisation of the entire temple space. The building of a temple becomes like the founding of a cosmos by homologising parts of the sacrificial room and eventually the temple itself to various parts of the universe. Building a temple is also likened to the implantation of a crop through such rituals as the germinating of grains, the use of paddy on the pedestal of the deities and other devices which homologize deities or temple parts and vegetation. Further, building a temple becomes the inauguration of a king in his domain by means of various rituals, some of them directly borrowed from ceremonies associated with kingship; the deity is treated like a king, the temple becomes his palace, the landscape it surveys becomes the 'king's' domain and the worshippers are his subjects (ibid.).

These are indeed powerful and profound symbols, which the devotee remembers as he or she enters the temple precinct.

UTSAVA: CELEBRATION OF REJOICING

The concluding part of the dedication ceremony includes various *utsavas* (celebrations of rejoicing and remembrance) which come close to the idea of thanksgiving. *Utsava* begins with *pradakshina* of the surrogate images (usually miniature bronze replicas of the major images in the temple), elaborately decorated with colourful garments, garlands and ornaments often carried in a palanquin or a large wooden chariot, accompanied with music, singing and a fitting finale (*aarati*). This kind of processional *utsava* may be repeated annually during major festive and auspicious days and is a regular feature of south Indian temple life.

The ceremony is concluded with the 'divine marriage' of the gods (*kalyana utsava*); here the gods and goddesses are given all the compliments, honour, festivity and respect of a human wedding. There then follows feasting, merry-making and much mirth, as the subjects celebrate the arrival and presence among them of the 'royal' gods. For the first Hindu gathering of its kind and size in Australia, a crowd of 2,000 assembled to witness the spectacular event and to partake of its

fig. 4.18: Frontal, Gopurum, Helensburg Temple, N.S.W.

fig. 4.19: Murgan Temple Sydney, N.S.W.

'sacraments'. The event, which was carried out with much pomp and ceremony, was described as an 'electrifying' culmination of years of yearning for a concrete symbol of the Hindu presence in Australia. So there it was, a structure and the first of its kind in Oceania-Australasia, fast becoming a pilgrim centre for Hindus from these and other regions.

fig. 4.20: Vishnu Temple Malibu, California

An important tourist attraction, it commands attention not only from the lay person, but also from students of religion and culture, embodying as it does the diasporic experience of a 'people in transit'.

What we have described was the first successful phase of the temple complex construction. The second phase, as noted above in Chapter 3, involved the installation of images of the *avatara*s of Vishnu (traditionally numbering ten), to fill the inside walls of the main hall. These comprise Matsya (Fish), Kurma (Tortoise), Varaha (Boar), Narasimha (Man-Lion), Vamana (Dwarf), Parashurama, Rama, Balarama, Krishna and Kalki, the horse-riding, spear-wielding destroyer-prophet yet to come. (The Buddha sometimes appears in place of Balarama, usually in northern practice; in the south the Buddha's function is generally considered to have been a neutral one.) The customary *stupa* or *dvajastambha*, the symbol of royalty and kingship over the sacred domain, the main entrance tower (*gopura*), as well as a large hall for cultural and educational purposes — incorporating an interfaith meditation centre — and quarters for priests, have also been added, as well as the separate shrines for Shiva and his consort, Parvati, and one for Subramaniam, also known as Murugan (the second son of Shiva). These, with the Ganesha shrine, constitute the second shrine complex, which have pleased the large number of Shaivas who have supported the temple project.

5

Religious Maintenance and Adaptation
An Example from the South Australian Hindu Diaspora

Heather Foster

Introduction

RAYMOND B. Williams (1992, 2004) identified different strategies within Hindu communities outside India, specifically in the United States, which enabled adaptation to the host community to occur while maintaining (and adjusting) religious beliefs and practices within the diaspora. John Hinnells (1998) subsequently proposed ten factors for change and continuity in diasporic religion. These approaches form a useful analytical tool for understanding the manner in which Hinduism has developed, and is developing, in South Australia. This chapter examines the development of diasporic Hinduism in the Australian cities of Adelaide and Whyalla, in the light of both Williams' and Hinnells' categories. A comparison of the strategies of the smaller Whyalla community is juxtaposed against the more developed and larger Adelaide Hindu community, highlighting the similarities and differences between distinctive communities in different circumstances. The scholarship by Williams and Hinnells is useful in providing a framework for understanding the developments within these communities in Australia.

Raymond B. Williams's Strategies

In a chapter entitled 'Sacred Threads of Several Textures: Strategies of Adaptation in the United States', Williams (1992) identified five different strategies used by the Indian and especially the Hindu community. These were: individual, national, ecumenical, ethnic and hierarchical. A brief explanation of each will be appropriate at this time.

INDIVIDUAL STRATEGY

The individual strategy, as the name suggests, is concerned with personal religious maintenance. It is operative when individuals involved in the immigration process preserve their '. . . religious identity through acts in private or its opposite in the private disregard for any religious heritage' (ibid.: 232). Maintained private practices included maintenance of a home shrine and the performance of family rituals.

NATIONAL STRATEGY

The national stage takes as its reference the colonial legacy, which superimposed a national identity on Indians. Williams describes the development of and support for numerous cultural organisations by the community. This is only possible once the community expands sufficiently to be able to maintain these organisations. Cultural organisations have a variety of different forms as they sponsor '. . . performances in film, dance, theatre and music, honour politicians and bureaucrats from India, observe all-India political and cultural holidays' (ibid.: 235). Although these organisations are theoretically secular in nature and promoting an Indian identity, Williams reports that they tend to become unofficially Hindu and include religious aspects within them and therefore function to assist in the maintenance of Hinduism in the diaspora.

ECUMENICAL STRATEGY

The ecumenical strategy includes a pan-Hindu emphasis. In this strategy, there is an emphasis and construction of the commonalities within Hinduism over diversity, including regional diversity. Temples are constructed around pan-Indian deities rather than regional deities, universally accepted texts such as *Bhagavad-Gita* are highlighted, and the festivals that are celebrated are also pan-Hindu (ibid.: 239).

ETHNIC STRATEGY

The ethnic strategy emphasises diversity, which occurs when a significant number of individual ethnic (regional/language) groups are found within the same location. Williams suggests that the combination of

> . . . ethnic and religious elements in personal and group identity has a powerful attraction for first-generation immigrants, more powerful than the union of Indian national elements with either secular elements or with an ecumenical Hinduism. — ibid.: 241

HIERARCHICAL STRATEGY

The final strategy of adaptation is hierarchical, which Williams describes as being concentrated upon loyalty to a living religious leader such as Sathya Sai Baba. This loyalty to a leader cuts across regional/ethnic groups (ibid.: 243). Let us now look at the ten factors that Hinnells has proposed.

J.R. Hinnells's Ten Factors

Hinnells suggested ten '[f]actors for change and continuity in Diaspora Religion' (1998: 821). As with Williams's work, it is clearly focused on the developing community rather than subsequent growth and maturation. This latter area of research Hinnells addresses in the same chapter, by using the work of Kim Knott. The ten factors Hinnells proposes are summarised below (ibid.: 821-26).

1. Where people come from?
2. The perceptions of the new country with which people come?
3. The nature of the immigration process.
4. What people were before they migrated?
5. What they were when they migrated?
6. With whom they migrated?
7. To where they migrated?
8. What people do in their lives after they have settled?
9. Who people are?
10. External factors.

Hinnells believes that both the country and region from which individuals migrate influence the changes in, and continuity of, their religion within the diaspora. This includes such aspects as the degree to which their religion may have previously evolved, whether they came from a rural or urban setting, and the 'twice migrant' (via another diaspora) experience. Perceptions of the new country may include feelings of concern and negativity, for example, ill feeling towards Britain due to its colonial past in India and concerns about strong conservative Christian influences.

The motivation for migration is also an influencing factor. As Hinnells suggests, those who migrate in order to advance their education or career are inclined to adapt more readily than those who feel forced to move for economic reasons. Education levels and religious knowledge also influence what occurs in the diaspora.

There is a significant difference between those who migrated in the early stages of a community and those who came at a later stage. 'When people migrated' and 'with whom they migrated', also includes such factors as the whether they came as a group, family or individual. The area in which they settled and the religious resources, if any, that might be available to them, are also determining factors.

Hinnells further suggests differing experiences for individuals due to the paths they follow. For example, women who remain in the domestic sphere differ, in the way in which they retain or change their practices, from women who work outside the home. Professionals will have differing experiences from non-professionals. Gender, education and specific careers were also determining factors for Hinnells. Finally, external circumstances, such as the media or negative stereotyping, were important influences on the diaspora community.

When looking at the ways in which the members of the Hindu community in South Australia have maintained their religion, I feel that it would be appropriate to do so in the light of the work both of Williams and Hinnells. A considerable amount of data regarding the maintenance of Hinduism amongst the Hindu community in South Australia was collected during the research for my thesis, entitled 'Accommodating Difference: The Cultural Construction of the Hindu Women of South Australia' (Foster 2002). As this article is concerned primarily with the establishment of the community rather than its maturation, early data collected is relevant to this process rather than more recent updated research, although this will be tapped into, to enhance the material where necessary.

Indian Migration to South Australia

The history of Indian migration to Australia has been extensively dealt with by scholars, including Bilimoria (1989a, 1996a, 1997) and de Lepervanche (1984). A history of Indian migration to South Australia has been reconstructed from primary sources; however, a brief summary of the major events is required in order to understand the development of the Hindu community. As Hinnells suggests, the profile of the people who came, their motives and circumstances influences the changes that occur.

There have been a number of small groups of Indians in South Australia from the mid-19th century. Initially, South Australia was one of the destinations for indentured labourers, followed by the arrival of small numbers of free labourers in the 1860s (Cigler 1986: 11; de Lepervanche 1984; Foster 2011). Indian immigration to South Australia was, however, effectively curtailed due to the introduction of the Immigration Restriction Act in 1901, more commonly known as the 'White Australia' policy. This policy was originally designed to stem the flow of Chinese migrants who were attracted to the Australian goldfield, but all non-white groups were denied access to Australia through the administration of a dictation test. Not only did it disadvantage the Chinese but also other individuals termed 'non-white'. Although the application of the policy was diluted in its last two decades of operation, it was not rescinded until the early 1970s and only remnants of the original wave of Indians were present in South Australia prior to the rescission (de Lepervanche 1984; Foster 1994; Bilimoria 1996a).

The most significant group responsible for the development of Hinduism in South Australia, and the last to migrate, consists of those who immigrated as individuals or small family units commencing when the Immigration Restriction Act was less stringently applied in the 1960s (Tinker 1977: 8-9; de Lepervanche 1984; Bilimoria 1996a), accelerating during the 1970s and continuing today. These immigrants tend to be urban Indians and, until recently, predominantly professionals. This professional group has immigrated to a number of countries, including the United States of America and Australia, thus the profile is similar between Hindus in the United States and South Australia.

The initial urban professionals filled a niche within Australian society, specifically within those professions in which insufficient numbers of Australian graduates were available in such fields as medicine and tertiary education. In more recent times, it would appear that the niche has changed, and Indians have been allowed to immigrate in order to fill positions within the computer industry, as well as in semi-skilled positions. There has also been a significant increase in the number of individuals coming to study at South Australian universities. Hence the profile of the community has started to change in the 21st century, although Hindus are still migrating to South Australia individually or in small family units (Foster 2007).

The different strategies Williams found within the United States can be verified in South Australia. As Williams suggests, a combination of these strategies can be identified at any time, with different strategies being applicable to different phases in the development of the community. It is worthwhile looking at the development of the communities and also to compare the urban setting of Adelaide with the smaller industrial city of Whyalla, north-west of Adelaide, in the light of Williams' categories. The changes and adaptations in these communities will also be discussed in light of Hinnells' ten factors for change.

It is the group of educated professionals who came as individuals from the 1960s who will be the focus of this analysis of the development of Hinduism in South Australia. I draw primarily on data collected as part of my doctoral studies, although subsequent research has also been included. The doctoral research consisted of an ethnographic study of the community generally, with a concentration on the women in the community. This involved participant observation of community events, both religious and secular, observations in domestic settings, and questionnaires and interviews, specifically with women, in both locations.

ADELAIDE AND WHYALLA

Adelaide is the capital of the state of South Australia and has a population of just over one million people. At the time of the study in the late 1990s there were just over 1,000 people identified as Hindus, which had increased to 13088 by 2011. Whyalla is the second largest city in South Australia. It is situated 396 km north of Adelaide on the upper Spencer Gulf. Although the Hindu population of Whyalla has since declined, the data was collected from the time when there were around 100 Hindus in the region.

The Development of Hinduism in South Australia

Many of the early migrants to Adelaide and Whyalla, from professional groups, continued Hindu practices individually, and in private, through the establishment and maintenance of home shrines and the celebration of festivals. Although this was a primary feature of Hinduism in the early stages when the community was very small, it remains the preferred means of practice by some individuals, even when a larger community was formed. Hinnells suggests that the area in which Hindus settle, as well as with whom they make the journey, influences the development of Hinduism and, in the case of both Adelaide and Whyalla, the lack of an established Hindu community, and migration taking place individually or as a nuclear family, affected the initial form in which Hinduism was maintained. In Adelaide, individual private religious maintenance still exists alongside other strategies, and it is also important for Hindu students, who live outside family units, and have come to study in South Australia, of late in increasing numbers. Many of these students frequently use the Hindu temple for their individual religious and cultural maintenance (Foster 2007).

With the fluctuating Hindu population in Whyalla, the maintenance of Hinduism has gone full cycle from being individual, through communal, to reverting to an individual activity as the numbers of Hindus in Whyalla declined with the restructuring of the industries that attracted Indian professionals.

As the communities in Adelaide and Whyalla increased in size, from the early stages, Hinduism was developed with pan-Indian and ecumenical parameters, and differences were glossed over in order for some sense of similarity to be highlighted (Foster 2002). Organisations evolved with pan-Indian cultural agendas. As the community expanded, Indian cultural events became a frequent part of the Adelaide landscape. Families vied to host visiting Indian dignitaries and artists, while community and private dinners for such Indian officials as the High Commissioner to Australia have always attracted great interest and support from the Indian community.

The very active Indian Australian Association of South Australia (IAASA) was established by three families in 1967, and by 1971 had developed and become formalised with a constitution (http://www.iaasa.asn.au/). It remains one of the prime voices for Indians in South Australia, as well as a springboard for leadership within the community. Most recently (August 2007), the South Australian Premier honoured the current president, Mrs Promila Gupta, at a prestigious reception celebrating the sixtieth anniversary of Indian Independence.

A variety of cultural events, the most significant being the annual *mela* (gathering) are sponsored by IAASA. It also organises Indian representation in Australia Day and Indian Republic Day events, both of which are celebrated on 26 January. Another celebration under the auspices of IAASA is that of Diwali. Although Hindu in origin, this festival is sponsored as a pan-Indian event by the Association, as well as being upheld within the family and ethnic/linguistic groups. It is an occasion when Indian Australians invite non-Indian friends to share in their community's culture. A number of other cultural organisations were formed in Adelaide such as Sruti, a group organising concerts by local artists, as well as larger functions featuring overseas artists. The number and focus of these cultural organisations have expanded with the increased numbers within the Indian community.

The central role played by IAASA has been modified in recent years and today it tends to be an umbrella organisation for cultural organisations with specific foci. It does provide a generic Indian focus for the maintenance of an Indian identity; however, at times it also incorporates religious aspects. For example, Hindu devotional prayers have preceded dancing or musical performances at IAASA events and, therefore, although seemingly secular, there are often religious undertones to the events. Christian Indians have their own association called Club India, which functions as an alternative to IAASA. Club India has representatives who liaise, and are associated, with IAASA committee. This seems to indicate that religion is a factor in the formation of Indian organisations in South Australia.

Indians from Whyalla, when the community developed in size and before the decline in numbers, also celebrated national events and conducted cultural performances, although in a limited form. This was initiated by individuals in the community on an informal basis, as no structured organisation existed. There was a connection between Hindus in Whyalla and Adelaide in a number of areas. Some Whyalla Indians belonged to IAASA in Adelaide as well.

Public religious activities for South Australian Hindus began with the celebration of festivals. While the community was still small, festivals were often held in private homes where groups of Hindus congregated for joint celebrations, regardless of individual difference in ethnic/

linguistic identification or in caste. Public venues were often too expensive for the community to hire. *Bhajan* (devotional singing) sessions within the homes of individuals developed, with the wider community being involved. As the community expanded, fortnightly meetings and specific festivals were held in the government-owned migrant centre, which was available free of charge.

The communities in both Adelaide and Whyalla included members with significant religious knowledge, and a number of brahmin men were able to act as religious leaders (*purohita*s) for the private and public rituals for the communities. This was an important element in the establishment and maintenance of Hinduism in the diaspora.

By the mid-1980s, Hinduism had become more established, with the opening of a Hindu temple in Adelaide. The ecumenical nature of this temple was demonstrated by the choice of Ganesha as the main deity. Ganesha was chosen as a compromise, being pan-Hindu rather than region-specific. The temple represented compromise and focused upon commonalities within Hinduism, therefore reinforcing the ecumenical ideals. The ecumenical or pan-Indian focus of the temple has remained to this day, although it also functions as the site for celebrations by specific regional groups (Foster 2007). The opening of the temple was important not only for communal worship, communal celebrations and private temple worship, but also for cultural activities such as dance, and as a centre for language teaching. The ecumenical form of Hinduism it provided has made it a focal point for Indian students.

In Whyalla, the emphasis on similarities rather than differences was even more important. Individual Hindus connected with others, by way of finding commonalities within their religious practices and assumptions, as a larger group. What Hindus in Whyalla held in common took on primary importance, due to the limited number in their community. Although a temple has not been built there, central meeting places, both private and public, have been used in order to celebrate pan-Indian religious and secular national events.

With the growth of the community, regional language affiliations have become increasingly important within the Hindu community in Adelaide. When the temple was extended, tensions arose as to the focus of the temple, since it was then seen by some to reflect a south Indian focus. The incumbent temple priest is from a Tamil-speaking background, and this has added to the north Indians' perception that it is becoming less ecumenical and more ethnically oriented. Worship is often split between times when Hindi or Tamil is the main medium for communication. Families often sponsor *puja*s (ritual worship), inviting members of their own social groups, and this can highlight linguistic differences within the temple.

A number of women who participated in the original interview process for the research suggested that they did not attend the temple at certain times due to their lack of understanding of the main language used on these occasions. Therefore, they felt outside the group (Foster 2002). From these accounts, it would appear that there were ethnic concerns within the temple. The temple was acting as a site of exclusion as well as of inclusion. That said, the main thrust of the temple is still ecumenical in nature, and considerable effort is being made to maintain this. The temple in this context performs a dual purpose as it is a site where an ecumenical form of Hinduism is maintained but, alternatively, it enables specific regional/linguistic groups to use this sacred space in order to reinforce a specifically ethnically oriented Hinduism.

It was not only in the temple that regional/linguistic affiliation was seen to be important. It was clear that festivals, for which the whole community in Adelaide would gather when it was small, were celebrated by different regional/linguistic groups, once the Adelaide community became large enough. For example, Bengalis come together to celebrate Durga Puja and Marathis celebrate Ganesha Chaturthi. Regional celebrations took on a heightened importance outside the family group, as the community expanded. For Diwali, as previously suggested, a series of celebrations often occurs. Family and friends may join together for one celebration, another will be held by the regional/language group, and the wider community will have a final celebration hosted by IAASA. The multiple allegiances and strategies for religious maintenance are evident in this pan-Indian festival, but it seemed to lack the level of importance that the other more specifically religious festivals engendered.

The performance of regional practices has assisted in the maintenance of a regional identity. There appeared to be a strong desire, within Adelaide, for more regional-specific Hinduism, rather than, or even as well as, an ecumenical Hinduism. Ecumenical Hinduism seemed to be appropriate to a specific stage of development in the community and provided an important strategy for religious maintenance, but it did not appear to supplant regional/language difference within Hinduism. That stated, subsequent generations might, in fact, reduce Hinduism to an ecumenical form, due to the lack of knowledge of the diversity within the religion, and lack of knowledge of regional difference. The use of regional languages may be a key to reinforcing regional identity. The lack of emphasis on teaching Indian languages to children, which was discussed by many of the early immigrants, may militate against the continuation of a regional identity. However, it does appear that, in more recent times, a reassessment has occurred, with a greater emphasis being placed on teaching Indian languages. The extent to which this will be taken up by subsequent generations is unknown at this stage. The continued development of regional/linguistic groups may also be determined by the subsequent growth in migration to South Australia and, therefore, the changes in size and regional configuration of the Hindu community in that state.

A close association with India and ease of travel enable many Hindus to maintain contact with their ethnic identity. Pilgrimages to sacred sites in India connected to family and regional deities are common practices for Hindus in the South Australian diaspora, and they assist the maintenance of a regionally specific form of Hinduism, thus confirming the place of the individual within a familial and ethnic context. The development, within the diaspora, of extensive gatherings of regional groups has facilitated an affiliation to a specific area of the subcontinent, and hence has reinforced diversity within the general South Australian Hindu community. Region-specific Hinduism appeared to be becoming more important, rather than less, within the Hindu community in Adelaide, certainly for the first generation immigrants.

The celebration of festivals within the Marathi community provides an interesting example of the way in which a regional language group functions within the larger Hindu community. For Marathas, the festivals of Ganesha Chaturthi and Dussera hold important places, and special celebrations are held for the community within private houses. For example, Ganesha Chaturthi, which continues for five days in Adelaide, involves, on the first night, a special *puja* at the temple, while the community meet for the next four nights at a private home where elaborate preparations have been made over a period of several months. When the Marathi community first started to celebrate Ganesha Chaturthi as a group, there were apparently eight to ten Marathi families in Adelaide, while it was reported that, at the time of the interviews, this number had increased to between 35 and 40 families (Foster 2002). One Marathi family had taken on the responsibility of hosting Ganesha Chaturthi each year for the Marathi community, while another family hosted Dussera. The family initially hosting the Ganesha Chaturthi, when numbers were more manageable, would host a dinner on one night for Marathis while, on an alternative night, non-Marathis were invited. At the time of the study, too many people (40 to 50 each night) attended for a family to be able to host a dinner. An ethnic strategy is still an important means of maintaining Hinduism, therefore, although accommodations have occurred over the years with increased migration.

Regional/language groups are also active across diaspora communities, echoing Bilimoria's findings regarding the importance of global diaspora networks (2007). Attendance by members of the Adelaide community was reported at a conference for Marathis (Brihan Maharashtra Sammelan — 'world conference of Maharashtrians') living outside India in Boston, in the United States, in 1997. In Australia, similar but smaller gatherings have occurred, drawing Marathis together from across Australia. For many, the desire to participate in ethnic cultural events is certainly evident.

Although caste did not appear to be operative in maintaining Hinduism or the formation of groups, one Tamil woman interviewed suggested that, because the Tamil community in Adelaide was now a large community, it was difficult for it to gather as a whole for festivals, and she believed it had split into lower and higher caste groups. There was no other evidence of specific caste gatherings in South Australia. In Whyalla, the community was so small that it did not appear that regional/language groups or castes were particularly operative.

The original study found interest in, and organisation around, different neo-Hindu concepts and *guru*s. In South Australia, one of the most prominent groups was organised around Sathya Sai Baba, who was the focus of worship and community activity for Hindu women and men, as well as attracting non-Indian devotees. For Hindus, Sai Baba worship was not a replacement for other forms of religious maintenance but, generally, an addition to it. A number of Sai Baba groups existed in Adelaide at the time of the study, attracting approximately 500 to 600 people, a third of them being Indian, with a total of seven centres being mentioned. Some had a greater number of Indians than non-Indians, although all were mixed. Worship, *bhajan* singing, the celebration of festivals and hosting guest speakers were all activities that were part of the centres.

There has been considerable division within the Sai Baba groups over the years, with different factions arising. New groups have formed when problems have arisen. The size of individual groups has fluctuated, with the Elizabeth (an outer Adelaide suburb) group at one stage acquiring a church in which to worship. When problems occurred over the incorporation of the group, the church was subsequently sold. Joint celebrations were held for such occasions as Sathya Sai Baba's birthday and these could attract around 200 people, with approximately half from an Indian background.

The situation in Whyalla was very interesting, as the community's religious life seemed to be organised by one individual, who could be described as an extraordinary woman. Her family was traditionally devotees of Shirdi Baba (an earlier incarnation of Sathya) but she did not see any distinction between Shirdi and Sathya Sai Baba. As this woman was highly revered and respected within the community, and due to her influence, Sai Baba had *ipso facto* become a central figure in the religious life of Hindus in Whyalla. Even for those members of the community who did not identify themselves as adherents to Sai Baba, community activities and worship were organised around Sai Baba. More recently, the Swaminarayan sect has become a focus for communal gatherings in Adelaide. Two specific groups have emerged with the members coming primarily from other diaspora communities, such as East Africa and the UK. Young men from a Gujarati background, especially, have been attracted to these groups as they are associated with this region. The groups have strong global networks and have been instrumental in assisting students coming to South Australia to study to maintain their Hindu identity (Foster 2010).

In the absence of a formal temple, the woman's family home had become the community temple. The deities were attended to on a daily basis and, when the woman was absent from Whyalla, other women attended the shrine. Her house (which she referred to as Whyalla's temple) was the centre for religious activity in Whyalla. *Bhajan* sessions, prayers, offerings of *prasad*, the celebration of festivals and special occasions, including such *samskaras* (rites of passage) as first feeding, were all performed at this 'temple'. The main focus of the 'temple' was Sathya Sai Baba, although deities other than Shirdi Baba and Sathya Sai Baba were represented in the shrine. Not everyone who used this space, or attended the functions, was a Sathya Sai Baba adherent, but it appears that the convenience of having a religious centre to use was more important than the specific orientation of the centre. The leaning towards Sai Baba was not considered an anathema to the Hinduism of the non-Sai Baba adherents. Women interviewed were often at pains to make the point that Sathya Sai Baba was not inconsistent with their Hinduism, although they may not have been adherents.

The woman responsible for setting up the centre and the temple was highly revered within the community as both a leader and the driving force behind the establishment of the centre. She was clearly loved within the community, and there were glowing testaments to her position in the community, including her contribution to its spiritual life. She has subsequently moved from Whyalla and, although the temple and centre have been taken over by another woman, the situation has changed since the time of the study. The number of Hindus in the city has decreased and, without the strong influence of this woman, other means of maintaining Hinduism seem to have returned. It was clear, however, that at the time of the study the respect for this woman and the energy she put into helping with the spiritual life of the Whyalla community was an important factor in maintaining Hinduism.

Although it is common for shrines to Sathya Sai Baba to incorporate different deities, one development to occur in Adelaide took this further with the installation of Lord Murugan. The meeting centre, which existed for a number of years, was in a stable at a private residence in suburban Adelaide and was sponsored by a wealthy family with a south Indian background who were adherents of Sathya Sai Baba. The explanation given was that a number of those attending the Sai Baba centre at their home were very fond of Lord Murugan and were keen to have him placed within the centre. The priest from the Ganesha Temple, also from a south Indian background, conducted the elaborate installation and continued to attend the god on a weekly basis. This seems to demonstrate a more ethnic influence on the community's sacred space in this centre. It is difficult to tell if this centre had become a substitute for the Ganesha Temple for the south Indian devotees, or an addition to it. In this case, Sai Baba did not cut across ethnic grounds but tended to reinforce them. This development contrasts with the temple that was established upon pan-Indian or ecumenical lines.

Summary

Williams's strategies of religious maintenance did provide a useful starting point for understanding the manner in which members of the Hindu community in South Australia maintained their religion in this specific diaspora. The different strategies were evident within the community in Adelaide; however, the Whyalla community, due to its smaller size, only engaged with some of them. Williams' strategies were only a starting point and did not reveal the whole range of maintenance strategies used. It is essential to acknowledge the importance of individuals and their particular interests and the influence they can have on the wider community. These individuals were not the strong personalities normally associated with community leadership but ordinary individuals who gained respect due to their religious practices and piety. They filled a void in the community in a unique way, demonstrating the manner in which the diaspora community provides space for the non-traditional development and maintenance of religion.

As my research involved interviews in both Adelaide and Whyalla, it provided an opportunity to compare different stages of development in two similar, although not identical, environments within South Australia. The Whyalla study may provide an insight into the way in which development took place in Adelaide during the very early stages of the Hindu community. This was confirmed, to a certain extent, by both the women and men who spoke about the early community in Adelaide.

There was a strong focus on both Sathya Sai Baba and ecumenical

Hinduism within Whyalla. The Sai Baba focus was due to specific circumstances. The lack of emphasis on regional difference generally is an important aspect of an emerging community. This is the case where regional/linguistic diversity amongst the residents, rather than regional similarity, is evident. Identity in Whyalla tended to be based on national and religious grounds, rather than regional or language difference. This certainly appears to have been the situation during the early stages of the development of the Hindu community in Adelaide.

When looking at the maintenance and adaptation of Hinduism and its development as a diaspora religion within Adelaide and Whyalla in the light of Hinnells' 'factors for change and continuity', what has been important is the profile of the Hindus themselves. The individuals who formed the community from the mid-20th century were generally from similar urban, educated, professional backgrounds, and had been exposed to modernity and Western concepts within India. The level of education was high for both men and women and they were entering Australia in order to take up professional positions. They tended to migrate in nuclear family groups or individually. Although some were 'twice migrants', they still fitted the educated professional profile. The experiences of those who went to live in Whyalla differed from those of the Adelaide Hindus, thus emphasising the influence of destination or place and the existing environment on the development, maintenance and adaptation of Hinduism.

The general professional group undertook the migration process in order to advance their own careers or education and were not forced to do so due to economic concerns. That said, some women were perhaps less enthusiastic than their husbands, although some men and women had made the journey alone. Even in the early stages of the community, before Indian students were actively sought by Australian universities, both men and women opted to come to Australia for study. There was high workforce participation by women due to their qualifications in this early group and this, as indicated by Hinnells, was an important factor in the adaptations that occurred.

Religious knowledge was sufficient amongst the community to enable the performance of important rituals, both within the household and for life cycle rites, ensuring maintenance of Hindu practices. As the community was wealthy, they were able to establish a temple where worship could take place and employ a religious expert from overseas. Although, as Hinnells discussed, religious knowledge was not always a means of gaining a leadership position within the community, and success in business or the professions often enabled individuals to gain positions where they provided a voice for their communities (1998: 833). In South Australia, involvement in organisations — religious, secular, cultural or multicultural — does promote individuals to leadership positions in the Indian community generally, and elevates them within the wider community.

The external circumstances in South Australia enabled the community to develop a comfortable relationship with non-Indians and this can be seen in the public events such as Diwali, the *mela* and Indian Independence Day celebrations. The large public celebration for the sixtieth anniversary of Indian Independence is a recent acknowledgement of this comfort.

The findings regarding the development of Hinduism in South Australia, although exhibiting some very specific characteristics did, in general, mirror Bilimoria's findings on the development of Hinduism in Australia.

Conclusion

Williams, Hinnells and Bilimoria provide a wider framework for interpreting and understanding the manner in which Hinduism developed, and was maintained and adapted, within Adelaide and Whyalla. As Hinduism is organic, it can retain relevance in different geographical settings, including diaspora communities. It not only connects these communities to their heritage but also provides meaning for their current lives, while linking them with other diaspora communities undergoing transformation. It will be interesting to see where this organic process leads in South Australia. Not only is religion developing a definite characteristic for subsequent generations of ethnic Indians in Australia, but the children of Hindus marrying outside their religious tradition also derive meaning from their own construction of Hinduism. These groups, as well as the increasing number of Indian students in South Australia, some of whom stay on, and new migrants, will ensure the development of interesting and diverse forms of Hindu assumptions and practices within South Australia.

6

A Statistical Profile of the Hindu Community in Australia

Philip Hughes

The Religious Profile of the Indian Diaspora

THE 2011 Census found that there were 295,362 people living in Australia who were born in India. Of these, 47% described themselves in the census as Hindus, a considerable proportion as Sikhs, and a large number as Christians. As shown in Table 6.1, some of the respondents indicated that they had no religion, while others failed to state a religion.

This profile of Indians living in Australia does not reflect the religious profile of the Indian population in India, of which 85% are Hindus. There are several reasons for these differences. The major reason is that the 'push' and 'pull' factors in migration are different for different groups of people. Minority religious groups may well experience more incentive to look outside India for their well-being, perhaps partly because they feel they do not fit well in the Indian culture. Some of them may well be members of families that already had roots outside India, but had settled in India for a period of time for work or because of pressures in their original homeland. This may be the case, for example, with some of the Jews who were Indian born but who have moved to Australia, although for centuries there has been a small, long established community of Jews living on the south-west coast of the Indian peninsula. Another reason may be that some groups have better connections with Australians, or even with Australian religious groups, which have helped them in the immigration process. For example, several Christian denominations have looked to India to find people to be priests or ministers in Australian churches.

Table 6.1: The Religious Identification of Indian-born People Living in Australia in 2011

Religion	*No. of Indian-born Living in Australia*	*All Indian-born Living in Australia (%)*
Hindus	139,632	47.27
Christians	69,855	23.65
Sikhs	55,312	18.73
Muslims	10,126	3.43
Buddhists	1,196	0.40
Jews	372	0.13
Baha'i	122	0.04
Nature religions and spiritualism	69	0.02
Other religions and miscellaneous religions	5,506	1.86
No religion	7,895	2.67
No Response	5,277	1.79
Total	**295,362**	**100.00**

Source: Australian Survey 2011.

It is likely that in a few cases, immigrants will change their religious identity after arrival in Australia. The Australian Survey of Social Attitudes (2009) asked people about their religious identity when they were eleven years old and what their religious identity was at the time of the survey. The sample of Hindus in the survey was quite small and thus does not provide a reliable basis for extrapolation to the whole population. However, some people who said they had grown up as Hindu indicated that they now had 'no religion'. There was little evidence of Hindus changing to other religions, although it is likely that this occurs occasionally. There were almost no cases in that survey of people who had grown up in another religion becoming Hindu, although this may occur occasionally through marriage, or through attraction to a particular Hindu movement such as the Hare Krishnas.

At the same time, as we discuss in some detail later in the chapter, Hindus have come to Australia from many countries around the world.

This chapter looks at the Hindu community, which intersects with the Indian community in Australia, but which is also significantly different from that community.

Change Over Time

As we have seen in the previous chapters, many Hindus who came to Australia in the 19th century worked as hawkers, travelling around the remote communities. Some came as labourers to work on sugar cane or cotton plantations. In 1880, there were about 3,000 Indians in Australia. However, the Immigration Restriction Act, 1901, also known as the 'White Australia' policy, restricted immigration from Asia and the numbers of Hindus declined. In 1911, the first federal census in Australia counted just 414 Hindus. The numbers dropped to 212 in 1933 and 244 in 1947.

For many years after Second World War, the Australian Bureau of Statistics did not count the number of Hindus in Australia, as they remained a very small part of the population. The next count took place in 1986. At that time, it counted 21,454 Hindus in the Australian population. The official dropping of the 'White Australia' policy in mid-1960s marked a turning point in migration from Asia. Many of the early Asian migrants were from Vietnam and were given visas on humanitarian grounds. As we noted earlier, in the mid-1980s, Australia began granting entry visas to people from around the world who fulfilled certain occupational categories, mostly professions such as doctors, engineers, and technicians, and to business people who could contribute significantly to Australia's economy. Many Indians took advantage of these visas and the Hindu population in Australia began to grow rapidly. Many of these migrants came with some financial resources and were quickly able to find well-salaried, specialised positions. Another form of immigration was through education. Many young Hindus came to Australia to study, particularly at tertiary level. Having obtained their qualifications here, many have stayed in Australia.

According to the 2011 Census, the very large part of the Hindu community was born overseas, as shown in Table 6.2. Most of the remaining members of the Hindu community were second generation Australians with one or both parents born overseas. There were very few Hindus born in Australia of parents not born overseas.

Table 6.2: Birthplace of the Hindus Living in Australia in 2011

Birthplace	*No. in the Hindu Community*	*Hindu Community* (%)
Born in Australia of Australian parents	3,887	1.4
Born in Australia with one or both parents born overseas	38,910	14.1
Born overseas	229,989	83.5
Born at sea or not described	2,751	1.0
Total	**275,537**	**100.0**

Source: Australian Census 2011.

Table 6.3 demonstrates the growth of the Hindu community from immigration. It is based on the Hindus living in Australia in 2011. It does not include those people who migrated to Australia and then moved on to another country.

In the late 1980s two military-style coups in Fiji led to many Indians leaving the country. Between 1986 and 1990, almost 6,000 of the Hindus now living in Australia left Fiji. In 1990, Fijian Hindus constituted almost one-third of the Hindu community in Australia. Since that time, there has

Table 6.3: Years of Immigration to Australia and Numbers of Hindu Immigrants

Years of Immigration	*No. of Hindu Immigrants to Australia*	*Hindu Immigrants* (%)
1910-60	236	0.1
1961-70	933	0.4
1971-80	4,144	1.8
1981-85	5,125	2.3
1986-90	15,041	6.7
1991-95	15,556	6.9
1996–2000	21,660	9.7
2001-05	42,245	18.8
2006-11	119,260	53.2
Total	**224,200**	**100.0**

Source: Australian Census 2011.

been a steady stream of Hindus coming from Fiji to Australia. In 2011, there were almost 26,000 Fijian Hindus living in Australia, constituting 11.5% of the total Hindu community. There was also political turmoil in Sri Lanka in the late 1980s. More than 3,000 Sri Lankan Hindus arrived in Australia between 1986 and 2000. They continued to come to Australia over the next fifteen years at the rate of a little under 500 per year. However, between 2006 and 2011, 4,000 Sri Lankan Hindus arrived in Australia. Altogether there are approximately 15,000 Sri Lankan Hindus in Australia, constituing 6.7% of the total Hindu community.

In the period from 2006 to 2011, there were a number of other groups of Hindus that began migrating in significant numbers. The largest of these were Nepalese. More than 16,000 Nepalese arrived in Australia in that period of five years. In 2011, they surpassed in numbers the Sri Lankan Hindu community, constituting 8.5% of all Hindus living in Australia.

It is likely that the economic problems in the United Kingdom have encouraged Hindus who had settled there to re-emigrate to Australia. According to the 2011 Census, more than 1,000 Hindus arrived in Australia from the United Kingdom between 2006 and 2011. The on-going economic problems in South Africa have probably been a major factor in the 1,000 immigrants who arrived in Australia from there between 2006 and 2011. Others have migrated from Bhutan, Bangladesh, Malaysia, Singapore and Mauritius, among other nations. Overall, almost 40% of the immigrant Hindu community in Australia in 2011 was born outside India (Table 6.4).

Information in the Census on languages spoken by Hindus living in Australia indicates where people have come from and the communities to which they belong. Table 6.5 shows the languages spoken at home by at least 100 Hindus. Sixty-six additional languages were spoken by another 2,714 Hindus. By far the largest language is Hindi. However, it is only spoken by 30% of the Hindu community. Thirteen per cent of the community speak English at home and approximately the same number speak Tamil. Other major Indian languages spoken are Gujarati, Telugu, Punjabi, Marathi, Malayalam, Bengali and Kannada. This information about language suggests that the largest group of Hindus have come from the Hindi-speaking northern parts of India. However, there are other major groups from the Tamil-speaking south (which would also include many Sri Lankans) and from the Gujarati-speaking area.

Table 6.4: Countries of Birth of Hindu Immigrants in Australia in 2011

Countries of Birth	*Numbers*	*Hindu Community* (%)
India	135,774	60.6
Fiji	25,737	11.5
Nepal	18,968	8.5
Si Lanka	14,959	6.7
Malaysia	4,249	1.9
South Africa	3,759	1.7
United Kingdom	2,490	1.1
Singapore	2,371	1.1
New Zealand	2,133	1.0
Mauritius	2,063	0.9
Bangladesh	1,880	0.8
Kenya	1,828	0.8
Bhutan	1,623	0.7
Indonesia	1,268	0.6
Other parts of Africa	1,178	0.5
Middle East	871	0.4
Other parts of South-East Asia	871	0.4
North America	708	0.3
Other parts of Europe	615	0.3
North-east Asia	308	0.1
Central Asia (including Pakistan)	222	0.1
Central and South America	162	0.1
Other	160	0.1
Total	**224,197**	**100.0**

Source: Australian Census 2011.

Where Hindus Have Settled

At the time of the 2011 Census, Hindus were most numerous in Sydney where they constituted 2.6% of the population. Hindus made up 2% of Melbourne's population and 1.7% of the population of Canberra. In fact, 70% of all Australian Hindus lived in either Sydney or Melbourne. There

Table 6.5: Language Spoken at Home by Members of the Hindu Community Living in Australia in 2011

Language	*No. of Hindus Speaking the Language*	*Hindus Speaking the Language (%)*
Hindi	81,892	29.7
English	36,948	13.4
Tamil	36,940	13.4
Gujarati	29,250	10.6
Nepali	21,766	7.9
Telugu	16,717	6.1
Punjabi	9,442	3.4
Marathi	7,773	2.8
Malayalam	5,938	2.2
Bengali	5,685	2.1
Kannada	5,383	2.0
French	1,180	0.4
Indonesian	1,171	0.4
Konkani	610	0.2
Fijian Hindustani	572	0.2
Mauritian Creole	513	0.2
Malay	436	0.2
Tulu	346	0.1
French Creole	328	0.1
Oriya	282	0.1
Sindhi	277	0.1
Sinhalese	234	0.1
Assamese	165	0.1
Italian	157	0.1
Fijian	130	0.0
Balinese	129	0.0
Vietnamese	109	0.0

was a substantial community of around 21,500 in Brisbane, just under 20,000 in Perth, and 13,000 in Adelaide. Altogether 93% of all Hindus lived in one or other of the capital cities. The high concentration of Hindus in Australia's state capitals reflects the fact that most recent immigrants begin their lives in Australia in these cities. As highly qualified professionals or business people, the cities are also the places where they are most likely to find work. In the period between 2006 and 2011, the Hindu community has grown most rapidly in Darwin, although it still numbers only 1,300 people. It grew at a similar rate, of more than 150%, in Adelaide and Perth. In Melbourne and Hobart, the community grew by just under 100% between 2006 and 2011. The community has grown least in Sydney, by just 61%.

Most Hindus are widely spread in the suburbs of the cities. However, there are a few suburbs in Sydney where there are large concentrations of them. According to the 2011 Census, 17,000 lived in Blacktown, another 15,000 lived in Parramatta and 10,000 in the Holroyd local government area at that time. The highest concentration, however, was in Strathfield

Table 6.6: Numbers of Hindus Living in the States and Territories and Capital Cities of Australia (2001-11)

State/City	*No. of Hindus in 2001*	*No. of Hindus in 2011*	*Increase (%)*
Australian Capital Territory	2,332	6,065	160
New South Wales	51,422	119,693	133
Sydney	*48,462*	*113,184*	*134*
Northern Territory	431	1,672	288
Darwin	*333*	*1,304*	*292*
Queensland	8,970	28,783	221
Brisbane	*6,813*	*21,419*	*214*
South Australia	2,531	13,621	438
Adelaide	*2,366*	*13,088*	*453*
Tasmania	491	1,621	230
Hobart	*274*	*906*	*231*
Victoria	24,328	83,008	241
Melbourne	*23,360*	*79,642*	*241*
Western Australia	4,966	21,063	324
Perth	*4,686*	*19,786*	*322*
Australia Total	**95,473**	**275,535**	**189**

Source: Australian Censuses

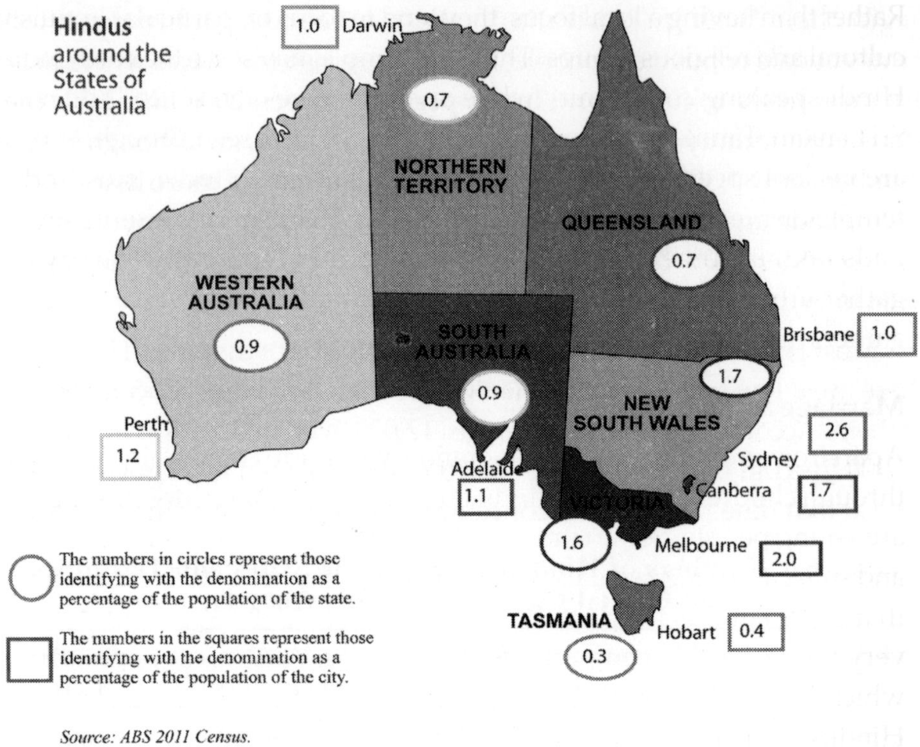

fig. 6.1: Hindus around the States of Australia

where 4,700 Hindus lived, but where they constituted 13% of the population. The Hindu community in Melbourne was less concentrated, with the highest numbers of about 7,000 in each of the local government areas of Casey, Monash and Wyndham. In none of these local government areas did they constitute more than 4.3% of the total population. Hindus are generally more dispersed than Jews or Muslims in Australian communities. Because most Hindus do not go to a temple as frequently as orthodox or conservative Jews go to a synagogue or as Moslems go to a mosque, they feel less need to live close to a temple. Indeed, the important religious centre for most Hindus is in the home. This means, however, that while temples play an important role in personal celebrations and community festivals, in most cases they do not serve local communities. Rather, on special occasions, they serve as regional centres.

Because the number of Hindus in Melbourne or Sydney has not been large, there have been just two or three temples serving the whole city.

Rather than having a local focus, they tend to focus on particular linguistic, cultural and religious groups. Thus, one temple may serve the north Indian Hindi-speaking community while another serves the south Indian and Sri Lankan, Tamil-speaking community. As we have seen, though, temples are far less specific in their foci in Australia than in India, most Indian temples serve one or a few gods. Most temples in Australia serve several gods and, in some situations, one section of a Hindu community will gather around one god at one end of a temple while a separate group gathers around another at the other end.

Marriage and Children

Apart from growth through immigration, the Hindu community has grown through children born into Hindu families in Australia. Most immigrants are young people. Some come as single people, others as young couples, and some as young families with young children. The 2011 Census found that of all Hindus in Australia, 76% were under the age of 40. This is a very young profile compared with the wider Australian population in which 54% of the population is under the age of 40. More than half of all Hindus living in Australia are aged between 20 and 40 years, as shown in *fig.* 6.2. The Hindu community is likely to grow rapidly between 2011 and 2030 through the birth of children.

Parents continue to be involved to some degree with their children's arrangements for marriage. In some cases, the parents in India will arrange

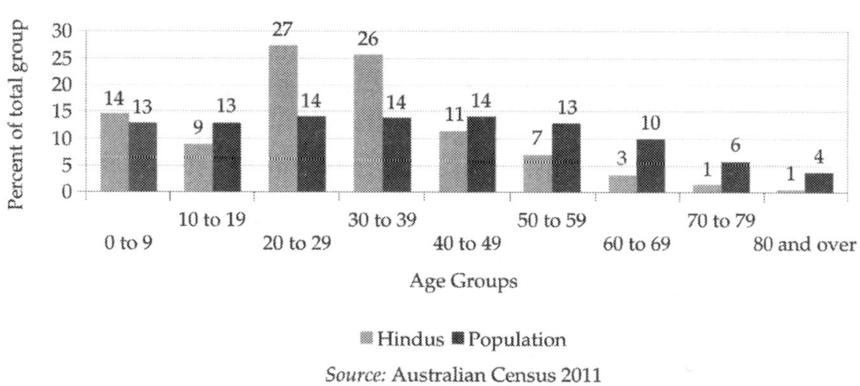

Source: Australian Census 2011

fig. 6.2: The age profile of the Hindu community compared with the Australian population

a marriage and the son will return to India from Australia to meet the bride. In other cases, some suggestions are made by the parents. Sometimes, the marriage is left entirely in the hands of their children. Few teenage weddings take place. The Census recorded only 75 cases in which a member of the Hindu community under the age of 20 was married. However, many marriages occur not long after that, and of all Hindus in their twenties, 51% were married compared with just 18 % of Australians. Another 1% had been through marriage and were divorced or separated. Among Hindus in their thirties, 88% were married, compared with 56% of Australians, and just 9% compared with 35% of Australians had never married. Three per cent of this age, compared with 8% of all Australians, were divorced or separated.

In 2011, there were 21,387 more male Hindus than female Hindus in the Australian population. This is largely due to more males migrating to Australia than females for work or for study. The discrepancy was particularly large among Hindus in their thirties, in which females account for only 43% of the Hindu community, and in their twenties in which females account for 46% of the community. This means that some men must either return to India or another country to marry, or they must marry outside the Hindu community.

De facto relationships are rare among Hindus living in Australia. Just 3,883 Hindus indicated on the census that they were living in a *de facto* relationship. This constitutes 1.4% of all Hindus and compares with 6.9% in the Australian community as a whole. Nevertheless, the fact that some Hindus have moved into *de facto* relationships shows a measure of Westernisation within the community. *De facto* relationships are rare in India. Proportionately, more Hindu women than men are in *de facto* relationships. As shown in Table 6.7, separation and divorce are also uncommon in the Hindu community.

Few Hindus living in Australia have large families. The 2011 Census indicated that, at the time of the Census:

- in 42% of families, there was one child,
- in 49% of families, there were two children;
- in 8% of families, there were three children; and
- in 1% of families there were four or more children.

More Hindu women than in the wider Australian population have children. Among all Australian women in their forties in 2011, 15% had no children, compared with 10% of Hindu women in that age bracket. However, 75% of Hindu women had had just one or two children, and only 15% had had more than two, compared with 50% of Australian women having had one or two children, and 35% having more than two. Because of the low number of separation and divorces, there are comparatively few one-parent families in the Hindu community. According to the 2011 Census, just 3% of the members of the community were living in the context of a one-parent family.

What Hindus Are Doing in Australia

As shown in the age profile in *fig.* 6.2, there were few Hindus over the age of 65 living in Australia in 2011. As shown in Table 6.8, almost half (48%) of all Hindus aged 15 and over were employed full-time and another 21% were employed part-time. Five per cent of Hindus were unemployed and looking for work. While this proportion is a little above the 3.5% of the wider Australian population unemployed and looking for work, it is a relatively small proportion of the population. Men were more commonly employed full-time, while many women preferred part-time employment.

Table 6.7: Marital Status of Members of the Hindu Community Aged 18 Years and Older

Marital Status	*Male Hindus*	*Female Hindus*	*Total Hindus*	*All Hindus* (%)	*Australians* (%)
Never married	37,554	18,060	55,614	20.2	27.7
Widowed	635	3,431	4,066	1.5	4.4
Divorced	1,985	3,040	5,025	1.8	6.8
Separated	1,276	1,445	2,721	1.0	2.5
Married	79,556	75,369	154,925	56.2	39.3
Not applicable (under 15 years of age)	27,455	25,729	53,184	19.3	19.3
Total	**148,461**	**127,074**	**275,535**	**100.0**	**100.0**

Source: Australian Census 2011.

Table 6.8: The Workforce Status of Hindus by Gender Living in Australia in 2011

Workforce Status	*Male Numbers*	*Male (%)*	*Female Numbers*	*Female (%)*	*Total Hindu (%)*	*Population (%)*
Employed full-time	72,728	60.1	33,754	33.3	47.9	36.7
Employed part-time	22,322	18.5	23,307	23.0	20.5	17.6
Employed, away from work	3,989	3.3	3,633	3.6	3.4	3.6
Unemployed looking for full-time work	2,944	2.4	4,010	4.0	3.1	2.1
Unemployed looking for part-time work	1,890	1.6	2,969	2.9	2.2	1.4
Not in labour force	15,956	13.2	32,514	32.1	21.8	33.0
Not stated	1,180	1.0	1,154	1.1	1.1	5.6
Total	**121,009**	**100.0**	**101,341**	**100.0**	**100.0**	**100.0**

Source: Australian Census 2011.

Of the 32,500 Hindu women not in the workforce, about half of them were studying, the majority of them at university. Other women were caring for young children. The census data suggests that most Hindu women resume working when their children are at school.

As shown in Table 6.9, because most Hindu families were relatively young in 2011, there were comparatively few Hindu children at secondary school. However, many young Hindus had temporary visas for study in Australia and were studying either at TAFE institutes or at universities. In fact, among all Hindus aged 15 and older, 8.5% were at university, compared with just half that proportion in the Australian population as a whole. Many of these people have come to Australia on temporary visas for study. Such visas are given for periods up to four years. For many people, temporary visas are a step to permanent migration and in 2008-09 one-third of the migration programme was made up of people who were granted permanent residency after initial entry to Australia on a temporary visa.[1]

Since Second World War, there has been a gradual change in the immigration focus towards a programme 'aimed primarily at meeting the labour market needs of the Australian economy'.[2] For a long time, apart from humanitarian entrants, there have been three major streams of migration: skilled, family and special eligibility. Since 2000, there has been a shift in the balance away from the family stream in favour of the skilled stream. While skilled migration made up 47% of the migration programme in 1996-97, it made up 67% of the programme in 2008-09.[3] Since 2009, there has been a further shift from independent migrants to those sponsored by an employer, or to people with skills considered to be in critical shortage in Australia such as medical and some IT professionals, engineers and construction trade workers.[4] Successful business people have also been encouraged to settle in Australia because of their potential to develop new

Table 6.9: Numbers of Hindus by Gender Compared with the Australian Population Attending Various Educational Institutions in 2011

Educational Institution Attending	*Male Hindus*	*Female Hindus*	*Total Hindus*	*Total (%)*	*Population (%)*
Pre-school	2,395	2,254	4,649	1.7	1.6
Infants/Primary	10,681	9,923	20,604	7.5	8.2
Secondary	6,823	6,492	13,315	4.8	6.2
TAFE	4,856	4,334	9,190	3.3	2.2
University	13,180	10,123	23,303	8.5	4.3
Other	6,743	5,729	12,472	4.6	0.8

Source: Australian Census 2011.

1 On *abhisheka* ritual details, see H. Daniel Smith 1978, *Padmasamhita*, p. 8.

2 Harriet Spinks, 'Background Note: Australia's Migration Program', Department of Parliamentary Services, 8 October 2010. http://apo.org.au/sites/default/files/AustraliasMigrationProgram.pdf. Accessed on 7 December 2012, p. 11.

3 Harriet Spinks 2010: 4.

4 Ibid.: 5.

business opportunities.[5] This means that most immigrants have arrived highly qualified or have come to obtain such qualifications in Australia. According to the 2011 Census, of all Hindus living in Australia, 43% had a university degree. Close to half of this group had a bachelor's degree and half had a higher degree. This makes the Hindus the most highly qualified religious group in Australia by a considerable margin. Thirty-six per cent of Jews had a degree, as did 14% of Christians and 15% of the Australian population. While there were fewer Hindu women with postgraduate degrees, the overall proportion of women with a university degree was not very different to that of the men: 42% compared with 44% (Table 6.10).

The major fields in which Hindus have qualifications are management and commerce. Both men and women are qualified in this area. Almost as many men, but far less women, are qualified in engineering. Information technology is also popular among men but less so among women, while many women are qualified in the areas of health, and society and culture as shown in Table 6.11.

There is some evidence that the Christian faith has encouraged people to look for qualifications and occupations in the 'people-oriented' occupations, such as health and education, and has discouraged people in

Table 6.10: The Level of Education by Gender of Hindus Compared with the Australian Population in 2011

Level of Education	*Males*	*Females*	*Total*	*Total (%)*	*Total Population (%)*
Doctoral Degree	2,881	1,605	4,486	1.6	0.6
Masters Degree	26,037	17,005	43,042	15.6	2.3
Graduate Certificate	3,202	2,559	5,761	2.1	1.4
Bachelor's Degree	32,686	32,674	65,360	23.7	10.9
Diploma	15,295	9,673	24,968	9.1	6.5
Certificate	10,636	6,129	16,765	6.1	14.6

Source: Australian Census 2011.

5 Harriet Spinks 2010: 4.

moving into technical or commercial occupations.[6] Many Christian denominations operate educational and health institutions and thus offer employment in those fields. These orientations are reflected to some extent in the fields of education of people who identify as Christian, compared with those who say they have no religion. Thus, 8.1% of Australians who identify with a Christian denomination have qualifications in either health or education, compared with 7.2% of those with no religion. On the other

Table 6.11: The Field of Education of Hindus by Gender Compared with the Australian Population in 2011

Field of Education	*Male Hindus*	*Female Hindus*	*Total Hindus*	*Hindus (%)*	*Australian Population (%)*
Management and commerce	26,466	21,950	48,416	17.6	8.1
Engineering and related technologies	24,297	3,980	28,277	10.3	2.3
Information technology	15,608	6,753	22,361	8.1	7.0
Health	6,157	10,398	16,555	6.0	4.7
Society and culture	3,966	9,438	13,404	4.9	1.3
Natural and physical science	4,068	6,107	10,175	3.7	4.1
Food, hospitality and personal services	6,537	2,789	9,326	3.4	3.3
Education	1,487	4,894	6,381	2.3	1.3
Creative arts	958	1,563	2,521	0.9	0.9
Architecture and building	1,144	615	1,759	0.6	1.5
Agriculture and environment	860	441	1,301	0.5	2.5

Source: Australian Census 2011.

6 P. Hughes, 'Religion and Occupation', *Pointers*, vol. 19, no. 1, March 2009, pp. 12-16.

hand, 0.9% of Christians, compared with 1.8% of the 'no religion' group, have qualifications in information technology. Thus, in a weak but significant way, occupational choices reflect religious interests and values. However, there do not appear to be any particular relationships between Hindu values and field of education preferences that are apparent in the Hindu community in Australia. The preferences reflect, to a large extent, the interests of the Australian government in offering visas.

Table 6.12 shows that while many Hindus are using their qualifications as professionals, there are fewer than one might expect who are managers and more who are labourers, given their level of qualification. This is particularly true among the women. The table suggests that some Hindus have not found work commensurate with their level of qualification. Nevertheless, given the young age of the community and the fact that many Hindus are recent immigrants, more may well find occupations appropriate for their level of qualification in future years.

Table 6.12: Occupations of the Hindu Community in Australia

Occupations	*Male Hindus*	*Female Hindus*	*Hindu Persons*	*Hindus (%)*	*Population (%)*
Managers	11,332	3,713	15,047	9.4	12.9
Professionals	30,985	19,527	50,513	31.6	21.3
Technicians and Trades Workers	14,546	2,729	17,274	10.8	14.2
Community and Personal Service Workers	5,087	8,587	13,672	8.6	9.7
Clerical and Administrative Workers	8,604	12,287	20,891	13.1	14.8
Sales Workers	7,616	6,233	13,847	8.7	9.4
Machinery Operators and Drivers	7,661	747	8,407	5.3	6.6
Labourers	10,990	5,681	16,672	10.4	9.4
Other/not stated	2,220	1,186	3,406	2.1	1.9
Total in Labour Force	**99,041**	**60,690**	**159,729**	**100.0**	**100.0**

Source: Australian Census 2011.

Table 6.13: The Industry-wise Areas in Which Hindus Are Working in Australia

Area of Industry	*Male Hindus*	*Female Hindus*	*Hindu Persons*	*Hindus (%)*	*Population (%)*
Agriculture, Forestry and Fishing	475	230	705	0.4	2.5
Mining	918	159	1,077	0.7	1.8
Manufacturing	12,494	3,404	15,898	10.0	9.0
Electricity, Gas, Water and Waste Services	1,535	489	2,024	1.3	1.1
Construction	2,631	612	3,243	2.0	8.2
Wholesale Trade	4,691	1,737	6,428	4.0	4.0
Retail Trade	10,003	6,222	16,225	10.2	10.5
Accommodation and Food Services	11,233	4,660	15,893	10.0	6.5
Transport, Postal and Warehousing	6,381	1,387	7,768	4.9	4.8
Information Media and Tele-communications	3,138	1,333	4,471	2.8	1.8
Financial and Insurance Services	6,210	5,454	11,664	7.3	3.8
Rental Hiring and Real Estate Services	741	410	1,151	0.7	1.6
Professional, Scientific and Technical Services	12,804	5,322	18,126	11.4	7.3
Administrative and Support Services	4,294	2,919	7,213	4.5	3.2
Public Admini-stration and Safety	4,803	3,505	8,308	5.2	6.9
Education and Training	3,215	4,552	7,767	4.9	8.0
Health Care and Social Assistance	7,869	15,442	23,311	14.6	11.6
Arts and Recreation Services	755	357	1,113	0.7	1.5
Other Services, inadequately described or not stated	4,850	2,497	7,347	2.0	6.1
Total	**99,040**	**60,691**	**159,731**	**100.0**	**100.0**

Source: Australian Census 2011.

Table 6.13 shows the industry area in which Hindus were working. While there are many working in health care and social assistance, and in professional, scientific and technical services, there are also many working in the retail trade and in accommodation and food services. Proportionately more Hindus than other Australians were working in information media and telecommunications, financial and insurance services, administrative support services and professional, scientific and technical services, and in accommodation and food services. It would appear that many, but not all, Hindus were working in fields similar to those in which they were qualified.

The Social Situation of the Hindu Community

It would appear from the labour-force status data that most Hindus living in Australia who are available for the workforce have employment. In 2011 Census, few people were looking for either full-time or part-time work. However, the occupation and industry information suggests that many people may not have found employment either in the industry of their training or at the level one might expect from their levels of education. Table 6.14 shows the personal weekly income levels of all Hindus aged 15 years and older and compares it with the income of the wider Australian population.

In comparing the Hindus with the wider population in Table 6.14, it should be noted that there are few Hindus of retirement age. There would be few of them on the standard aged pension, and thus comparatively few in the bracket of Au$ 200-299 per week. Fifteen per cent of Hindus indicated that they were not receiving a personal income at all. Many of these people would be students who were engaged in full-time study at school, university or TAFE and who would be supported by their families. The table indicates that many Hindus received around Au$ 600-799 per week. Many of these people would be engaged in part-time work. In all the higher income brackets, the proportion of Hindus is higher than that of Australians. However, in interpreting this, one must take into account the fact that Hindus have less than half the proportion of people retired. One must also take into account the fact that Hindus were more willing than other Australians to provide an indication of their personal weekly income. The table shows that many Hindus have a reasonable income on which to live. Certainly, their income levels are much higher in Australia than they would be in India or most other parts of Asia.

Table 6.14: Levels of Income among Hindus in Australia Compared with the Australian Population

Weekly Income Levels (Au$)	*Male Hindus*	*Female Hindus*	*No. of Hindus*	*Hindus 15+ (%)*	*Wider Population 15+ (%)*
Negative	448	669	1,117	0.5	0.6
Nil	9,887	23,443	33,330	15.0	7.6
1–199	4,523	8,527	13,050	5.9	7.4
200–299	6,081	7,214	13,295	6.0	10.4
300–399	7,513	7,240	14,753	6.6	9.9
400–599	11,956	10,728	22,684	10.2	11.6
600–799	15,854	11,001	26,855	12.1	10.4
800–999	13,334	8,298	21,632	9.7	8.3
1000–1249	12,158	7,500	19,658	8.8	7.9
1250–1499	9,962	5,162	15,124	6.8	5.5
1500–1999	12,688	5,576	18,264	8.2	6.5
2000 or more	14,108	3,715	17,823	8.0	6.2
Not stated	2,497	2,269	4,767	2.1	7.9
Total	**121,009**	**101,342**	**222,351**	**100.0**	**100.0**

Source: Australian Census 2011.

Another indication of objective well-being in Australia is given by accommodation tenure. Most Australians dream of owning their own home. In 2011, just 9% of Hindus had achieved that dream compared with 26% of the Australian population. Many Hindus had a mortgage. However, a much higher proportion of Hindus (45%) compared with the wider population (26%) was renting (Table 6.15). Indeed, more Hindus were renting their accommodation than most other religious groups, apart from the Sikhs, Muslims and the Latter-day Saints. This reflects the fact that such a large proportion of the Hindu community has recently arrived in Australia, so the tenure situation could change in the future. However, it may also reflect a lower importance among Hindus of owning a home. While these values may rarely be made explicit, this lower priority to owning a home may reflect the emphasis placed within Hinduism on the transitory nature of human existence, values reflected archetypally in the wandering Hindu mystic.

Table 6.15: Tenure of Home for Hindus in the Australian Population in 2011

Tenure Type	*No. of Hindus*	*Hindus (%)*	*Total Australian Population (%)*
Own outright	25,619	9.3	25.6
Own with a mortgage	112,903	41.0	37.9
Rented	124,634	45.2	25.9
Other	12,378	4.5	10.6
Total	**275,534**	**100.0**	**100.0**

Source: Australian Census 2011.

Hinduism and the Hindu Community in Australia

Hinduism, as it is expressed in Australia, is shaped by the nature of the Hindu community as it has formed in Australia. The analysis of the Census data shows that the Hindu community is diverse in its background. Some members of the community, coming from places such as Fiji and Sri Lanka, have come to Australia primarily to escape ethnic persecution. They have come so that they can live without the political pressures of their homeland, and where they can freely express their culture and their religion. This is similar to other groups who have fled persecution, such as some of the Lutherans and, more recently, Coptic Christians from Egypt and Bahá'ís from Iran.

Most members of the Hindu community, though, have migrated to Australia for a better life economically. They have taken the opportunities provided by the current visa arrangements to obtain better pay for their level of qualification than they could find in India or in some of the other countries where they have been living. The census data shows that, at least in some measure, many Hindus have found jobs that provide a good income. They have settled here with their families and are raising their children here. While they have retained the identification as Hindu, one might ask how much meaning it has for these people.

Anecdotal evidence suggests that some Indians have chosen largely to dissociate themselves from their Hindu traditions. They have done so partly because they believe that is expected of them in the new, supposedly secular, environment, or that they have come from secular environment. They find it easier to pursue a liberal existence without the challenges, ambiguities and ambivalences of Hindu traditions. However, there will be occasions when even these lapsed Hindu Indians will show support for the aspirations and activities of their fellow Hindus, especially where common concerns about settlement, immigrant, educational and public representational issues are being negotiated. Many Indians and Sri Lankan Tamils who have migrated to Australia come from educated, semi-middle-class urbanised backgrounds in which, as in most secular contexts, religion and matters of public life are kept apart. Thus, while a Hindu may not outwardly display his or her religious leanings, in private life there may well be a definite space and scope for spiritual pursuits.

The Australian Survey of Social Attitudes (2009) provides a picture of religious activities by Australian adults. While the Hindu sample was too small to provide highly reliable information, the fact that 48% of them said they were involved in some form of public worship or religious activity at least once a month suggests many Hindus are active in public expressions of their faith. Many Hindus participate in festivals at the various Hindu temples around Australia. Many go there on special personal occasions; for example, to remember the death of parents or to celebrate birthdays. Hindu missions are active in sponsoring lecturing tours from various *gurus*, youth camps and study classes, as a study of websites, such as that of the Chinmaya Mission in Australia (www.chinmaya.com.au) reveals.

Migrants in general tend to be more active religiously than the wider population, especially those who have more recently arrived.[7] They look to religious groups to provide them with connections into a community that shares their values, their sense of identity, and, very often, their language.[8]

The nature of the religious community also determines to some extent how religion will be expressed. People of different educational backgrounds often look for different resources in their religious faith. In India, Hinduism developed largely from rural village settings in which fertility rites and community-binding festivals were important aspects. In Australia, some well-educated Hindus, living in an urban environment in which they feel they have some distinctive values that have their sources

---

7 P. Hughes, 'The Impact of Recent Immigration on Religious Groups in Australia', *Pointers*, vol. 22, no. 4, December 2012, p. 6.

8 G. Bouma (ed.), *Many Religions, All Australian: Religious Settlement, Identity and Cultural Diversity*, Christian Research Association, Melbourne, 1996.

in their Hindu heritage, are looking for resources that will help them to find a sense of community with others who share those values, and will help them to train their children in those values. Hence, alongside the temple celebrations, they look for teaching about how Hinduism might help them to live, for both themselves and their children. Some look for meditation practices, such as *yoga*, which will give them a sense of inner peace in a stressful, urban world. They look for small group activities through which community can be formed. While Hindu temples help to maintain community in localities in India, Hindu activities become a means whereby community is created across a region in Australia.

Many religious communities in Australia have been formed partly to carry the identity of new immigrants:[9] the Lutheran community carried the German identity, the Presbyterian community the Scottish identity, the Greek Orthodox community the Greek identity, to name just a few. So the Hindu community is carrying the Indian identity. Some of the Protestant denominations have also carried the identity of sub-groups within the community: people with a particular sense of their place in the wider society. The Brethren and, to some extent, the Baptists, have identified themselves against the wider society through their religious faith. Hinduism is currently carrying an ethnic rather than sub-group identity. As noted in the statistics of language, there are several major linguistic sub-groups within the Hindu community, and there is some tendency, particularly as the Hindu community becomes larger, for those sub-groups to be reflected in the worship of different gods, and, to a lesser extent, the development of separate temples and in the celebration of different festivals. As the profile of the Hindu community in Australia continues to develop through continuing immigration, and as families continue the settlement process and focus increasingly on bringing up their children in a new context, so the expression of Hinduism will continue to change.

9 Bouma (ed.), 1996: 69.

Sikh Community in Australia

7

Sikh History and Migration

Carmen Voigt-Graf

History of the Sikh Religion

SIKHISM was founded by Guru Nanak (1469–1539), who was born at Talwandi, now known as Nankana Sahib, in the Punjab province in present-day Pakistan. According to tradition, Guru Nanak was bathing in a stream when he heard a call from God. He disappeared for three days, presumed drowned. When he reappeared, his first words were 'There is no Hindu; there is no Muslim'. Guru Nanak regarded his revelations as transcending both Islam and Hinduism, proclaiming the oneness of humanity; he also emphasised the unique role of the *guru* to lead the religion's followers (Lewis 2002: 1176). Throughout his life, he held steadfastly to the vision of a common humanity in which all barriers of race, caste, creed, gender and ethnicity are transcended.

Accompanied by a Muslim musician named Mardana, Guru Nanak began a long and winding journey, a sort of 'prophet's pilgrimage'. He travelled all over India and beyond, to Assam in the east, Sri Lanka in the south, Ladakh and Tibet in the north, and westwards to Mecca and Baghdad. He spent twenty years this way, spreading the message of love, peace and equality (ibid.: 1175). He visited major spiritual centres of all faiths — Hindu, Muslim, Jain, Buddhist, Sufi and Christian. He engaged in dialogue with various faith leaders, to encourage people in perceiving the truth within them. He did not hold in high regard vain rituals, which he believed led people astray and distanced them from the essence of religious teachings.

In spreading his message, Guru Nanak relied on the Hindu and Muslim religious identities and vocabulary, since these were easily known and understood. It is because of this that some scholars say that Sikhism is a synthesis of Islam and Hinduism. This is far from the truth and misrepresents the significance of his message. He never tried to create a following as a person. He did not claim that only he was the saviour. Guru Nanak told both Muslims and Hindus to become true believers, in order to achieve salvation.[1] Thus, a community developed around Guru Nanak and his followers began to call themselves 'Sikhs', meaning students or disciples.[2] Even though it was meant to form a bridge between Islam and Hinduism, Sikhism quickly became a distinct community with its own scripture and institutions. Guru Nanak had pronounced that:

> Only they who dwell on the Lord's Name, earn the real merit of their toil (they are liberated, their toil over). Their faces glow with the glory of the Light Divine, and many more are liberated in their company. — *Sri Guru Granth Sahib*, p. 8 (hereafter *SGGS*)

Guru Nanak preached that there is only one God. 'God is *Ek* (One)', he said. He used the numeral 1 to emphasise this. His cardinal doctrine is:

> There is one God, eternal truth, Creator Being, without fear, without enmity, timeless, formless, not-born, self-existent and realised by His own Grace. The true One was there at the beginning, was true throughout the ages, is true now, Nanak says will be true in the future. — *SGGS*, p. 1

---

1 Guru Arjan, the fifth Sikh Guru, later echoed these sentiments:

I do not keep the Hindu fast nor the Muslim Ramadan;
I serve Him alone who is my refuge
I serve the One Master who is also Allah
I have broken with the Hindu and the Muslim,
I do not worship with the Hindu nor like the Muslim go to Mecca,
I serve Him alone and no other,
I will not pray to idols nor say the Muslim prayer
I shall put my heart at the feet of the One Supreme Being
For we are neither Hindus nor Musslman.

Likewise, Guru Gobind Singh had also emphasised the independence of the Sikh religion, stating that 'the different paths of Ram, Rahim, Puran[a], and Quran, I do not accept'.

2 For details on the history of the Sikhs and their belief system, see Cole and Sambhi (1978); Fenton, Hein, Reynolds, Miller, Nielsen, Burford and Forman (1993); Grewal (1990); W. Hew McLeod (1968, 1976, 1989, 1997) and Singh (1963, 1966).

God is viewed as *sagun* (with attributes), but also as *nirgun* (without attributes). To regard God as *nirgun* is to think of God as formless and infinite. God manifests Himself in His Creation. The finite form in which God manifests Himself is not to be worshipped.

Central to Guru Nanak's teaching is the affirmation of this Ultimate Reality. The purpose of life is to seek liberation. This is possible through love, and *naam simran* (meditating on God's name) as the methodology and a way towards this objective. However one's *haumai* (ego) may stand in the way. Through their ego, people see themselves as being distinct from God. They become separated from the Universal Will and mistake what is unreal from the real. One is dominated by passions and instincts such as *kaam* (lust), *krodh* (anger), *lobh* (greed), *moh* (attachment) and *ankhar* (pride). *Haumai* is the chief cause of one's suffering. It is the opposite of *naam* (essence of God). *Naam* will not reside in the mind as long as ego is there.

How can ego be overcome? Guru Nanak rejected all outward forms of piety and all forms of austerities, penances, pilgrimages, fasts, or asceticism. In his *Japji Sahib* (the Sikh prayer) he says that it is only possible to overcome ego through total self-surrender to God and complete faith in His *Hukam* (Will).

fig. 7.1: Guru Nanak

After his travels, Guru Nanak founded a village at Kartarpur on the banks of Ravi River. Here he set about restructuring the religious and social life of the people. The people gathered at his *dharamsala* (a place of worship) for *sangat* (holy fellowship of people) who gather for the sole purpose of prayer. Guru Nanak also started the practice of *langar* (a communal kitchen). People sat together in a *pangat* (row) to eat. These were ordinary people who mixed together without reference to caste or status. All acts were performed in the spirit of selfless service (*sewa*). This helped to emphasise the unity and equality of humankind.

The community was brought to gather through *sewa*. Sikhism teaches that it is good to serve others. It is a way of showing love to fellow human beings. Service has to be performed without expectation of any reward or benefit. Guru Nanak said 'One who performs selfless service without the thought of reward shall attain his Lord and Master' (*SGSS*, p. 110). *Sewa* is rendered physically through good actions and deeds, mentally in thought and with wealth by providing resources for community needs. This was the glue that bound the community together. People came together and built community facilities and mixed freely, prayed and ate together, thus bringing about equality and social cohesion not seen before Guru Nanak's time. Today wherever the Sikhs are, they built their *gurdwara* (temple) through *sewa* and provide community services.

The Sikh Gurus were social reformers. Their message was that humanity is one and there is no caste, creed, high or low, nor is there any colour or race bar. There is no caste in the hereafter so we should regard all the same. Guru Nanak identified himself with the lowest of the low. 'Nanak seeks the company of those who are lowest of the low. He has no desire to compete with the rich and powerful' (*SGGS*, p. 15). Equality is not only important in terms of worldly relationships but the emphasis was that, in spiritual development of the individual, God dwells in every heart. All can have God's Grace. Guru Nanak was concerned with the plight of women. He disapproved of discrimination against them. Sikh *gurus* therefore promoted gender equality and set about bringing change and improving the status of Indian women. In the *Guru Granth Sahib* (or *Adi Granth*), the feminine principle is considered to be eminently important. The equality and oneness of humanity for Guru Nanak cut across not just caste and racial lines but across gender as well. Both men and women came to hear the preaching of Nanak, and they sat side-by-side. They also took a common meal together and participated in the common worship in the temple congregation. Nanak believed that there was no task too large or too small for a woman to undertake on equal footing with a man, an uncommon attitude for the time. Motherhood was also thought by him to be something very sacred and, unlike in Hinduism, there was no pollution associated with childbirth. Bearing children and preserving the tradition are the sacred endowments that God bequeathed to woman in the original covenant. In the tradition of the *gurus*, practices of infanticide, *purdah* (veiling), child marriage, polygamy, *sati* (widow-immolation) and banning widow re-marriage are all condemned. A woman has value as an individual, for she is seen 'neither as a goddess to be worshipped in some hidden sanctuary nor as a temptress to be left behind' (Singh 1993: 58). Women are the 'conscience of man'. Nanak would cite a hymn from the *Guru Granth Sahib* that valourised the status of a woman in no unflattering terms:

> *Of woman are we born, of woman conceived,*
> *To woman engaged, to woman married.*
> *Woman are befriended, by woman do civilisations continue.*
> *When a woman dies, a woman is sought for.*
> *It is through woman that order is maintained.*
> *Then why call her inferior from whom*
> *All great ones are born?* — cited in Singh 1993: 30

THE MEANING OF 'GURU'

One feature of Sikhism that is found in other Eastern religions is the idea and importance of the *guru* (teacher). Sikh Gurus are taken to be 'Enlighteners'. The holy teacher is not thought of as an incarnation or manifestation of God — although some Sikhs do believe that Guru Nanak and the nine successor Gurus were the embodiment of Divine Light — but as guiding people in the ways of Truth. They are comparable in later beliefs to the Messengers of God. The more general belief is that the ten Sikh Gurus emphasised that they were human beings who worked as communicators of God and that they should not be worshipped as God (Bilimoria 1996a, 1997), although they are revered deeply. The holy scripture of the Sikhs, the *Guru Granth Sahib*, is said to be revealed through the Gurus. Gurus taught and practised the principles and practices of

fig. 7.2: The Golden Temple, Amritsar

Sikhism in an exemplary way. Guru Arjan, the fifth Sikh Guru, led the community from 1581 to 1606. He completed the construction of the lake (*sorvar*) begun by Guru Ramdas at Amritsar, the centre of Sikhism. In it he built the Harmandir Sahib, popularly known the Golden Temple. In 1604, he compiled the *Adi Granth Scriptures* (the First Holy Book) of the Sikhs, and included the compositions of the first four Gurus and those of Muslim and Hindu *pir*s and *sant*s (saints). However, Guru Arjan was its major contributor. Guru Gobind Singh, the last in the line of the ten *guru*s, in 1706 added to the *Adi Granth* the compositions of the ninth Sikh Guru, Tegh Bahadur and brought it to a completion. Just before his death in 1708, he declared the work 'the Guru', hence the *Guru Granth Sahib*.

The *Guru Granth Sahib* is installed on a dais that is erected as a sacred throne (*takhat*) in Sikh *gurdwara*s, and is itself treated as a living presence of the *guru*'s spirit. Through it, Guru Nanak is thought to continue his teachings to the Sikhs, and it plays a pivotal role as witness to and conferrer of blessings in all Sikh ceremonies.

Many of Sikhism's major social reforms are also attributed to Guru Gobind Singh. Building on the institutions begun around 1469, he founded the *khalsa* (a brotherhood or a united community of the pure and faithful), through his famous initiation ceremony of *amrit* (nectar) of the *panj pyare* (five beloved ones) on 30 March 1699. Sikh history has it that on Vaisakhi

fig. 7.3: *Ikk Oankar*

(Baisakhi) 1699, in Anandpur, Punjab, Guru Gobind Singh gathered his Sikh followers and tested their loyalty to the newest Indian religion. With a drawn sword in his hand, he challenged who would come forward and offer their heads in self-sacrifice to him. He took the first volunteer into a tent and came back out with a bloodied sword. Whilst many of the 80,000 gathered departed, four more came forward. The Guru then emerged with his beloved five (*panj pyare*) from the tent, re-attired in saffron-coloured robes and turbans. Thereafter the *panj pyare* received *amrit* (water to which his wife Mata Sahib added *patasha*s, sugar crystals that became life-giving ambrosia) which the Guru stirred with his two-edged sword. After initiating the *panj pyare*, the Guru received the same initiation. This significant ceremony of overcoming the most debilitating of all emotions – fear – also gave birth to a new and martial race: the *khalsa*. He prescribed the use of five manifest articles of faith, the 'five Ks'. These include uncut hair (*kes*), a comb (*kanga*), a steel bracelet (*kara*), a sword (*kirpan*) and a pair of breeches (*kachh*). The small sword in a strap suspended at the waist is a major symbol in the emblem of the Sikh faith; it is not a signifier of military or combative confrontation but, rather, signifies the protection of *dharam*, or the moral norms of the community, bonded in a spiritual union. The Sikhs were now *sant-sipahi*s (saint-soldiers), having a dual role of becoming spiritual personalities and soldiers prepared to fight against oppression and tyranny. The Guru also prompted equality of the sexes and proscribed caste among his followers, thus forming them into the united community of the *khalsa*.

After Guru Gobind Singh's death, ongoing conflict between the Sikhs and the Mughal empire continued. In 1799, the Sikhs captured Lahore and made it the capital of the Sikh kingdom, dominating the Punjab and other areas of north-west India. During Ranjit Singh's rule of the Sikh kingdom, between 1799 and 1839, large numbers of farmers converted to Sikhism (Lewis 2003: 1177). After being defeated by the British in 1849, the area that had been under Sikh rule, became part of British India. Sikhs continued to increase in number during the Raj, because of the special favours accorded to Sikhs in the army and the civil service (ibid.: 1177). A key theme throughout Sikh history has been their struggle for their own religious and ethnic identity amid Muslim and Hindu persecution.

Sikh Beliefs and Practices

The life goal of Sikhs is the realisation of Akal Purakh (The Timeless One, the Divine, that some render as 'God', although not in the strict monotheistic sense of Personal Deity; it may even bear 'Non-Dual' connotations, as in *advait*).According to the teachings of Sikhism, this may only be achieved if one's livelihood is earned through creative, productive and honest labour (*kirt karni*). It also occurs through being in tune with the infinite through meditation on divine qualities, so that one becomes filled with the Divine's presence (*naam japna*), and through sharing the fruits of one's earnings with the needy (*vand chakna*). Sikhism teaches people to be contented, humble, merciful, truthful and helpful to others. Moreover the five evils of carnal appetite, anger, greed, attachment and ego (*haumai*) must be avoided in order to attain such a realisation. However, self-realisation does not equate to salvation or admittance to heaven, but rather is a means of reaching God-consciousness through reaching one's own full potential. The principles and the eventual attainment of self-realisation are held to have been demonstrated through the lives of the ten Gurus who sacrificed their lives in the service of the people and the Divine.

Other Sikh principles are *sangat*, which advises Sikhs to associate with like-minded strong-in-faith people and abstain from hedonistic or materialistic lifestyles; *pangat*, which emphasises equality between all

fig. 7.4: The *Guru Granth Sahib*

humans regardless of caste, creed or colour; *sewa*, which refers to service to others; and *simran*, which means meditating and staying in tune with the Divine (Bilimoria 1996a, 1997). Entry into the Sikh religion is open to all and conversion is symbolised through *khalsa* initiation ceremony, as described earlier, that involves the conferring of the 'five Ks' and affirmation of the *khalsa* symbols on the part of the initiated. Henceforth, initiated Sikhs are obliged to wear on their body the 'five Ks'. Moreover, male Sikhs are encourged to suffix their name with 'Singh' (lion) and females with 'Kaur' (princess or lioness).

While the central focus of worship is the Timeless One, the *Guru Granth Sahib* is the focus of the rituals and religious ceremonies enacted in the presence of the congregation. The *granthi* (appointed presider) reads selected passages and chants from the verses in the text. Any layperson is authorised to lead the signing, reading and making of supplication for the congregation. *Gurdwaras* are important venues for the gathering of Sikhs and for dissemination of the teachings of the Sikh Gurus. While Hindus are often happy conducting their devotional worship (*puja*) and prayers at home, Sikhs feel the need to congregate and offer worship together. At the *gurdwara* no worship as such is offered, since the Sikhs do not believe in images. If anything, Sikhs worship the formless non-dual Divine Principle who is considered to be both transcendent and immanent in a panentheistic cosmo-theogonic understanding. The Universal Progenitor is believed to be manifest right across His creation, from the microscopic to the macroscopic realms of the universe. Devotional singing (*kirtan*) is done toward this all-pervading Supreme Presence. While being unequivocal in its belief in the oneness of God and the rejection of image worship, Sikhism nevertheless draws upon some features of Indic dharma traditions, including the idea of the cycle of rebirths and *karma*.

Migration among Sikhs

Sikhs have a one-and-a-half century long history of migration to Australia and to other nodes of what has become a global Sikh diaspora. Sikhs are the exception to the rule of immobility that is found elsewhere in India. Nearly two-thirds of the total Sikh population come from a farming background; more than 80 % of them are Jat Sikhs (Jaijee 1999: 11), who also form the majority in the Punjabi diaspora.

In 2000, an estimated 24 million people lived in Punjab, of whom some 15 million were Sikhs. About one million Sikhs lived in other parts of India and some two million Sikhs lived abroad (including 600,000 in the United Kingdom and 300,000 in the United States and Canada each) (Bains Pers. Comm. 1999). This means that some 11% of Sikhs live abroad, compared to 2% of Indians as a whole. The impact of migration is even larger when looking at a smaller geographical scale. Emigration from the region of Doaba has occurred on such a large scale that in a village of 200 households, almost all of the 80 or 100 Jat Sikh households have at least one relative in a Western country, mostly in the United Kingdom, Canada and the United States. Two or three households have a relative in Australia. Among the factors accounting for their exceptional mobility patterns are the turbulent history of their home region as well as the impact of Sikhism, which is less bound to Punjab's soil than Hinduism is to India's.[3]

---

3 Much of the information on the migration and settlement history of Sikhs is based on findings from fieldwork that was conducted as part of a Ph.D. thesis in geography looking at the migration and transnationalism →

Current estimates (to 2015) indicate that there are some 25 million Sikhs; the majority still live in the Punjab, while the rest are spread across other parts of the subcontinent, with over 2 million in the diaspora.

PUNJAB'S TURBULENT HISTORY

The greater Punjab region is primarily an alluvial plain bounded by the Indus River to the west, the Yamuna River to the east, the Shivalik foothills to the north and the Rajputana desert to the south. The name Punjab is derived from the Persian words *punj* (five) and *ab* (water), referring to the five rivers Jhelum, Chenab, Ravi, Beas and Satluj (or Sutlej) that run through it. Its political boundaries have in the course of history expanded and shrunk. The location of Punjab on the invasion route into India from Afghanistan and Central Asia meant that waves of traders, immigrants and conquerors swept through the plains, transforming Punjabi society and leaving a distinctive mark on its people. Today, many Sikhs attribute their adventurous spirit and strong will to survive under difficult circumstances to the tumultuous history of Punjab (Voigt-Graf 2002: 101-02).

When Punjab was under Sikh rule between 1799 and 1849, few people left the region. Punjab's inclusion into British India in 1849 started an emigration flow that has continued to this day. The reasons for Sikhs looking for opportunities abroad lay in the hardship that many farmers faced as a consequence of British rule. The middle layer of the peasantry,

---

← experiences of three groups of Indian migrants in Australia, one of which were Punjabis (Voigt-Graf 2002). The core of the research consisted of in-depth semi-structured household interviews with Punjabi migrants in Australia and of the kin of migrants in Punjab. Between 1998 and 2000, 32 Punjabi households were interviewed in Australia (20 in Sydney and 12 in Woolgoolga) and 28 in Punjab. The findings from the household interviews were complemented by other sources of information. These included participation in social activities in Punjabi households and communities, key informant interviews, expert interviews and the analysis of census data and other statistics. Some 30 persons provided expert knowledge on a variety of aspects. They included academics, government officials, religious and community leaders in Australia and India.

Although this research study focused on Punjabis rather than Sikhs, the vast majority of the respondents were Sikhs. Only three respondents in Sydney, none in Woolgoolga and six in India were Punjabi Hindus. Names of respondents were changed to guarantee their anonymity.

rather than the landless masses, joined the ranks of the migrants. They went overseas as free migrants and not as indentured workers, in contrast to Indians from many other regions of India. Additionally, ten years of famine in the Punjab region (1869-79) increased Sikh migration in the 1880s, as many families had become indebted during the famine. Moreover, as a result of their loyalty to the British colonialists during the Great Rebellion of 1857, many Sikhs were recruited into the British army, exposing them to opportunities in various parts of the British Empire. In the early days of the 20th century, Punjabis migrated to North America, Malaya, Hong Kong, Burma, Australia, New Zealand, the United Kingdom and East Africa (Cohen 1997: 110).

When British rule ended in 1947, the subcontinent was divided into two countries defined predominantly on the basis of religion. Partition divided the region of Punjab between Pakistan and India. It occasioned the greatest and one of the most violent mass migrations recorded in history (Zolberg, Suhrke and Aguayo 1989: 126-79). Between August 1947 and April 1951, when the borders were finally closed, some 14 million people had migrated between India and West Pakistan. An estimated one million were killed in the slaughter that accompanied the migrations (Jaijee 1999: 322). About 2.5 million Sikhs poured out of Pakistan into India. This mass influx of refugees triggered another wave of Sikh emigration, mostly to the United Kingdom.

In 1956, the Indian government began to create linguistic states in India, although a Punjabi-speaking state with a Sikh majority only came into existence in 1966. Today, Punjab is the sole state in India where the majority of the population are Sikhs — 63 % in 1991 (1991 Census of India, State Profile). The Indian state of Punjab (henceforth referred to as Punjab) was left with the Satluj, the Beas and part of the Ravi, an area of 50,362 km^2 and at the time of the 1991 census, a population of 20,282,000 (*1991 Census Handbook*: 2). Just outside Punjab's borders lies the Union Territory of Chandigarh, which is the shared capital of Punjab and Haryana. Partition left Punjab's former capital Lahore in Pakistan, which resulted in the decision of the Indian government to build a new town. In 1991, its population was 642,015 (*1991 Census of India*, Series 28: 38).

Punjab is administratively divided into 17 districts and includes three 'folk' regions: Doaba, Malwa and Majha. These are separated from each other by rivers and have each developed specific characteristics reflected linguistically in dialects (Gosal 1984: 25). The most important region in regards to Sikh migration is Doaba, a name derived from *do* (two) and *ab* (water) and referring to the area between the Beas and the Satluj. This is the region from which the vast majority of Sikh migrants in Australia, as well as in other settlements of their global diaspora originate (Voigt-Graf 2002: 100).

Punjab is one of the smallest states of India and some Punjabis feel that they were treated unfairly in the process of the reorganisation of states. Conflicts mostly revolve around the allocation of water resources. While there were grievances about their treatment by the central government, only a small number of radical Sikhs in the diaspora demanded an independent Sikh state of Khalistan before 1984. Events in that year, however, radicalised many Sikhs in Punjab and abroad. In June the Indian army invaded the Golden Temple and 40 other *gurdwara*s, claiming that they had been used to store the weapons of Sikh militants. In November 1984, the assassination of Indira Gandhi by Sikh bodyguards triggered off a massacre of Sikhs in Delhi and other Indian cities, leading to an escalation of violence.[4] Many Sikhs sought refugee or asylum status in Western countries, including Australia.

Until as late as the early 20th century, religious lines were not drawn as rigidly as they are today, and Punjabis strategically emphasised different aspects of their identity, such as language, religion, caste or regional origin (Dusenbery 1995: 190; 2008). Traditionally caste endogamy was practised across religious lines and marriage alliances between Sikh and Hindus of the same caste, for example, were common. This situation changed in the wake of 20th-century political events. Already, in colonial times, the formerly more flexible identity markers of religion and caste had become frozen, as a result of the insistence of the British colonial administrators on clear-cut categories. The categories became increasingly loaded with political meaning. With impending partition of the subcontinent, Sikhs began to assert that they belonged to the Punjab and the Punjab to Sikhs (ibid.: 25). In the wake of the 1984 events, Sikhs around

---

4 Details on the crisis in Punjab are provided by Juergensmeyer (1988) and Singh (1995).

the world have increasingly been concerned with the movement for an independent Sikh state of Khalistan. In the diaspora, Sikh culture and religion have been revived. Sikh nationalist ideologies circulate widely over the Internet (see e.g. www.khalistan.com and www.khalistan.net) and are manifest in a number of Sikh organisations with global membership. This has affected the relations of Sikhs with other Indians, including Hindu Punjabis. In short, ever since the incorporation of Punjab into British India, the history of the area has been tumultuous. This has been one reason for the high number of Sikh migrants.

THE IMPACT OF SIKHISM ON MOBILITY

Sikhs regard mobility as a virtue, in contrast to Hindus who are bound to the Indian soil by their religion (Voigt-Graf 2002: 102). Guru Gobind Singh pronounced that wherever five Sikhs are gathered in the presence of the *Guru Granth* there too would be the eternal Guru. In other words, it is affirmed that Sikhism is not affected by relocation. The attitude of Sikhs is foreshadowed in a story recorded in the *Janam-sakhi*, a book that records incidents in the life of Guru Nanak (see below):

Migration as a Blessing in Sikhism

> *The story says that one evening, after a long day on the road, Guru Nanak and his companions arrived in a village and asked for food and shelter but were turned away by the mean-spirited inhabitants. A mile or so on they came to another village. Here the residents came out and welcomed them conducted them to a clean, comfortable room, brought the best food they had and when the Guru was rested, they asked him to teach them.*
> *The next day Guru Nanak and his companions set out again. Seeing the rejecting village in the distance, the Guru said: "May these people always remain settled where they are, may they never be disturbed or uprooted", and then turning to the good village he pronounced: "May all these people be scattered".When his companions remonstrated at this strange blessing he explained its meaning: "virtues should be spread around and not confined to a small place or just a few individuals".* (Jaijee 1999: 324)

The history and culture of Punjab as described above have made Punjab's population one of the most internationally mobile in India. The particular routes that have led Punjabis to Australia are examined below.

Origins of the Sikh Community in Australia

SOJOURNING IN AUSTRALIA

Two major scholarly studies of Sikhs in Australia were carried out by de Lepervanche (1984), based on her study of the Sikhs in Woolgoolga in northern New South Wales, and by Bilimoria (1996). Further additions to the literature of Sikhs' diasporic experience have been made by Rajender Gabbi (1998), Voigt-Graf (2001) and Gurdarshan Singh Gill (2010). A brief history is presented here from these studies.

The first Sikhs were brought privately to Australia after the 1830s, when they worked for minimal wages as shepherds and farm labourers. Despite the fact that employers did not record the actual ethnicity or origin of workers, Sikh immigrants can often be identified through their surname 'Singh'. The latter half of the 19th century saw the arrival of Afghans, colloquially known as 'Ghans' (see Chapter 2). Although most were Muslims, the group also included Sikhs and Hindus. The cameleers who were brought in the 1860s from Afghanistan, which at that time was under Sikh rule, included many Sikhs. During this period,word of mouth was a key form of recruitment (Gabbi 1998). Many Sikh migrants were farmers who sought their fortune in Australia before returning to Punjab. In the 1890s, nearly 250 Sikhs worked on the cane fields in Queensland, while others worked clearing bushland or growing grass for sheep grazing. Some Sikhs moved southwards and settled in the coastal towns of New South Wales (ibid.).

After the passing of the Immigration Restriction Act, 1901, new migration from India became impossible, though re-entry for those already living in Australia was not denied. Most of these pioneering Sikhs led an early version of a transnational way of life, determined by slow and expensive transport links. They could only afford to visit their ancestral home region a few times during decades of wage labour in Australia, but they wrote letters and almost all of them ultimately retired in Punjab. For these early migrants, the village in Punjab remained home, and savings from Australia were remitted or brought back on their visits in order to support the extended family in their daily lives and to increase the family's landholdings (Voigt-Graf 2002: 105-06; 2003: 147-49). Sons tended to join their fathers in Australia, sometimes replacing the grandfather who would return to India for retirement. The key to Australia was thus passed on from father to son, and many families kept their links to Australia for two or three generations before a family member permanently settled there.

The grandfathers and fathers of many respondents in Woolgoolga, who were interviewed in 1999, had been sojourners in the late 19th and early 20th centuries (see Voigt-Graf 2001; 2002: 105-07). Hearing of work opportunities in Australia, the grandfather of 75-year old Kulbir Bains from Jalandhar district was the first family member to migrate in 1885, working on a sugar cane farm in northern New South Wales. Kulbir's father joined the grandfather, arriving in Australia with the last ship from India before the start of the 'White Australia' policy in 1901. As Kulbir remembered:

> When I was a boy, every couple of months we got a letter from my father in Australia. He also came to visit us two or three times over the years . . . I came to Australia under the permit system in 1947. I could get a visa because I was a British subject and because I had a permit from my future employer in Australia, which my father had organised for my brother and me. He had organised this before the troubles started in India so when the violence began [following partition of the subcontinent in 1947], I got on a ship. I settled in Gordonvale [in Far North Queensland]. [. . .] My father went back to India in 1951 and stayed there for 21 years. He only returned to Australia after my mother died in 1972.

Asked about his own marriage and visits to India, Kulbir explained:

> My marriage was arranged through a relative in India and I got married in 1949. My wife first stayed in India and I visited her in 1952 and again in 1955. After that visit, I brought her and my two daughters out to Australia. . . . My next visit to India was only when my mother died in 1972 and then for my daughter's wedding in 1982. Two years ago, I went back to visit my relatives.

Kulbir is the first in his family who is permanently settled in Australia, along with his wife and children, and who has no intention to retire in Punjab. His family's migration from Punjab to Australia is a typical narrative of over 100 years of transnational biographies linking Punjab and the east coast of Australia.

CONSOLIDATING A RURAL PUNJABI COMMUNITY IN WOOLGOOLGA[5]

The first Sikh is recorded to have settled in Woolgoolga, in northern New South Wales, as a farm worker in 1939. In 1950, four or five Sikh families lived in town (Gabbi 1998: 133) and one of them bought the first banana farm owned by a Sikh in the area. Kewal Rattan came to Australia in 1954 and was among the early settlers in Woolgoolga. From owning a small plot of land in Woolgoolga that his father had bought in 1957, the family property has grown to become one of the largest Punjabi properties in the Woolgoolga area. Today, it includes four big houses and a total of 80 acres of farmland.

The population increased to 274 Punjabis living in and around Woolgoolga in 1973 (de Lepervanche 1984: 14-15). Today, some 600 Sikhs live in Woolgoolga where they make up over 10 % of the population. The number of Punjabis in the area has increased mostly due to immigration

fig. 7.5: The Sikh *gurdwara* at Woolgoolga (photo: Philip Hughes)

[5] I am particularly indebted to Rashmere Bhatti, from the Woolgoolga Neighbourhood Centre, for her time and patience in answering all my questions about the Sikh community in Woolgoolga.

fig. 7.6: Inside the *gurdwara* at Woolgoolga (photo: Philip Hughes)

along family chain migration paths (Voigt-Graf 2002: 106-11). Marriages are particularly important in perpetuating migration. Ever since Sikhs came to Australia, they assumed that the appropriate place to recruit spouses for their offspring was from those families into which they would have married had they not moved abroad. Sikhs follow the rules of caste endogamy and *gotra* exogamy. This means that marriages are arranged between people of the same caste, e.g. Jats, but not of the same patrilineal descent group (*gotra*), nor from that of one's mother or any of one's grandmothers. According to the rule of village exogamy, marriages are not arranged between two partners of the same village. In addition, the rule of patrilocality applies, whereby couples take up residence with the husband's family. The rule of village exogamy has been transferred to Woolgoolga and only very rarely are marriages arranged between two Woolgoolga Sikhs. Since the range of prospective partners is wide and no particular obligations with respect to accepting or making offers of marriage alliances exist, marriage arrangements for offspring are often governed by the long-term interests of the family (Ballard 2001). For this reason marriage alliances can serve as strategic steps towards opening new migration routes, especially from India to Australia but also from one diasporic node to another.

Parents, other senior relatives and sometimes the wider Sikh community in Woolgoolga are involved in identifying potential spouses for young Sikhs, with the final say usually given to the couple. Sandeep Singh tells how his marriage to Paramjit was arranged:

> When it was time for me to get married, my parents started looking for a spouse. They asked our relatives in Doaba whether they knew of a girl that was suitable for me. They also told the community in Woolgoolga and people made suggestions. I wanted a girl from India because I thought that she would be better able to instruct our kids in Punjabi culture. . . . It was through a family here in Woolgoolga that contact to the girl's parents was established. My father travelled to Punjab to meet the family and he found that it was a good family. That's when they started arranging our marriage. Before everything was finalised, I went to India with my parents and met my wife and her family. . . . I could have refused to marry her but my parents would have been very offended and the family in Woolgoolga that recommended her would have been offended too.

Most marriages of Woolgoolga Sikhs are arranged with families in India, despite the fact that Punjabi women prefer to marry Australian Sikhs. The traditional pattern of patrilocality has given way to a system whereby the spouse from India — male or female — migrates to Australia. Dharmbir Grewal moved to Woolgoolga after his marriage:

> My father had started looking for a wife for me in Punjab and informed our relatives about it. My father's second cousin's husband knew that his nephew in Australia was looking for a husband for his daughter. I didn't really want to move abroad because all my family and friends are in Punjab. But my father wanted me to move because then I could maybe help my younger brother to migrate too. I would have preferred to go to the United States because I know some people who have moved there. But I thought that Australia was not bad because at least there is land available. That was important for me because I am a farmer. I wouldn't work in factories like most Punjabis in Britain. . . . My father-in-law visited us in Punjab and he and my father arranged the marriage. I never met my wife before our wedding in Punjab.

> After our marriage they sponsored my migration to Woolgoolga. For the first two years we stayed at my in-laws place which was hard because I don't get on with them. Then they helped us to buy our own place so it's better now.

Dharmbir's case demonstrates how the traditional rule of patrilocality is broken in order to open migration doors from India to Australia. The psychological strain associated with such a move is often considerable. Since his in-laws sponsored and paid for his migration, Dharmbir felt obligated towards them even though he did not get on with them.[6] For his wife, the advantage of marrying someone from India was that she was able to stay in Woolgoolga close to her own family, an option that the traditional rule of patrilocality does not offer. On the other hand, Dharmbir is more traditional in outlook than most Punjabi men raised in Australia. Punjabis from India are also regarded as being less able to support their wives economically. For this reason, his wife might have preferred to marry an Australian Punjabi. If she had married a Punjabi from Sydney or Brisbane, she would have been expected to move there after her marriage.[7] From her point of view, the disadvantage of marrying someone from India is thus balanced out by the fact that she continues to live close to her own family.

In the past, little time passed before new Woolgoolga residents sponsored the migration of their parents and siblings, thus continuing the chain migration networks. With the cut in the 1990s in the numbers of migrants accepted into Australia through the family migration stream, this has become increasingly difficult.

---

6 The average costs for the visa application and the move were around Au$ 8,000. In Dharmbir's case, being sponsored to migrate to Australia, and the help he received by his in-laws to set himself up in Australia, can be interpreted as a form of dowry. Dowry, the gift from the bride's to the groom's family, is the token that seals the goodwill between the two families. Traditionally, it was one of the main points during marriage arrangement negotiations. The practice has however become increasingly symbolic among Woolgoolga Punjabis (see also Bhatti and Dusenbery 2001: 166-76; 2008).

7 Sikh girls from Woolgoolga are popular spouses in the eyes of Punjabi men in Sydney and Brisbane because they are more traditional than girls that grew up in cities. It is therefore easier for girls from Woolgoolga to find a partner in Australia than it is for Sydney or Brisbane girls.

In many cases, what started as the migration of one Sikh in the 19th century, has resulted in the settlement of more than 30 of his descendants in Australia today. Since none of the older generation today seriously considers retiring in Punjab, the number of Punjabis will increase more rapidly than in earlier times when generations replace each other rather than settling together in Australia.

Most respondents or their parents came to Australia for better economic and educational opportunities. In Doaba particularly, many families do not own enough land to provide all sons with a sufficient heritage.[8] While the oldest son usually stays on the farm and looks after his parents, younger sons often choose a professional career and migrate to towns in Punjab or overseas.

While Woolgoolga is the largest rural Punjabi settlement in Australia, other pockets of Sikhs are found along the Queensland and NSW coasts. More recently, Punjabis have moved into the agriculturally prosperous Riverina in southern New South Wales and to the irrigated lands along the Murray River in South Australia.

The consolidation of the rural Punjabi community in Woolgoolga is a special case. Punjabi migration to Sydney and Melbourne involves larger numbers.

SETTLING IN URBAN AUSTRALIA

Of 26,427 Punjabis in Australia, 9,873 live in Sydney and 8,593 live in Melbourne (Australian Bureau of Statistics, 2006). Most are recent migrants who have arrived since the abolition of the 'White Australia' policy.

Many recent migrants entered Australia under the skilled migration programme. An economically important sub-group of these professionals are the highly qualified twice migrants from Singapore and Malaysia. While all Punjabis in Woolgoolga are Sikhs, the vast majority of them being Jat Sikhs from Doaba, Sydney Punjabis are considerably more diverse in terms of religion and country of birth.

According to the 2011 Census, approximately three-quarters of Sikhs

---

8 By law, daughters inherit an equal share of their parents' property. Socially, however, this is not acceptable, as daughters also receive a dowry on marriage.

living in Australia were born in India (see pages 236-38). Most others were born in Australia, while substantial numbers migrated from other nodes of the Punjabi diaspora, particularly from South-East Asia and the United Kingdom. The diversity of birthplaces, and the fact that many Sikhs were born in countries other than India and Australia, point to considerable flows of people between various nodes of the Punjabi diaspora and the presence of twice and thrice migrants (Voigt-Graf 2001: 253-58; 2002: 111-14; 2003: 148-49). Many India-born Sikhs lived in other countries before migrating to Australia. Awtar Nahil is an example of a thrice migrant:

> I was born in Jalandhar district and lived in India until I completed my BSc. In 1953, I moved to Uganda and worked as a teacher. Employment opportunities at that time were much better in Africa than in India and wages were higher. I chose Uganda because my elder brother was already living there. . . . In 1973, we were kicked out from Uganda and went to the United Kingdom. One year later, we came to Australia. I had always admired Australia because I am a keen sportsman myself. Migrants are much better treated in Australia than in Britain. That's why we came to Australia. While we lived in Uganda, we had always planned to go back to Punjab for retirement but since we came to Australia I know that we are going to stay here.

Despite the existence of some complex migration biographies like that of Awtar, most Punjabi respondents in Sydney migrated directly from Punjab. Most respondents came for political, economic or educational reasons, or a combination of these. In contrast to the Woolgoolga Punjabis, many Sydney Punjabis entered Australia with independent skilled visas.

The chain migration networks of Sikhs in Sydney are not as well established as those in Woolgoolga. Fewer Punjabis in Sydney have relatives who arrived before or after them in Australia. Most migrated to Australia as couples or young families, while some arrived as singles, later sponsoring the migration of spouses. The process of marriage arrangements is similar to that in Woolgoolga and most marriages are arranged within Australia or with India.

SOJOURNING AT UNIVERSITIES AND THE CASE OF PAU

A special case of migration from Punjab to Sydney is that of former staff of the Punjab Agricultural University (PAU) in Ludhiana. After Second World War, under the Colombo Plan scholarships were granted to students from poorer Commonwealth countries to enable them to obtain higher education in countries like Australia. By 1970, Australia had trained 1,001 Indian students under the scheme (Gabbi 1998). A considerable number of them were Punjabis. This migration — albeit temporary at first — constituted the first wave of educated Punjabis to Australia. Gurcharn Singh Sidhu, who published an article on Sikh migration to Sydney (Sidhu 1999), was among the first batch of five Punjabi students who were awarded postgraduate scholarships. All five returned to the Punjab after the completion of their Ph.D.s, later occupying key positions as professors at PAU. These returning Ph.D.-holders were crucial in determining future migration of students and academics from PAU to Australia:

> At first it was a trickle and then it became almost a flood with not only recent graduates from PAU but also many of its faculty. So great has been the recent migration from PAU that the joke is that every Singapore Airlines flight from New Delhi to Sydney brings yet another member from PAU and that pretty soon an alternate PAU campus could be set up here. — Sidhu 1999: 13

Today, PAU has around 1,400 academic staff while an estimated 250 families of former staff live in Sydney. At PAU, Australia is widely regarded as a safe, clean and prosperous country with good educational opportunities. More specifically, two factors were responsible for the migration flow. First, in the early 1990s visa application procedures were quick and most applications successful. Second, internal administrative rules of PAU were favourable for migrants. Staff members could take up to five years leave without pay while their positions would be kept vacant. They thus had the chance to migrate abroad on a trial basis, knowing that if they were unsuccessful, they could get their former positions back. As a result, many departments have suffered greatly from the vacancies, especially as it is almost impossible to hire someone on a temporary basis in India.

Subeg Jaggi was one of the former academics interviewed in Sydney, where he worked as a train-guard. He had been a lecturer in the Department of Plant Pathology for 16 years before migrating to Australia in 1996 with his family:

> We came to Australia to offer our children a better life and also because one never knows how bad the situation in Punjab will get again. We chose Australia because I had friends here and they had told me that Australia is good. . . . I quite like it but my family moved back to India in 1998 because they did not like it. My kids did not like their school because there is no respect for teachers in Australia. And my wife could not find a job. In India she was a teacher and in Sydney she only got casual factory work. [. . .] I have not yet decided whether I stay or return to Punjab. I like some things in Australia but there are many things that I don't like. There is too much leniency towards drugs in Australia and everybody smokes. People don't have respect for each other. There are so many people with bad manners and bad attitudes. When I work in the trains, I often hear dirty language and people are drinking and sometimes urinating in the trains. . . . I could get back my former position at PAU because I am still on leave. I don't know whether I want to go back there because my former colleagues would make fun of me and they would be ahead of me in the department and I would find that very humiliating.

Six months after this interview in Sydney I visited PAU in Ludhiana, and to my surprise I met Subeg there. He works again in his former department but has not yet made up his mind where to settle eventually. His case demonstrates the difficulties of migrating and returning.

Some recent developments have reduced the extent of migration of PAU staff to Australia. First of all, visa procedures for Australia now take up to five years. Canada, for which procedures currently take about two years, has become the preferred destination country. More importantly, numbers have been reduced by a policy change at PAU. Staff members travelling overseas on a residence visa are asked to retire from their positions before leaving. This forces them to make up their minds before migrating.

AUSTRALIA'S POPULARITY COMPARED TO OTHER DIASPORIC NODES

An important question in regards to Punjabi migration concerns the popularity of Australia compared to other potential destination countries. Many Punjabis rank the various nodes of the Punjabi diaspora according to their popularity. This became obvious during interviews in Australia and India, as well as through other indicators. Looking at the situation in Punjab, the majority (16 of 28 respondents) had no intention to emigrate. Nine respondents were planning to move abroad and six had already applied for residence visas (five for Australia and one for Canada), while seven were undecided whether or not to try to emigrate. The popularity of Australia among the respondents was primarily a result of the sampling method of this survey, where all respondents had relatives in Australia. Gurdev Singh's answer was typical:

> I haven't applied for residency abroad but I am thinking of applying for Australia because my sister lives there. I think the US is the best country because career opportunities are best there. Canada is good too. The living standard is high but the climate is bad. The best thing about Canada is that it is easy to sponsor family members. One of my friends just moved back from Canada because he didn't like the winter. For me, Australia would be best because my sister could help me settling there. That's the main reason why I would apply for Australia.

Asked about the United Kingdom, Gurdev says:

> The British colonised us and that's why I don't want to live there. There is also too much racism there. For me, I would only move to the US, Canada or Australia. New Zealand receives migrants too but the economy is not good and there are no chances for migrants.

In his answer, Gurdev ranked several potential destination countries. Like Gurdev, most respondents regarded the United States as the most favourable country in terms of economic opportunities, though were concerned about safety problems. Canada was often considered the second best option, in particular because of its generous family migration programme, its high living standard and its potential role as a stepping-stone to the United States. North America is followed by Australia and the United Kingdom. While the United Kingdom was the preferred destination in the 1960s, it is today largely regarded as unattractive due to problems with racism and fewer economic opportunities compared to North America and Australia. New Zealand was also considered unattractive in terms of economic opportunities. Non-English-speaking countries were rarely looked at as potential destination countries.

fig. 7.7 Remembering Vaisakhi by Sikhs in New Zealand (indianewslink.co.na)

The ranking of countries also becomes obvious in the process of marriage arrangements (Voigt-Graf 2002: 117-19). Overseas Sikhs from higher-ranking countries can make more demands. A dowry paid for a daughter's wedding to a Sikh settled in the United States is on average higher — other conditions being equal — than that paid to an Australian Sikh. Another indication of the ranking of countries is the occasional breaking of the rule of patrilocality. As already discussed, husbands from India routinely join their wives abroad. Likewise, if a marriage is arranged between a boy from a non-Western country such as Malaysia and a girl from a Western country such as Australia, the boy usually moves to the girl's place. Sometimes even marriages between two Western countries result in the breaking of the patrilocality rule, as Prianka of Sydney explains:

> My parents and brothers and sisters are all here in Sydney. Only one of my brothers moved to the US after he got married to a Punjabi girl there. He wanted to move to the US anyway because he thought he could find a better job there. So when my parents looked for a spouse for him, they specifically looked in the US. They contacted distant relatives of ours and they knew of a family that was looking for a husband for their daughter. That's how my brother met his wife.

In the case of Prianka's brother, a marriage was used to strategically open a migration door to a more attractive country. If a marriage is arranged between two Western countries and the boy comes from the country that is regarded as less attractive, such as Prianka's brother's marriage between a girl from the United States and a boy from Australia, patrilocal rules are not always broken. The fact that they are occasionally broken, points to a hierarchy in countries.

The diversity of birthplaces of Australian Sikhs suggests considerable flows of people between various nodes of the diaspora. It may also underline the existence of a hierarchy of diaspora nodes, in which Australia ranks above the United Kingdom and South-East Asia, because considerable numbers of Punjabis born there now live in Australia. Even though the United States and Canada both have a substantial Sikh population, few Sikhs born there live in Australia. This may point to the higher ranking of Canada and the United States in the hierarchy of preferred destinations, as few Punjabis born there are prepared to move to Australia.[9] The countries of birth of Australian Punjabis thus seem to confirm the popularity ranking of destination countries. To confirm this assumption, a comparison with the birthplaces of Punjabis in North America, the United Kingdom and South-East Asian countries would be necessary. If birthplaces indicated hierarchy, which in all likelihood they do, some Australian-born Punjabis would live in North America, whereas few would live in the United Kingdom and South-East Asia. Ballard's research, among Punjabis in the United Kingdom; points to substantial migration flows of highly educated British-born Punjabis to Canada and the United States for employment reasons. Marriages across the Atlantic are also popular among British Punjabis (Ballard 2000: 16). Another indication of the popularity ranking of countries is linked to the social status an Australian Punjabi family receives by hosting overseas kin. The prestige for the hosts depends on the source country of the visitors, with the highest status increase derived from hosting relatives from the United States.[10]

---

9 The fact that few New Zealand-born Punjabis live in Australia is linked to the comparatively small number of Punjabis in New Zealand, rather than to New Zealand's popularity ranking (see Bilimoria 2013b).

10 Even though the United Kingdom is not seen as an attractive settlement country, it retains a comparatively high social prestige, especially among rural Punjabis in India and Australia. Punjabis in Woolgoolga receiving →

In short, Sikh migration to Australia has become increasingly diverse over the last century and a half. Starting with migration from a few villages in the Doaba region, when young Jat Sikh men left for Australia and led commuting lives between Australia and their natal villages, there is now a variety of migrants. Nowadays, migration flows from Punjab to Australia are largely composed of professionals from urban areas but also include students, skilled workers and semi-skilled labourers, and temporary migrants, with many twice migrants among them. Finally, many Punjabi migrants who arrive in Australia do so not as individuals but in cascading chains along paths of kinship, friendship and colleagueship.

fig. 7.8: Sikh wedding (*photo:* Sukh)

← visitors from the United Kingdom derive considerable social status. In addition, Woolgoolga youths look at the Punjabi youths in the United Kingdom with envy, because 'they are cool'. Similar sentiments are not found among Sydney's Punjabi youths.

8

It's a Small World: Two Graves

Jayant Bhalchandra Bapat and *Manpreet Kaur Singh*

Two Graves (Jayant Bhalchandra Bapat)

AUSTRALIAN history is full of fascinating accounts of ordinary people who came here to make a better life for themselves and succeeded in spite of overwhelming odds. This was especially true in the case of the South Asian hawkers. They came alone leaving behind their families, suffered incredible hardships, often relied on a poor meal of nothing but bread and pickles, were humiliated and looked down upon by the white society and had no permanent place to stay. Most of them would carry their goods in a large sack on their back and travel long distances to sell them. Some of the lucky ones later bought a small horse cart in which they travelled hundreds of kilometres everyday and slept at night. In the cart they carried exotic goods for sale, such as silks, dress materials, toys, jewellery and so on, to remote communities, many of which were associated with fossicking for gold. The money these hawkers made was sent back to their families; it was the sole source of support for many of them.

It was a something of a chance event that led me to the graves of two of the Victorian hawkers, Ali Buc (Bux) and Gunga Singh. I was holidaying with my wife at a hotel in Dunkeld. On our arrival at the hotel, we were given a wonderful folio book of black and white photographs with the title, *A Dunkeld Portfolio*. While browsing through its pages, I came across an intriguing photograph of a grave. The modest inscription on the headstone as could be read from the image declared its interred resident simply as 'Ali Buc, Indian Hawker'. The grave looked totally neglected and appeared to be on its own (see photographs under 'Dedication'). I decided to contact the tourist information bureau the next morning.

I have always found Australian country folk to be very friendly and ever smiling. The lady at the desk at the tourist bureau the next morning was no exception. She was, however, totally unaware of the grave and could not tell me where it was situated, but she had a bright idea. There was a woman in her late eighties who lived with her son on a nearby farm and she would know. She rang this person straightaway. As expected, the old lady was able to tell us where the grave was. She made it a point to tell us that it was a long way from all of the Christian graves, in a corner of the Dunkeld cemetery. While I was browsing through the tourist literature at the tourist office, the phone rang again. It was the same old lady who had forgotten to tell me to go to Hamilton as well and inspect the grave of Gunga Singh, another Indian hawker. She also offered to send me more information about these two hawkers and told me about Len Kenna and Manpreet Kaur Singh. I quickly went to Hamilton cemetery and photographed the grave of Gunga Singh.

Within a few weeks, I got a large envelope in the mail. It was from Mrs Terry Nicholson, the lady mentioned above, and it contained information about Len Kenna, an Australian historian, who had grown up in Hamilton and remembered a Sikh hawker called Gunter Singh who visited his home frequently. Mrs Nicholson also mentioned that a charming young lady called Manpreet Kaur Singh from SBS (Special Broadcasting Service) had come and interviewed her. Back in Melbourne, I wasted no time in contacting Manpreet. She was kind enough to come and see me at my home and gave me a fascinating account of her researches into the Indian hawkers. Perhaps the most important and well-known example was that of Pooran Singh who had lived in the Warrnambool area. Here then is the story of Pooran Singh in Manpreet's own words.

The Remarkable Story of Pooran Singh's Ashes

(Manpreet Kaur Singh)

I have been managing the Punjabi programme for SBS Radio since 1991. I met Len Kenna, a historian, nearly fifteen years ago and was fascinated by the history of Indian hawkers that he had painstakingly collected over the years. Len has written plays about these hawkers in country Victoria and has personal childhood memories of interacting with them. He clearly remembers turbans drying on the washing-line in his backyard and the aroma of the wonderful curries and johnny cakes that a Sikh hawker named Gunter Singh made for his family, when he camped in Hamilton. Over the years, I have interviewed Len a few times on SBS Radio and written about his work for international publications. These, in turn, have brought me a wealth of information from people around the world but especially from small country towns in Australia, about how local Australian residents mingled freely with Indian hawkers.

An article I wrote for *India Today*, which was republished on the website Sikhchic, and still generates great interest among people of Indian origin around the world.

I have now collected many photographs, anecdotes and valuable pieces of oral history that have thus come my way over the past few years and am currently working on the story of Bud Singh, another Sikh hawker who lived in Yerranderie (NSW) and whose name is about to be commemorated on a special plaque at local hospital in Camden.

It were Len who told me about the ashes of a hawker called Pooran Singh that were still being held at the funeral parlour in Warrnambool where his funeral service was conducted decades ago. Len introduced

fig. 8.1: Plaque to Pooran Singh

me to Alice Guyett-Wood, the owner of the parlour, and I met her in May 2010 to interview her for SBS Radio. Once the story was aired, it took on a life of its own, connecting people from India, Australia and England together with a legendary cricket star, on a goodwill mission that is best described as "the Pooran phenomenon". Luckily for me, SBS took this on as a special project and I was able to travel to India to document this landmark journey via many platforms – radio, video, blog and other content on air and online.

Pooran Singh was a Sikh from the village of Bilga in Punjab, who landed on Australian shores as a young 30-year-old man in 1899. Like many other Punjabis of his time, he worked as a hawker, selling goods from his horse-cart, travelling from one country town to the other. He had left his family behind in Punjab and spent the remaining 47 years of his life in country Victoria. He died on 8 June 1947 at Warrnambool & District Base Hospital, Victoria, aged 77 years.

Pooran Singh's funeral was conducted by Guyett's Funerals, who have run their family business in Warrnambool over a very long period (for at least three generations). The present owner of the funeral parlour is Alice Guyett-Wood. It is possible that her grandfather presided over Pooran's funeral service in Warrnambool. Pooran had left instructions that, according to Sikh tradition, he desired to be cremated, not buried. His body was therefore sent to Melbourne by train to the only crematorium at that time, which was in the eastern suburb of Springvale (The Necropolis). Records at Guyett's Funerals indicate that he was cremated on 10 June 1947 at 11.45 a.m. Interestingly, the records state his religion as 'Hindoo' (a generic term for all Indian nationals of the time), and that an amount of over £53 was paid for the funeral service, which would have been roughly six months earnings for an average hawker in those days. It must be noted that cremations were very rare back then (see p. 74); Pooran's cremation seems to be the only one recorded in Warrnambool for the year 1947. Incredibly, Pooran's ashes were preserved by three generations of the Guyett family in deference to his wish that they be sent to India and dispersed in the Ganges River.

I broadcast Alice Guyett-Wood's interview on 24 June 2010. Alice recalled that, just before her father Jack Guyett died in 1986, he shared with her his sentiments about Pooran's remains in their care:

> We should have done something about Pooran's ashes. We should have sent them to India because he wished them to be immersed in the River Ganges.

There was no written instruction to convey this wish, but it was passed down through the generations of the Guyett family. When asked why they still kept the ashes, even after six decades, Alice simply said:

> We didn't have the authority to dispose them off, so we just held them. In fact, I had thought that we may even go to India one day and fulfil Pooran's last wish.

Len Kenna and his research partner Crystal Jordan had a copy of Pooran Singh's will, which revealed that he had grown to be quite a wealthy man. When he died, his assets amounted to £2,376, clearly a result of many years of diligent saving. The money was distributed according to Pooran's wishes to his relations in India by the executors of his will, with some money going to a few local residents of Warrnambool, who presumably took care of him in the last stages of his life. But nearly £1,500 was sent to India, with £360 apiece for each of his four nephews Gurbachan Singh, Chanan Singh, Milka Singh and Kartar Singh. The will named them as the sons of Sultani Ram of Upper Bhopa, Bilga, who was Pooran's brother.

The 'White Australia' policy was officially enforced in Victoria in 1901, which excluded all non-whites from entering the country. However, Len Kenna believes that many thousands of Punjabi hawkers were already living and working in Australia by then, having arrived earlier as 'coolies' and camel drivers (see Chapter 2 and Appendix B, pp. 354-68). Len also thinks that the hawkers were embraced by all sections of the local population in Victoria. The children loved them since they played games with them and told them incredible stories; the women loved them because they brought them exotic goods as well as items of daily need, and showed them a great deal of respect; the men loved them because they played good cricket! The Australian countryside is dotted with memorials and remains of these men, even though they are almost forgotten in the annals of history. Sadly, a majority of the hawkers lived lonely, desolate lives, travelling long distances alone to sell their wares, seldom getting an opportunity to be with their compatriots, and almost never reuniting with their families back home. But Pooran's story was destined to have a happier ending.

Alice Guyett-Wood got fairly emotional while talking about Pooran Singh's ashes: she was keen for them to make their final journey back to India. 'After 63 years, I think it's about time that they were returned', she said. It was truly amazing to see that this Australian family had respected the last wishes of an Indian hawker whom they did not know personally. It was clear that Pooran had become an integral part of their family history. Incredibly, even the trustees of the Warrnambool cemetery extended this respect to Pooran Singh, who they regard 'as their own'. In the late 1980s, they decided to commemorate Pooran's presence in Warrnambool by installing a plaque at a memorial wall at the cemetery, with his ashes safely placed in a niche behind it. When Alice brought up the possibility that the ashes may soon be returned to India, the trustees reportedly said, 'We'll send the ashes back, but we'll still keep the plaque on the niche wall, because Pooran *was* here!'

There is yet another Punjabi hawker who is commemorated at Warrnambool cemetery — a search of the records revealed that Milki Ram Gandhi, also of the village Bilga in Punjab, who died at Warrnambool in 1930 and a prominent grave and headstone mark his final resting place in the cemetery.

On 25 June 2010, my article about Pooran Singh's ashes was published in the Indian daily, the *Hindustan Times*. It took just one day to trace Pooran's extended family to an obscure village in Punjab called Uppal Bhopa. The family had built their house in 1950 with the money Pooran had bequeathed to his nephews. The house still stands today and proudly bears the inscription, 'S. Pooran Singh, Australia. 1950'. I believe that the two inscriptions about Pooran Singh summarise the spirit of this entire story – the plaque at the Warrnambool cemetery in country Victoria which says 'Pooran Singh, Indian Hawker, died June 1947', and the second one in the ancestral house in a remote village of Punjab saying, 'Pooran Singh, Australia, 1950'.

This amazing Oceanic-Indian 'find' was featured prominently in Indian newspapers. Things moved very rapidly after that. Upon hearing this amazing story, Kapil Dev, the Indian cricket legend, decided to visit Australia to collect Pooran's ashes, arriving in Melbourne on 22 July. Harmel Uppal, Pooran's great-nephew, flew in around the same time from the United Kingdom. The dignified and emotional ceremony of handing over the ashes to Kapil Dev and Harmel Uppal took place on

fig. 8.2: Ashes of Pooran Singh

fig. 8.3: Immersion of the ashes of Pooran Singh

25 July at the Warrnambool cemetery, witnessed by hundreds of people who had specially travelled from Melbourne, to be part of that historic moment. Importantly, this took place at a time when the world media was saturated with stories of violence against Indian students in Melbourne. Kapil Dev talked of building a "bridge of goodwill" through this story, by demonstrating how Australians have loved and respected Indians since they first arrived in Australia. Alice Guyett-Wood and her brother Brian Guyett handed over the ashes that their family had preserved for 63 years. After collecting the ashes, Kapil Dev, Harmel Uppal, Len Kenna, his research associate Crystal Jordan and I flew to India amidst wide-spread media attention. The ashes were finally dispersed into the Ganges at Haridwar on 31 July 2010 (*figs*. 8.2 and 8.3).

The impact of Pooran Singh's final journey to his homeland has been deep and far reaching. It is a story of mutual respect that cut across cultural and historical divides – revealing a little known part of Australia's pre-federation multicultural fabric. It has added a new historical dimension to the relationship between Australia and India and has fostered a unique feeling of closeness between the two countries.

Many country towns around Australia are looking at their history to document their 'Indian connection'. The radio documentary 'Pooran's final journey' was chosen a finalist at the 2010 UN Media Peace Awards, in the category 'Promotion of Multicultural Issues'. Educational Services Australia has commissioned the blogs that I wrote during "Pooran Singh's final journey" as a resource for high school students in Australia, to promote understanding of Australia's multicultural and multiracial history. Significantly for all those cricket lovers for whom 'Ashes' has had a very different meaning until recently, a small Victorian town called Warrnambool, a Punjabi migrant named Pooran Singh, historians Len Kenna and Crystal Jordan, Australia's SBS Punjabi radio programme and the Indian cricket legend Kapil Dev have changed that forever! Pooran Singh's memory will forever remain in the hearts and minds of many locals in Warrnambool and, incredibly, even though I was present at the moment when we immersed Pooran's ashes in the holy Ganges, I'm certain that some part of Pooran will continue to remain with us, right here in Australia.

9

Sikh Practices and Gurdwara in Australia

Carmen Voigt-Graf with *Purushottama Bilimoria*

SIKHS in India and elsewhere are conscious of being a distinct community, in terms of their religion and their ethnicity. They remain grounded in the teachings and prescriptions promulgated by the tenth Sikh Guru, Guru Gobind Singh (as we saw in Chapter 7, pp. 184-86). In the West generally, Sikh practices have adapted to the secular environment and facilities available. During the early 1980s when trouble erupted, Punjab was besieged by radical Sikh factions seeking establishment of a separate state of Khalistan. Sikh communities throughout the world responded in different ways. Some Sikhs, particularly the youth and more zealous members, began to propagate a more orthodox way of life for all Sikhs. The rediscovery of the past glories of Sikhdom, its affinities with neighbouring Muslim states, and the possible results of a deep politicisation of the religion, contributed to growing confidence among the Sikh leaders and lay members alike. Even some of those who had a nominal sense of being a Sikh, became involved in and spoke for the 'Sikh struggle'. The reactions to the political crisis in Punjab revealed the differences between India-direct Sikh migrants and twice migrants from South-East Asia and East Africa, some of whom publicly distanced themselves from Indian Sikhs. In addition to such differences in political outlook, Sikh life in Australia differs considerably between rural and urban areas and is therefore discussed separately.

The existence of *gurdwaras* is generally a good indicator of the presence of a well-established Sikh community. In Australia, all major cities have at least two if not more *gurdwaras*. In addition, there are *gurdwaras* in some small towns. In New South Wales, there are two *gurdwaras* in Woolgoolga, one in Murwillumbah in northern New South Wales, with a Sikh population of some 200, and one in Griffith in the Riverina catering

fig. 9.1: *Gurdwara*, Craigeburn, Melbourne (photo: Philip Hughes)

for some 100 Sikh families. Likewise, the small towns of Edmonton and Gordonvale in Far North Queensland have *gurdwaras*, as do Renmark and Glossop in South Australia. Whether in urban or rural areas, Sikh communities struggle to maintain their ancestral culture in the diaspora. Compared to other Indian communities in Australia, the presence of an older generation of Punjabis — a result of their long history of migration to Australia — helps with the cultural maintenance.

Sikh Practices and Life in Rural Australia

In regards to interactions between Sikhs and the wider Australian society, there is considerable social distance between the two. The situation in Woolgoolga is particularly revealing because there are only two main communities in Woolgoolga Punjabis and Anglo-Australians (for more details on Sikh practices and life in Woolgoolga, see Voigt-Graf 2001: 258-63; 2002: 130-33). Sikhs are a sizeable part of the population and they have been there long enough to consider Woolgoolga their primary or only home. While relations between Sikhs and Anglo-Australians are largely trouble-free, social interaction is limited. It is a common assumption of Sikhs that Anglo-Australians drink too much, have brought drugs to Woolgoolga and are generally of loose morals. Sikhs reject their Anglo-

fig. 9.2: Berkeley students at *langar* at Gurdwara Sahib El Sobrante, CA (photo: P. Bilimoria)

Australian neighbours' lifestyles, which they view as being too individualistic and hedonistic and lacking a sense of family life and respect for elders. There are also some practical problems of interaction, such as the vegetarianism of many Sikhs, which they think rules out their attendance at Anglo-Australian functions. Many Sikhs stress the long history of Indian culture compared to what they regard as a young and almost non-existent Australian culture. A feeling of moral and cultural superiority is often implied. Ethnic boundaries are thus patrolled in order to keep people within the Punjabi community. Surinder Kaur's sentiments and concerns are shared by many Sikhs in Australia:

> Culture is very important for us. Our main concern is to keep our culture and we are afraid that our children will lose our culture and language. That's why we take them to India every two years. We really want them to keep the link to Punjab.

In Woolgoolga, the Punjabi population is comparatively uniform, most being Jat Sikhs from Doaba. Due to their large numbers, they have successfully transplanted their culture to Woolgoolga. The community at large is conservative and most have adhered to traditional marriage customs. Only about fifteen Sikhs in the whole area are married to Anglo-Australians. Hence intermarriage is not as common among Sikhs as perhaps among the larger Indian immigrant community and Australian-born Indian adults. Punjabi is spoken in all households though half of the respondents also use English with their Australian-raised children. All children are able to converse in Punjabi though often unable to read and write the Gurmukhi script. Among the older generation, knowledge of Punjabi is often better than English. There is however a growing intergenerational gap, with many Australian-raised Punjabis attempting to carve out greater freedoms for themselves. So far, however, parents and the more traditional community members have retained the upper hand. The pressure to conform is high because the entire family loses honour if one member behaves inappropriately.[1] Close kin in Punjab also suffer from lost family honour if their relatives in Australia behave inappropriately, as gossip travels back to Punjab. Sikhs in Punjab have therefore a considerable interest in their overseas relatives' behaviour.

Even those Sikhs who have sufficient critical distance from the Woolgoolga community to realise the enormous social pressure, find security in being part of the community and having all their cultural needs easily met, such as Paramjit, who reflects:

> Sometimes I wish I had more freedom but then there are many advantages of living in Woolgoolga. It's just like in India. When I do my shopping I meet other Punjabi women and we stop for a chat. On Sundays, I can just go to the *gurdwara* if I feel like it. In Sydney, they have to drive a long way. That's why we feel sorry for Punjabis in Sydney or Brisbane. It's so easy here and being

[1] Expectations on women are particularly high. The only fully acceptable role for them is to be happily married. The arrangement of marriages is an indicator of family honour because the negotiations depend on the status of the families involved. Thus, if a Punjabi man wants to marry his daughters or sisters into good families, his success depends on his family's reputation. An individual not living up to the traditional image thus risks not only her own marriage chances but those of others in the family. If a woman gets divorced, not only she but also her children, parents, siblings and to a lesser extent her more distant relatives lose honour. The siblings and parents are also likely to feel pressure from the community to talk to the woman and make her reconsider her decision (see also Bhatti and Dusenbery 2001: 124-28; 2008).

> part of the community makes me feel secure. [. . .] My sister for instance lived in Sydney but she moved up here again when she had her first kid. She only wanted to stay for a few months so that we could help her with the baby. It's more than five years now.

The first *gurdwara* in Australia was opened in Woolgoolga in 1968. Soon thereafter, a dispute broke out over the use of chairs during *langar* (traditional communal meal) breaking with the tradition of sitting on the floor.[2] A second *gurdwara*, therefore, the Guru Nanak Sikh Gurdwara, opened in 1970. This initially modest building on a hill, at the southern end of Woolgoolga, was replaced in 1994 by a purpose-built *gurdwara* that has since become the most famous of Woolgoolga's landmarks. The social lives of Woolgoolga Sikhs revolve around the two *gurdwara*s and most families have joined one of the two temple societies. The Sunday ceremonies in the Guru Nanak Sikh Gurdwara regularly attract some 500 worshippers and are followed by *langar*. In addition, Punjabi language and Sikh religious classes are organised to instruct young Woolgoolga Sikhs on the foundations of their religion and culture.

There is a visible Punjabi presence in the streetscape of Woolgoolga. Apart from the two *gurdwara*s, there are two Indian restaurants and one street is called 'Arkan Avenue', a symbolic gesture to the Arkan family, members of which were among the pioneering Punjabi settlers in the area. Moreover, Sikhs have fought symbolic struggles for local belonging. These include the right to hold street processions and the wearing of the *kirpan* (the symbolic small sword worn by Sikh men), and a battle before the Anti-Discrimination Board to be granted access to the Woolgoolga RSL (Return Soldiers' League) Club wearing a turban. (Sikhs do not cut their hair as it is seen as a gift of God. Men cover their hair with a turban, which is not removed in public.) Sikhs in Woolgoolga have also supported the battles of Sikhs in other parts of Australia, such as when a Sikh was not allowed to join the ambulance service in Cairns because of his turban. This shows their commitment to fight for local belonging, not only in Woolgoolga but also more generally in Australia. Woolgoolga in particular is a very visible node of the Punjabi diaspora.

In short, Sikhs in Woolgoolga have developed a strong sense of local

---

2 The chairs were finally removed in 1994, following an order from the highest Sikh authority in Amritsar after the visit of a high priest to Woolgoolga.

belonging, while at the same time managing to preserve their traditional culture. Eleven of the twelve respondents in my survey were homeowners, which in itself shows a commitment to a long-term residence and local belonging. Moreover, all twelve respondents felt at home in Australia, more than anywhere else, and were not planning to return to India. In this, they differed from the Sydney Punjabis whose answers were more diverse. Only twelve of the twenty respondents in Sydney considered Australia their home.

Despite their local roots, it is interesting that one of the most important social divisions within the Sikh community in Woolgoolga is based on the area of origin in Punjab. In the past, almost all Woolgoolga Sikhs came from the Doaba region but the numbers of 'outsiders' have gradually increased through marriage arrangements with families from other parts of Punjab and subsequent chain migration. Today, about one quarter of Woolgoolga Sikhs come from the Malwa and Majha regions of Punjab. However, they continue to be regarded and treated as outsiders. One respondent from the Malwa region who grew up in Woolgoolga recalled that she was made to feel an outsider even at school: 'The other girls said to me 'you are from across the river. You are not one of us', and they called me Malwa.' The phenomenon is interesting because it shows that the geography of Punjab on a very local level continues to influence social relations among Punjabis in Woolgoolga, even among those born and raised in Australia. Only in a small rural community, like Woolgoolga, with a relatively homogeneous population that has to a considerable extent kept its former village ways and mindset, is a situation like this thinkable. In Sydney and other Australian cities, where the Sikh population is much more diverse in terms of regional origin, country of birth and caste, local rivalries between adjacent districts in Punjab pale before the overall diversity.

A Diverse Sikh Community in Australian Cities

Urban areas attract a different kind of Sikh migrant, one with a more professional and cosmopolitan outlook. An important distinction within the Sikh community in urban areas in Australia is that between India-direct migrants and twice migrants, which is also reflected in the variety of associations and places of worship (for more details on Sikh life in Sydney, see Voigt-Graf 2002: 136).

In Sydney, the first Sikh association was established in 1969 in the suburb of Parklea, though initially no purpose-built *gurdwara* was constructed. Less than ten years later the community split and a group of predominantly East-African Sikhs formed a separate association in the suburb of Revesby. Both of these associations split again to increase the number of *gurdwara*s in Sydney to four, with the other two in Austral and Turramurra. The *gurdwara* in Turramurra was opened in 1980 and is frequented by Punjabis from Singapore and Malaysia. A purpose-built *gurdwara* was opened in Parklea in 1997. The largest single donor was a Sikh from Singapore. Many Sikhs have an interest in promoting Sikhism globally as well as in establishing connections with other communities that can be drawn upon for future marriage arrangements or business dealings. In respect of the hospitality extended to the community, the *gurdwara* is also a place of refuge for the needy and it serves as a temporary hostel for itinerant guests.[3]

For some time, Melbourne boasted three major Sikh collectives, each with its own *gurdwara* and variations in services. An earlier worship-hall was disbanded after an unresolved legal dispute in 1992. Victorian Sikhs have consolidated their identity around two *gurdwara*s. In December 1993, one of the two Sikh groups in Melbourne invested Au$ 1.3 million and converted a massive former mail-sorting centre so as to house a congregation of up to 1,000 people. In 2009 a large new purpose-built *gurdwara* was opened at Craigieburn, to the north of the city. Each weekend *langar* (food from the community kitchen) inside the *gurdwara* is served to the congregated patrons and guests, sponsored by a Sikh family. Three *raagi*s (musicians) are brought from India on a rotational basis to perform regularly, to help lead devotional singing and chanting during regular prayer services. Each temple attracts a cross-section of Sikh immigrants from the different regions.

As is the case for Hindu priests in Australia (see Chapter 3), Sikh leaders are not locally trained, as there are no institutions offering training in ancient and classical recitations. As we have seen, training for Hindu temple priestcraft takes place mostly in India, although the community priests learn a modicum of rituals and rites necessary for social ceremonies.

---

3 In 1998, a new *gurdwara* was opened in Australia and the construction of a new building has commenced in Revesby as well.

Other kinds of leadership training among Sikhs are more random and community leaders emerge out of their own educated background to ascend ranks within community groups or associations. It is on-the-spot training for most of them. In any event, the *Guru Granth Sahib* is written in Gurmukhi script, and a substantial majority of Sikhs are able to read this.

The congregations of some *gurdwara*s are split between more orthodox and less orthodox factions. The major differences in outlook, however, are between Indian origin Sikhs and twice migrant Sikhs. While many Sikhs from South-East Asia have retained the custom of wearing turbans, decades of residence in the multicultural societies of Malaysia and Singapore have affected the outlook of Sikhs who have come to Australia from those countries. They are generally more cosmopolitan, Westernised and affluent than Sikhs who have come directly from India. Many also have strong leanings towards the Punjab; it is a distinctive feature of modern Sikh migrants to have a degree of commitment to, and concern about, the political situation in Punjab. Thus, the distinguishing feature of the Indian Sikhs is that, much like Sikhs in Britain and North America, in Australia they have tried to form a lobby to monitor and respond to events, especially those connected with the Sikh struggle for greater autonomy in Punjab. However, not all Sikhs here have welcomed the issue of a separatist movement bent on establishing Khalistan.

Many Malaysian and Singaporean Sikhs are culturally not as closely linked with Punjab as they are with multi-racial Malaysian or Singaporean society, and they keep somewhat aloof from their Punjabi counterparts. In the wake of the unrest in Punjab in the mid-1980s, South-East Asian Sikhs distanced themselves from Indian Sikhs, afraid that the political crisis in India might reflect adversely on all Sikhs in Australia. It remains to be seen whether these differences within the Sikh community will persist into the future, or whether kinship and religion might in the long run be stronger than the diversity of migrant experiences. Generally, however, the political overtones of Sikh religious congregations of the 1980s have all but disappeared, as liberal and more orthodox Sikhs together have taken control of the local organisations. The emphasis is increasingly towards maintaining cultural identity, conducting ceremonies and rites according to the Sikh scriptures, and strengthening ties with India.

In addition to religious associations around the *gurdwara*s, all major cities are home to a number of Punjabi cultural associations, which include formal and informal associations, general cultural associations, caste-based associations (such as the Ramgarhia Welfare Association in Sydney) and an alumni association of former PAU students and staff.[4] Most associations organise between three and five cultural and social functions per year, which are attended by the bulk of their members. In Sydney, these functions usually include barbecues, harbour cruises and other get-togethers for their members, special events for children, and often a cultural evening that is advertised within the entire Indian community. There are also Sunday classes in which children can learn the Punjabi language. The recently reorganised Sikh Association of Victoria provides particular incentive, especially for adolescent Sikhs, to become involved in community activities, ranging from cultural dinners to sporting events (e.g. *kabaddi*, holding your breath and trying to escape a ring of opponents) to *gidha* (folk dance) and 'Bangra Beat Nites', the latter a fusion of traditional Punjabi music and dance with reggae and rap rhythm. A handful of Sikh leaders have been involved in bringing together the plethora of 'Indian' community groups under a fledgling Federation of Indian Associations. But this leadership has been resisted by the internecine Indian associations and factional infighting among the elites from within the Indian community.

Apart from the regular gatherings in the *gurdwara* on Sundays, and the personal festivals such as naming children, initiation into the Sikh community (*amrit*), marriage and funerals, there are a range of public festivals. Most of these celebrate the birth or death or one or other the Sikh Gurus. Among the major festivals is the celebration of Guru Nanak's birthday (*Guruparb*), which usually occurs in October or November each year, Guru Gobind Singh's birthday on 5 January and *Vaisakhi* which falls on 14 April marking the founding of the *khalsa* by Guru Gobind Singh. The installation of the *Guru Granth Sahib* in the Golden Temple is celebrated on 1 September and its declaration as the eternal Guru for Sikhs on 20

---

[4] One important event in the Sikh calendar in Australia is the Sikh games held annually at Easter. Sikhs from around the country meet to compete in various sports. Other than these games, there is little interaction between Sikh associations in the various towns, with most contact being restricted to kinship networks.

October. The martyrdom of Guru Arjan is remembered on 16 June and the martyrdom of Guru Tegh Bahadur on 24 November. These festivals are often celebrated by a 48-hour non-stop reading of the *Guru Granth Sahib*. The readers take turns, reading for two hours at a time. There is also usually a prayer service and a celebratory meal. There may also be lectures and prayers (Gurdarshan Singh Gill and Ranjit Kaur 2010).

Cultural and Economic Transnationalism of Australian Sikhs

While Sikhs have planted local roots in Australia, they have managed to retain many aspects of their traditional culture. Close contacts with relatives in Punjab are one reason, another being the establishment of *gurdwaras*, and cultural, religious and recreational associations in Australia. Today's technologies have greatly increased cultural links with India. Bollywood movies for instance are released in the diaspora shortly after their first screening in India. Diasporic Sikhs invite cultural and religious performers to their overseas settlements, the trips often entirely paid for by diaspora members keen to remain culturally connected. Moreover, as noted above, most Sikh temple priests are trained in India. Furthermore, many individuals perform important life rituals in both countries. Wedding ceremonies of diasporic Sikhs, for example, usually take place in Punjab, with a second ceremony held later in Australia. These examples indicate a transnational cultural existence and the importance of transnational networks along which cultural goods and performers travel in all directions (for more details on Punjabi transnational activities, see Voigt-Graf 2002: 119-50).

Economic transnational activities manifest themselves on the kinship level as well as the level of the wider economy in Punjab. In the past, when only single men migrated to Australia, they sent most of their savings home to support their families and acquire economic assets, especially land. Some invested in the family farms, by buying tractors and other machinery, or by funding the construction of a tube well in their natal village. Over time, this has led to over-mechanisation of Punjabi agriculture, with the result that today some 30% of tractors in Punjab are not in use (Gopal Krishan, Pers. Comm., 12 April 2000). In addition, 1,400,000 tube wells in Punjab have led to a considerable depletion of the subsoil water table. Today, most Jat Sikh farms in Punjab are well equipped and there is little need for further assistance in this regard. It was the Green Revolution in Punajb that made such a prosperous and productive environment for all residents of the region.

Remittances from the diaspora have also contributed to inflated land prices and a housing boom, particularly in the Doaba region where most Sikh migrants come from. Travelling through the region, one cannot but notice the presence of large vacant mansions, of privately sponsored public works such as elaborate entrance gates to villages and newly-refurbished *gurdwaras*. Of 32 Sikhs surveyed in Australia, 23 retained a house in Punjab. Sometimes, this was a share in the family house. In other cases, the house was solely owned by overseas Punjabis and was generally vacant and looked after by a relative. Hardly ever is it rented out because it is felt that tenancy laws in India favour the tenant too much. Most houses owned by overseas Punjabis are therefore not a source of income but are status symbols and places to stay in during return trips.

The main factor determining whether and how much money was remitted by Australian Sikhs was the existence of close relatives overseas — the closer the relatives the more likely it was they received support — and how needy they were. Since most relatives of Australian Sikhs are from an urban professional or a relatively wealthy Jat Sikh farming background, few depended on remittances for their daily maintenance. In regards to the rural households in Punjab, the absence of one son who would otherwise have to be fed from the family farm was of a much greater economic benefit to the peasant household in India than remittances could ever be. This explains why few respondents in this survey sent regular remittances to Punjab. Some households in Punjab received occasional remittances, such as for special family occasions or when they needed additional money for a specific purpose.

In addition to supporting their relatives, most overseas Punjabis retain property in India, often in the form of a legal share in the family farm or house. In most farm households, the eldest son stays in India and looks after the family farm and his parents. If a younger brother has moved overseas, he continues to legally share the family farm but usually does not receive any income from the farm. If all sons have migrated overseas, the land is often given to a more distant relative, such as a cousin or nephew, who would usually pay rent for the land. One respondent in

Doaba for example was looking after 10 acres of land that he jointly owned with his brother, who lived in Canada. He was also renting another 10 acres from his cousin in Woolgoolga.

Cultural maintenance in Australia would be impossible without the construction of transnational linkages and a constant flow of cultural goods and people from the subcontinent. In both Woolgoolga and Sydney, the first generation of migrants has maintained a strong commitment to the culture they left behind. In Sydney, few second generation Punjabis have yet reached adulthood. It remains to be seen to what extent they will adhere to their cultural traditions after they start independent lives. The second generation in Woolgoolga has so far largely followed in the footsteps of their parents.[5] The system of arranged marriages to Indian-raised spouses is particularly important in this regard and it has ensured that the traditional culture survives longer in the diaspora. Sikhs in urban areas are less conservative than their rural counterparts, their community is less tightly knit and social control is less restrictive. As a result, cultural changes have occurred more rapidly. For instance, the children of only six respondents in Sydney are able to converse in Punjabi, compared to all children in Woolgoolga. The second generation particularly in urban areas are generally less concerned with maintaining the cultural heritage. In matrimonial advertisements, for instance, some young Indians stress that they are 'fun-loving' and 'like to enjoy life to the max', whilst 'caste is no bar'.

The Sikh Gurdwara[6]

Sikhs, like all South Asians in Australia, have endured many hardships, and experienced prejudice on account of their colour or religious background. They have persevered despite social and cultural alienation. In the broader context of mainstream Australian society, the Sikh *gurdwara* with its 'Word as God', symbolises the struggle of maintaining a distinctive community within a decidedly multicultural and ethnically plural environment. There is a certain austere sophistication about the Sikh temple set aside for purposes of worship. Unlike the Hindu temple, the appearance

5 There is nevertheless an obvious generational gap in terms of values and tastes (see Singh 2001: 236-37).

6 This section on Sikh Gurdwara is written by Purushottama Bilimoria, drawing on various extant studies.

of the Sikh temple is of more recent origin, that is to say, with the emergence of the Sikh religion. The Sikhs themselves refer to their temple as *gurdwara* (occasionally transliterated as *gurudvara*), literally meaning 'the doorway to [the dwelling place] of the *guru*'. The latter epithet, *guru*, in this instance does not refer to any personal *guru* or line of teachers, from long past or living, but rather to the *Guru Granth Sahib*, the holy scripture of the Sikhs, that symbolically brings together the teachings of the ten *gurus* under one canon, and so is revered and worshipped in the temple as both the supreme *guru* and Divine presence in a single moment. The presence of *gurdwaras* is both a sign that there is in the vicinity an established Sikh community, and a symbol of their solidarity (certain degrees of factionalism and inter-community schism notwithstanding).

STRUCTURE AND ARCHITECTURE

First, a little on the structural significance of the *gurdwara*. Except for the major *gurdwaras* that serve vast throngs of the Sikh population scattered across Punjab and other regions of north-west India (for example, in Delhi), most *gurdwaras* are modest buildings, without the elaborate ornamentation and display of shifting architectural styles that one sees with Hindu temples or Christian cathedrals. The *gurdwara* has modestly small domes (sometimes incorporated into the front fa®ade of the building), but is otherwise generally devoid of massive domes, spires or decorative pillars, or a *sanctum sanctorum*, at some remove from the congregation, where an image of a god (or several gods) might be installed for purposes of worship and visual edification. The exception is the landmark iconic *gurdwara* in Amritsar, which stands as a pinnacle among all Sikh *gurdwaras* with its gold-covered semi-domes and pillars (built stylistically closer to the then flourishing Mughal mosque, with a hint of the north Indian Hindu temple), and long since a desirable site of pilgrimage for all Sikhs at least once in their lifetime. Most *gurdwaras* do not attempt nor intend to replicate its style, particularly outside the subcontinent, and yet one cannot fail to recognise a *gurdwara* by its distinctive architectural fa®ade (see image of the Woolgoolga and Melbourne *gurdwaras* in Australia (*figs*. 7.5 and 9.1).

There are indeed features about the spatial *loci* in the broader context of the host environment and the tensed sensitivities of the community concerned, that are striking in their own ways and are of some significance to consider. Tavleen Kaur, basing her study on the construction of the largest *gurdwara* in the United States, in San Jose, California, suggests that 'from the perspective of spatial theory, the *gurdwara* is what Homi Bhabha calls the third space', and as such stands apart from the cultural grid of the urban sprawl.[7] What this implies is that the *gurdwara* is something of a geographic and temporal anomaly in the eyes of municipal politics surrounding its construction inasmuch as it resists assimilation to the heterotopia space around it by its somewhat gothically unconventional and towering physical appearance. And yet the pioneer Sikhs who arrived along the West Coast of North America in the early 1900s appear to have set a dubious trajectory towards 'Becoming America'. This latter is suggested in the very naming of a heterotopic-style museum exhibit created by contemporary Sikhs in the same location in Yuba City in the same state (which boasts among the earliest Sikh settlements in the US) narrating their own history and projecting the grand 'American Dream' possibly desired by the community *or*, more cynically, hoisted upon them by the host community. The *gurdwara* resists being utilised for the kind of narrativisation and alien futuristic dream as the museum-exhibit tends to.

There are nevertheless other features of the *gurdwara* that have very specific religiously-nuanced symbolic significance that may serve to remind the adherent of some elements of the essential teachings or faith of the Sikhs, or bring to the present awareness something from their collective historical memory as a people who have lived elsewhere and moved over generations to another, distant, location. In principle, a *gurdwara* can be established inside any building or premises that has roof above it and space large enough to serve two kinds of purpose: the purely religious and the social. The first purpose entails a large enough open space called a *darbar* or *diwan* hall within the enclosure of the premises that is set aside for the community members to congregate for worship and recitations centred around the *Guru Granth Sahib*. The *darbar* has doors on all four sides, indicating that the temple is open to people of all castes and creeds, and that it is not exclusive to Sikh members or the initiated. A raised platform called *takhat* (throne), within a canopy decorated with cloth,

[7] Homi Bhabha, *The Location of Culture* (1994); Tavleen Kaur, 'The Limit of Public Spatial Expression: Negotiation of Religion, Law and Secularism among Diasporic Communities', paper present at Sikholar Conference, Stanford University, Palo Alto, CA, February 2013 (unpub., courtesy of P. Bilimoria).

houses the *Guru Granth Sahib*, brought out from an adjoining room where the holy book is kept at night (see Chapter 7, p. 189; p. 233 below).

We may note that the service involves more often than not singing by a group (*raagis*), with the accompaniment of music played on a harmonium; the congregation is expected to join in the hymnal singing (*kirtan*). Collective worship is called *diwan* and can take place any time on any day. As the members enter the *darbar*, each one bows in front of the *Guru Granth Sahib*, making a simple offering and then greeting the congregation in a low voice with the words, *waheguru ji ka khalsa, sri waheguru ji ki fateh* (the Sikh vows allegiance to the *guru*, sovereignty belongs to the *guru* alone). The service begins with the singing of a hymn called *Asadivaar*, composed by Guru Nanak. Other hymns from the *Guru Granth Sahib* are then also sung, accompanied to the sound of the musical instruments being played at the same time (Magloff 2005).

SOCIAL SPACE AND LANGAR

The second purpose of the *gurdwara* is served by a large adjoining space, or an extension to the building (sometimes fulfilled by the common basement space in most urban buildings), where members meet to participate in community activities, which could range from gathering for festivities to partaking of food (*langar*), for which a suitably equipped kitchen is built-in. Devout members often sponsor such *langar* service. Outsiders, regardless of caste, race or creed, are not prohibited from taking the food in the Sikh *gurdwara*: indeed, they are welcomed. Other social functions cover a range of life-cycle rites, such as marriage, infant-naming ceremonies, religious service for the departed, and these are accompanied by recitations from the *Guru Granth Sahib*. A library and learning area is also part of the open social space, where classes in Sikh teachings and perhaps also the predominant language of the Sikhs, Punjabi utilising the Gurmukhi script, are presented. As the most recent census data has shown, Punjabi is the fastest growing language in Australia. It is partly due to the local *gurdwaras*, as well as the sizeable increase in the number of Sikhs and Punjabi-speaking people choosing to settle in Australia, that this momentum to retain and disseminate the language among its own people, particularly the second and third generation, is kept up. There is one more social function that may be added to a *gurdwara*, although it is not that common in Australia, namely, providing guest accommodation for intermittent travellers within the community who may have come from another state or from overseas.

As Marie de Lepervanche describes in her careful study of the Sikhs in Woolgoolga, there are five main ceremonies the Sikhs recognise as part of the life-cycle rites:

> When a baby is four to five weeks old the mother takes the infant to the *gurdwara* to be named. Here the *granthi* [the officiating priest] opens the *Granth Sahib* at tandom and the first letter of the first word on the opened page becomes the initial letter of the child's name. When the *granthi* announces the initial, members of the family suggest appropriate names and eventually choose one. Before marriage, a betrothed boy and girl may meet each other with family and other kin at the temple. Then prayers are said and the families exchange gifts. Marriages are also solemnised: special hymns are read and the couple circumambulates the holy book. Throughout the service the priest chants and the congregation responds. Guests go to the couple and give them gifts of money; they also shower them with flower petals and bedeck them with garlands. On two occasions I saw the bride's mother give the groom a coconut for fertility and luck. At funerals, mourners do not take the body into the temple, as in Christian rites, but after a death a service is held in the *gurdwara* and sometimes also in the house of the deceased. At one funeral I attended, prayers were said at the funeral parlour and at the crematorium in addition to the *gurdwara* service.
>
> — de Lepervanche 1984: 166

While the construction of the *gurdwara*, particularly in the diaspora, does not call for an elaborate architectural feat, and none of the items within the temple exhibit the ornamental styles of Hindu temples or Christian churches, there is nevertheless a distinctive quality or presence that marks off a Sikh place of worship. The outside fa®ade may boast a style of architecture that modestly recalls the synthesis of Hindu and Muslim places of worship. It will be marked by a yellow or orange triangular flag called the *nishansahib*, and light, which reminds all that the light of the Divine is ever present and that everyone is welcome at any time. Displayed on the flag is the symbol of Sikhism, the *khanda*. The interior of the temple may be adorned with a simple canopy flanged across by decorative cloth, the *khalsa* symbols, and a raised altar that serves as the 'throne' (*takhat*), indeed the royal *sanctum* for the *Guru Granth Sahib*, the holy book, during the period of the service. No lamps, candles, incense, bells or other such items are permitted. The Holy Granth is continually revered with the waiving of a whisk or feathered fan by the *granthi* (priest). The loyal worshippers, as they enter the temple hall, walk straight to the *sanctum* and make a gesture of bowing to the majesty of the Guru by touching their forehead on the ground. As they step backwards to take a seat on the floor of the hall, they make a modest offering, usually of coins or a note by the altar.There is also a resting place from nightfall for the *Guru Granth Sahib*, known as the *sachkand*. As the *Guru Granth Sahib* is isomorphic with the formless Divine Principle that pervades the whole universe, there is no holier place than the *sachkand*.

During the public service, the priest continuously fans the *Guru Granth Sahib*. He then reads from the ornamentally covered holy book, which is opened by the *granthi* only at the time of religious service and certain rites. There may be long readings (which could last for a number of days depending on the nature of the service or festivities being observed), and there may be short ones lasting an hour to two hours. As we have seen, priests (*granthis*) and *raagis* are often brought from a major *gurdwara* on the subcontinent to conduct recitations and expound the meaning of the portions of the holy book being recited.

In the two temples in northern New South Wales that de Lepervanche studied, towards the end of the service, 'the whole congregation joins in the *Ardas*, or Sikh prayer, which invokes divine grace and recalls the past tribulations and triumphs of the wider Sikh community' (p. 164). The ceremonies conclude with distribution of *karah parsad* (a sweet made from semolina cooked in ghee) which the members eat from their cupped palms; this is called *bhog*, the concluding ceremony of a Sikh ritual. This is followed by announcements about house-keeping matters, the names of the sponsors of the day's *langar*, birthdays of members or their children, and the ensuing classes that are held for the younger generation. We end this chapter with Sikh invocation of the *guru* (p. 231):

waheguru ji ka khalsa, waheguru ji ki fateh

10

A Statistical Profile of the Sikh Community in Australia

Philip Hughes

THE Australian census, which is conducted every five years, provides the most detailed information that is available about the composition of the Sikh community in Australia.This chapter is based on analysis of the 2011 and previous censuses. It should be noted that the census can provide information about those who identify themselves as Sikh, but it does not provide any information about people's religious practices.

Change Over Time

There were Sikhs in Australia in the 19th century, but the numbers are unknown. The censuses that were held in the various Australian states did not clearly distinguish the various people from South Asia, mostly classifying them all as 'Hindoos'. (As indicated earlier, this classification was widely used in British India, Great Britain and its global colonies, and in North America as well.) The first reliable count of Sikhs in Australia occurred in 1991. At that time, the Australian census counted 7,795 Sikhs living in Australia.

Further information about the origins of the present Sikh community can be gathered from the information about the time when they arrived in Australia. That information, from the 2011 Census, is presented in Table 10.1.

Very few Sikhs arrived prior to 1970. A few arrived between 1971 and 1985. From 1985, the numbers began to increase. A huge number arrived in the five years from 2006 and 2011 and the size of the Sikh community more than tripled over that period. The Sikh community grew considerably faster during those five years than did any other religious community, growing at double the speed of the Hindu community.

Table 10.1: The Year of Arrival in Australia of Sikhs Living in Australia in 2011

Year of Arrival	*Number of Sikhs*	*Percentage of Sikhs*
1910-60	101	0.2
1961-70	202	0.3
1971-80	1,064	1.8
1981-85	1,115	1.9
1986-90	2,261	3.9
1991-95	2,659	4.5
1996–2000	3,671	6.3
2001-05	7,368	12.6
2006-11	40,112	68.5

Source: Australian Census 2011.

One of the early Sikh communities in Australia was Woolgoolga, on the New South Wales coast, 26 km north of Coffs Harbour. Of the 371 Sikhs who were born overseas living there in 2011, 64 arrived prior to 1970. Some Sikhs trace their history several generations in Australia before the 'White Australia' policy in 1901. They began to gather in Woolgoolga during Second World War because of labour shortages and the relaxation of the prohibition of non-European labour in the banana industry. After the war, they began to develop their own banana plantations. The 2011 Census recorded that 661 Sikhs were living in Woolgoolga and has one of the highest concentrations of Sikhs in Australia.

Apart from Woolgoolga, there are several other rural towns with a number of Sikhs including Griffith, Renmark and Coff's Harbour. These are exceptions to the general patterns of Sikh settlement in Australia. Most Sikhs have settled in the major cities rather than in rural areas. The largest Sikh community is to be found in Melbourne and in 2011 consisted of almost 28,000 people. The second largest was in Sydney, with 18,800 people, as shown in Table 10.2. While there are several thousands of Sikhs in Brisbane, Perth and Adelaide, and just over 1,000 in the Australian Capital Territory, there are very few in Hobart.

Within the various cities, Sikhs are spread quite widely. The local government area with the highest number of Sikhs was the Sydney area of Blacktown, where 6,821 Sikhs were resident in 2011. However, the Sikhs only constituted 2.2% of the population there. The highest suburban

Table 10.2: Numbers of Sikhs Living in the States and Territories and Capital Cities of Australia 2011

State/City	*No. of Sikhs*	*Percentage of Total Population (%)*
Australian Capital Territory	1,059	0.30
New South Wales	21,706	0.31
Sydney	*18,800*	*0.43*
Northern Territory	244	0.11
Darwin	*176*	*0.14*
Queensland	9,428	0.21
Brisbane	*7,132*	*0.35*
South Australia	5,289	0.33
Adelaide	*4,587*	*0.38*
Tasmania	219	0.04
Hobart	*150*	*0.07*
Victoria	29,441	0.55
Melbourne	*27,874*	*0.70*
Western Australia	4,911	0.22
Perth	*4,751*	*0.28*
Australia	**72,297**	**0.34**

concentration of Sikhs was in the Greater Dandenong in outer Melbourne, where they constitute 2.7% of the population. In Melbourne, Sikhs are spread widely in a range of suburbs across the city, from Brimbank in the west, Whittlesea in the north, to Casey in the south-east. There is no evidence of Sikhs developing 'Sikh ghettoes' in Australia.

Immigration Patterns

Because of the extent of recent Sikh immigration, less than 1% of all Sikhs in Australia were born in Australia of Australian-born parents. Another 15% were born in Australia with one or both parents born overseas. The remaining 84% were born overseas as shown in Table 10.3.

The majority of Sikhs have come to Australia from Punjab, India. However, many have come from other places, reflecting the fact that many migrants move country several times. The Sikh communities in places

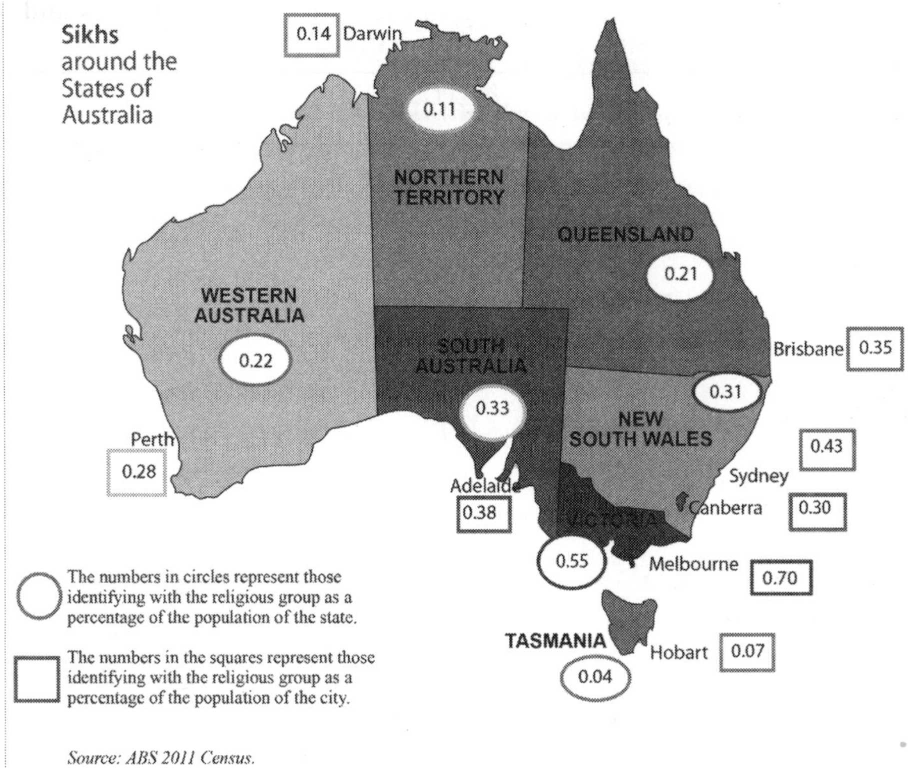

fig. 10.1: Sikhs as a percentage of the population in the states, territories and capital cites of Australia 2011

Table 10.3: The Region of Birth of Sikhs Living in Australia in 2011

Region of Birth	*No. of Sikhs*	*All Sikhs Living in Australia* (%)	*All People Living in Australia* (%)
Born in Australia with parents born in Australia, or parents' birthplace unknown	437	0.6	51.0
Born in Australia with one or both parents born overseas	10,485	14.5	18.8
Born overseas	60,512	83.7	24.6
Birthplace not known	863	1.2	5.6
Total	**72,297**	**100.0**	**100.0**

Source: Australian Census 2011.

such as Malaysia, Singapore, Kenya and Fiji have become sources of members of the Sikh community in Australia (Table 10.4).

Table 10.4: The Country of Birth of Sikhs Living in Australia in 2011

Country of Birth	*No. of Sikhs*	*Total Sikh Community (%)*
India	55,312	76.51
Malaysia	1,738	2.40
England	838	1.16
Singapore	806	1.11
New Zealand	422	0.58
Kenya	405	0.56
Fiji	286	0.40
Canada	78	0.11
United States of America	49	0.07
United Arab Emirates	48	0.07
Scotland	46	0.06
Thailand	41	0.06
Pakistan	37	0.05
Tanzania	31	0.05
Indonesia	29	0.04
Afghanistan	29	0.04
Vietnam	27	0.04
Philippines	24	0.03
Uganda	22	0.03
Kuwait	20	0.03
Hong Kong	20	0.02
Myanmar	13	0.02
Italy	12	0.02
Other parts of Europe	52	0.07
Other parts of Asia	39	0.05
Other parts of Africa	29	0.04
Other parts of Oceania	10	0.01
South America	3	0.00
Total	**60,509**	**83.70**

Source: Australian Census 2011.

According to the Census, close to 5,500 Sikhs (8% of the community) indicated that they spoke English at home. In comparison 80% of the community spoke Punjabi. Another 6% spoke Hindi at home, in most cases indicating that they or their parents used to live in northern India outside the Punjab. The remaining 6% of the Sikh community spoke a wide variety of languages reflecting the various parts of the world from which they had come, as shown in Table 10.5.

Table 10.5: The Language Spoken at Home by Sikhs Living in Australia in 2011

Language	*No. of Sikhs Speaking this Language at Home*	*Sikh Community in Australia* (%)
Punjabi	57,641	79.73
English	5,460	7.55
Hindi	4,213	5.83
Indo-Aryan not further defined	1,709	2.36
South Asian languages, not further defined	1,232	1.70
Malay	140	0.19
Urdu	91	0.13
Italian	35	0.05
Thai	35	0.05
Vietnamese Fijian	34	0.05
Hindustani	22	0.03
Gujarati	17	0.02
Indonesian	14	0.02
Mandarin	12	0.02
Tamil	10	0.01
Other European languages	27	0.04
Other Asian languages	66	0.09
Other languages	63	0.09
Not stated, inadequately described, or non-verbal	1,522	2.10
Total	**72,296**	**100.00**

Source: Australian Census 2011.

While few Sikhs speak English at home, more than half indicated on the census that they spoke English very well. Eight per cent indicated that they did not speak English well or not at all. It was a little more common for women to indicate they could not speak much English.

Marriage and Children

As the majority of Sikhs living in Australia arrived between 2006 and 2011, the age profile is highly skewed. Compared with just 14% of the Australian population as a whole, 43% of the Sikhs were in their twenties in 2011. Just 14% of the Sikh community were 40 years of age or older, compared with 47% of the Australian population. There were some young Sikh children under 10, but few Sikhs in their teenage years.

There is also a large disparity in gender in the Sikh community, with just 30,000 women (42%) compared with 42,200 men (58%). It is more common for single men than single women to migrate to Australia to seek work. In many cases, parents back in India arrange marriages and the men return to India for the wedding, before bringing their brides back to Australia.

According to the 2011 Census, there were just 3,972 female Sikhs in Australia who had never married, compared with 14,122 males who had never married. There were also more married male Sikhs than married

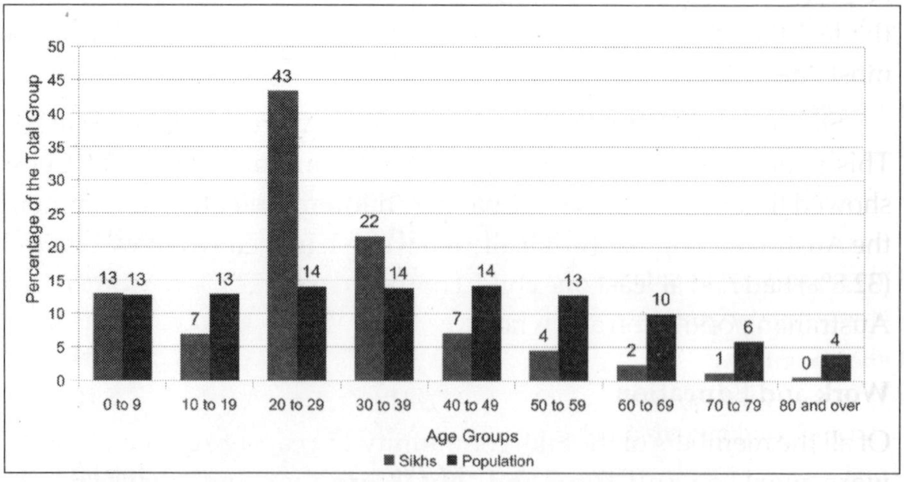

Source: Australian Census 2011

fig. 10.2: Age profile of Sikhs compared with the Australian population

Table 10.6: The Marital Status of Sikhs by Gender Living in Australia in 2011

Marital Status	*Male Sikhs*	*Female Sikhs*	*Total Sikhs*	*Sikhs (%)*	*Australians (%)*
Never married	14,122	3,972	18,094	25.0	27.7
Widowed	168	625	793	1.1	4.4
Divorced	500	682	1,182	1.6	6.8
Separated	380	392	772	1.1	2.5
Married	20,544	18,870	39,414	54.5	39.3
Not applicable (under 15)	6,513	5,528	12,041	16.7	19.3
Total	**42,227**	**30,069**	**72,296**	**100.0**	**100.0**

Source: Australian Census 2011.

female Sikhs. While a few male Sikhs may have married outside their religious community, it is likely that some Sikhs had wives overseas, mostly in India, at the time of the 2011 Census. Some would be in the process of arranging for their wives to join them in Australia. Others may be in Australia temporarily, expecting to return to their family in India.

Divorce is relatively uncommon among Sikhs. A total of 1,182 Sikhs indicated on the census that they were divorced: 1.6% of the community compared with 6.8% of the wider Australian community. While this may be partly related to the young age of the Sikh community, it also reflects the fact that divorce is not accepted as readily among Sikhs as among most Australians (Table 10.6).

Sikh families were similar in size to other Australian families in 2011. This is partly because of the age of the community. The 2011 Census showed that Sikh women were having children earlier than is common in the Australian population. Of all Sikh women in their twenties, one-third (32.8%) had had at least one child, compared with 22.5% of women in the Australian population as a whole.

Work and Education

Of all the members of the Sikh community 15 years of age and older, 37% were working full-time and 30% were working part-time. The unemployment rate was low: only 2.2% were looking for full-time work and 2.3 looking for part-time work at the time of the 2011 Census. However, 22% of the Sikh community 15 years and older were not in the workforce. These figures were quite different for men and women as shown in Table 10.7.

In the Australian population, similar numbers of women work full-time and part-time. However, most men who are in the labour force work full-time and just 12% work part-time. While some working part-time are doing further studies on a part-time basis, it may well be that many have taken part-time work because they have not been able to find full-time work.

In total, 7,074 Sikh men and 6,349 were women involved in some form of tertiary study. About one-third of them were in university,

Table 10.7: The Workforce Status of Sikhs by Gender Living in Australia in 2011

Workforce Status	*Male*		*Female*		*Total*	*Population*
	No.	(%)	*No.*	(%)	*Sikh* (%)	(%)
Employed full-time	16,432	46.0	5,861	23.9	37.0	36.7
Employed part-time	11,062	31.0	7,168	29.2	30.3	17.6
Employed, away from work	1,736	4.9	1,011	4.1	4.6	3.6
Unemployed looking for full-time work	588	1.7	727	3.0	2.2	2.1
Unemployed looking for part-time work	591	1.7	801	3.3	2.3	1.4
Not in labour force	4,531	12.7	8,440	34.4	21.5	33.0
Not stated	6,513	2.2	532	2.2	2.2	5.6
Total	**35,715**	**100.0**	**24,540**	**100.0**	**100.0**	**100.0**

Source: Australian Census 2011.

Table 10.8: Numbers of Sikhs by Gender Compared with the Australian Population Attending Various Educational Institutions in 2011

Educational Institution Attending	*Male Sikhs*	*Female Sikhs*	*Total Sikhs*	*Total (%)*	*Population (%)*
Pre-school	516	424	940	1.3	1.6
Infants	2,082	1,763	3,845	5.3	8.2
Secondary	1,440	1,222	2,662	3.7	6.2
TAFE	2,168	1,581	3,749	5.2	2.2
University	2,550	2,581	5,131	7.1	4.3
Other	2,356	2,187	4,543	6.3	0.8

Source: Australian Census 2011.

another third at a TAFE institution and the final third were in other forms of education, such as community-based or industry-based courses, including language schools as shown in Table 10.8.

Many Sikhs are highly educated. Almost 30% of the total Sikh community in 2011 had a university degree. This compares with 15% of the wider Australian population (Table 10.9).

Sikhs, like the Hindus, are particularly well qualified in the area of management and commerce and in engineering and related technologies. Many others are skilled in information technology. But there are also a high proportion, particularly among women, who are qualified in society and culture, health and education (Table 10.10).

Table 10.9: The Level of Education by Gender of Sikhs Compared with the Australian Population in 2011

Level of Education	*Males*	*Females*	*Total*	*Total (%)*	*Total Population (%)*
Doctoral Degree	269	191	460	0.6	0.6
Masters Degree	3,526	3,899	7,425	10.3	2.3
Graduate Certificate	528	474	1,002	1.4	1.4
Bachelor's Degree	6,716	5,731	12,447	17.2	10.9
Diploma	7,796	3,860	11,656	16.1	6.5
Certificate	4,185	1,981	6,166	8.5	14.6

Table 10.10: The Field of Education of Sikhs by Gender Compared with the Australian Population in 2011

Field of Education	*Male Sikhs*	*Female Sikhs*	*Total Sikhs*	*Sikhs (%)*	*Australian Population (%)*
Management and commerce	4,832	3,403	8,235	11.4	8.1
Food, hospitality and personal services	4,967	2,727	7,694	10.6	2.3
Engineering	4,488	425	4,913	6.8	7
Society and culture	1,962	2,469	4,431	6.1	4.7
Information technology	2,765	1,183	3,948	5.5	1.3
Health	848	2,000	2,848	3.9	4.1
Education	559	1,862	2,421	3.4	3.3
Natural and physical science	572	797	1,369	1.9	1.3
Agriculture and environment	730	119	849	1.2	0.9
Creative arts	359	445	804	1.1	1.5
Architecture and building	272	79	351	0.5	2.5

Source: Australian Census 2011.

While many Sikhs are well educated, the work they reported in 2011 did not reflect their levels of qualification. Thirty per cent of them had university qualifications, but only 20% of them were managers or professionals. Close to 40% of Sikhs were machinery operators and drivers, or labourers. In 2011, many Sikh males were working as taxi drivers or drivers for the post office, or as couriers (Table 10.11).

This is partly a result of the fact that the community is very young. Recent immigrants have been willing to take whatever work was available to them. Over time, it is likely that many of these people will find work that is more compatible with their qualifications.

In 2011, employed Sikhs were heavily concentrated in the transport, postal and warehousing industry sector, in accommodation and food, and in health care and social assistance. More than 40% of Sikhs were

Table 10.11: The Occupation of Sikhs by Gender Compared with the Australian Population in 2011

Occupation	*Sikh Males*	*Sikh Females*	*Sikh Persons*	*Sikhs (%)*	*Population (%)*
Managers	2,490	883	3,373	7.8	12.9
Professionals	2,736	2,686	5,422	12.5	21.3
Technicians	4,052	1,067	5,119	11.8	14.2
Community and Personal Service	1,817	2,865	4,682	10.8	9.7
Clerical and Administrative	1,827	1,645	3,472	8.0	14.8
Sales	1,629	1,661	3,290	7.6	9.4
Machinery Operators and Drivers	8,192	294	8,486	19.6	6.6
Labourers	5,637	2,567	8,204	19.0	9.4
Other/not stated	846	375	1,221	2.8	1.9
Total in Workforce	**29,226**	**14,043**	**43,269**	**100.0**	**100.0**

Source: Australian Census 2011.

employed in these three industry sectors. Given their qualifications, one would expect that their presence in manufacturing and professional, scientific and technical services, and in information media and telecommunications, might increase in future years (Table 10.12).

Income Levels

Few Sikhs have come to Australia to escape political or religious persecution, although the freedom to worship in their own way makes Australia a desirable destination. More impelling, however, is the fact that incomes are much higher in Australia than most Sikhs would be able to earn in India or in most other parts of the world. Sikhs have had a reputation as being entrepreneurial. They are prepared to work and have looked for opportunities for developing businesses in many places around the world, such as Thailand, Singapore, Malaysia, Kenya and Britain. Many Sikhs have come to Australia in their search for a good return for their labour. The census information on personal income provided a measure in 2011 of how well they were doing (Table 10.13).

Table 10.12: Industry in which Sikhs are Employed Compared with the Australian Population 2011

Industry	*Sikh Males*	*Sikh Females*	*Sikh Persons*	*Sikhs (%)*	*Population (%)*
Agriculture, forestry and fishing	1,162	505	1,667	3.9	2.5
Mining	73	16	89	0.2	1.8
Manufacturing	3,084	916	4,000	9.2	9.0
Electricity, gas, water and waste services	189	66	255	0.6	1.1
Construction	725	97	822	1.9	8.2
Wholesale trade	1,253	344	1,597	3.7	4.0
Retail trade	2,419	1,502	3,921	9.1	10.5
Accommodation and food services	3,677	1,979	5,656	13.1	6.5
Transport, postal and warehousing	7,273	403	7,676	17.7	4.8
Information media and telecommunications	399	181	580	1.3	1.8
Financial and insurance services	766	640	1,406	3.2	3.8
Rental, hiring and real estate services	169	70	239	0.6	1.6
Professional, scientific and technical services	1,045	577	1,622	3.7	7.3
Administrative and support services	1,332	884	2,216	5.1	3.2
Public administration and safety	1,528	549	2,077	4.8	6.9
Education and training	374	873	1,247	2.9	8.0
Health care and social assistance	1,110	3,472	4,582	10.6	11.6
Arts and recreation services	137	57	194	0.4	1.5
Other/inadequately described & non-stated	2,510	913	3,423	7.9	6.1
Total	**29,225**	**14,044**	**43,269**	**100.0**	**100.0**

Source: Australian Census 2011.

Table 10.13: Personal Income Levels of Sikhs Compared with the Australian Population 2011

Weekly Income Levels (Au$)	*Sikh Males*	*Sikh Females*	*Sikh Persons*	*Sikhs (%)*	*Population (%)*
Negative	235	327	562	0.9	0.6
Nil income	2,891	6,224	9,115	15.1	7.6
1–199	1,375	2,020	3,395	5.6	7.4
200–299	2,523	2,497	5,020	8.3	10.4
300–399	4,335	2,585	6,920	11.5	9.9
400–599	6,438	3,099	9,537	15.8	11.6
600–799	6,409	2,540	8,949	14.9	10.4
800–999	3,861	1,440	5,301	8.8	8.3
1,000–1,249	2,422	1,038	3,460	5.7	7.9
1,250–1,499	1,296	736	2,032	3.4	5.5
1,500–1,999	1,327	712	2,039	3.4	6.5
2,000 or more	1,294	426	1,720	2.9	6.2
Not stated	1,309	897	2,206	3.7	7.9
Total	**35,715**	**24,541**	**60,256**	**100.0**	**100.0**

Source: Australian Census 2011.

Table 10.13 indicates that 22% of Sikhs compared with 16% of all Australians aged 15 years and older have a personal income of less than Au$ 200 per week. Women are twice as likely as men to be in this situation. While many of these people are students studying at school or at university, others are women who are keeping house or looking after children. Half of all Sikhs (51%) compared with 40% of the Australian population have an income level between Au$ 300 and 1,000 per week. There are comparatively few Sikhs (15%) compared with the Australian population (26%) with a personal income of Au$ 1,000 or more per week. This reflects the fact that the community is very young and many Sikhs have not had an opportunity to become established in their work, and that many of them are taking part-time and semi-skilled work that does not reflect their levels of education. However, it is likely that this picture will change in the future as the community ages.

Impact of the Social Profile on the Religious Community

Because the community is relatively small and young, it is not yet clear how the shape of the diaspora community is influencing the practice of Sikhism in Australia. Sikhs do not need elaborate temples for their worship and are readily able to adapt existing halls for that use. As the community has expanded in recent years, the number of Sikh *gurdwara*s has rapidly grown. Some have been existing small buildings, but there have also been some large purpose-built *gurdwara*s, such as the one on the edge of Melbourne at Craigeburn.

Many Sikhs do attend the weekly services at the *gurdwara*s. Like many new immigrant groups, they look for ways in which they can build community among people who share their language, their values and their heritage. The *gurdwara*s provide a focal point for the building of these communities and, hence, religious faith becomes a vehicle for the affirmation of their identity. While there is no statistical evidence at this time, it is likely that many Sikhs are even more focused on their religious communities than they would be in India, given their relative isolation in the Australian community.

Many Sikhs feel some tensions between that sense of identity and the traditions associated with it and their adopted homeland. Observation at a *gurdwara* makes it evident that Sikhs in Australia vary in how strictly they keep to the Sikh dress codes and rules about not cutting hair.

Since 1971, increasing numbers of Australians have been describing themselves as having 'no religion'; in the 2011 Census, 22% of Australians described themselves that way. At the same time, involvement in religious organisations has been declining. The Australian Survey of Social Attitudes (2009) found 16% of the sample of adult Australians involved in a religious organisation monthly or more often. This is down from about 23% of Australians in 1993 and 30% in 1969.[1]

It has been noted that business people have left the Christian churches over recent decades. In general, those people who see the development of the economy and material production as personal priorities attend less

1 P. Hughes, 'Are Australians "Losing Their Religion"', *Pointers*, vol. 20, no. 2, June 2010, p. 1.

fig. 10.3: Sikh youth Kirtan programme in Leamington, UK
(*Source*: Manvirsingh.blogspot.com.au)

fig. 10.4: Punjabi Bhangra dance: a diaspora delight

frequently than those for whom family life and social justice are major foci.[2]

Nevertheless, there is little evidence currently that many Sikhs in Australia are questioning their faith or dropping association with it. The business orientation of many Sikhs is not seen as being incompatible with the values of their religion. Looking at the religious identity of those people living in Australia and speaking Punjabi in the 2011 Census showed that 81% of those people identified themselves as Sikh, 13% as Hindu, a few as Muslim and a few as Christian, but only 1.2% described themselves as having 'no religion'. While it is possible that Sikhs from others parts of the world have dropped their religious identity, few Sikhs from the Punjab have done so. As we have seen, the Sikh faith both incorporated and rejected aspects of Hindu and Muslim faith and culture, and the community has always been required to maintain its identity over and against larger majorities. It may well be that this heritage will assist Sikhs in the development of an Australian identity that retains the core of the community's religious and cultural values.

---

2 P. Hughes, 'Values and Local Church Mission', *Australian Journal of Mission Studies*, vol. 5, no. 2, December 2011, p. 50.

General Reflections on the Indian Diaspora in Australia

11

11

Diversity of Indian Identity in Multicultural Melbourne[1]

Salim Lakha, Michael Stevenson and *Surjeet Dhanji*

Introduction

THIS chapter explores the expression of Indian identity in Melbourne, which in 2011 had the largest concentration of India-born population of all the capital cities in Australia.[2] The Indian presence in Melbourne is increasingly evident, both in the workforce and through the proliferation of Indian restaurants and grocery shops. The chapter questions the notion of a singular Indian cultural identity, and instead emphasises the heterogeneity of Indians in Melbourne. It argues that varying discourses in India and Australia strive to forge the idea of a unified Indian culture and community that cannot be sustained in the face of diversity and contradiction. Indeed, from the earliest nationalist stirrings in the 19th century, the question of who should be included in the Indian nation has been a matter of controversy amongst nationalists (see Chatterjee 1993: 109-10). In the past, the status of Muslims in the Indian nation has been the source of bitter conflict, and recently militant Hindu nationalists have mobilised around this issue, asserting that there is only one Indian identity,

---

1 We are grateful to Moinak Biswas (Jadavpur University) and Rashmi Desai (Adjunct Research Fellow at Monash Asia Institute) for their helpful comments on the paper. This paper was originally written in 1999–2000 before the significant influx of students from India and further settlement of Indian migrants.

2 The population of India-born Indians in Melbourne in 2011 equalled 166,595 persons compared to Sydney where it numbered 87,874 (ABS 2011). Melbourne's Indian population constituted 56% of Australia's total Indian-born population of 295,362 (ABS 2011).

and that it is derived from Hinduism (see Bhatt and Mukta 2000).

Historically, the Indian National Congress as the leader of the nationalist movement aimed to create a unified, secular nation and establish an independent state committed to making India a modern, world power. During recent years, the rapidly expanding Hindu revivalist nationalist movement has given a new twist to Indian unity by propagating the slogan 'one nation, one people and one culture' (*The Economist* 1998: 32). As many commentators on India have argued, the homogenising ambitions of militant Hindu nationalism underestimate the cultural diversity of India. By any standard, the country represents a unique multicultural milieu, with at least sixteen major languages, a population professing many faiths, and a myriad of local communities displaying significant cultural, linguistic, geographical and even ecological complexities.

Notwithstanding this diversity, the attempts to forge a singular identity continue both in India and overseas, including in Australia. Political considerations exert an important influence amongst those in Australia who promote the idea of a single Indian identity. An editorial in *India Link* (12 June 1995), an Indian community newspaper published in Sydney and circulated nationally, raised the perennial question 'Who is an Indian?' The editorial expressed its dissatisfaction with an official Australian publication that described the Indian community in terms of 1991 census classification. According to this classification, Indians were defined by their country of birth rather than their origin or ethnicity.[3] The editorial argued that the official enumeration of Indians underestimated their numbers because it excluded members of the various

[3] Defining Indians by place of birth, i.e. those born in India raises certain anomalies. It includes people of British ancestry born in India and who later migrated to settle in Australia. Similarly, it includes Anglo-Indians born in India but excludes people of Indian origins born outside India. In contrast to the 1986 Census of Australia, which provided information on ancestry, the 1991 and 1996 censuses did not do so. However, the censuses since 2001 have resumed collection of information on ancestry, revealing that in the 2011 Census, 390,894 persons claimed Indian ancestry, apart from the few who named their ancestry in terms of a particular Indian state or as Sikh. (See Chapter 3 for details on the geographical background of the people from the Indian diaspora in Australia.) In 2011 the number of people claiming Indian ancestry ranked eighth highest in the national population.

diasporic Indian communities settled in Australia; for example, those born in and originating from Fiji, Africa, Indonesia and many other parts of the world. It asserted that the distinction between Indians on the basis of those born in India and those born outside India was meaningless because all people of Indian origin share a common pool of culture. The political agenda of the *India Link* editorial is revealed in the following argument:

> Given the multicultural debate in Australia it is important for Indians to lobby to enlarge the definition of Indians living here. In the first instance, it builds numbers and numbers are what matter. A larger community has a greater say in convincing the mainstream about its needs. If the Indian definition is enlarged their numbers would automatically double or increase even more.
>
> — 1995: 12

Interestingly, the editorial supported its view by citing similar comments from a federal member of parliament who was present at the launch of this publication about the Indian community in Australia. Indian spokespersons in Australia often raise this issue and, at a public forum in Melbourne some years ago, a leader of one of the major Indian diasporic communities expressed the same view as that of the editorial.

There are some who wish for a greater unity amongst all Indians regardless of whether they were born in India or somewhere in the far-flung diaspora, irrespective of the many and varied differences between their compatriots. They express some angst, and even unhappiness, about the sheer vigour with which diversity is being pursued. Nevertheless, for the moment, a singular identity eludes those who entertain political aspirations.

The homogenisation of peoples of non-Anglo-Celtic background, according to several commentators, is associated with the discourse of multiculturalism in Australia, which adopts an essentialist view of culture and equates ethnicity with culture (Jayasuria 1997: 6-9). Langer, in her study of Salvadoran refugees, concurs with this criticism of multiculturalism when she asserts that multiculturalism represents immigrants in terms of 'ethnic culture' without reference to their historical background (1998: 165). Under multiculturalism, differences are distinguished on the basis of culture, which leads to both a 'fetishisation of "ethnic culture" and the construction of culture as a homogeneous category (ibid.: 175). Langer questions the notion that ethnic groups represent 'cohesive communities bound by fixed cultures' because such a characterisation does not correspond with the cultural reality of the late 20th century, which is marked by hybridity (ibid.). Similarly, Ram criticises what she refers to as the liberal conceptualisation of multiculturalism, which involves a way of dealing with cultural contact where an individual culture is viewed as a cohesive unit (1996: 134). The official discourse on multiculturalism is, therefore, unable to account for the complex and diverse ways in which identities are forged.

Though we generally agree with the view that identities are contextual and subject to change, our research reveals that such change has its limits, as explained below. The arguments about fragmented identities, which these days are very popular amongst writers who debunk essentialist notions of identity, overlook the immigrants' desire for stability in unfamiliar circumstances. As we demonstrate, this continuity is actualised through the particularities of cultural expression, which provide an anchorage for migrants. We believe there is a duality in the process of identity formation because on the one hand there is fragmentation through increasing group differentiation, yet on the other there is a striving for continuity of identity within each group.

The two important expressions of identity that we deal within this chapter revolve around food and language. Both the accounts of our informants and the extensive network of Indian associations confirm the significant meaning that people attach to food and language. As one young Indian immigrant recounting his experience of settlement in Melbourne remarked: 'If one is able to speak one's own language and eat the food then one derives some contentment in a strange land'. The rich symbolic associations connected with food and language offer a sense of continuity in the diasporic context of displacement. As our informants and interviewees constantly emphasised, food and language provide the means of establishing closeness and a sense of belonging. The ethnographic evidence on Sikhs in Melbourne, which is presented below, strengthens this argument further.

In the first place, the chapter draws on Salim Lakha's many years of participation in Indian community life in East Africa, Britain, Australia and Canada. It also draws on Michael Stevenson's understandings of diaspora experience in Melbourne and many conversations with Indian friends. Furthermore, this chapter draws on Surjeet Dhanji's observations and research amongst the Sikhs in Melbourne, as well as her first-hand knowledge of Sikh communities in East Africa and Britain. Second, this chapter is also based on in-depth interviews we conducted in Melbourne with ten people during August–October 1999. Those interviewed were from different states in India and engaged in a variety of occupations, such as medicine, business, teaching and research, driving instruction, and technical work. In the chapter, we focus on the cultural practices of Indian migrants who were born in India and settled in Melbourne. However, as discussed below the activities in which Indians participate include both those born in India and those who originate from the diaspora. These practices reveal a rich cultural landscape marked by substantial heterogeneity. It is through these heterogeneous cultural practices that people articulate their identity, maintain their links with their birthplace or homeland in India, and experience a feeling of closeness that is central to their imagining of being an Indian. Importantly, these cultural practices are not necessarily bounded by a single identity marker, although sharing a common language often exercises a decisive influence.

Previous research by Bilimoria and Ganguly-Scrase (1988a), which deals with Indians in Victoria, was based on a large-scale questionnaire survey that elicited information on a wide range of cultural and social issues. Their definition of who constitutes an Indian includes those born outside of India as well as those born in India (ibid.: 8-9). They provide a detailed picture of the Indian community taking into account certain aspects of identity formation such as the use of language, religious affiliations, marriage preferences, and the differences between the India-born and overseas-born Indians who maintain close and regular contact with India (ibid.: 73-95). This chapter, however, strives to analyse the dynamics of identity formation and its manifestations. In this study we have chosen to combine a small number of in-depth interviews with our own observations of Indians (India-born and others) in Melbourne over many years and in many contexts. We have also benefited from the rich ethnographic account of Indians in Woolgoolga, New South Wales, by Marie de Lepervanche (1984), who examined the dynamics of race and class in regional Australia. However, her study focuses primarily on experiences of the Sikhs, who represent an earlier wave of immigrants to Australia and who have engaged mainly in agricultural occupations. The research did not concentrate upon issues of diversity relating to Indians of different cultural, religious, linguistic and geographical origins. Our chapter is concerned with post-colonial immigrants from India or 'new immigrants' who are primarily from professional backgrounds (Helweg 1992: 77-78), and whose experience of Australia is shaped significantly by the multicultural milieu in which they live. It is this multicultural environment that offers them the space to express their cultural identities.

Prior to 1948 the flow of migrants from the Indian subcontinent was numerically insignificant and their settlement very dispersed, which vitiated the growth of a distinct cultural identity (Bilimoria 1996a: 13). Our observations reveal that today Indians of varied cultural, linguistic backgrounds participate vigorously in their associations in Melbourne. From the accounts of our informants, it was also evident that their participation in language-based and religious associations did not necessarily detract from their engagement with Australian mainstream culture and institutions. They therefore conform to Helweg's typology of 'new migrants', who are comfortable in both Indian and Western surroundings (1992: 80). In this study, however, we have chosen to examine the multiplicity of identity expressions primarily, but not solely, amongst India-born Indians because their practices question the homogenising discourses of identity emanating from both India and Australia. In addition, where it illuminates an issue, we draw on personal ethnographic knowledge of Indians born outside India and who may not necessarily live in Australia.

Language

In India linguistic difference corresponds largely with political, geographical and cultural difference because the various states of India are carved out along linguistic lines. Though Hindi is common to the northern part of India, various states are connected to a dominant language that defines the cultural identity of the people who traditionally belong to that region. A further complexity is that even within the dominant language there may be considerable dialect variations depending upon where particular groups dwell. The relationship of dialect and space is of great importance even though we do not explore the issue in the chapter. In Melbourne, this geographical and linguistic difference is reproduced through many of the local Indian associations that cater for people originating from the different Indian states. For example, of the 23 member associations of the Federation of Indian Associations of Victoria (FIAV), eleven of these are cultural-linguistic associations.[4] In addition, one is solely a language association, namely, Hindi Niketan, which aims to promote the Hindi language and literature. Several other cultural-linguistic associations are not affiliated to FIAV, either because they are small, informal organisations or because they are not registered. The membership of FIAV is however subject to change over time, with some groups departing and new ones seeking affiliation. Both Marathi and Gujarati literary groups, which meet periodically, and where only the respective languages must be used, are informal groups that have small numbers of literary-minded members.

The co-existence of an umbrella organisation joining together cultural-linguistic associations amongst Indians overseas is not peculiar to Melbourne. In the city of New York, for example, which has a substantial Indian presence, groups corresponding to those in Melbourne have been established since the 1970s. Thus, as in Melbourne, there are Gujarati, Maharashtrian, Bengali, Malayalee and other similar associations concerned with manifold religious and secular activities (Khandelwal 1995: 180).

The various associations in Melbourne are important sites of cultural activity and provide the communicative space where the heterogeneity and multiculturalism of India are represented and expressed. The celebration of various seasonal festivals, such as Onam from Kerala, Poila Baisakh from West Bengal and Bihu from Assam, is conducted by the respective associations, namely, the Malayalee Association, Bengali Association and the informal gathering of Assamese people, even though their numbers in Melbourne are low. Similarly, religious celebrations like Navaratri and Durga Puja are organised by the Gujarati and Bengali associations, respectively. Occasions commemorating the birthdays of local heroes, for example, Shivaji in Maharashtra, and the poets Rabindranath Tagore and Kazi Nazrul Islam in Bengal, are also celebrated by these

[4] See FIAV Newsletter, August 1999.

associations. The national celebrations such as Independence Day and Republic Day, however, are hosted by FIAV or the Australia India Society of Victoria, which is a longer established organisation compared to the former, but caters for both Indians and Australians in Melbourne and maintains its autonomous status *vis-à-vis* FIAV. Hence, at the Independence Day celebration held by FIAV in Melbourne in August 1999, around 400 people attended the dinner function, including prominent dignitaries such as the Indian High Commissioner, a federal government cabinet minister, the leader of the Australian Democrats, a minister from the Victorian government and an Australian Labour Party parliamentarian in Victoria.

In the case of some groups, for example, the Gujarati and Bengali associations, the commonality of shared language and cultural practices transcends national and even religious boundaries. Thus the Gujarati Association encompasses within its fold people of Gujarati origin from India as well as those deriving from the Gujarati diasporic communities in various parts of Africa, Fiji and elsewhere, who have settled in Melbourne. Some Muslims of Gujarati origin, from different parts of the world, have also attended annual Hindu religious functions like Diwali. Muslim participation in such events is inspired by shared cultural and linguistic bonds, and by the need for warmth and closeness in a city where the familiar circle of family members and friends is absent. In the search for friendship with people who spoke the same language, a Gujarati-speaking Muslim family from Pakistan attended the functions of the Gujarati Association. Thus in Melbourne many different kinds of Gujaratis have been able to share and enjoy a common communicative space, thereby enlarging each other's lives.

In the same vein, spoken Punjabi is common not only to Sikhs, Hindus and Sindhis but also to the Muslims in the Punjab region of India and Pakistan. In Australia Punjabi speakers draw a familiar sense of belonging to a common culture despite different political and geographical boundaries and places.

Interestingly there are manifestations of diverse cultural tendencies expressed in Gurmukhi — the written language of the Sikh scriptures (*Guru Granth Sahib*) — which is more poetic than spoken Punjabi. Gurmukhi literally means from 'the mouth of the *guru*, the disciple or teacher'. Guru Gobind Singh, the tenth and last spiritual leader of the Sikhs, was a prolific poet, equally at home in Persian (Farsi), Sanskrit and Punjabi. For instance, the *Zafarnamah* is a letter written in Persian to the Mughal Emperor Aurangzeb. It lays out the doctrine of just war (Cole and Sambhi 1978: 55-57). Guru Gobind's love of poetry can be seen in compositions in the *Adi Granth* (scriptures), which he shared and composed with some of the 52 poets at his court. The *Adi Granth* is distinctive among the world's scriptures in its inclusion of non-Sikh hymns. Hindu and Muslim writings are included in what is called the *bhagat bani*. Hindus and Muslims, Sufi Baba Farid, *pir* Kabir (born a Hindu but raised as a Muslim) and Bhagat Ravidas (a Hindu cobbler) are amongst the fifteen individuals whose writings occupy a revered space within the Sikh faith, propagating its message of universality to its adherents. Guru Gobind Singh held recitations of poetry (*kavi darbars*), in a variety of languages every full moon. Thus it is easy to understand why it is incumbent upon all Sikhs to learn Gurmukhi so that they can read and understand the scriptures — the *gurus*' literature and rich poetry, and the parables they tell. Youngsters are also encouraged to learn Punjabi for cultural maintenance and bridging the intergenerational gap (see Chapter 9, p. 221).

Sikh temples (*gurdwaras*) usually run weekend and holiday schools to expose youth to learning Gurmukhi, devotional singing (*kirtan*) of sacred music (*gurbani*) in classical *raag* form, and taught to play traditional instruments, the harmonium, *sitar* and drums (*tabla*). Such learning is often followed by a wholesome Punjabi breakfast or tea. It is at commemorative Sikh festivals that these youngsters will show off their learning by reciting poetry, singing hymns, in solo or in chorus, accompanied by music. Promising students are invited to perform with their peers during *kirtan* or oratory programmes. In keeping with technology and modernity, *gurdwaras* have installed video screens that show words to the hymns being recited — both in English and Punjabi — so that all members of the congregation regardless of religion can participate in *kirtan*. Outside the *gurdwara*, social gatherings, such as recitations of poetry and music festivals, will see large numbers of Punjabi-speaking people from different nationalities and ethnic backgrounds speaking the language that brings them together.

The Bengali Association similarly attracts both Hindu and Muslim Bengalis from India and the neighbouring country of Bangladesh. The confluence of Hindu and Muslim Bengalis in the Bengali Association in Melbourne is particularly significant because it transcends a major difference, i.e. religion, which is burdened by the bitter and violent memories of the partition of Bengal at the time of Independence in 1947. With some surprise, a Bengali informant of Indian origin, observed that in Melbourne Bengalis from India and Bangladesh freely attend the functions hosted by their respective associations, and that furthermore the social interaction between the two communities is increasing. People of the younger generation from the two groups also interact with each other, though their socialising depends upon their parents' predilection for interaction with people from one or the other community.

Importantly, both the Bengalis from India and Bangladesh participate in the cultural activities organised by the Bengali Association, as evidenced in the staging of *jatra* (Sanskrit *yatra*), which is a genre of popular drama. It is normally held on a stage that is open on all sides, leaving the actors exposed to the audience. The *jatra* involves varied themes connected with the daily lives of ordinary people and therefore evokes a strong rapport between the actors and the audience. Even though the themes of *jatra* may be somewhat different in Melbourne compared to Kolkata, the style of the presentation is the same. In 1998 the theme of *jatra* resonated strongly with all the Bengalis. It dealt with the predicament of many a family in India, dramatising the dilemma faced by a young man seeking to work overseas in the face of opposition from his mother, as well as his father, who had different ambitions for his son's career. Furthermore, migration and the diasporic experience are now themes that are increasingly woven into the narratives of Bollywood cinema.

Melbourne is providing the space where Bengalis from India and Bangladesh have easier access to each other's cultural activities and styles. Being away from home, there is also greater potential for socialising between them, since both are minority communities in the diasporic context. In Australia a particular type of syncretic Bengali identity has been able to emerge, facilitated by the shared cultural–linguistic background of the Bengalis from India and Bangladesh. The existence of this shared cultural background does not suggest that there are no tensions between the two groups. What is significant, though, is that in Melbourne there is capacity for the expression of a form of radical heterogeneity that transcends the national and religious boundaries that are more deeply etched on the Indian subcontinent.

One of the issues emerging from this investigation into Indian identity in Melbourne is the significance of the relationship between language, place and identity. The question of geographical propinquity is pertinent. As with Hindus from West Bengal (India) and Muslims from Bangladesh, belonging extends beyond a mere sharing of common geographical space. So, beneath the surface of the national and other political–regional boundaries, there is a wider Bengali terrain, which is imbued with profound cultural and historical meanings that are shared, thereby forming a basis for mutual identification. In the same vein, one of our southern Indian Muslim informants explained cultural variations in India by reporting a conversation he had at his home over dinner with a Hindu friend from Bihar in the north. His friend felt that Hindus in northern India had more in common with the Muslims in the north than the Hindus from the south.[5] Though contemporary Hindu–Muslim tensions arising from the escalation of militant Hindu nationalism, especially in the north, cast a profound shadow over this claim, these tensions do not detract from the many areas of cultural commonality that bind Hindus and Muslims and that are able to be explored in Melbourne. Popular music and film are two significant forms of shared cultural interests, besides the myriad of everyday social interactions. Despite these commonalities our informant also remarked upon the immense cultural diversity of India by comparing it to Europe. He stated:

> India is like Europe. Each state is like one of the European states, so there is very little in common [between them]. But to the geographical subcontinent the name India is given.

According to our information and observation, the prevalence of this kind of radical heterogeneity amongst South Asian diasporic communities is not unique to Melbourne but may be found in different places at different times. Two comparative examples illustrate this phenomenon, with

---

5 The languages of the north are Indo-European in origin, while those of the south are Dravidian. This difference is connected to a profound cultural divide with deep historical roots. In the post-Independence period, this split has given rise to passionate conflict over language use.

reference to Indians and Pakistanis overseas. The first involves a south Indian Hindu acquaintance, a computer professional in Melbourne, who worked for some time in the United States.[6] When he was departing the United States, a Muslim Pakistani family he had got to know well hosted a farewell dinner party for him. Their hospitality, despite the perennial political differences between India and Pakistan, did not surprise him. He remarked that the tensions between Indians and Pakistanis exist only on the subcontinent, whereas away from the subcontinent the relations between the two nationalities are cordial. Further, he added it was the politicians in the pursuit of power, rather than the people, who fomented the conflict in the name of religion. Such diasporic unity at the personal level has not eluded Bollywood, as evidenced in a recent popular film dramatising the culture-shock and betrayal experienced by a mixed group of ordinary South Asian immigrants (Indians/Pakistanis/Hindus/Muslims/Sikhs) in the materialistic milieu of New York.[7]

The second example relates to my own experience as a student at university in a small city in the north-east of England during the late 1960s and early 1970s, where I was a participant in the relationships between a group of Muslim Punjabi students from Pakistan and an Indian Hindu Punjabi student.[8] From my contact with these students over a three-year period, it was evident that the bonds of language, food and music played a major role in bringing them together. Their relations were in no way strained by ritual differences amongst them, such as those connected with the consumption of alcohol at dinner gatherings and in the student union. The bonds between them were reinforced by the fact that several of them studied the same course and they were all away from home. However, my own involvement with the group was neither owing to communication in a common language (Urdu and Punjabi which they spoke

[6] Computer professionals are the most mobile of professional groups in India because they are recruited to work on contract in many parts of the world (see Lakha 1992; Mir, Ali, Biju Mathew, and Raza Mir 2000). Their mobility raises interesting questions pertaining to identity formation, which need to be explored by further research.

[7] The film referred to is *Aa Ab Laut Chalen*, which was shown at the State Film Theatre in Melbourne in April 1999.

[8] This information is based on the personal account of Salim Lakha.

are not my native languages), nor to shared national origins, but rather mainly because of my nostalgia for north Indian *ghazal* (lyric poem) and popular music, and a craving for Indian food, after the regular monotony of the bland diet served in the hall of residence in which I lived for two long years.

They treated me as both an insider and an outsider. I was accorded insider status because of my Indian origins and the fondness for Indian music and food. It did not matter to them that my historical and social links with the Indian subcontinent were tenuous because I belonged to a diasporic Indian community and my family had been settled in East Africa for over three generations. At the same time, however, I was also an outsider because I mostly communicated with them in English. My native language is Gujarati, which they neither spoke nor understood sufficiently to allow meaningful communication. This account serves to illustrate that though language is an influential factor in forging a cultural identity, the articulation of this identity occurs in diverse situations, so communicating in a common language is just one means albeit an important one. Food, music, ethnic origins and various cultural codes also promote a sense of closeness in a wide range of social situations.

Food

It is of course well known that food carries a rich set of meanings because of its ritual connections and the social context of its consumption. Within people's homes, and at various community gatherings, particular food items have association with specific religious and secular festivals. Amongst the Indian and Pakistani Muslims, the celebration of Eid and other religious events is marked by serving *biryani* (a rich dish of meat and rice). In Melbourne Eid is celebrated by Indian and Pakistani Muslims as a community function at their religious/cultural centre, where *biryani* is one of several South Asian delicacies served to mark the occasion. It is also served to mark wedding celebrations, and though it is generally associated with Muslim cuisine, it is widely consumed by non-vegetarian Hindus in social rather than religious contexts. One of our female informants fondly reminisced about the special way in which Muslims in India prepare *biryani*.

Sweet food has a special meaning for all, as it is regularly distributed

fig. 11.1: A Muslim family celebrating Eid festivals
(photo: Tasneem, Melbourne)

to friends and family members to mark all auspicious occasions. The offering of prayers (*puja*) in Hindu homes and in the Sikh *gurdwara* in Melbourne is followed by the distribution of *prasad*. The rites of passage from weddings to the birth of a child also involve distribution of sweets. Generally, any joyous occasion is accompanied by the consumption of Indian sweets.

Food plays a particularly important role in Sikhism. In contemporary temples in Melbourne there are the two usual primary spaces, the communal eating area, 'the kitchen', and the space where communal prayers and singing take place. Guru Nanak, the first of Sikh Gurus, institutionalised the concept of a community kitchen, or *langar* ('alms house for the poor and needy') in Persian; 'the cooking place' in Sanskrit (Patwant Singh 1999). *Langar* (the ritual communal meal and space) (Voigt-Graf

2010), therefore, has in reality many layers of interconnected meanings. It was the *guru*'s belief that the basis of mankind's misery lay in a lack of cohesion and the accompanying poverty and he thus inculcated the concepts of *sangat* and *pangat*. The former refers to the congregation or association of like-minded people that help Sikhs attain spirituality, the latter to participating in the *langar* (ritual meal) whilst sitting on the floor in a row. *Pangat* expresses the Sikh principle of equality, brotherhood and humility. It is here that a mutual understanding of equality, corporate unity, essential religious and social service is created. The *guru*'s disciples not only sit together in *sangat* to pray but also sit together in the *langar* to share the food.

Guru Nanak intended to uproot the caste system. By providing food and refuge for the poor and destitute, the *langar* was aimed at effectively levelling social differences in society. *Sangat* plays an important role in defining the Sikh community's development and social welfare. The congregation participates in the *langar*, which is open to all. The *langar* is a unique practice of Sikhism and is crucial to establishing a Sikh identity. It has become the cornerstone of equality and fraternity, and expresses the longing for an egalitarian society. Guru Amar Das, the third Sikh Guru, enshrined participation in the egalitarian, communal, ritual meal: *pehle pangat, pichhon sangat* (broadly translated as 'first eat together, then combine as community'). He made it obligatory that all visitors dine in the community kitchen prior to seeing him. Thus non-Sikhs are made to feel 'at home' in the *langar*.

The maintenance of the *langar* is a feature of the social corporate responsibility of Sikhs. Every Sikh is expected to take part in the running of the kitchen and the *langar* is a place where Sikhs serve each other. A Sikh may pay for the expenses, *daswandh*, bring provisions, *daan*, or personally contribute labour of love, by cleaning utensils, fetching water or fuel, or taking a hand in cooking and distributing food. Thus *sangat* and *pangat* provide various avenues of Sikh service to community: collecting funds to buy rations of food, cleaning grains, chopping vegetables, cooking food and distributing it. Humility and hospitality are achieved through serving water, cleaning utensils, or clearing the dining hall. All of these services are provided on a purely voluntary basis.

The *langar* requires great organisational abilities and skills, and can be likened to a community project requiring considerable tolerance, accommodation, co-operation, facilitation and sagacity. It symbolises Sikh recognition of equality, brotherhood and the spirit of social service that strengthens unity. The meal remains simple and humble reflecting the staple diet of Sikhs: lentils, a vegetable and *phulka*s or *roti*s (unleavened bread). This food is traditionally grown by Sikhs in Punjab (the bread basket of India). In times of good harvest, there may be two vegetables, yoghurt, a *cachumber* (mixed salad mildly spiced), plain rice and, inevitably the best part of the meal, the *khir* (sweet rice). Somehow the food at the temple always tastes better than that cooked at home. The explanation often given is that the food has been cooked with devotion and dedication. Although Sikhs do eat meat, meat is never cooked within the *gurdwara* precinct, ensuring that the congregation only eats that which is available and affordable by all.

On more joyous occasions, such as the 'naming ceremony', baptism, marriage, commemoration of the birth of Guru Nanak or Vaisakhi (the formation of the Sikh faith and the Sikh New Year), desserts and Indian sweetmeats such as *jalebi*s, *ladoo*s or *burfi,* plus ice-cream, may also be served dependent on the congregation's contributions.

Volunteer men and women jointly cook meals in huge cauldrons called *degh*s, which require some dedication and stamina to keep stirring. The *langar* space is organised into different areas much like a chain of spontaneous tasks from the cleaning and preparation of lentils, chopping of vegetables, to cooking in the cauldrons on gas fires. In another area, mounds of dough are prepared for *roti*s, making of dough balls, rolling them into circular shapes, tossed on to a huge griddle and then finally popped into wicker baskets inlaid with a cloth to keep them warm. Several women including children will divide themselves into teams to keep up the tempo, from the gathering of a small mound of dough to the making of the final *roti*. The deep sinks denote the washing up area where all utensils used to cook the meal, as well as the ones used to eat in, will be washed and returned to their respective places.

Meals are prepared simultaneously as prayers are recited in the prayer hall in the *gurdwara*. Before prayers are completed, a tenth portion of the meal is blessed, this portion being reserved for the tenth Guru. It is then returned, to be mixed with the meal. In addition to this, *khrah*, a mixture of semolina, flour, ghee and sugar (commonly known in India as *prasad*), is distributed to all worshippers, symbolising human equality. After the prayers and *prasad*, worshippers and visitors proceed to the *langar* to eat in common. The consumption of the meal is itself a ritual process, as is the cleaning up afterwards. For Sikhs, egalitarian closeness in this ritual is of prime significance. In Melbourne on special occasions such as the Sikh New Year (Vaisakhi), which coincides with the harvest season, as well as Guru Nanak's birthday, one can see in the various Sikh temples more than several hundred people partaking of the food in the inclusive *langar*.

It is clear from the above discussion that food is imbued with multi-dimensional symbolic value. Indian social gatherings, whether at home or outside, are replete with food. The lavish range of foods offered at social functions in people's homes, besides expressing warmth and closeness, is meant to display the considerable culinary and management skills of the wife. The quantity and the quality of the food also serve to enhance the prestige of the hosts. It is therefore not unusual for such functions to assume a competitive character, where the quantity of food, and the number of new items introduced to the menu, are the main criteria for judging both the success of the occasion and the domestic virtues of the hostess.

The proliferation of Indian restaurants and grocery shops is a conspicuous expression of the increasing heterogeneity of Indians and their cultures in Melbourne. As some of our older informants observed, it was difficult to obtain Indian spices and groceries in Melbourne when they arrived here in the 1960s. They were restricted in their consumption of Indian foods or alternatively they were compelled to obtain their supplies from India and South-East Asia. From our observation and experience, the range of spices and other ingredients available in Melbourne was limited even during the mid-1970s. Similarly, there were few Indian restaurants before then and they mostly offered Punjabi, that is, north Indian dishes. To widespread dismay it was impossible to find regional cuisines or the wide variety of Indian snacks and sweets available either in India, or places such as London with large Indian communities. The introduction of the *tandoor* (clay oven) for the cooking of *tandoori* dishes around the late 1970s introduced a new era of Indian cooking in the restaurants.

A major shift in Indian restaurant cuisine in recent years is the offering of Gujarati and south Indian food and the availability of north Indian *chaat* (snack meals). The shift to regional diversity is evident in the names of the newer restaurants. Thus Lakshmi Vilas (with a name typically south Indian for a restaurant) serves south Indian food, whereas Guru Da Dhaba (Guru's popular roadside stalls) and Kake Di Hatti (Uncle's Shop) offer popular north Indian snacks at weekends.[9] Eponymous eating places in Delhi are famed the world over among the Indian diaspora and backpacking visitors. Various grocery outlets around the city sell a wide range of Indian sweets, as well as spices, other foodstuffs, Ayurvedic medicines, and the ubiquitous videos of Hindi, Punjabi and Tamil films.

Although Melbourne does not have an extensive Indian shopping strip or centre comparable with London, Toronto and Los Angeles, or the Vietnamese shops in Victoria Street, Melbourne, a small South Asian concentration has emerged in Dandenong. New York City also has an Indian business centre, in the suburb of Jackson Heights, Queens (Khandelwal 1995: 185). In Melbourne, in addition to take away food shops, groceries and videos, Dandenong also has shops that sell women's colourful fashion wear. The location of the shopping centre in Dandenong is probably explained by the relatively larger concentration of Indians and other South Asians in and around that part of Melbourne. Nevertheless, overall, the Indian population in Melbourne is widely dispersed and thus it is difficult to equate a particular neighbourhood or suburb with an Indian presence.[10] This is in stark contrast to London

[9] Since the initial research for this paper, the names of some restaurants have changed, for example, Guru Da Dhaba has been replaced by a differently named Indian restaurant on the same site. Also, many more Indian restaurants have opened up, with the rapid growth of the Indian population in Melbourne.

[10] There is now (2010) a shift to some suburbs/localities displaying a marked concentration of Indians and South Asians more generally. The suburb of Clayton is one example, where more grocery shops and restaurants have appeared, especially in the main shopping centre close to the railway station, as a result of a growing number of Indian students and migrants residing in the suburb. Interestingly in outer Melbourne, a housing estate in the suburb of Point Cook is referred to as Mumbai Cook because it is reported that of the 1,500 homes 'every third or fourth home is an Indian family' (Johanson 2010: 9).

where certain areas are not only associated with Indians, but also with Indians from a particular region as, for example, in the case of Wembley in London, which has a large Gujarati population.

Food provides a continuing link with India, as well as expressing Indianess in the multicultural milieu of Melbourne. Amongst our informants, all those we interviewed ate Indian food at home. An Anglo-Indian informant deriving from south India, who has resided in Melbourne for 30 years, said that at home the family ate both Indian and Western food, and that he himself was particularly fond of south Indian food. He also frequented a south Indian restaurant in a nearby suburb and took pride in claiming that his son, who previously shunned Indian food, and now in his twenties, had recently taken to eating hot curries.

Paradoxically while people will assert that there is common Indian-ness arising from having been born and raised in the profoundly multicultural land that is India, it is clear from their personal accounts that these first generation India-born immigrants pursue their own religious, caste, cultural and linguistic identities with a passion even where food is concerned. An instance of this is a band of families who hold regular Bhav Bhojan (friendly dinner). These families have been meeting for the last 30 years. They speak the Marathi language, cook and eat Marathi food, all come from Maharashtra, and are a separate entity from the Maharashtra Mandal (a cultural association), which organises plays in the Marathi language, as well as concerts and festivals that are celebrated back home in Maharashtra. This friendly gathering around food provides the communicative space within which a particular cherished identity is articulated and a sense of enduring closeness is created.

A noted group of diasporic Indians from East Africa, belonging to different Indian linguistic/regional backgrounds, also has dinner parties in Melbourne where group members speak some Swahili, the *lingua franca* of East Africa and indulge in Indian food. At one of their parties, in an Indian restaurant in Melbourne, their East African–Indian identity was expressed through an exchange of Swahili phrases and the listing of the Indian menu in the Swahili language. Needless to say, the evening was peppered with convivial and nostalgic reminiscing about life in East Africa. Observation of India-born Indians, as well as diasporic Indians from East Africa, who have settled in Melbourne and in other parts of the world, including Britain, Canada and the US, shows that Indian food is a crucial part of sociability. During functions in middle-class homes, the elaborate preparation of food and the wide range of dishes offered are comparable to the practice in India and East Africa where domestic help was readily available to assist in the cooking. The preparation of some foods in advance of the event and refrigerating them reminds people that they are now living in a new homeland.

A key feature of culinary practice is the synthesis of Indian and Western foods, which is brought about by a greater health consciousness in conformity with publicity about healthy living. As a consequence some households have moved from the consumption of *ghee* (clarified butter) to vegetable oils in order to maintain a healthy diet. One informant of Maharashtrian origin explained that his Marathi-speaking acquaintances and friends hardly ate *puri*s (small puffed bread) because they are deep-fried and therefore regarded as unhealthy. According to him healthy eating was prompted particularly by the younger generation of Indians, who are 'fanatically health conscious'. Thus the incorporation of pasta and salads as part of Indian diet is not uncommon. Many Indians in Melbourne eat less oily and less spicy food than formerly, which is a trend that is also observed amongst some Indians from East Africa living in Canada. On the whole the predilection for spices continues, so that spicing is incorporated into Western style meals. During a visit to one of the relatives of Salim Lakha in the United States, a regular pre-dinner conversation and relaxation was accompanied by the consumption of red wine, popcorn and the Gujarati *dhokla* (steamed, spiced lentil flour cake). In East Africa red wine and popcorn did not feature as part of the snack and the *dhokla* was accompanied by tea.

Heterogeneous Identities

The prevalence of heterogeneous cultures and identities, both in their continuity and their differing contexts, is widely observed and commented upon in the literature on South Asian diasporic communities (Baumann 1996; Lewis 1997: 129; Vertovec 1995: 144). It is rightly argued by Mankekar (1994: 363) that identities are conjunctural rather than stable and unified. Similarly Hall (1996: 4) observes that in the 'late modern' context identities are 'increasingly fragmented and fractured'. Others also recognise that identities are not constant but are shaped by the material circumstances of daily existence and the narratives that people recount (Brah 1996: 183). Collectively, these writers argue against an essentialist view of identity by drawing attention to the constructed and indeterminate nature of identity. With the conventional anthropological understanding of culture as bounded and essentialist coming under increasing criticism (see Calgar 1997: 169-70), there is greater stress upon the shifting contexts within which identity is imagined, forged and articulated. As is widely acknowledged now, one is more likely to encounter competing and multiple identities under contemporary transnational conditions rather than a single totalising identity (Smith 1998: 202-05).

In the case of Melbourne, the social demographics of migration have had substantial influence on the forging of identities according to two of our informants. One has an intimate knowledge of Indians in Melbourne because he has lived here for over 30 years and has been actively involved with Indians through his role as a priest and a marriage celebrant. He explained that during his early years in Melbourne people from different parts of India mixed freely with each other. However, as the population of Indians increased there was a growing tendency for people to congregate and socialise on the basis of their cultural-linguistic and birthplace backgrounds, as well as through their respective associations. He referred to the process as ghettoisation. Another informant — a Muslim, who has also lived in Melbourne for nearly as long — confirmed this, but with reference to the relations between Hindus and Muslims. He claimed that earlier in Melbourne there was greater socialising between Hindus and Muslims, but over time as more people arrived the interaction between the two groups became less frequent.

Some of the evidence from Britain confirms a similar trend in the pattern of socialising amongst migrants there. A study of South Asians in Bradford, for example, found that, during the early period of 'pioneer migration', the male members of different communities (Hindus, Sikhs and Muslims) either shared their living quarters or lived within the same neighbourhoods. Later as they established their families and community structures, the Hindus and Sikhs tended to disperse away from the Muslim 'concentrations' (Lewis 1997: 130). The arrival of families in Britain also strengthened religious practice and with the growth in population through immigration, places of worship proliferated (Ballard 1994: 18). As the settlement process consolidated itself, religious and sectarian commonalities became the bases upon which different South Asian communities distinguished themselves (ibid.).

In Melbourne, demographic growth and the setting up of family-based households provide only partial explanation for the character of social interaction between Indians from different cultural and religious backgrounds. Cultural distinctions related to ritually defined consumption habits have also exerted some influence on the pattern of socialising. According to a Muslim informant, the non-consumption of alcohol amongst Muslims contributes to reduced socialising between Hindus and Muslims, as well as between Muslims and others. He attributed the decline in social interaction between Hindus and Muslims in recent years to an increasing trend towards the social consumption of alcohol at various functions by Hindus in Melbourne. Although it is difficult to ascertain definitively whether abstinence from the consumption of alcohol is related in any way to the reduced social interaction between people from the two communities, our observation suggests that the attitude to the consumption of alcohol may have hardened in recent years. For example, at the time this research was conducted, a secular social function was hosted by a liberal-minded Indian Muslim of East African origin in an Indian restaurant in Melbourne, where no alcohol was consumed or served to the guests who were Muslims of Indian and Pakistani origins. While there were a few Anglo-Australians present, there were no Hindus.

This generalisation regarding social interaction between Hindus and Muslims, however, should not be interpreted rigidly because, as one of our Muslim informants observed, he and his family regularly shared meals with Hindu families. He stressed that a sense of compatibility was significant to him rather than religious difference. When asked about the question of alcohol, he explained that his Hindu and Australian friends had come to understand not to follow the Australian custom of bringing a bottle of wine when invited to meals. While people may choose to use alcohol to symbolise their identity positions, there are many axes of social interaction through which people can structure their sociability with each other; alcohol and its meaning is only one of them. For example, there is now an Indian cinema house in the city that specialises in showing Indian

Hindustani films.[11] Indians and Pakistanis from all kinds of backgrounds enjoy seeing these films. Similarly, when Indian musicians stage musical performances in Melbourne, they attract many people of diverse cultural, linguistic, national and religious backgrounds.

It is also significant that South Asian Muslims, mainly Urdu-speaking Indians and Pakistanis, have established their own mosque and community centre in Melbourne, commonly referred to as the UMMA (United Migrant Muslims Association), where they pray, socialise and conduct language and religious instruction. Whilst the centre welcomes Muslims of all nationalities and backgrounds, it is largely patronised by Urdu speakers from India and Pakistan. They articulate a common identity derived from linguistic and religious affinity. This identity is distinct from Hindus, as well as from Muslims from outside South Asia. The centre symbolises a new configuration in which Indian and Pakistani Muslims have forged their own unity that transcends the bitter national divisions of South Asia.

The founding of the UMMA reveals that language is an important means of creating the community and constructing an identity. A Muslim informant, who was at one time an official of UMMA, stated that because Urdu is a common language of many South Asian Muslims in Melbourne, they felt that they should have their own centre. He explained that when South Asian Muslims visited mosques belonging to other Muslims, such as those from the Arabic-speaking nations, they did not quite feel part of that group. Referring to the establishment of UMMA as a separate organisation from other Muslim groups, the informant commented that 'language is by far the most important difference because not everyone can speak Arabic or English. Ladies and gents prefer to communicate in your [*sic.*] mother tongue.' Whilst there may be common religious affiliation or identity, cultural commonality is decisive. Of the elements of cultural commonality, the most important it seems is language. Though Bangladeshi Muslims are from South Asia they are not closely associated with UMMA because they are Bengali speakers. They have their own *imams* (religious leaders) and mosques in Melbourne. Similarly, there are several Hindu temples where the differences between them have their

---

11 Hindustani is a mixture of Hindi and Urdu, which is readily comprehended by Hindi- and Urdu-speakers on the Indian subcontinent and by many who are part of the South Asian diaspora across the globe.

origins in language, region and nationality (Bilimoria 1996a: 31-40). As noted above, there are also a number of Sikh temples where the pleasure of speaking Punjabi is available to all.

Sikhs in Melbourne congregate at various *gurdwaras*, where they express their religious and broader cultural identity. Newly-arrived migrants and students find anchorage here in these temples. It gives them a sense of belonging, a 'coming home of sorts'. The things they value most are best understood in terms of the food, language, music and dance that are part of the distinct Sikh identity. The distinctive feature of the forging of Sikh identity is the constant emphasis on inclusiveness, both in the structuring of the rituals and in the temples. Hence *gurdwaras*, since the times of the third Guru, have a doorway in each side, open to all four castes. Unlike in Hinduism, these groupings are all considered equal partners (Cole and Sambhi 1978: 25). Despite the underlying principles of equality, there are also factions within the different Sikh groupings striving to forge a common identity (see Chapter 9, p. 224).

Cultural heterogeneity amongst Indians does not necessarily indicate a rejection of national identity. Paradoxically, heterogeneity and unity co-exist. This was cogently demonstrated by a Muslim informant, who expressed alienation from India as well as identification with it. On the one hand, his account of India conveyed a sense of marginality because he felt Muslims are discriminated against in employment, especially in the public sector, and as a consequence have to rely upon their own initiative and resources to survive. He claimed that he did not intend returning to India permanently because he had had a traumatic experience during a Hindu–Muslim riot in the neighbourhood where he lived. In the riot the family house was attacked and the event had left a deep psychological scar. On the other hand, despite the alienation and the trauma suffered, he continues to regard himself an Indian because India is his birthplace and he has friends there, both Hindu and Muslim. The house he lived in is still there and so are some of the neighbours. On his visits to India he gets together with the neighbours to share memories of the 'good old times'. During these visits he enjoys watching films, talking in the Urdu language (his native language) and eating at good restaurants. For him, attachment to birthplace, memories, the peculiarly Indian ways of dressing, eating, talking, and watching films, have an important bearing on what constitutes an Indian identity. For example, he explained how viewing a film in India was an altogether different experience to seeing it in Australia:

> The atmosphere of watching a movie in India is different. The big billboards, large numbers of people around the cinema, all the talking going on inside, and when you come out there are different kinds of people all around. Somebody wearing a suit, someone in a loincloth, and you stand on the corner and see a lot of amusement. After the movies you go and talk to your friends about it.

Even chewing *paan* (betel leaf) was a different experience in India! Thus the example of this informant's narrative shows how everyday cultural practices have an experiential meaning that profoundly shapes both cultural-linguistic and national identities.

Other informants also spoke strongly of the powerful memories they carried of their friends, relatives, homes, neighbourhoods and food in India. It is these memories that sustain a sense of belonging to India. Though the feeling of belonging is not embedded equally in our informants, it is nevertheless strong enough to create a longing for the past and the place within which this past was enacted. This longing is strengthened where people have close relatives and friends in India. In the case of one informant, it was especially heightened by the difficulties experienced in securing stable employment in Australia. Furthermore, the sense of loss was not compensated by her spouse's secure employment position in Australia.

Conclusion

One way or another, Indians in Melbourne are expressing their identities with great vigour through their cultural and social activities. As stated above, ten Marathi families have been meeting every six weeks for over 30 years to enjoy Marathi food. Interestingly, given the discourse on fragmented and unstable identities, this does manifest a certain stability and continuity of identity. Nevertheless, identities are conjunctural. The Bengalis from West Bengal and Bangladesh have also come together to express their cultural unity through combined enactment of *jatra*. Those south Indians who have a taste for classical music indulge their passion through the Carnatic Music Circle, which holds concerts that are patronised by music lovers. Thus, the Marathis, Malayalees, Bengalis, Gujaratis and other Indians all practise their distinct Indian-ness in Melbourne.

The cultural adherence of Indians in Melbourne does not confirm Vasta's observation that well-educated, skilled Asian migrants with high-levels of English competency are inclined to 'socio-economic assimilation' rather than retaining their cultures (1996: 61). Indians in Melbourne, as in Australia generally, have a high level of educational attainment and proficiency in the English language. According to the 2011 Census, 93% of the India-born population spoke English 'well' or 'very well' (ABS 2011). Also, over 67% (15 years of age and over) had qualifications up to a bachelor's degree or higher (ABS 2011). (For details of educational attainment of Hindus see Chapter 6, and of Sikhs see Chapter 10.) Whilst they are entrepreneurial and seeking upward socio-economic mobility, they also demonstrate a strong attachment to their own cultures. For example, one of our informants explained that when she was in India she did not regularly go to the temple, but since arriving in Melbourne, she visits the temple more often, so that her children have some exposure to their own culture. Although not everyone may go to the temple, in their own ways the Indians we interviewed, and many others we know well, are active consumers and promoters of both popular and classical forms of their culture. Interestingly, a survey of Indians (India-born and others) in Victoria revealed that over 72% of them were involved in a community association, and the primary form of communal activity amongst Indians was cultural (Bilimoria and Ganguly-Scrase 1988a: 101).

In Melbourne, India-born Indians tend to be high caste and possess all the attributes of solid middle-class status. Combined with this, as we have stated previously, they are dispersed over many different suburbs. They feel comfortable, secure and not embattled as a victimised minority group. They are therefore freer to pursue their cultural activities and not pressured to form a politico-cultural bloc against other groups.

Several of our informants found Melbourne's multicultural milieu refreshing. One was appreciative of the close interaction in his workplace between people of different cultural backgrounds, whilst another was readily absorbed into a book-reading circle through a colleague in the department where she is a postgraduate student. Another informant, who acquired carpentry and other construction skills after migrating to Australia, explained how one of his Australian neighbours had taught him all the skills necessary for household repairs. Beyond these personal contacts, there is also a deeper interest in India among Australians, which is illustrated by the presence of many European Australians at the various Indian music and dance performances that are held in Melbourne.

Generally though, our informants felt that people in Australia viewed India either as an exotic land of elephants and snake charmers or as poor and backward. One person claimed that Australians only showed interest in those Asian countries that were economically successful, such as Japan. An Indian friend once confided that he found the hype about Asia and Asian Studies in Australia offensive because it was not accompanied by a genuine interest in the culture of Asian countries. One of the informants stated that she felt Indian because no matter how long you lived in Australia, people always asked where you were from. Perhaps her feelings draw attention to the limits of multiculturalism. In Australia, Indians are constantly reminded of their Indianess, and this is heightened when they are represented as Indians in the Australian media and other public spaces. These representations are not always favourable and vary, from Orientalist constructions to those that are profoundly offensive to cultural and national pride.

Whilst Indians in Melbourne are engaged in a rich cultural life, they experience aspects of deracination. The weakening of cultural influence over the second generation is a major issue. For example, the children of our informants communicate in English with their siblings, although they converse with their parents in Hindi, Urdu, Tamil or one of the other Indian languages. For instance, the survey of Indians in Victoria showed that the preference for communication in English was pronounced amongst young Indians, 75% of whom preferred to speak in that language. Their reluctance to communicate in Indian languages was attributed to the 'pressure of monolinguism' and the fear of appearing 'different' (Bilimoria and Ganguly-Scrase 1988a: 76-77). A female acquaintance from one of the Indian communities in Sydney stated that her young children were reluctant to communicate at home in their native language, Kutchi (a dialect of Gujarati), especially after her son inadvertently replied to his teacher at school in Kutchi and felt a great sense of embarrassment.

A further issue for the parental generation is the question of courtship and marriage as it relates to their children. For many parents it is a cause of endless concern because they find it difficult to accept the uninhibited mores of the wider society. This was highlighted during our research by one of the informants, who was counselling a young Indian woman estranged from her family because of a relationship they did not approve. There is profound anguish amongst the parental first generation about the possible loss of their children to the egocentric ways of mainstream Australian culture. While the object of our research at this stage is not about the second generation, a recent work offers an illuminating analysis of the complexities of identity formation amongst second-generation Indian women (Joshi 2000).

Most of our informants do not expect their children to choose an Indian partner because they realise that they no longer have any say in the matter. However, with the advent of instantaneous and cheap Internet connectivity, and websites such as 'shadi.com', the traditional mode of marriage arrangements has been somewhat overcome by 'virtual' on-line reality for some. Marriage partners are now 'facilitated', as opposed to arranged, with all parties communicating in virtual time, with cyber technology differentiating and transforming contemporary migratory experiences in Australia (Costa-Pinto 2010; see also Mitra 2005). Costa-Pinto's paper provides useful insights into the interaction between gender and technology in fostering intimacy within the transnational familial networks between Australia and India, as well as globally (2010: 10). It differentiates between earlier female migrants who are comparatively less familiar with cyber technology and recently arrived migrants who are more technologically savvy. The latter take advantage of both worlds (Australia and India), enabling them to adjust to their new environment in Australia with greater ease compared to their earlier female counterparts (ibid.: 26).

Our chapter does not strive to provide a comprehensive account of community social life and its politics. We are aware of disputes and struggles within individual associations and umbrella organisations. The issues raised by these conflicts are worth investigating but they are beyond the scope of this chapter. While community politics possess their own drama, what sustains individuals and groups are their rich cultural repertoires.

In conclusion, what distinguishes our ethnographic study from subsequent research on Indians in Australia is that it explores the expression of cultural identity in the context of multiculturalism and reveals the diverse nature of this identity. We acknowledge the important contribution made by recent scholarship, which expands the thematic boundaries of research on Indians in this country and draws attention to major changes in the composition of the Indian population here. Since our initial research, which was conducted in 1999–2000, there have been major shifts in the social and demographic structure of the India-born population in Australia (Singh and Cabraal 2010: 231). For example, the large presence of Indian students in Melbourne was not a significant phenomenon then. In recent years, their rapid and substantial influx has attracted much media and scholarly debate, especially with the rising incidence of violent attacks on Indian students. Research by Bass (2006b), Singh and Cabraal (2010) and (Marginson, Nyland, Sawir and Forbes-Mewett 2010) provides useful insights into the motivation behind the migration of Indian students to Australia and their experiences of the education system and racism here. Singh and Cabraal (2010) also make a major distinction between the earlier influx of India-born migrants, who were the subject of our initial research, and later arrivals, i.e. the students. Whereas the former constituted professional migrants from metropolitan centres, many of the latter student arrivals had their roots in rural India or smaller urban centres with relatively low English language proficiency (ibid.: 19). Needless to say, the social and class implications of this change, for the Indian population in Melbourne (and other Australian cities), require further exploration.

The question of identity is still pertinent, as revealed in a recent study on Indian migrants in Sydney. Naidoo (2007) demonstrates that Indians in Sydney create multiple identities in negotiating their diasporic situation. In short, they decide against choosing a singular Indian identity that is based in an imagined cultural tradition. Nevertheless, Indian migrants do draw on their own cultural diversities to adapt and flourish in Australia, thereby creating viable flexible identities.

12

Religiosity in a New Land
Women's Strategies for Daily Living

Selena Costa-Pinto

Introduction

THE socio-cultural-religious context of migration affects the lives of migrants from the moment of arrival in a new land and on a daily basis. In this chapter, I analyse the transformation in religious commitment and practice from my subject position as an Indian woman migrant in Australia. My analysis is focused on religious behaviours such as rituals, temple and church attendance, and customs involving prayer, food and dress.

In the first part of this two-part chapter, I explain my focus on religious commitment and practice, and discuss the two main reasons why Indian women migrants in Australia turn to religion to counter feelings of alienation and isolation. In the second part, I analyse the strategies for religious commitment that enables these women, and others like them, to manage their daily living in a new land. Both sections of the chapter will be supported by data collected in Melbourne between 2002 and 2008.

Current immigration policies favouring skilled migrants have resulted in a burgeoning Indian presence in Australia. In general, India-born migrants in Australia are a well-educated group, with the men being at slightly higher levels than the women. As with other migrant groups in Australia, such as the Italians (Vasta 1991), the majority of Indian women arrived as dependents — wives, mothers, daughters — of male migrants. Their everyday lives in Australia can be described as 'middling transnationalism' (Conradson and Latham 2005; Smith 2005), due to their transnational dimension and their middle-class origins in India.

Despite educational levels that are generally higher than women in the total Australian population, and white-collar employment including jobs in financial and IT sectors powered by global elites, Indian women continue to be seen as migrant women of colour. This historically lower-class position in Australian society exacerbates what Vertovec (2009: 140) describes as 'the situation of being migrants from another place and, thereby, of being minority "others"'. One way of managing this situation, in order to carry on with their everyday lives in a new environment, is by constructing personal narratives.

Following the observation of Bouma and Brace-Govan (2000: 160) that in Australia 'religion is almost entirely lacking as a category of description or analysis, usually being masked by ethnicity', I did not set out to focus on religious affiliation. Instead, I selected three ethnic groups, Anglo-Indians, Sikhs and Tamils, on the basis of their population sizes according to census data provided by the Australian Bureau of Statistics. These three groups represent three different religions, Christian, Sikh and Hindu, respectively. All the Anglo-Indians were Catholics and all Tamil interviewees and the overwhelming majority of Tamils surveyed were brahmin by caste.

Narrative evidence was obtained through in-depth interviews with 24 women that included eight from each of the three ethnicities. Socio-economic data was generated from a survey of 224 women that consisted of 83 Anglo-Indians, 82 Sikhs and 59 Tamils. As with the interviewees, survey respondents were selected through 'snowball' sampling, based on ethnicity (Anglo-Indian, Sikh or Tamil), as well as marital (at least one marriage) and migrant (first generation migrants living in Melbourne) status.

The Role of Religion

There are three bases for the significance of religion in the lives of Indian women migrants. The first is that migration exposes individuals to stressful situations that generate personal insecurity (Rees 2009). Religion is often significant in migrant lives as a counter to feelings of alienation and isolation in a new land. A major review of Australian religion and spirituality found that 'migration brought people (to Australia) who were more religious than they would have been had they stayed where they were raised' (Bouma 2006: 73). Furthermore, Vertovec asserts that the experience of being a migrant 'often stimulates a mode of religious change through heightened self-awareness' (2009: 140).

The second reason for the significance of religion with regard to Indian migrants is the differences between sending and receiving countries. In India these women subjects were nurtured in a pluralistic society that contrasts with the multiculturalism they encounter in Australia. Bouma and Singleton (2004) describe multiculturalism in Australia as extending equality and freedom to all regardless of ethnicity, race or religion. However, on another level, Bouma (1993: 17), asserts that 'Australians are obviously more ready to be ecumenical about cuisine than they are to be multicultural about religion'.

Third, like women everywhere, these women migrants were nurtured to assume gendered roles in society. Further, their pre-migration religious nurturing in India occurred within an environment of intraculturalism (Bharucha 1993: 151), and the socio-cultural inclusiveness of that country's majority religion, Hinduism.

'INTRACULTURALISM' AND THE INDIAN SETTING

Multiculturalism in India is better described as 'intraculturalism' (ibid.), which refers to the ties and tensions, noise and chaos of diverse cultures occupying the same space within the overall shared culture of a given nation state. It differs from interculturalism, a term that describes cross-cultural interaction across national boundaries or between different nationalities in any given country.

The characteristics of intraculturalism as described by Bharucha, and due to which the women experience inclusiveness in Indian society, are fourfold. It respects cultural differences in the wider community and does not seek to keep minorities in their place. Second, it seeks the challenge, stimulation and even the reformation of the dominant culture by the minorities. Third, it recognises that — following Benedict Anderson's 'imagined community' (1991) — the citizens of any given community share, horizontally, values and attitudes regardless of their own culture or its position in the wider community. Finally, it resists, in the post-colonial tradition, the hegemonies — both national and global — of the wider community's institutions of cultural domination.

Simply put, this is a setting in which all faiths are regarded as equal under the umbrella of the majority religion, Hinduism, which itself is riddled with diversity derived from cults, sub-cults and spill-overs from minority religions within the community (Nandy 2001: 125-41). Some commentators argue that even 'European philosophies of nationalism, based on ideas of blood, soil, purity and the Volksgeist' (Nussbaum 2007: 5) have contributed to this diversity. For minority religious groups, such as the Muslims, Christians and Sikhs, this intracultural environment is generally comfortable and inclusive, despite being challenged from time to time, often violently, and for political reasons. This is particularly true for middle-class and urban-based individuals such as these women subjects.

Before contrasting Indian and Australian forms of 'multiculturalism', it is important to cite the difference in usage between the terms 'ethnicity' and 'community' in India and in Australia. In Australia's mainstream networks 'ethnicity' is generally understood in two ways. In the formal sense it is determined according to immigration department regulations by country of birth, and informally, as in social interaction, by ancestry. However, in India the elements of 'ethnicity' as understood in the Australian context refers to 'community' and includes groups with common attributes such as language, religion and region of origin. Hence what is 'multicultural' or 'multi-ethnic' in Australia is called 'intercommunal' in India.

The Indian migrant community in Melbourne embraces 'ethnic' differences that are classified as 'communal' in India, 'ethnic groups' that are called 'communities' in India and individuals of Indian 'ethnicity' who are described as belonging to the Sikh/Tamil/Anglo-Indian/Goan/Gujarati/Parsee, etc. 'community' in India. This largely semantic problem has been resolved in this chapter by describing such an individual as being of Sikh/Tamil/Anglo-Indian ethnicity, belonging to the Sikh/Hindu/Catholic religion, respectively, within the Indian migrant community.

The women's pre-migration religious nurturing in India's intracultural environment is integral to my argument that migration enhances religious awareness, commitment and practice because migrants turn to religion to counter feelings of alienation and isolation. I will discuss this nurturing within two contexts. The first is their life experiences prior to migration and the second concerns the nature of Hinduism itself. The former makes them aware of differences and similarities between the main faiths of India. Consciously or unconsciously, they generally understand Hinduism as placing ritual above belief, Christianity and Islam as being strict about dogma, and Sikhism as emphasising the teachings of its *gurus*.

Most Anglo-Indians were educated in 'convent' schools run by Catholic missionaries or in co-educational schools run by Christian trusts (D'Souza 1976). Hence, Anglo-Indian women left school with a strong sense of religious beliefs and rituals that was largely affirmed at home.[1] Thereafter, religious activity centred on weekly Sunday worship, usually conducted in English. This was a significant social event for which Western dress that met certain norms of modesty was acceptable.

In general, Sikhs in India adhered to the religion's egalitarian orientation, and most grew up in close proximity to Sikh temples (*gurdwaras*). However, this did not necessarily result in greater religiosity. On the contrary, as N2,[2] a Sikh interviewee, reported, 'my other two sisters (in India) are not religious at all. I mean they do go to the *gurdwara* every now and then. But not as much as I do'.

In India, Tamil women put great emphasis on religious rituals of praying, fasting, making vows, or going on a pilgrimage for special favours (Caplan 1985: 77-8). S4 confirmed that had she not migrated from India to Melbourne, 'I would have been very sheltered and caught up with all the festivals and the rituals'.

The women's religious nurturing in India occurs under the umbrella of India's majority religion, Hinduism, and is further associated with two elements. The first of these is the three roles of biological reproducers, community participators and ethnic group signifiers that characterise the lives of women in general (Yuval-Davis and Anthias 1989: 1-15).

Indian women migrants conflate the first two roles, that of reproducers

---

1 Anglo-Indians are Eurasians of primarily British and Indian ancestry born in India.

2 I have used codes rather than pseudonyms to protect the identity of respondents and to avoid the arbitrariness of assigning names to subjects without consulting them. Anglo-Indian interviewees carry the code A, Sikhs code N and Tamils code S. Informed consent was obtained from each interviewee in accordance with Monash University's regulations for ethical research and Ph.D. research projects.

of ethnic group members and participators in the community's ideological reproduction and transmission of culture. Not only are they the biological reproducers, but also the main socialisers of children, and are seen as the ethnic group's 'cultural carriers' (ibid.: 9). The narrative evidence suggests that Indian women migrants, particularly if first generation arrivals outside the workforce, are often less assimilated socially and culturally within wider society. Hence they are able to transmit and transfer to the young the ethnic group's social, cultural and religious heritage, as well as its hopes, ideals and ways of living.

In their third role as signifiers of ethnic/national groups, women embody these hopes and expectations, often constituting the difference between their ethnic community and other migrant, or non-migrant, groups. For instance, the women's narratives indicated that across ethnicities and religions they revered Indian national figures such as Mahatma Gandhi and Mother Teresa. They also upheld goddesses of the Hindu pantheon who epitomise qualities of modesty, chastity and meekness, as well as resilience, intelligence and wealth.

The second element of the women's pre-migration nurturing in India is the nature of Hinduism itself. Hinduism is rooted in the history of India and Indic civilisation, and has been presented as 'an umbrella term given to a vast range of traditions and beliefs' (Brown 2006: 139). Brown asserts that 'there is certainly no single Hindu faith or pattern of observance in South Asia or in the diaspora' (ibid.: 139). Yet it is acknowledged as the majority religion of India, a position it has retained through two processes. First, it manages challenges from other religions through cultural syncretism or assimilation as sub-cults, which occurred with Buddhism and Jainism (Heredia 2007). Alternatively, it adopts tolerance towards beliefs and practices of religions such as Islam and Christianity that resist assimilation. This achievement is due to the intrinsic diversity and inclusiveness of Hinduism (ibid.).

Singer's study of modern and Western practices among industrialists and business leaders from traditional Hindu, Muslim and Christian religious backgrounds in Madras (Chennai) city is pertinent. Singer (1972: 341) found that the Hindu participants privileged beliefs over conduct. However, Hindu religious leaders emphasised the 'sociological foundation' of Hinduism 'which avoid(s) pollution and transmit(s) from generation to generation the proper way of life' (ibid.). Thus, regardless of how it is perceived by its followers, according to its patriarchy, Hinduism is a world religion that prioritises rituals over beliefs.

The diversity within Hinduism coupled with this emphasis on rituals has an impact on religious practices among minority religious groups such as the Catholics and the Sikhs. For instance, India's Catholic hierarchy initiated a process of 'inculturation' in the 1970s that introduced decorations, furnishings, postures, gestures, prayers and hymns that 'take their inspiration from the cultural and religious heritage of India'.[3] Indeed, the Catholic Church hierarchy in India leaned towards liberation theology (Freire 1970) and 'Indianisation' in religious rituals. Hence it was in alignment with the socialist orientation of successive Indian governments and the intraculturalism of the majority Hindu population. From the 19th century, the Sikh hierarchy has acted to root out Hindu practices from *gurdwara* worship, indicating that similar processes had been at work in Sikhism prior to that period. The Muslims, also, have not been immune to interreligious exchanges, as evidenced among the Sufis (Baldick 1989: 36, 95) and the non-Muslim devotees who even today venerate *pir*s (holy men) at Muslim shrines such as the Chishti Dargah in Ajmer, about 390 kilometres south-west of Delhi.

In short, multiple religious identities bound together by mutual tolerance and a code of ethics that might embrace rituals as well as beliefs are quite common among Indians (Nandy 2001). Such responses were promoted early in the country's freedom struggle by Mahatma Gandhi, written into independent India's Constitution, and aggressively pursued by secularist/socialist governments.

On the macro level, this has kept the country relatively peaceful, given the multiplicity of religions, ethnicities and political parties lobbying for power under a democratic rule of law (Sen 2006). It involves continuous

---

[3] From the report of the proceedings of the All India Seminar on The Church in India Today, Bangalore 1969, published by the Catholic Bishops Conference of India (CBCI), Ashok Place, New Delhi. As a result of this report Vatican-approved adoption of Hindu rituals such as the *aarati* before a blessing, and the *anjalihasta* as a greeting within the Catholic Mass were introduced (Report of the General Meeting of the Catholic Bishops' Conference of India, Ernakulam, 7-16 January 1970).

engagement between the diverse traditions of the Hindu majority, the non-Hindu minority, and the everyday demands of modern living. At the micro level, individual reflexivity and community flexibility are crucial. It is noteworthy that non-Christians in India revere Mother Teresa as 'the saint of Calcutta [Kolkata]'. At the same time, according to my evidence, the three roles of Indian women, whether Hindu or not, and particularly in the diaspora, as reproducers, participators and signifiers of their ethnicity, are influenced overwhelmingly by Hindu practices, and occasionally even beliefs.

This conflation of Indian identity with Hindu culture, values and ideals raises the spectre that all Indians are basically 'Hindu' in identity, and ethnicities, including religious beliefs, are layered over as palimpsests. This view underlines the Hindu revivalist nationalist movement, Hindutva, which has been defined as 'the newly emergent monolithic global Hinduism' (Kannabiran 1998: WS-56) and has a robust following among the Indian diaspora.

Amartya Sen (2005: 253-54) proffers three reasons why the Hindu nationalists' interpretation is incorrect. The first is that identity is not a matter of discovery, but one of choice based on reason. Identity can be drawn from a range of possibilities that are increased by events such as migration. At one end is what is assigned to an individual such as religion, which is inherited at birth. At the other is what the individual prioritises at any given moment, such as nationality, gender or ethnicity.

Second, from the earliest of times India has been a multi-religious society that has welcomed Jews, Christians, Parsees and Muslims as traders and settlers (ibid.: 253). Thus, the conflation of any socio-cultural element such as cow worship, a largely Hindu canon, with the Indian identity excludes all other religions and denies their crucial contribution to India's history and cultures.

Third, Hindus can be defined by ethnicity or by belief. Central to Hindu culture is a rich tradition of heterodoxy that divides Hindus by beliefs into sects, cults and sub-cults, yet unites them in ethnicity (ibid.: 354). Beliefs, therefore, are only one of many attributes of a Hindu, ethnicity being another. On migration a seismic change occurs that appears to shift perceptions of religious beliefs and rituals across and within ethnicities.

THE POST-MIGRATION AUSTRALIAN ENVIRONMENT

The second reason why these Indian women turn to religion to counter their feelings of alienation and isolation concerns the level of displacement they experience on migration. In Australia, culturally shared norms are significant for the intensity and style of religious practice and belief, the relations among different religious groups, and the religious differences among them (Bouma and Singleton 2004: 17). This significance generates Vertovec's 'heightened self-awareness' (2009: 140) and occurs in two spheres — the 'public' and the 'private' — of the women's lives.

In India, the women were nurtured according to 'private' religious awareness, commitment and practice within a 'public' sphere dominated by Hinduism. In Australia, however, the cultural context within which religious groups operate and religious diversity is managed in 'public' or the 'mainstream' is largely Anglo-Celtic. According to Jamrozik, Boland and Urquhart (1995), there is a lack of structural and personnel diversity in the institutions that comprise this hegemonic core, some commentators arguing that at the practical level multiculturalism is merely 'a celebration of costumes, customs and cooking' (Gunew 1993).

The 'private' sphere for Indian women migrants encompasses their own migrant community, and extends to their roles as wife, mother and worker (Bhattacharjee 1997). In an engagement with Catherine MacKinnon's text (1989), Annanya Bhattacharjee defines 'home' for the Indian woman in the diaspora at three levels: the family home, the extended ethnic community to which she belongs, and India as portrayed within the Indian migrant community.

When placed in a different environment often a first response is a conflation of the traditional with the contemporary, as Singer's (1972) study of Indian businessmen in Madras city concluded. He found that apart from small differences in detail 'a similar industrial code and set of beliefs' emerged across religions (ibid.: 340). Singer observed that in order to satisfy religious heads who represent the patriarchy within their respective communities, the businessmen resorted to strategies that allowed a balance between social obligations and personal priorities in matters of religious practice and belief.

Similarly, I argue, these women migrants evolve a code of traditional and non-traditional strategies that reflects both the pre-migration Indian setting in which they were nurtured and the post-migration Australian situation in which they find themselves. All have been adapted from practices in India so as to satisfy the patriarchy in the 'public' and 'private' spheres of their lives in Melbourne. For instance, some migrants have extracted the socio-cultural elements of regular worship in India and conflated these with occasional social interaction. Carnatic music concerts can serve this purpose for some Tamil women such as S1. Her 'main reason' for attending these religious music concerts is 'because you meet people there'. Within Anglo-Indian networks this might revolve around 'bingo evenings' and 'trivia nights' in Church halls. Though religion played a lesser role in the everyday urbanised, middle-class lives of most of these women when they lived in India, this entirely social connection to one's religious group is viewed as being in line with 'mainstream' trends in Australia. As A3, a young Anglo-Indian, observed, 'Here it's like, it [religion]'s no big deal'.

However, a second group of women has grown in spirituality in Australia, motivated, as one explained, by the 'fear and insecurity of migration'. This response is supported by a major review of Australian religion and spirituality, which reported that 'migration brought people [to Australia] who were more religious than they would have been had they stayed where they were raised' (Bouma 2006: 73). Like the first group, they have also undertaken a similar process of distilling the fellowship elements of their networks, but they have chosen to conflate these with traditional religious worship. N5, a young Sikh, explained her *gurdwara* attendance in this context: 'I feel we are more keen on it now because this is the one way we attach to our country and to our religion.'

To examine the complexities associated with enhanced religious worship, I return to Gunew's interpretation of multiculturalism in terms of costumes, customs and cuisine. These three aspects encapsulate the socio-cultural nature of Indian religiosity and its impact on the negotiation of religion and culture in 'public' and 'private'.

Costumes

Traditional costumes for Indian women are based largely on the common-sense requirements of a time and place that existed in India's cultural and historical past. On migration and in the 'public' sphere, all except for a few recently arrived, older women adopt Western dress. As N1 said, 'I'm just too lazy and it's so comfortable in just pants'.

There are two underlying elements to this view. The first is that dress codes have been de-linked from religion and ethnicity in contemporary, middle-class, urban India. Many of the non-Anglo-Indian women migrants insisted that they had rejected traditional dress even before migrating. All agreed that Western dress worn on a regular basis is not unusual in India today, with modified traditional styles for temple visits and celebrations of religious festivals and ceremonies. As S5 noted, even for concerts at the Music Academy in Chennai, the seat of traditional Carnatic music, women now wear north Indian styles such as the *gharara/choli* (skirt/ blouse) instead of the *sari* because they 'match with the Western clothes'.

Second, some early arrivals had adverse responses to Indian dress codes. The Anglo-Indian habit of 'Sunday best' for weekly worship caused A5's husband some embarrassment and his family much amusement on a visit to a small West Australian town. A5 reported that Sunday worshippers noticing a well-dressed stranger in their midst 'wanted to know if he was gay!'.

For others, tensions centred on their workplaces. N3, a gynaecologist who came to Melbourne in 1972, described one such encounter:

> I went in my *sari* for my interview. The medical superintendent looked at me and said, 'how do you do obstetrics in that garb?' And I said, 'In India we deliver babies, and a lot more babies than in Australia, wearing the same outfit. All you do is hitch it up, and off you go.' I never went back for a second interview with that guy.

Even though S1, who happened to be an ANZ bank employee in the 1980s when the bank had large interests in India, met with a different response, she soon gave up traditional dress. She said:

> Like I can remember once I wore a *sari* for something and the manager said, 'What's this?' I said, 'I'm wearing an Indian dress'. And it was actually navy blue with white dots you know, so he said, 'Oh!' I said, 'It's part of ANZ corporate wardrobe' (*laughs*).
>
> *Oh, so did he believe that?*
>
> Of course not! No, he just laughed. So he used to say, 'So what

are you wearing tomorrow? Your corporate wardrobe?' (*laughs*).

However, in their three 'homes', which include temple visits, large Indian social gatherings and celebrations of festivals such as Diwali, the women revert to traditional dress. For all intents and purposes these occasions are 'private' because publicity and invitations are through Indian networks only. Non-Indians, including local politicians, who attend in the spirit of multiculturalism are accepted as 'honorary' Indians for the occasion. More importantly, it is at such times that diasporic women are on display as embodiments of the ethnic group's reproducers, participators and signifiers (Yuval-Davis and Anthias 1980: 1-15).

Cuisine

With regard to cuisine, it is the Tamil brahmin women who are universally challenged due to their vegetarian diet, which is dictated by religious belief and ritual. Some, like S2, who came to Melbourne immediately after marriage in the 1970s, have abandoned this canon despite admitting, 'I still have an aversion to the red meat'. She explained:

> Like sometimes at work if there is a lunch and whatever, and there is no food available, I won't be anti-social. So I just have a bit of chicken or whatever, but I still prefer the vegetarian.

She recalled the first time she ate meat when her Indian–Australian, Tamil brahmin husband, who 'has always been a meat eater', goaded her into doing so:

> I remember once he took me to one of the restaurants and he said, 'Ah', he was teasing me, and he said, 'Ah yes, you can eat this *pappadam*, it's not a meat', or something. And I was really, sort of, it bothered me. I said 'Alright, go get me a Kentucky chicken', I said. And I started eating chicken.

In the 'public' sphere, this group feels socially constrained, given the Australian practice of family barbecues and dining out. However, as vegetarianism gains popularity in the West and more non-Hindus and non-Indians adopt it, dining out is becoming easier. Besides, from the narratives it was not entirely clear whether food and its associated religious canons was the only social constraint. For instance, A6, an Anglo-Indian, with no food restrictions at all also found socialising difficult. She explained that the problem ran deeper: 'we can't afford to socialise and go out and drink and have fun. At the same time try to raise a family and ask them to adopt certain values.'

Customs

Many of the socio-cultural practices that Indians take for granted have religious origins of which they are unaware because they are so imbued with 'intraculturalism'. On relocation to the diaspora after migration they are free to re-assess these practices and accept or reject them. For instance, A3, a career-oriented 26-year-old Anglo-Indian Catholic, rejected alcohol consumption, which is anathema to Muslims, Indian nationalists and Gandhians. She said:

> friends, people at work would want to go out on a Friday night and just party and do that sort of stuff. And I would agree to do it. But their means of fun was like getting really drunk at a pub and that was something I would not do. I would not try to be like them for them to accept me.

Since the largely Catholic Anglo-Indians belong to a 'mainstream' religion in Australia they are the only group whose socio-cultural-religious responses straddle both 'public' and 'private' spheres. Being Westernised, cultural hurdles are few, and most assimilated well. Being Catholics, many benefited from individual and organisational support such as schools, parish associations and welfare agencies. In India, they were used to high levels of beliefs and rituals in 'public' and 'private' religious worship. In Australia, however, two main groups emerge.

The first group is lured by Australia's materialism and consumerism into low levels of religious ritual and belief such as attendance at Sunday Mass on an irregular basis. The second group responds by falling back on religion and deepening personal beliefs. However, they do not embrace more rituals because everyday demands limit time for worship, and in their new environment religious practices and rituals are not priorities (Bouma 2006). Instead, this group embraces individual spirituality and small group gatherings. A third, older and smaller group of Anglo-Indian migrants experiences a surge in ritual and belief as they reach retirement. In this respect they are not unusual in Melbourne's wider population, as A3 observed that 'most of the people that go to church at least in the parish that I go to are all elderly people. I very rarely see young ones there.'

In general, 'public' and 'private' socio-cultural-religious traditions are set by the group's experience prior to migration and passed on by succeeding generations. But difficulties with negotiating cultures in a new environment often result in a group response of defensiveness, in which religious interpretation is usually left to the community's patriarchy. However, first generation migrants, such as these women subjects, are relatively recent arrivals in Melbourne, hence their patriarchy tends to be less rigid. Most of these women reported that over time they had become relatively free from the structures and controls of the patriarchy, which could suggest confidence as well as an infusion of Western individualism. S1 said:

> When I came here initially maybe I would think a bit of what the community thought. But I think over time I'm only now interested in what my immediate family would think about anything I get into. I couldn't care less what anyone else thought (*laughs*).

Besides, due to the 'middling transnationalism' of recent arrivals they do not connect immediately with Indian migrant community networks in Melbourne. As N6, a young IT professional, said: 'I've never felt that they're the ones having an impact on my life or anything like that'. Instead, they turn to their traditional patriarchal extended family in India, even on religious matters. One Anglo-Indian woman even went to the extent of checking with her parents in India before forming a *de facto* relationship in Melbourne. She insisted, 'No matter where I would have been, had my parents not approved of it I would not have, never done it. No.'

In general, the Sikhs alone maintain a high level of ritual practice and religious belief, which is similar to a Sikh church (Singh 1963: 62). This is due, in large part, to the all-inclusive fellowship and hospitality associated with *gurdwara* worship and attendance in the 'private' sphere, as well as the distinctive dress code that sets them apart in the 'mainstream' public environment. Though these gatherings are often more about fellowship than piety, they are largely conducted within the precincts of the *gurdwara*. Thus *gurdwara* gatherings are distinct from the social interaction of Anglo-Indian Catholics and Tamil Hindu functions, which are mostly cultural occasions.

Sikh fellowship, however, does not obliterate divisions of caste, class and more particularly migration histories that create factions (Cole and

fig. 12.1: South Indian Hindu woman worshipping in home shrine (Source: http://yadavhistory.com/yahoo_site_admin/assets/images/Naray16.319172441_std.jpg)

Sambhi 1978). But despite such internecine politics, *gurdwara* attendance brings 'a nice warm feeling' to N2, is 'an anchor' that 'play(s) a major role in my life' for N3, and for N4, it is 'a huge network thing for us'.

Due to its diverse socio-cultural nature, Hinduism does not embrace the concept of a congregation as in Catholicism and Sikhism. Hence the affirmation of religious worship and rituals afforded by art forms such as Carnatic music and Bharata Natyam dance become attractive. They are rooted in myths, themes and traditions, combining religious rituals, cultural awareness and social interaction.

Visits to the main Hindu temple in Melbourne confirmed what one interviewee asserted, that temple attendance in Melbourne is more popular among non-Indian Tamils. Indeed, S8 admitted, 'my home is my temple', S3 and S7 participate in *bhakti* worship through Carnatic music hymn singing on Sundays, S2, S4 and S6 participate in a Bharata Natyam dance group, and S1 and S5 are active in a Carnatic music circle. Further spiritual needs are met by regular visits to the temples of family deities in India. On a daily basis though, some like S4 turn to Westernised versions of Indian spirituality for sustenance. She said,'I think it made me stronger, it made me search deeper into life and it gave me the spiritual growth as well.'

Strategies for Coping

As the evidence above indicates, the transformation of religious awareness and practice between source and destination countries is a significant aspect of migration. However, variations in style and intensity between different ethnic groups and individuals persist, depending on religious nurturing and migration experiences in both sending and receiving countries. Analysis of the evidence indicates that migrants are eclectic, crafting traditional and non-traditional strategies for different settings.

TRADITIONAL STRATEGIES FOR NON-TRADITIONAL SETTINGS

Traditional strategies for coping with levels of displacement in Australia draw on the women's religious nurturing in India.

Assimilation and Tolerance

With regard to assimilation, A4, a reflexive woman, who came to Melbourne 20 years ago, said, 'I think you need to assimilate and you still need to get in touch with the person within you. I think a good mix of both'.

'Tolerance' in the Australian context is celebrated as a form of liberalism, whereby all ethnicities are allowed equal and appropriate access to the structures controlled by the mainstream Anglo-Celtic culture (Stratton 1998). This liberalism is a far cry from the cultural pluralism that may have been the original point of multiculturalism. Stratton asserts that official multiculturalism, as a political policy, is more conservative than it is liberal, in retaining its Anglo-Celtic core.

In Australia, either the ethnic group must retain a level of 'oppositionality' to the mainstream Anglo-Celtic culture and forever describe itself in terms of how it differs from that culture, or, alternatively, it must remain eternally petrified in a cultural mould that may no longer be practical or comfortable but must nevertheless be maintained in order to retain its 'ethnicity' (ibid.). My narrative evidence and survey findings suggest that every day, in practical terms, this core is shifting due to changes in Australia's immigration policy and the migrants it attracts.

The women's experiences of 'intraculturalism' and Hinduism's inclusiveness towards other belief systems condition them towards assimilation and tolerance. At the same time even within the diaspora, non-Hindu individuals, including A5, an Anglo-Indian, and N1, a Sikh, draw inspiration from national figures such as Mahatma Gandhi, whose philosophy and teachings are strongly rooted in Hindu scriptures and traditions.

Sikh participants emphasised that they still 'remember and say' the Catholic prayers they learned from nuns in India. N3, who studied in such a 'convent' and married a Hindu explained that she was unfamiliar with Punjabi and Sanskrit, the languages of the Sikh and Hindu scriptures, respectively. Hence, she said, 'my communication with my Sikh God and sometimes Hindu God is "Our Father who art in heaven, hallowed be thy name"'. To her this was merely 'swaying with the wind a bit'. Others like N6 pointed to close friendships with Muslims as proof of religious tolerance.

Religion and Racism

One of the major sources of isolation for Indian women migrants in a largely white environment is racial discrimination. In the caste-ridden, post-colonial, middle-class society that these women have left behind such discrimination is largely — and safely — embedded in religious rites and rituals or abrogated by legislation. At the same time, norms and forms of everyday behaviour in the socio-political arena that involve caste are negated by aggressive affirmative action public policies. Nevertheless it can be assumed that Indian women migrants arrive in Australia with their own experiences of discrimination based on colour, culture, religion and race, even if these are only relatively benign forms of colour prejudice against darker skin shades. A2 summed up her experience in India thus: 'That is such an important thing in India — fair or dark. And I'm thinking you don't have to come to Australia to face that.'

The understanding and practice of caste in India is based on the concept of colour and indeed, the Sanskrit word for 'caste', itself of Portuguese/ Spanish origin, is *varna* (colour). The nexus between caste, colour and race is strengthened by the association of each *varna* with a colour ranging from white for the Brahmin to black for the lowest Sudra caste. While this might confirm the impression that caste is indeed a racist concept, with skin colour as its defining marker, the fact remains that there are innumerable exceptions of dark-complexioned brahmins and light-skinned shudras. Further, there is much academic debate to challenge the connection between caste, colour and race (Thapar 1966). Nevertheless, a widely propagated theory among South Asians, across ethnicities and particularly in the United States, is that the elite (upper caste/class) are 'Aryan' and by extension 'Caucasian' (Mazumdar 1989).

Due to its resonance with India's caste system and the association of dark skin colour with lower caste origins, experiences of discrimination in Australia are particularly intolerable for these middle-class women. As in India, in Australia, too, dark skin colour is generally regarded as a lower-class attribute. But unlike India, the praxis between colour and race is different. Just as ethnicity has always been associated with migrants, 'culture' in Australia has always been tied to ethnicity and race/colour (Hage 1998; Stratton 1998). These women are therefore often uneasy and confused — particularly as upper-caste Indians are nurtured to be inordinately proud of their ancient roots — when exposed to discrimination in Australia that is directed against culture rather than colour. The strategy employed to counter this problem is denial, as was suggested in my survey evidence. The majority of Sikhs (about 68%), Tamils (nearly 68%) and Anglo-Indians (almost 76%) denied any experience of racism.

What emerged in conversations with survey respondents and interviewees alike was that the term 'racism' is ambiguously understood. Second, there is a widely held view that racial discrimination is an outcome of ignorance and therefore best ignored. Such responses were similar to those reported by de Lepervanche (1984). According to her Sikh respondents entrenched ignorance in a poorly-educated host society was the cause. Positioning themselves as more enlightened they deliberately ignored discrimination, just as N5 encouraged her husband to do when he experienced it at work. She said:

> I just make him understand, 'No, it's just your thinking, you're just thinking in your mind because once you have that in your mind, you're gonna always think like that. You shouldn't think like that when it's not proved, why should you think like that? The more you think, the more you'll feel. So better not to think like that (*laughs self-consciously*).

Thus by assuming the moral high ground, as it were, Indian migrants take control of a basically intolerable situation, even while appearing to 'go with the flow'. S2, a medical doctor, acknowledged that a 'handful of Anglo-Saxon patients' in her practice 'absolutely refuse to see a "curry doctor"'. But she insists with complete self-confidence, 'I'm not offended by it anyway'.

NON-TRADITIONAL STRATEGIES FOR TRADITIONAL SITUATIONS

Embedded in their religious nurturing in India are the bases for the non-traditional strategies that the women evolve to cope with levels of displacement in Australia. These are similar to those of the industrialists whom Singer studied in Madras City.

Compartmentalism

Compartmentalisation (Singer 1972: 320-25), in the case of these Indian women migrants, involves the separation of two contesting sites, the 'private' sphere or home life from the 'public' sphere or 'mainstream' life, and further, the division of the 'private' into three 'homes'. Each involves sets of different practices. The 'private' inevitably emphasises traditional Indian rituals and the 'public' leans more towards what is 'Australian', and Westernised. Compartmentalisation, therefore, comes down to the delineation of what is ethnic and non-ethnic, Indian and non-Indian. Leakages occur between spheres and across compartments, creating tension that leads to eventual change, often across generations.

The process of compartmentalisation is best illustrated in the lives of the Tamil women because of their strict observance of ritual purity at home. While this may be done to appease older relatives who live with them, or the patriarchy with whom they interact socially at cultural events, it is also of their own choosing. Like their counterparts in Madras these migrants see ritual purity as fulfilling a duty for the welfare of their families (Caplan 1985). In reality, however, outside the home, particularly in Australia, and indeed within the home, even in India, ritual pollution is so endemic in modern living that M.N. Srinivas described the 'ordinary ritual status' as one of 'mild impurity' (1968: 121).

Women in the diaspora may strive to maintain a 'pure' status in the 'private' sphere of one 'home' — their family home. But they have no control over their other two 'homes', nor the 'public' sphere of the non-Indian community. For instance, S3, like most Tamil brahmin women, follows a strict vegetarian regimen at home. She also ensures that every Sunday morning her sons perform the purifying ritual of an 'oil bath' before they join their father in reciting the prayers required of brahmin boys who have been anointed at the Sacred Thread ceremony. During the other six days of the week S3 ensures that the boys are immersed in the study and sports activities of Australian school boys.

For social events in the 'private' sphere the dress code is traditional, with explanations provided when the code is broken. At one event the lone woman in Western attire explained that she had come directly from her son's school. Clearly, it was a case of 'cross-compartmentalisation' and no disrespect or disloyalty was intended. Similarly, S2 wears traditional *saris* in contemporary designs that she buys on her regular visits to India, even though in 'public', which includes her workplace, she finds this dress too 'cold' and 'cumbersome' for use.

Vicarious Ritualisation

Singer's second strategy involves vicarious ritualisation (1972: 331-35) and implies the continuation of religious practices and rituals but in abbreviated and conflated forms. For instance, celebrants are often requested to shorten marriage ceremonies and combine blessings of new homes with welcoming rites for new babies. This strategy is based on two assumptions. The first is the ritual neutralisation of the 'public' sphere. This involves the cessation of religious rituals and practices outside the home and designated place of worship, except when practical and convenient. Hence religious rituals are adapted into more user-friendly forms. For instance, N2, a Sikh, who spends a great deal of time in her car uses a CD to pray on the morning school run, while her Hindu peers listen to *bhajans* (hymns). At the same time, as Singer also observed (ibid.: 325-29), images of the god Ganesh may be discreetly displayed at one's work station alongside family photographs.

The second aspect concerns the secularisation of ritualisation (ibid.: 329-31). Often unfamiliar situations arising in new settings fall outside the prescribed parameters of religious practices or rituals with no basis for comparison. Once this principle is accepted the second assumption, which is replacing ritualisation by secularistion in the non-religious context becomes easier to embrace. For instance, the office-going woman in the 'public' sphere of paid employment is a modern phenomenon for which no traditional practices exist. Hence there is room for flexibility with regard to dress codes and, at a deeper level, social interaction across gender and caste as well.

In another context, many food sanctions are rejected in the 'public' sphere but strictly observed in the 'private'. Further, in the 'private' sphere of the family home the vegetarian canon is not broken when S7 eats eggs in Western (and secular) cuisine such as cakes, but is violated and therefore forbidden when eaten in a traditional preparation, such as a *sambhar* (which is similar to *dhal*).

Re-Interpretation

The third strategy, about redefining the essentials in order to meet the demands of the new setting, is called re-interpretation (ibid.: 335-42; Bilimoria 2007). As S. Radhakrishnan (1927: 18) observed, 'All sects of Hinduism attempt to interpret the Vedanta texts in accordance with their own religious views'.

In the Indian context, when re-interpretation of religious traditions becomes necessary, the faithful consult a priest (*pandit*), who is a highly learned brahmin well-versed in the religious texts. In Melbourne the newly-formed committee of the Ganesh Temple contacted the chief *pandit* of the Kanchipuram temple near Chennai, India, for guidance. But for more mundane matters such as the observance of holy days through fast and abstinence rather than worship, women in the diaspora decide for themselves. They may choose to observe such occasions in thought rather than deed, often citing sacred texts to support their choice. When pressed they may consult with or engage the services of a local Hindu priest from one of the temples.

At another level, as in India, festivals such as Christmas, Guru Nanak Gurpurab (usually in November) and Diwali are celebrated through attendance at Midnight Mass, recitation of the Akhand Path and Lakshmi Puja, respectively. For Indians in Melbourne such events are important occasions for social gatherings. For celebrations conducted in the 'private' sphere of the family home, and often even within the second 'home' of their extended ethnic community, the women may invite the equivalent of the parish priest to attend.

For the Sikhs this could be a *granthi*, who can be anyone able to read the Gurmukhi script of the *Guru Granth Sahib*. For the Hindus the celebrant could be a man of the brahmin caste who is able and willing to conduct the ritual. One such priest, since deceased, was a beef-eating, retired academic in 'mainstream' society who saw this function as a social service to the Indian community. On days when he was booked as celebrant he assumed ritual purity by reverting to a strict vegetarian diet.

Across the three religions there are numerous examples of re-interpretation that occur at both the group and the individual level. For instance, many in the Sikh community have cut their hair. N4 dismissed the fact of uncut hair (*kesh*) being one of the five marks of Sikh identity saying, 'you have to see the history of how it happened'. According to her the five emblems of Sikh identity were created for 16th-century warriors. She said:

> I personally don't think having the hair or cutting the hair has got absolutely any bearing on how much of a Sikh you are, because the core values of Sikhism is [*sic.*] not about hair.

Others such as S4 claim they are more 'spiritual than ritual-orientated' and re-interpret their Hindu religion accordingly. Her narrative given below suggests that this is an on-going, difficult process that is not easily articulated:

> *How important are these religious festivals and rituals for you?*
>
> The festivals and the religious rituals themselves are probably not such a major issue for me, but spirituality is part and parcel of my life.
>
> *How do you define it?*
>
> Well the rituals are something where you believe that OK you get up in the morning, for instance. Today is an auspicious day. Like you've got to, like for instance, Guru-Purnima day or something like that. People might believe like on Guru Purnima day you've got to fast, or you've got to actually do this, do that. For me fasting, or not having onions — for instance, in India you won't have onions on special days — is probably not such an important thing. But, yes, the auspiciousness of the day is important. Yes, if it's Guru-Purnima day it's actually respect for the Guru and I, so

> I, I'm more spiritual than ritual.
>
> *So you would have the onions but you would remember the day?*
>
> Definitely, yes.
>
> *How would you remember that the day . . .?*
>
> Only because somebody would have told me it's . . .
>
> *How would you make it auspicious?*
>
> It's a special day in terms of, I come from a spiritual background and I have continued having that spirituality in Australia. And that has been my anchor over the years. That has fundamentally been my anchor.

Conclusion

The migration narratives reveal that based on their religious nurturing in India the women evolve strategies that are traditional and non-traditional, and suitable for different settings. These enable them to cope with feelings of isolation and alienation in Australia, generating a sense of security on which they rely throughout, and in all aspects of their migrant lives.

For A4, an Anglo-Indian, this security comes from the basic familiarity of a ritual, regardless of the level of belief. She said that though migration was 'scary', 'adventurous' and 'new' with 'lots of good feelings, lots of sad feelings too':

> I remember thinking through it all that there's one thing that has not changed all the way through and that's been church. Because the Mass remains the same whether you're in India or whether you'd come here.

For N4 *gurdwara* attendance is important for religious worship, and also for its social and cultural affirmation. She said, 'it gives me that sense of belonging. It just, and also like I said, it's the hub of my social life. This is where it all started.' S8, a Tamil, finds security in a set of beliefs related to duty (*dharma*) and destiny (*karma*) (Singer 1972: 329-31). When things go well, she said, 'I believe that God has made these things go well for me, it is a blessing'. About the bad times, she said:

> I have my turbulence sometimes. I am a normal human. Sometimes

> I can have that jittering thing. But again I pray. I don't have anybody else to go for help. . . .

In this chapter, I set out to analyse the role of religion in helping migrants cope with the alienation and isolation they feel in a new land, with particular focus on 'middling transnationalism' from Asia (India) to the West (Australia). To do this I used narrative evidence and survey data from three groups of Indian migrants in Australia, namely Anglo-Indian, Sikh and Tamil women. I have shown that these women use their middle-class attributes and transnational connections to craft strategies for individual and ethnic group interaction in the 'private' and 'public' spheres of their everyday lives. They draw on their pre-migration nurturing in India and their post-migration experiences in Australia to achieve this. All the strategies involve socio-cultural practices, along with religious rituals and beliefs, that are adopted, discarded or modified for the sole purpose of making sense of their lives in a new land and on a daily basis.

Religious awareness, commitment and practice in a new land, therefore, is drawn from two sources — the migrants' nurturing in their country of origin, and the social environment in their new homeland. The first accounts for differences between migrant groups of similar religious affiliation but different religious environment, such as the Catholic Anglo-Indians and Italians in Australia. The second explains differences in terms of beliefs and rituals between and within India-born and Indian-descended diasporic groups, in a particular destination country or across the global Indian diaspora, of different religions and ethnicities, of similar religion but different ethnicities, and of different religions but similar ethnicity.

13

Indian Students in Australia

Margaret Kumar and *Purushottama Bilimoria*

THIS chapter has two parts. The first draws on the information presented by Indian student data, as well as media reports, to examine how Australia as a nation addresses the issues facing overseas students, and Indian students in particular. It is important to note that there were a number of factors affecting Indian students in their academic sojourn in this country. The issues confronting these students were far and wide ranging, spanning a continuum of problematic factors, from education abroad to violence against them, to Australian government policy, education providers and soft courses, and to permanent residency and visa applications.

Part A also identifies the dilemmas that faced both the Australian and Indian governments in dealing with these problems. It is hoped that a discussion of these issues will be to the betterment of the students and the stakeholders. Part B considers the 'learning anthropology' of Indian students in Australia, by drawing on interactions with such students in light of certain studies relating to the nature of their 'being'.

PART A

Education Abroad

There are various reasons why Indian students seek education abroad. In their study, Johnson and Kumar (2010) outline the burgeoning of a growing middle class in India that puts greater value on higher education. The issue however is where to go to seek such an education. As discussed by Fischer (2010: 2-3) some 220 million Indian children are enrolled in elementary and secondary schools but India's 400 universities can provide places for only 12% of this number. For this reason, many Indian students seek higher education overseas. Recently, *The New Education Act* of the Indian government has promised substantial increases in funds. However this is not sufficient in proportion to the growth in the number of individuals seeking a higher education.

As a result of this drive to secure higher education, there has appeared over recent years advertising campaigns by overseas countries to publicise the benefits of an overseas education. The recruiting of Indian students to universities abroad is so competitive that independent agents are employed in India to this end (Fischer 2010: A1-A22). Some examples that he reports are:

> In Delhi, test-preparation companies put signs on light poles promising help and a passport to a secure future.[1] There are also overseas-admission counsellors with floor to ceiling posters in the lobbies of high-rise office towers promising a better tomorrow for today's aspiring generation. In small offices over a local McDonald's, on the backs of taxis, and on central thoroughfares, agents, advisers and college recruiters ply their services. 'Study in Australia! Master your test! Foreign education delivered!' Correlating with this are newspaper advertisements consolidating a collective recruitment for Australian universities.

Australia is a country actively seeking to recruit students. This came about as a result of the Hawke government viewing education as a commodity of trade. In September 1985, the government formally adopted the 'Policy on the Export of Education Services', as part of a wider policy to boost the country's foreign exchange earnings. Universities and colleges were encouraged to increase their incomes and earn foreign exchange by charging full fees to private overseas students. This development also indicated that there were stages to the market ideology in the constructing of the international student (Kumar 2004).

In the move implemented by the Hawke government, the conceptualising and constructing of 'the international student' took on an ideological and complex meaning that went deeper than that portrayed in the Colombo Plan (ibid.). The literature documenting this development (Williams 1989; International Education and Development Services Program (IDP) 1995) shows that the marketing of education was started in 1986 by private intensive English-language-training institutions (ELICOS

---

[1] From their own experience, the editors note that such signs are put on light poles in almost every major city and town within India.

centres) and a few private universities and colleges. In 1987 and 1988, universities, technical and further education institutions and technical schools also began to recruit fee-paying students from overseas. This gained momentum when the government announced in 1988 that the subsidised private overseas student programme would be phased out by 1990 (Kumar 2004: 62). As a result of this initiative, international students have been coming to Australia for education in increasingly large numbers. In the period 1994–2000, these numbers increased from 100,000 to just under 200,000. In the period ending April 2010, they increased to 451,016 (Australian Government Education International 2010).

Historically, the number of Indian students was also increasing at a rapid rate. In 2002, there were 11,364 students (Australian International Education Network (AEI) 2002). By the year 2008, India ranked second to China, in the number of students who chose Australia as a place of education with 19.1% of all overseas students. In addition, India was the second largest source country by volume of enrolments (13.5%) and by volume of commencements (12.6%) (AEI 2009). By April of 2010, India was still considered one of the two largest markets in the higher education sector, with 10.7% enrolments and 6.73% commencements (Department of Education, Employment and Workplace Relations 2010). It is important to note that in more recent times other factors have encouraged Indian students to choose Australia as a location of higher education. For instance, as part of the move to recruit students, the Australian government has offered transition visas, leading to permanent residency, to students upon completion of their studies (Singh and Cabraal 2010; Gunawardena, Wilson, Georgakis and Bagnall 2010).

International education has been said to contribute Au$ 17 billion to the Australian economy.[2] It is also said to be Australia's second most valuable export after metals, according to a report by Harrison, Austin and Millar.[3] Apart from its monetary value, international students contribute markedly to the traffic of knowledge that comes about through the diversity of cultures, education systems, skills and talent (Kumar 2011). However, it is important to acknowledge that in the past few years there

2 N. Craig, *The Sunday Age*, 23 May 2010.

3 D. Harrison, P. Austin and P. Millar, *The Age*, 7 July 2010.

was a lull in this scenario. This was attributed to problems faced by Indian students, one of which was the issue of violence.

Problems Faced by Indian Students

VIOLENCE

It is also important to explore the historicality of the violence directed at Indian students.

In a recent report Craig discussed possible contributing factors for this violence, such as racism, a lack of security and safety, a lack of understanding about Australian and Indian cultures and victimisation.[4] Several research studies substantiated these factors. For example, Singh and Cabraal (2010) reported that 32 Indian students died in Australia between 2003 and 2009. In 2010 an Indian international student, Nitin Garg, was murdered (Masson 2010). While some of these reports may be exaggerated, there certainly were underlying problems (ibid.: 462; Mullins 2010). One has to remember that the victims have been international students who were here as 'guests' of the Australian society. This understanding led to a report that strongly asserted that, 'international students need protection and that it was not the laws that were damaging Australia's reputation but that these laws were not being enforced'.[5] Of notable significance was the fact that universities acted to address the growing security fears of Indian and other overseas students and to safeguard the multibillion dollar international education industry.[6] In understanding this violence, one must look at Australian government policies.

GOVERNMENT POLICY

Kumar (2004: 75) has pointed to the ambivalent nature of the Australian government policy towards international students. From aid to trade to internationalisation, there was a whole suite of policies that related to 'students from overseas' or 'international students'. Some of these were interpreted in ways that have proven to be detrimental and damaging to both the Australian and Indian governments.

---

4 N. Craig, op. cit.

5 Bonny Symons-Brown, *AAP Australian National News Wire*, 27 August 2009.

6 Josephine Tovey, Amrit Dhillon, Jonathan Pearlman and Eric Jensen, *Sydney Morning Herald*, 6 November 09.

A consequence of the historical development in policy was the number of reports that pointed to the host country not meeting its end of the transactional understanding of education as a trade commodity. In May 2010, N. Craig in *The Sunday Age* reported that Australia's promotion of its international market was unco-ordinated and lacked leadership and strategy. He also quoted Stephen Connelly, the president of the International Education Association of Australia, raising a number of concerns over how the policy for international students had been implemented. His key emphasis was that the violence against Indian students was a reflection of the dearth of policies relating to the quality of education and experience of international students. What could be regarded as a lack of direction, in both Australia and India, became evident in other areas of concern. One of these was the practices of education providers and the courses they offered.

EDUCATION PROVIDERS AND COURSES

A number of concerns had been raised about the questionable nature of education providers, in the sense of private vocational colleges and the courses they offered. The concerns raised came from various members of the community, ranging from people in authority, advocates of students, as well as the students themselves.

In August 2009, journalist Peter McCucheon reported that hundreds of private colleges had been offering hairdressing, cooking and accounting over the previous four years.[7] In the same report, lawyer John Kotsifas stated that some students were told to take some holidays but that they would be marked as present, because there were no teachers. Another incident discussed in the programme was that of an Austech cooking school, which enrolled 1,500 students but had facilities for less than 200. Federal authorities ordered a Brisbane-based college of technology to halt enrolments until it had put in place a system to record whether students were actually attending classes. In the same report, Gurmel Singh, a student who attended a Brisbane college teaching hospitality management, said that when he went there, there were not enough lab computers, no resource materials, the kitchen had not been built and there was no drinking water.

---

[7] 7.30 Report, ABC Television, 13 August 2009.

These examples may be representative of many such cases. Anecdotal evidence from several sources had shown that this may be so. The Australian government responded to such issues by putting in place stringent requirements for colleges catering for international students.

PERMANENT RESIDENCY AND IMMIGRATION LAWS

Closely linked to education providers and courses was permanent residency. A by-product of the education industry was the federal government's move to tackle Australian skill shortage by allowing overseas students to stay in Australia once they had completed their studies. On the Indian side, particularly in Punjab, several dishonest practices regarding the meeting of the criteria for students to come to Australia have surfaced. Concerns were raised both in Australia and in India about immigration scams providing access to permanent residency rather than quality education.

A television report in 2009 stated that:

> . . . an investigation into the overseas student industry has revealed that thousands of Indians are being enrolled in dodgy courses in Australia, while others are paying up to $ 20,000 for a good result in the IELTS (International English Language Test System) exam. In the Punjab — the main feeder community for Indian students in Australia, three people were arrested for impersonation and forgery after they were caught sitting the IELTS exam. Other scams have involved operators in the Punjab arranging contract marriages for aspiring immigrants to partners who have passed the mandatory test. For an additional fee agents have arranged bank accounts and loans to satisfy immigration law that demands that students have the means to support themselves for the duration of their stay.[8]

Some international recruiting agencies were investigated for fraud.

HOUSING AND ACCOMMODATION

Concerns were also been raised about housing and accommodation facilities for foreign students. In this regard, Stephen Connelly, the president of International Education Association of Australia, said that housing and transport should be addressed together with migration, education and

[8] 7.30 Report, ABC Television, 13 August 2009.

diplomatic goals 'not only should we develop housing strategies for international students but work on integration between international and domestic students at the same time.'[9]

Repercussions for the Parent and Host Countries

The repercussions of these issues were felt by the governments of both countries, as well as the parents of the students in India. In an article entitled 'Countries Agree on Students', Amrit Dhillon reported that the Indian Prime Minister Manmohan Singh and the then Australian Prime Minister Julia Gillard had discussed the Australian government's efforts to curb violence against Indian students and that the former was appreciative of what was being done.[10] In collaborative talks, former Prime Minister Gillard stated that institutions that failed to meet standards would be shut down, irrespective of what happened to the number of Indian students in Australia.

Of equal importance, the influence of Indian parents could not be understated. A sense of panic has set in for some of them. Parents who spent Au$ 30,000 a year in tuition fees in Australia, were sending their children to the United Kingdom, the United States or Canada because they no longer considered Australia a safe place.[11] Up to this point safety had been a major selling point for Australia's education industry but that reputation had been shattered in India by the widespread publicity about the attacks on students, along with revelations about disreputable vocational courses and visa-related scams. The seriousness of these issues resulted in a move by the Greens party to seek a senate inquiry into international education.[12]

Discussion with Indian officials showed several discrepancies. One of these was a reduction in staff in missions abroad. This meant that several measures put in place had to be stopped. One of these was the process of screening and interviewing students to see that they met the criteria of what could be termed 'the traditional student', i.e. an individual who is sent overseas to study for higher education with the proviso that they

[9] As reported by N. Craig, op. cit.

[10] Amrit Dhillon, *The Age*, 9 March 2009.

[11] Matt Wade and Heath Gilmore, *The Age*, 31 July 2009.

[12] Josephine Tovey, Amrit Dhillon, Jonathan Pearlman and Eric Jensen, *Sydney Morning Herald*, 6 November 2009.

return. As a result of the loophole that was created, students were able to work through agents rather than mission abroad officials, and original documents were not viewed. Thus, it was difficult to check who was the bona fide student.

In the Australian government's move to recruit students to raise its economy, it could be said that the principles guiding recruitment were interpreted in various ways. A repercussion of this particular loophole raised issues both for the parent country, India, and the host country, Australia. In Australia, this led to the 'birth' of private providers, some of whom had bypassed the federal government's guidelines. In India, this move led to a concerted drive by Indian agents to recruit students. According to Indian officials, there was no regulation of agents representing foreign education institutions. Both the parent country and the host country presumed that these agents were regulated when in reality, that was not the case.

The dearth of firm policies on the part of the Australian government led to various interpretations by the departments and private operators. Resulting from this, some institutions set up by private providers did not have the infrastructure, facilities and courses that were relevant to an Indian market. For example, according to official sources, some private operators had been able to bypass federal government guidelines and, in the past, there was ineffectual regulation of such providers. There were several factors that contributed to the problems discussed above. It has been reported that the Australian missions overseas did not have enough staff or resources to properly scan the student applicants. As a result of such loopholes, some applicants were able to work through agents of questionable repute rather than government officials. Further, in order to attract overseas students, many courses such as hairdressing, auto-mechanics and patisserie were offered, which are not relevant to Indian needs and which were also easily available within India.

Understandably, these issues will take some time to unravel and sort out. They highlight the shortcomings of international student recruitment. It can be argued that the issues began with the mishandling of the Colombo Plan and the administering of several policies (Kumar 2004). One factor has been the desire of the Australian government to fulfil the shortage of unskilled labour. This is seen in the taxi, cleaning and seasonal short-term market and fruit-picking industries. Another factor is the student who is struggling to make ends meet. In a study carried out by Bass (2006b: 14) it became evident that to meet living expenses and repay loans many students took poorly paid jobs night-time jobs to meet living expenses and repay loans. Adding to this was the fact that businesses were often run by migrants who by paying cash in hand did not leave a paper trail of underpaying their workers. A further case in point as pointed out by Bass is that students themselves were competing for these jobs and the ones who demanded the least amount of money were the ones who got employed. What has resulted is a vicious cycle of rule and regulation that needs to be examined from the planning to the implementation stage.

A drive by both the Australian and Indian governments indicates their intent to thoroughly address the factors affecting Indian students. Ultimately, further questions need to be asked: What is the appropriate system for recruiting students and providing quality education that meets the needs of Indian students? Should a pedagogical system be interlaced with a market economy? How does Australia approach the protocols guiding housing, accommodation and use of the international student labour force? It is important therefore to also explore the learning anthropology of Indian students, to which we now turn.

PART B

The Learning Anthropology of Indian Students

This section argues that Indian students like any student in higher education institutions overseas, progress in their journey of learning through an anthropological system that contributes to their being. It is hoped that this discursive exploration will contribute towards a better understanding of the Indian student, and subsequently lead to an interrogation of how curriculum and academic study can be improved to enhance student experiences and learning at a university. Further, in understanding how an Indian student learns, we invoke the concept of *topos* (place) in the learning behaviour of students. We choose a narrative approach in writing this section, as much of what we narrate stems from our professional experience of interacting with students, as well as drawing on our personal experiences of being brought up in a society that has undergone similar experiences.

BACKGROUND

Before we can discuss the core of what constitutes Indian international students, there is a need to assess the legacy that is built around international students in general. This we do from several studies. An important factor influencing the way international students adjust to study in higher education is the issue of transition as seen in the work of Kumar (2011), who discusses the fact that what might seem like rote learning and a lack of critical thinking skills could in fact be a developmental process of learning. This process involves a student 'shuffl[ing] through' the subtleties and nuances of the varying educational systems they have experienced, as well as the linguistic functions of form before a meaning is derived in the English language. As indicated by Biggs (1999), a reason for this may be the ethos, style and task demands of Australian and British universities, which may differ from the learning backgrounds of international students. Also significant, as pointed out by Watkins (1996: 115), is that the way Asian students combine the processes of memorising and understanding is different from that of a Western student. On this note, it becomes evidentially important that memorisation is an important process of learning (Hess and Azuma 1991; Marton, Dall'Mba and Tse 1996). Equally relevant is the fact that a number of students achieve better results with more understanding (Stevenson and Stigler 1992), thus signalling that both memorisation and the deeper approaches of understanding are significant patterns of learning behaviour in international students.

On another level, the impact of culture on learning behaviour has been considered in both a positive and a negative light. For example, Gow, Kember and McKay (1996) in a study carried out through action research signify the importance of the 'cultural' in deep learning approaches. Conversely, issues of how culture is viewed as a hindrance to learning are seen in the work of Biggs (1989, 1991, 1999) and Kember and Gow (1991), who point out that certain student groups are often associated with evidencing behavioural patterns of cultural passivity and a lack of creativity towards their learning. Yet, there are other studies that indicate very strongly that this would be the case if results are viewed only from a Western perspective (Tang 1993; Volet and Kee 1993; Ward, 2001; Watson 1997). Implicit in these studies is an underlying factor. It is that there are certain dilemmas for the student in how to use the knowledge he brings with him.

What also becomes apparent is the need to consider international student learning with a proactive approach rather than a reactive one. What this further denotes is that, while these studies have looked into ways of amending what is seen in a Western learning environment to be unacceptable to progressive learning, they have not looked into the deeper issues of the history, background and culture of the incoming student, and how these affect learning. They have not explored students' behavioural patterns towards their learning and whether these learning patterns create pathways that contribute to their world-view and progression of being. In taking these issues to a particular cohort, we now explore how they relate to Indian students. This we begin by contextualising the Indian student.

CONTEXTUALISING THE INDIAN STUDENT

In contextualising the Indian student, we draw attention to the general and to the particular in the term 'Indian students'. This cohort of students is further qualified by the name tag 'international students'. To discuss Indian students on a general scale is misleading. To define Indian students as coming from the subcontinent only is a misnomer. This is because the term 'Indian student' embodies a cultural and historical legacy in the persona of the individual, regardless of where she or he is physically located in terms of place of residence.

It is not our intention to discuss why this might be the case. Suffice to say that as part of a conscientious historical movement, as determined at either a macro level by government policy and decision, or at a micro level of individual decision-making, Indians have dispersed across the world, and many now call their place of home a physical space that is distinctly different from the subcontinent. So the term 'Indian students' to refer to a category of students who display particular physical characteristics is misleading. Our purpose in foregrounding this issue is to acknowledge the paradox we are creating. Nonetheless, we are using the concept to provide an understanding of Indian students who are mainly from the subcontinent, and to explore their learning from the point of view of a cultural/international dichotomy.

CULTURAL/INTERNATIONAL DICHOTOMY

We propose that Indian students have a cultural/international dichotomy in their persona that determines their ways of knowing and ways of being. Within this dichotomy, issues including history, culture and enculturation, ways of learning and methods of giving and receiving information, are of great significance to the being of Indian students. We call these issues 'essentialisms' in the behavioural learning patterns of the students.

In explaining this further, we borrow from Spivak (1993: 3) when we say that each individual is an essentialist to some degree. In taking the premise further, we are invoking the use of *topos*, in relation to the meaning of place (Literary topos 2013), as being a strategic essentialism in the lives of Indian students. Accordingly, it becomes necessary to acknowledge the importance of Indian history and how it provides a macro overview of the culture of Indian society, which subsequently helps in the students' enculturation to a *topos*.

Studies undertaken by Spivak (1988), Guha and Spivak (1988) and Choudhary (2008) emphasise the importance of historical periods for both determining and influencing the life and living of Indians. Of note is Choudhary's discussion that higher education in India has always been a socio-historic journey from tradition to modernity (ibid.: 69). The components that make up this journey include the ancient, medieval, colonial, post-Independence and contemporary, thus indicating the many phases through which Indians attained an essentialism that is conducive and therefore seen as productive to higher education for individuals who are from the subcontinent.

The use of essentialism in the behavioural learning patterns of Indian students will only be productive if it is used in a strategic sense, in deconstructing how the students are positioned in relation to our understanding of their behavioural learning patterns. To do this we need to think differently. In order to do just that, we need to take the 'risk of essence' (Spivak 1993: 3). The discussion that follows is based on that premise.

In this regard, we refer to Choudhary (2008: 51), who outlines the significance of Hinduism, Buddhism and Jainism as religions that are essentialisms in the being of Indian individuals. Within these constructs, the values of the Buddha, Mahavira, the great-emperor Ashoka and the great poets, such as Kalidasa, in ancient India were influential in creating, transforming and transmitting knowledge to Indians. This objective of transmission of knowledge was promulgated from the highest level in the Vedic period through the Brahmanical and Buddhist educational systems. Choudhary points out that the Brahmanical system was influenced by religious values, while the Buddhist system was a form of education that was secular in nature (ibid.: 69). He also emphasises the importance of *madrasa*s that were developed by Muslim scholars in the medieval period.

According to Choudhary, these phases of civilisation were seen as agents of change, in that they led to positive change for the whole country (ibid.: 57-70). In this sense, Choudhary outlines the wholeness and diversity of the traditional systems of higher education as being both religious and literary in character, with subjects such as medicine, astronomy, music, dancing, logic and law being some that students studied. However, he also puts forward the case that even though, in this early period, Indian universities were renowned seats of higher learning, under the colonial era, education was not used for sustainable development but to create a new class for the purposes of carrying out British rule. To this end, the six universities that were set up from 1857 to 1916 were established on the pattern of the University of London.

At the risk of seeming pedantic and painstakingly meticulous, it is important to re-emphasise that higher education was seen even in this early period as an essentialism in the 'fabric' of Indian society. In fulfilling this aim, Indian education incorporated a Western model alongside what could generally be said to be an Indian one to further enhance higher education. The result of this incorporation was seen in the fact that by between 1950-51 and 2006-07 universities in India increased from 28 to 369 and colleges from 578 to 18,064 (ibid.: 63).

All these factors, combined with the integration of states in the post-Independence period (ibid.: 70), sponsored a modernisation of India's education system made up of the components of a modern, Western social ethos and colonial legacies, whilst still maintaining in many instances a traditional higher education based on religion and ties of culture, caste and kinship. In exploring these phases of Indian civilisation, and the key roles they played in developing the country through the micro level development, as seen through the religions and their influence on the cultural being of its citizens, it becomes evident that both culture and its enculturation process began to provide a foundation for the anthropological approach to the learning behaviour of Indian students. Significant in this was the inherent value of Indian history and its influence on the being of an Indian international contemporary student.

THE INDIAN INTERNATIONAL CONTEMPORARY STUDENT

In the constituting of an Indian international contemporary student, we evoke the use of the 'differential' in relation to an essentialism. The differential allows one to take positions that reverse, displace and seize the apparatus of the value form. The operation of the value-form thus makes every commitment negotiable (Spivak 1993: 62-63). We use this definition in the positioning of Indian students, wherein the being of the Indian student is a composite-value form that is determined by their historical and cultural background as well as by contemporary practices. This becomes evident quite early in interaction with students, as discussed below.

Culturally, the student is defined by various representations. As outlined above, these have been defined by history, which subsequently has evolved into culture and enculturation. The culture that they 'inherit' and the enculturation that takes place constitute essentialisms in the being of these individuals. In the being of the contemporary students, 'cultures are patterns or schemas which are implicit in social practices and diffuse enough not to have to impinge on [a student's] consciousness' (Ram 1999: 215). Interactions with many Indian students show that they are able to draw on their essentialisms, which form part of their background learning, to draw on the present forms of learning. In this way they are taking the 'risk of essence' in a positive sense, to draw on their present learning. Included in this risk of essence are the differentials applied to meet the demands of the present. These differentials may be in the form of cultural practices, which, composite in themselves, are drawn upon without conscious reflection.

A further differential is the significance of parental guidance. In this regard, it is essential to point out a study by Johnson and Kumar (2010), who discuss the significance of parental guidance in the 'nurturing' of children to achieve higher education. Again the element of *topos* becomes evident, in that the guidance shows that the values chosen and the factors put in place lead to students seeking this form of education. In many instances, as Johnson and Kumar point out, the curricular of some schools in India are geared towards enabling Indian students to have a smooth transition to tertiary education in spaces that are away from home in another country.

Closely related to this is a further differential. This is that, as a result of being 'nurtured' to seek higher education overseas, many Indian students 'come to Australian universities with a global cosmopolitan imaginary already developed' (Rizvi 2005: 5). In extending this factor of a 'global cosmopolitan imaginary' further, it is our argument that this 'imaginary' is never stationary for the student. For the Indian student has a world-view that is always in transit, as determined by India's many phases of civilisation and leading to the anthropological experiences she/he experiences. For many students, learning is a journey that takes them through a myriad of such spaces. Being in Australia is but one step towards the many phases of the journey they have undergone in the search for a likely *topos*, as denoted by their historical background, as well as the many phases they are likely to undergo until they reach another *topos* that is conducive to their needs. Thus, for many of the students, their stay in Australia is what we term 'a learning sojourn' in their spectrum of being a global person.

The sense of being global also becomes evident in the way Indian students 'connect' with their home country. Points for discussion, in their interaction with parents, relatives and friends back home, may be a daily narration of what is happening there, asking for opinion and giving advice (ibid.). However, in this process, there is also a giving of new information, in the sense of a traffic of knowledge 'passing through', or how the student begins to transit into the new space of higher learning. Especially relevant here is the sense of *topos* within the student's spectrum of life and living. This *topos* is global in that, within its framework, their positioning, both in India and in Australia, is equally balanced (Johnson and Kumar 2010: 219; Kumar and Ang 2008).

The issue of language and its relationship to English is another differential that is significant in the contemporary being of Indian students. The official language of India is Hindi. However:

> The English language has a similar status and is also used for many aspects of education, politics and commerce as a language of communication. There are many other official languages and each state is free to decide its own regional language for internal administration and education, so there are 18 official languages spoken throughout the country. These are Assamese, Bengali, Maithili, Nepali, Telugu, Marathi, Tamil, Urdu, Gujarati, Malayalam, Kannada, Oriya, Manipuri, Punjabi, Assamese, Kashmiri, Sindhi and Mizo. The Sanskrit language is recognised as the official language of religion and is used in rituals and ceremonies and as part of daily prayers. Overall, there are 24 different languages, each spoken by a million or more persons as well as other 'languages' not officially recognised and a vast range of dialects. — Indian Languages 2010

In effect, the influence of these languages becomes a significant essentialism in students' behavioural approaches to learning.

Interactions with students have shown that an Indian student, by virtue of his persona, as determined by the historical background of culture and enculturation, is multilingual. Very often their repertoire of speaking skills is interspersed with several dialects. The majority of them have had formal education delivered through several systems, ranging from the cultural to religious to highly academic. In relating this to the language or language varieties students have within their repertoire of speaking and learning skills, interactions with students indicate the need for them to explain their relationship to both learning and the use of the English language as a medium of academic learning, as well as how these two issues relate to the language or language varieties they speak and very often think in. How they draw upon this learning to undertake further learning in higher education in the English language can sometimes be classified as a differential that is incommensurable. However, as Ram has shown, incommensurability can only be understood if we resort to language as an entire and primary modality of constructing a shared world for the speakers of that language (1999: 215).

Summary and Conclusion

In summary, a question we may ask is how do we make efficient use of the anthropological learning of our Indian international students. As

fig. 13.1: Students from India (Source: *Youths of India Abroad*, 27 June, 2014)

educational practitioners, we need to contextualise the traditions, beliefs, practices and customs that contribute to the being of the Indian student. It is through recognising that their background and experiences from home are interchangeable with experiences being faced in the new *topos* of the new country that learning is enhanced for the student (Kumar 2011). As outlined above, the degree of differentiality is reliant upon how the 'world' of the country they come from can be diffused into the 'world' of the country they are in.

It thus becomes necessary to seek to understand identity and cultural formations as 'historically structured but contingent, culturally patterned but dynamic and always politically contested' (Rizvi 2005: 3). For practitioners and educators, this means being acute to the diversity of the many states the students come from, the languages and dialects they speak, the differing customs, cuisines and cultures they practise. In fact, it would be fair to say that many of the Indian students who come to university are like any other international student, meeting other Indian students for the first time. Thus, to classify them as belonging to a general cohort of Indian students is misleading and creates both confusion and dilemmas for the student. In this sense, we need to take the 'risk of essence' in recognising the irreducibility of these students.

14

Changing Attitudes Towards the Hindu and Sikh Communities among Australians

Philip Hughes

Early Attitudes to Religions Other than Christianity

WHEN the British convicts and soldiers first arrived in Australia, they assumed they were bringing with them 'civilisation'. The convicts may have been people who had failed the social system in their homeland but they were still part of what they considered to be a civilised society, superior to any other around the globe. Most early European settlers regarded the Aboriginal people as entirely uncivilised, and barely human. The fact that they did not wear the clothes of 'civilised' people, or live in 'civilised' houses was evidence enough. The Asian people who came to Australia during the Gold Rush and in the following years were seen as little better. They were regarded as uncivilised. Mostly, the European settlers looked down on them and had little to do with them. This was true of the Chinese miners, the Afghan camel drivers and the Hindu pedlars.

At the heart of this attitude was a confidence that the white Australian Christians had superior knowledge of the world. In those days, Christianity was considered to be synonymous with civilisation. The missionaries who took the Christian faith to the Aboriginal people often saw themselves as introducing not only a new religious faith but also civilisation. It has been remarked that:

> The 'Christianising' and 'civilising' aims were often mentioned together, as if they were inseparable — to them, the rejection of pagan ways was as important as the rejection of pagan religion.
>
> — Harris 1990: 78

Within this understanding of 'civilisation' was the belief that human beings were progressing over time. 'Civilisation' represented the goal of this progression. It was seen as the goal that all human beings might expect to attain, given time and opportunity. The European nations saw themselves as much further advanced in this development than any other peoples, close to the peak of what was possible. Thus, they were benevolently helping other peoples to 'catch up'.

This progressive development was represented, for example, by medical success — the ability to treat successfully many diseases and conditions which had been previously untreatable — as well as industrial technology, such as harnessing of the power of steam, the development of machines for weaving cloth and, later in the 19th century, the development of the telephone, and still later, electricity, electronics and computer technology. These were all signs of European superiority. As inheritors of the Enlightenment, most Europeans had little time for what they considered to be the primitive superstitions of the religions of the East.

The British displayed these attitudes in India, justifying their colonisation in terms of 'civilising' people they regarded as primitive, by imposing British forms of law (rule of law) and order and the introduction of new forms of technology.

The Hindus and Sikhs who came to Australia in the 19th century were treated similarly. The white Australians tolerated them as labourers or as pedlars. But there was no suggestion that these people might bring religious traditions that were valuable in themselves or might even be of interest to Australians of European background. As noted above, there was a reluctant acceptance of a few Hindus and Sikhs as agricultural labourers and domestic servants, but the people of European origin had no time for what they considered as the practice of 'Hindu idolatry'.

Attitudes began to change in the years following the 'Great War'. When Europeans reflected on the terrible human costs of what we now refer to as the First World War, there was little basis for feeling superior to other peoples. As confidence in European civilisation fell, so did confidence in the Christian faith as its foundation (Howe 2003).

Within this period of questioning, following the Great War, some Australian intellectuals began to explore new ways of thinking about life. In doing so, they began to look more seriously at Eastern religions.

However, Buddhism attracted Westerners more readily than Hinduism or Sikhism. The philosophical nature of Buddhism, and its lack of requirement of belief in God or gods, was attractive to intellectuals who were increasingly influenced by the positivist and empiricist philosophies that were dominating thinking in British philosophical circles. The earliest known Australian Buddhist group of Westerners, the Little Circle of the Dharma, was formed in Melbourne in 1925 by Max Tayler, Max Dunn and David Maurice (Kelly 2007).

A second Buddhist group, set up in Melbourne in 1938, was led by Leonard Bullen, who used exclusively English terminology, rather than Pali or Sanskrit for the presentation of Buddhist teaching. The early appeal of Buddhism was evident in that the group promoted Buddhism as a workable school of psychology for modern problems. The study group was short-lived, however, perhaps due to the outbreak of the Second World War (Adam and Hughes 1996: 7-8). Other Western intellectuals in Australia rejected religion altogether. In 1918, the first Rationalist Society was formed in Melbourne. Similar groups were formed in other capital cities in the following years and a loose coalition of such groups, the Rationalist Society of Australia, was formed in 1938.

Nevertheless, Hindu-based or derived spiritual and cultural artefacts did begin to permeate the wider Australian landscape, whether through the Theosophical Society's urban meetings, visiting diplomats such as Rt. Hon. Srinivasa Sastri (Chapter 2, p. 67), or, more significantly, from 1930s, the explosion of Indian Dance repertoires in theatres across the nation and performative classes. These were introduced and choreographed by the legendary Louise Mary Lightfoot, with her accompanying Indian dance maestros, Shivaram from Kerala and Rajkumar Priyagopal Singh from Manipur (Bilimoria 2015). But educating Australians about the creative versatility of Indian culture — even within the context of the Empire, indeed the 'Jewel in the Crown' — was a slow and sporadic process, for some time yet.

The Second World War did not have quite the impact on Christian morale that had been experienced after the First World War. Indeed, there was a significant up-swing in the vitality of Christian groups throughout Australia. Many of the migrants who arrived in Australia in the immediate post-War years turned to the churches to find people with similar values, backgrounds and languages to their own. Inglehart (1977) has suggested that, throughout the Western world, there was a strong desire for stability after the Depression and the War, and the churches offered that. In this period, there was an explosion of suburban life around the capital cities and an explosion of family life. The churches provided a moral foundation and practical facilities for the development of family life.

Questioning Tradition

The children who were born in those years following the war, however, began to question some of the traditions of life as they grew into teenagers and young adults. They had been brought up in families and education systems that encouraged questioning. One of the catalysts for the questioning of tradition was the Vietnam War. Conscription into the army strengthened the issue. Many young Australians did not believe that Australia should be in Vietnam. Many felt that the war could not be justified. Christianity also came under considerable criticism, not least for prohibiting sex outside marriage, a tradition that seemed quite unnecessary when contraception was now readily available.

Within this context, there came a much wider movement to explore other paths to a 'good life'. Many turned to a range of drugs to explore inner experiences while some turned to other religions. The fact that celebrities such as the Beatles explored what Hindu *guru*s might have to offer was one of the factors that put Eastern religions on the radar for many young Australians. They travelled across the world in their thousands, looking at other cultures; they absorbed the sights, colours, sounds and smells of Eastern countries; they explored Eastern religions and rituals.

Hindu *guru*s began making their way to the West and many Westerners flocked to hear what they had to say. The visit to Australia of Swami Ranganathananda of the Ramakrishna–Vivekananda Mission in 1964 led to the foundation of the Vedanta Society of New South Wales. In the 1970s, members of the Hare Krishna sect were a common sight, processing and chanting around the streets of Melbourne and Sydney (see Chapter 3, p. 84).

While there was some fascination with Hinduism as represented by the migrating *guru*s and by the Hare Krishna movement, very few Westerners described themselves as Hindus. Buddhism remained more attractive to Westerners, and it has been estimated that, by 1991, perhaps 10,000 Anglo-Australians had decided to describe themselves as Buddhists on the Australian census (Adam and Hughes 1996: 42).

This new openness to Eastern religions occurred at the same time as changes in the immigration policies in Australia. As Australians increasingly explored the East, they became more accepting of people from the Eastern world migrating to Australia. In the early 1970s, the White Australia policy was discarded. Many of the first Asian immigrants to Australia were Buddhists and Christians from Vietnam. Then, in the 1980s, Hindus, first from Fiji, and then from India, began to arrive in significant numbers. Sikhs also began to arrive from India, Malaysia and other places. Thus, Australians began to see the traditional practices of Hinduism and Sikhism in their home context.

Openness to a Variety of Religious Practices and Philosophies

The Australian Survey of Social Attitudes (2009) is a major source of information about Australian's attitudes to religions. The survey was conducted by the Australian National University in conjunction with the International Social Survey Program. A random sample of 1,724 Australian adults responded to a wide range of questions about religion and spirituality.

The survey asked people about their religion when growing up and their religion at the time of the survey. Only 0.5% of the Australian population indicated that they had converted to a religion other than Christianity. This compares with 0.9% of the sample who had grown up in a religion other than Christianity and had converted either to Christianity or, the majority, to 'no religion'. The survey demonstrated that the dominant movement in the Australian population was from religion, whether it be Eastern or Western, to 'no religion', a move that had been made by 35% of the sample who had grown up as Christian and 20% of those who had grown up in another religion, such as Hinduism. The sample was not sufficiently large to indicate whether large numbers of Hindus and Sikhs were among those who had moved to 'no religion'.

While comparatively few people of Anglo-Australian background had indicated a change in religious identity, other surveys have shown that some have been willing to explore Eastern religious practices. The Well-being and Security Survey (2002), conducted by Edith Cowan University, Deakin University and Anglicare Australia, asked a random sample of 1,514 Australian adults, in some detail, about their religious and spiritual practices. While just 0.4% of the sample described themselves as Hindu and 1.3% as Buddhist,

- 19% said they had practised *yoga* or *tai chi* within the last twelve months, 4% doing so often;
- 16% said they had practised Eastern meditation in the last twelve months, 3% doing so often;
- 9% said they had read material on Eastern religious philosophies in the last twelve months; and
- 4% said they had attended a seminar or group on Eastern religious philosophies in the last twelve months.

Of those who practised *yoga* or *tai chi*, about half described themselves as Christian, another third as having 'no religion', and the remaining 17% as being of another religion. Of those practising Eastern meditation, just over one-third described themselves as Christian, one-quarter said they had 'no religion', and around 40% identified with a religion other than Christianity or described themselves as 'spiritual but not religious'. While many approach *yoga* and Eastern meditation simply as techniques for reducing stress or improving health, these figures indicate openness to Eastern religious practices among people who describe themselves as Christian or as having no religion.

In a similar way, there have been changes in the understanding of religious knowledge. In the past, religions were regarded as alternative systems. Most people identified with one religion and saw them as mutually exclusive. In recent decades, many Australians have come to regard religions as traditions, from which they can adopt, from time to time, a variety of beliefs and practices that might be personally helpful or relevant.

The Well-being and Security Survey put the following statement before respondents:

> The best way to develop spirituality these days is to take on board whatever is helpful from different spiritualities or religions.

Thirty-one per cent of Australians agreed with the statement, 35% were not sure, and 34% disagreed. While many Australians were not ready to embrace what different religions might offer them, approximately one-third indicated that they were open to the idea.

Many Australians are positive about people of other religions. The 2009 Australian Survey of Social Attitudes asked about the willingness to accept and respect people of a different religion to their own.

- 78% said that they would accept a member of another religion marrying a relative.
- 69% said they would accept a member of another religion as a political candidate.
- 67% agreed that 'We should respect all religions' and
- 58% agreed that 'All religions in Australia should have equal rights'.

Further questions were asked in the survey about people's attitudes to people of various religions. The survey showed that nearly half of all adult Australians were neutral to people of most religions. Many others were positive towards people of other religions, but the proportion who were positive varied considerably. Not surprisingly, given the proportion of people who identified themselves as Christian, more than 50% of Australians were positive about Christians. Around one-third of Australians were positive towards Buddhists, and about one-quarter of the population was positive about Jews, atheists and Hindus. Seventeen per cent of Australians said they were positive about Muslims as shown in *fig.* 14.1.

As *fig.* 14.1 shows, there was a range of levels of acceptance of Hindus in the Australian community. Those people who were most accepting were people with high levels of household incomes and those who saw themselves as being of higher social classes. While just 10% of those with incomes between Au$ 200 and 300 per week felt positive towards Hindus, more than 30% of all those with incomes of Au$ 700 per week or more felt positive. Similarly, while just 6% of those who described their social class as 'lower' felt positive, more than 30% of those who described themselves as 'upper middle' or 'upper' class were positive.

It is likely that those with higher incomes feel less vulnerable to economic competition and social competition from others. Indeed, among these people with high levels of income would be people looking for reliable employees. In contrast, those with lower incomes feel more vulnerable to all potential competitors, so people of different backgrounds and religion from their

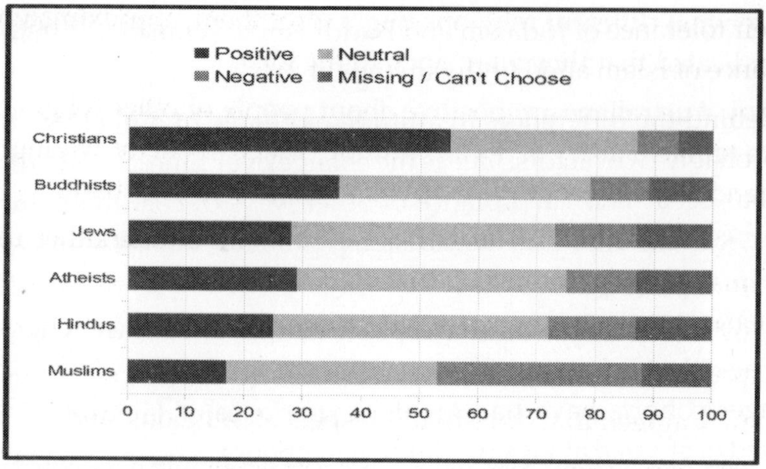

Source: Australian Survey of Social Attitudes 2009.

fig. 14.1: Proportions of positive and negative attitudes towards people of various religions among adult Australians

own are more likely to be experienced as a threat. Hindus, along with people of other religions such as Islam and Buddhism, are experienced as potential competitors for work, income and a place in society.

Apart from social class, education is a significant factor in the acceptance of Hindus. Twenty per cent of those without post-school qualifications were positive towards Hindus as were 18% of those with a trade qualification or apprenticeship. In comparison, 38% of those with a diploma or degree were positive. This pattern was also found in attitudes towards people of most other religions, including Islam, Buddhism and Judaism. It was also found in relation to atheism. People with higher levels of education tend to be more open to and tolerant of the variety of ways of thinking and of conceiving the world. Fifty-four per cent of those with a trade qualification or apprenticeship said they respected other religions compared with 73% of those with a university degree.

A third factor affecting the levels of acceptance of Hindus is age cohort. The Australian Survey of Social Attitudes (2009) found that younger people were more tolerant than older people. Just 10% of those aged over 80 years were positive towards Hindus compared with around 32% of those aged under 40 years. Again, similar patterns were found in relation to other religions, although there was some variation in its strength from one religion to another. The difference between younger and older people in their tolerance of Judaism and Buddhism was much less than in their tolerance of Islam and Hinduism (*fig.* 14.2).

Behind the differences in attitude of people of different age groups are probably two factors. One is the change over time, already discussed, that has occurred in acceptance of other ways of conceiving the world. Older Australians continue to display, to some extent, the attitudes that were prevalent prior to the 1970s, in which the Christian faith was frequently seen as being exclusively true.

The other factor evident in those of different age groups is that younger cohorts have had greater experience of Hindus. More have worked or studied alongside Hindu neighbours. Since most Hindus have arrived in Australia since 1985, few people over the age of 45 would have had Hindus as fellow students and would be less likely to have them as peers in the workplace.

A final factor that affects the level of acceptance is the religious orientation of the person himself or herself. It may be assumed that people who were deeply steeped in their own religion would be less tolerant of those of other religions. However, in Australia, that is not so. Of those who attended church monthly or more often, 35% say they felt positive to people of other religions. In comparison, among Australians who did not attend religious services at all, just 18% said they felt positive. In

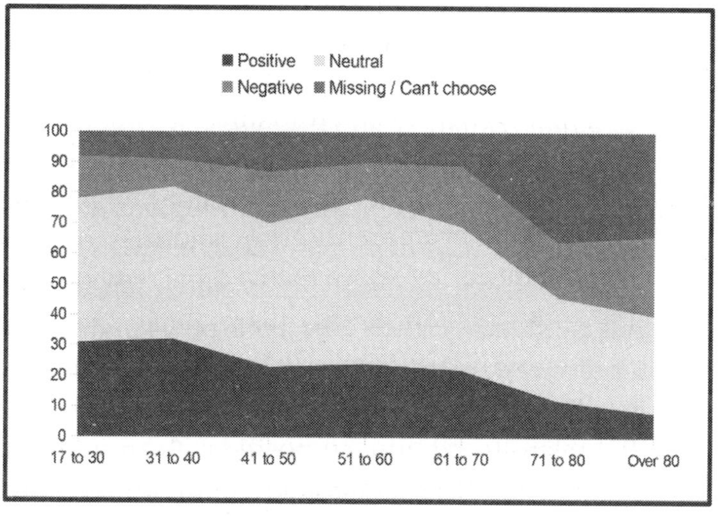

Source: Australian Survey of Social Attitudes (2009).

fig. 14.2: Attitudes towards Hindus among Australians by age group

general, those Australians who are interested in religion are more accepting of people of other religions than are those Australians who are not interested in religion at all. There are some exceptions to this. There are a few people involved in more exclusive religious groups, such as the Pentecostals, who are less tolerant of people of other religions. Nevertheless, even among the Pentecostals, only 29% indicated that they were not positive towards Hindus.

In summary, then, the major factors in acceptance of Hindus in Australia include low levels of competition for jobs and social standing, and tolerant attitudes towards people of different religions that have developed through changes in the understanding of religious truth, particularly since the late 1960s in Australia, as a result of high levels of education and through an interest in religion.

There were no questions about attitudes to Sikhs in the Australian Survey of Social Attitudes. While it may be surmised that similar factors would be evident in positive and negative attitudes towards the Sikhs, there is no survey evidence available. One difference between Sikhs and Hindus in Australia is that Sikh dress very clearly identifies, especially turbaned, Sikh men. Difference in dress ensures that the distinctiveness of the group is always apparent in public settings. Such distinctiveness may well make acceptance a little more difficult for some Australians.

Among the factors that have been found to be related to people's tolerance of immigrants, for example, are general positive attitudes to civil liberties, people's views of the economic situation in their region and their own economic situation, and the personal experience of having friends in the immigrant group (Kehrberg 2007). These factors will often be significant in the way that people of other religions are viewed. The personal experience people have of people of other religions is an important factor. These experiences may be positive or negative. If people see people of other religions as threats to their jobs, their power, or their freedom, then the experience may be negative. If people see people of other religions as bringing a positive diversity and richness to their life-experience as friends, then that experience may be positive. A positive attitude to multiculturalism, as distinct from ethnocentric attitudes in which minority groups are expected to assimilate, makes a difference to the level of tolerance (ibid.: 277). The experiences people have had of diversity have worked itself out in quite different ways in various political, economic and historical circumstances (Bouma 2011: 59-61).

Several social factors have probably contributed to the acceptance of Hindus in the Australian community. One factor is that the Hindus have been widely distributed through the suburbs of the largest cities. The community has not formed ghettoes but, rather, Hindus have interspersed widely with the wider Australian population and across the landscape.

Another factor that has assisted the acceptance of Hindus into the Australian community is the high level of education and the specialised occupations that most Hindus have. In 2006, the Hindu community was more highly educated than any other religious community, with 51% of all Hindus 15 years and older having university degrees. One-third of all Hindus had a professional occupation. Many Hindus had come to Australia to fill specialised occupations in which there were inadequate Australians to fill the positions. Thus, they have competed less with Australians for jobs compared with some other immigrant groups.

A third factor has been the open and inclusive nature of Hinduism. Being diverse within itself and offering many ways to the divine, Hinduism has not been seen as a rigid set of rules or an exclusive set of doctrines. Hindus have participated in the multifaith councils and conversations that have evolved in Australia, and people of other faiths have found it easy to dialogue with Hindus.

A factor that has hindered the acceptance of Hinduism is the belief in many gods. Australians are generally increasingly sceptical of the existence of God or gods. The multitude of Hindu gods is particularly strange and difficult for many Australians to understand. These factors are not present for Sikhism, with its belief in one Divine Principle, its focus on a sacred text, and its lack of unfamiliar and unusual images or icons and idols. In principle, the portals of Sikhism especially its *gurdwaras* and offering of *langar-prasad*, is open to anyone and everyone, regardless of ethnicity, caste or faith.

There are other factors, however, which may have hindered the development of positive attitudes towards Sikhism in Australia. There have been no particular Sikh practices comparable to the Hindu yogic practices, which could be easily adopted by Australians without the adoption of the religion as a whole.[1] Sikhism is also not as open and inclusive as Hinduism, partly because of its authoritative regard for its own scriptures. The factors of distinctive dress and rituals may well be hindrances in the acceptance of Sikhism among Australians. Nevertheless, Sikhs have also participated widely in interfaith activities in Australia.

The fact that many Australians, especially younger people, are respectful of other religions and accepting of people of other religions, but are not converting to those religions, suggests a different approach to religion and spirituality among most Australians from that which existed in the 19th and 20th centuries until shortly after the Second World War. Consistent with the turn to what the Canadian philosopher-theologian, Charles Taylor, has christened 'Secularity' or the 'Secular Age', many younger Australians now see religion not as a matter of 'truth', but as a matter of personal preference, a lifestyle choice. If you want to believe in reincarnation, that is fine (Hughes 2007: 129). If you prefer to believe that there is nothing after death, that is fine too. Indeed, recent research into young people's attitudes to religion has shown that most young people approach religion as a personal matter. '[Religion] is something they can turn to for help if they feel the need. Whatever is good for you, whatever works is fine. Whatever you believe is up to you' (Hughes 2007: 148). While that means Australian young people are open to a variety of religions, it also means that they are not inclined to take religion very seriously. It is not central to their thinking or high on their list of priorities. The majority of young Australians are not deeply concerned about religion and feel that religion should not be taken 'too seriously'. Asked in surveys in schools if religion was harmful if taken to extremes,

- 52% thought that it was,
- 30% were not sure, and
- 18% thought it was not (ibid.: 149).

While many Australians have a positive view of multiculturalism and of cultures other than their own, racist attitudes surface from time to time.

---

[1] Though some popular Sikh teachers in recent years, especially in North America, and also with Western converts to Sikhism, have set up their own yoga centres, Punjabi music schools, and regular retreats for *Kundalini* practices, such as the 3HO — Healthy Happy Holy Organization of Yogi Har Bhajan Singh. Their presence in Australia, however, has not been negligible.

The race riots involving approximately 5,000 people that occurred in Cronulla, Sydney, in December 2005 are an extreme example. Those riots were focused particularly on Lebanese and people of middle-eastern backgrounds. Nevertheless, the language surrounding those riots, including that used on public radio by the presenter Alan Jones, shows that racist attitudes still abound in Australia.

Balbinder Singh Bhogal of Hofstra University, New York, in reflecting on the Oak Creek shootings in the United States, of Sikhs in their *gurdwara*, has argued that colonial views remain current in the Western world:

> Though the language of civilized vs. barbaric may no longer be in vogue given the influence of cultural relativism, the colonial mindset resurfaces in the distinction drawn between secular rational moderns and irrational religious primitives.
>
> — Bhogal 2012: 338

He suggests that this is evident in some of the responses to the Oak Creek shootings, in the fact that Western cultures allow white-supremacist attitudes to develop in someone like the Norwegian Anders Breivik, and in the way vigilantes patrol the southern US border. He suggests that many people regard those from the world once colonised by the West as 'outsiders', and as under-dogs, and that this perspective legitimises 'a level of violence and righteousness in equal measure' (ibid.: 337). The preoccupation in Australia with border controls, particularly in relation to people seeking to reach Australia by boat, might be interpreted as reflecting racist attitudes, although a significant part of it the motivation appears to be not to exclude people, but to have control over entry.

Bhogal goes on to argue that, as a result of the way that religions such as Hinduism and Sikhism were branded by the West, Europeans saw themselves as having a superior critical consciousness. While Hindus and Sikhs were seen as involved in myth, ritual and superstition, the West was viewed as superior in its multiculturalism and rationality. In this way, the West's so-called 'secular culture of oppression and hate' has been normalised. Bhogal suggests that a new frame of 'cultural comparativity' is needed for the differences between Hindus and Sikhs, for example, and Europeans 'not to be perceived as a threat or a virus, but precisely that which enhances the whole that remains invisible otherwise' (ibid.: 338).

The Roots of Change and Continuing Challenges

Bhogal may be right that some elements of colonial thinking survive in Western nations, and that many Australians of European origin do not see Indians as their equals. It has been reported that 58% of adult Australians believe that all religions in Australia should have equal rights, 23% of Australians do not agree with that view, and 18% do not have an opinion either way. Nevertheless, there has been a very significant shift in opinion and the openness to people of other religions since the colonial attitudes of the 19th century. At the root has been a decline in confidence in Christianity, partly in the face of the involvement of Christian nations in war, the decline of European empires, and partly in the face of the growing impact of science. On the other hand, secular views can also involve an intolerance of religion, and particularly 'non-European' religion, as seen in the lower levels of acceptance of Hindus by those who hold 'no religion' in the 2009 Australian Survey of Social Attitudes.

However, the critique of tradition *per se*, and the search for new ways of experiencing life, that developed in the Western world in the 1960s and 1970s, has played a major role in developing tolerant attitudes. The delight that many young Australians have taken in travel and in exploring the variety of cultures, religions, cuisines and lifestyles has contributed to that openness that is now evident among many Australians. Within the new ways of thinking about tradition have been changes in the ways of thinking about the truth of religion. Many Australians see religion as part of culture, or as a personal preference, rather than something that is true or false in an objective way.

With each new wave of migrants to Australia, there has been some wariness. But, in general, most Australians have come to accept and even to celebrate the variety of cultures that have become part of Australian multiculturalism. As Australians have come to understand these different cultures, many have come to feel positively about them. That process has been a little easier with some religions than others. For example, the inclusive attitudes that many Hindus and Buddhists have in relation to religion have assisted dialogue and mutual acceptance.

In a world of uncertainty, fundamentalist attitudes, whereby one decides that a particular religion is exclusively correct, do persist. Understanding beliefs, and appreciating the common human values of people from different cultural and religious backgrounds, is therefore critical for developing harmony in a multicultural society.

15

Concluding Reflections
Indian Religious Diaspora in the Post-secular Era

Purushottama Bilimoria, Jayant Bhalchandra Bapat and *Philip Hughes*

THE story of the Hindu and Sikh diaspora in Australia is the story of the interaction between two entirely different cultures and their ways of thinking. In Australia, the Indian-rooted Hindu and Sikh traditions have interacted with the Australian culture, with its predominantly Western, Christian origins. Hinduism and Sikhism in the diaspora have also found themselves in a different kind of plural context from that in India, a context in which pluralism means individual choice and even the individual construction of personal 'faiths', drawing on a variety of religious resources.

This book has examined, in a variety of ways, the effect of this interaction on both the Indic and the Australian cultures. Here, we have seen our role as bringing together the threads contained in the preceding chapters, in order to consider their significance, both for the on-going development of Hinduism and Sikhism within Australia, and for Australia's future as a multi-ethnic community.

The story began in the 19th century, with small groups of Hindus and Sikhs seeking a livelihood in Australia. Almost all of those who came were men, hoping to make some money in the expanding economies of the Australian colonies. The mining of gold had brought new wealth and spawned the development of many towns and cities. At the same time, farming was expanding rapidly and the export of wool to Europe, in particular, was proving a lucrative trade.

The Hindus and Sikhs who arrived in Australia in the 19th century were not offered a wide range of options. It was not possible for most of them to buy land. However, a number of Hindus and Sikhs became pedlars, marketing small goods to isolated farms. Hindus and Sikhs were tolerated, but most Western people saw them as inferior, as only partially civilised. There was little chance of integration. Indian religion was seen as inferior to Christianity and not worthy of interest.

When the economic situation tightened at the end of the 19th century, and unemployment became common, attitudes hardened against these adventurous and resilient people from South Asia. They were encouraged to leave Australia's shores and any newcomers from their part of the world were prohibited. Only a very small group of Hindus and Sikhs were able to remain in Australia. Because lived mostly as isolated individuals, or in a few small family groups, their practice of religion remained within their private lives, in the context of their homes.

The cessation of the 'White Australia' policy in the mid-1970s meant that the diasporic pattern has developed a very different form. Partly because of the numbers of Hindus and Sikhs arriving in Australia, and partly because of the greater openness among people of European background to the religions of the new arrivals, there has been considerable interaction between Australians of European background and Hindus and Sikhs. Such interactions have had an influence on the Indian faiths, and the Indian faiths have had an influence on the Australian cultural environment.

The Significance of Context for Indian Faiths

CHANGES IN RELIGIOUS SALIENCE

One of the most immediate impacts of immigration is that it raises questions of identity. In simple terms, immigrants are forced to ask themselves 'who am I?' While they may have distinguished themselves from others in their homeland by their respective region, language, occupation, class or caste, as well as their family connections, these distinctions mean little or nothing in the new context. Immigrants become poignantly aware of their ethnicity, their language, or their way of pronouncing it, and their cultural practices and customs, which distinguish them from the people around them. Within this context, they become aware of their very different religious background and the different ways in which they express and practise their religion. Thus, religion becomes part of that which distinguishes them from others within the new context, and therefore a more prominent part of their identity. It has been noted that many Hindu and Sikh immigrants who come to Australia from relatively secularised environments in India take their religion more seriously in the new country. As they become aware of it as part of their identity, so it becomes more important to them. It is not just a set of customs that they may have taken for granted in their homeland.

This increased interest in religion comes about in several ways. One is that Australians will ask about it: children from India may be encouraged to give an account of their religious customs and festivals in the school; neighbours and colleagues in the workplace will ask about the new immigrants' religious beliefs and practices.

A second way in which interest in religion is increased is that new decisions have to be made. Will time be requested in the workplace for the celebration of a religious festival? What provisions will be made in school for the religious heritage of the child? Will children be encouraged to go to special classes to learn about their religious background? On what religious sensitivities will the person insist within a hospital or when a person dies? Many of these decisions would not arise within the homeland where the religion is embedded in the local way of life. But the very fact that these decisions emerge in the new setting adds salience to religious heritage.

A third way in which interest in religion is enhanced is that it often becomes the focus around which immigrants gather. Religious festivals and times of worship bring people of common religious heritage together. People find their sense of community around people who share their values, their view of life and their religious heritage. Hence, the religious community becomes conscious of its distinctiveness.

Nevertheless, both surveys and other research suggest that this heightened awareness of religion among new immigrants weakens over time. Gradually, immigrants get to know Australians outside their faith community. They begin to identify themselves more with the people and culture of their new context. A trip 'home' sometimes demonstrates how much they have changed from the people they left behind when they emigrated. They become aware that they are now Australians, rather than immigrants from South Asia.

This process continues into the second generation. Indeed, some second generation immigrants find themselves caught between the homeland culture, as practised in the home, and the Australian culture in which they find their friends and with whom they wish to identify. They have to make difficult choices: while some find their identity in their distinctiveness from the Australian culture, others find their identity within the Australian culture. The involvement of second generation immigrants in their religion is often not as pronounced as among first generation immigrants. The importance of religion as part of their identity sometimes fades.

Religious salience may fade even more if the second generation immigrant marries a person of a different religious tradition. It becomes harder for them to maintain the distinctiveness of their religious customs and less important to do so for their sense of identity.

CHANGES IN RELIGIOUS ORGANISATION

In the new context, people from different Hindu and Sikh traditions find themselves working, living and worshipping alongside each other. Within the home context, there would be many temples from which they might choose, and even different festivals in which they might be involved. This is not the case in the new context. There are fewer options even in the larger Australian cities. Hence, different religious traditions may be merged with each other. This has been most evident in the building of some of the Hindu temples. While Melbourne and Sydney have different temples for people from the north and south of India, most Hindu temples contain images of a variety of gods, including gods who would normally be worshipped quite separately in the Indian context. People from different Hindu traditions are forced to collaborate, and, in many instances, forced to compromise. They cannot all have their favourite gods in the most prominent position. They must make space for the rituals associated with gods other than those to whom they would normally pay attention.

The development of leadership within the diaspora communities is often a challenge. The structures whereby leaders operated in India no longer work in the new context. New structures have to be created, sometimes in ways where there are no easy precedents to follow and no clear power structures to acknowledge. Hence, there is often a jostling for positions of power and authority within the diaspora community. People are keen that their particular traditions receive appropriate recognition, so they strive to give them a place.

Many of the priests who serve the Australian temples are brought from overseas for that purpose. They are able to conduct the appropriate rituals. Yet, again, for them, there must be compromises that they did not have to make in their homeland temples, as they serve people who have a variety of customs, backgrounds and even spiritual needs. They might also find themselves in difficult situations, as they do not necessarily understand English or the new Australian context of those whom they serve.

Over time, as temples are built and as new structures begin to emerge to train religious leaders within the context of the diaspora, decisions are made and organisational issues are settled. The new structures that emerge, however, are often quite different from those of the homeland. As people of different traditions celebrate and worship together, new customs and practices emerge within the new organisational structures.

CHANGES IN BELIEF AND PRACTICE

Within the new context, the very nature of religious faith changes. Rather than being an expression of a national identity, religious belief becomes an expression of personal, or sub-group identity. Religious faith becomes more personal, rather than simply participation in a larger community. As such, the faith is no longer dominated to the same extent by the religious organisation. The individual must make his or her own decision about what to believe and what to practise.

What is meaningful in the new context also changes. Within the Australian social context, for example, caste is not relevant. Thus, religion as a protector of caste is not an issue. The social role that Sikhism has performed in providing an alternative to Hinduism, in the rejection of caste and in the focus on the authority of the book, the *Guru Granth Sahib*, does not bear the weight that it did in India.

The context puts pressure on practice in various ways. Festivals cannot be so easily celebrated in the streets of the cities. More attention must be given to the interests of those who do not share the faith.

In relation to Hinduism, funerals have been required to conform to Australian norms. Open pyres have not been allowed. In most places in Australia, cremations have to occur within crematoriums; and temple priests are called upon to perform the funerary rites, which is not their usual calling in India.

The importance of festivals that involve particular locations inevitably declines. Thus, washing oneself in the Ganges is not possible for most Indians living in Australia. Its importance fades in the new context.

It is inevitable that Hindus and Sikhs will find a new sense of what they have to offer and in what ways their faiths are distinctive within the Australian context. Future generations will identify the distinctiveness of their faiths in new ways and will do so in relation to the Australian cultural context. Some immigrant communities have been aware of the strength of their community life, in comparison to the lack of a sense of community and the low levels of commitment to family or family values they perceive among Australians. Some immigrant communities have been scandalised by the lack of a sense of the spiritual, overshadowed by the stark materialism and consumerism of Australian culture. Consequently, they have found their sense of identity over and against Western individualism and consumerism.

On the other hand, there has also occurred some de-mystification and rationalisation of religious faith within diaspora communities. The academic Sikh community in the United States, for example, has begun to adopt some of the forms of literary criticism and postcolonial/postsecular theorising that have been used in Western Christianity and postmodern theology to obtain new or progressive hermenutical understandings of their history, beliefs and scriptures. Elements of religion that might be considered superstitious have been rationalised or historicised.

Over the coming decades, both Hinduism and Sikhism will evolve. As they do so, they will be shaped, to some extent, by the new or altered contexts. They will also find their distinctiveness within the new Australian context and thus continue to have an impact on the Australian ethno-religious landscape and its visions for a polychromatic citizenry. On a more general note, with Indians comprising one of the largest and fastest-growing communities in Australia, there is great scope to harness societal links to strengthen political and business ties as well between the two former colonial outposts. It is essential to build constituencies to champion Australia-India relations in both countries during future potential phases of trouble, which could occur in any bilateral relationship.

The Influence of the Diaspora Hindu and Sikh Communities on Australia

The major influence of the diaspora Hindu and Sikh communities in Australia has been to add to the multicultural and multi-faith nature of Australian society. Numerically, the Hindu and Sikh communities are still quite small. Together, they make up little more than 1% of the Australian population. In many parts of Australia, especially outside the major capital cities and large regional towns, Australians have little awareness of these communities and may never have met a member of them.

Even in Melbourne, Canberra and Sydney, where these communities are well over 1% of the population, many Australians will not have had the opportunity to meet or interact with members of these communities, and they will have little awareness or understanding of their religious traditions. They might occasionally catch a glimpse of a Hindu temple or a Sikh *gurdwara* as they drive past on a freeway. Many will see them as strange buildings and will have no way of identifying what they are or to what communities they belong.

Nevertheless, most Australians are well aware that they now live in a religiously pluralistic context. They are aware that people around them believe quite different things to themselves. They might not know the faith of the people who wear turbans, but they will be aware that it is a faith that is different from their own.

In some contexts, the awareness of the multiplicity of religious faiths has put the issue of spirituality on people's agendas. It has encouraged them to think about religious faith in contexts in which it would not previously have occurred. Sometimes they become aware that people are celebrating their religious festivals. Sometimes they are aware that people are making choices about food or clothing that reflect their religious heritage, and thus they become aware that religion is a part of life that is important to people.

In communities such as schools, the presence of people of a variety of the world's religions helps to put religion on the agenda. Schools must take seriously the provision of opportunities for education in and celebration of various religions. They will therefore present opportunities to enable students to better understand each other and the backgrounds from which they come.

The presence of Hindu and Sikh communities has raised questions for Australians about how they relate to the multiplicity of religions. How do they relate to people who have a different understanding of the world? There are some Australians who, in the face of other religions, reassert their own understanding of the world more strongly. They see themselves as having the truth and believe that they must seek to convert others to their way of thinking. This applies to both some Christians and some atheists. On the other hand, others are encouraged to understand the diversity, and to accept that people from different religious backgrounds can live harmoniously together. Indeed, it has been noted that the majority of Australians now have some respect for all religions.

The plurality of religions raises questions about how can — and should — that plurality be managed? Are there points at which respect must cease or at which people should be forced to confirm to common Australian patterns of life? Certainly, this has been an issue with funeral practices. Governments have had to decide what was necessary in the interests of public health and propriety and to what extent Australian customs could be varied. Plurality of religions has also raised the issue of what the minimal values are with which diaspora communities should be expected to identify. There has been re-affirmation from time to time that respect for the equality of all human beings, for example, and the expression of that equality in democracy, is necessary.

fig. 15.1: Unity in diversity

While putting faith on the agenda, the multi-faith nature of Australian society has introduced the notion that the nature of religious belief is relative. People become aware of others operating comfortably in society on the basis of quite different world-views and religious systems of belief. Hence, the sense has developed among most young people in Australia that they must make up their own minds about what they believe about religion. The awareness of the multiplicity of possibilities means that there are options and the tenets or practices of particular religion cannot be imposed.

It is not clear whether, in the long term, the presence of diaspora communities of the various world religions will have the effect of strengthening or weakening overall religious faith and commitment in Australia. The presence of a variety of religious communities has raised the issue of religion and spirituality for people who might not otherwise have thought about it. On the other hand, the variety has led to the sense that religion is relative and is a personal choice. Most young Australians see religion as something they either choose, or choose not to be, involved in. That is the predicament or rather prerogative of the 'Secular Age' (Taylor 2007).

The Future of Religion in Australia

The Indian diaspora will continue to grow for some years to come. The numbers involved will depend on the vagaries of Australian immigration laws. The laws will be developed in relation to both 'push' and 'pull' factors. Changes in climate, for example, could be among the 'push' factors that force people to look for parts of the world that are not so subject to difficult climate conditions, whether they be floods or droughts, or the ravages of tornadoes. Among the 'pull' factors may be the desire for increased new immigrant workers to serve an increasingly local ageing population. On the other hand, the capacity of Australia to cope with a larger population and its demand for water and other natural resources will continue to be debated.

The rates of continued immigration will have an impact on the extent to which the diaspora communities remain fresh and the extent to which they are oriented primarily towards those who have recently arrived from overseas. As long as immigrants arrive, there will be a role for the religious communities to help them find a place to belong and with which to identify. If immigration rates slow, however, the links between ethnic heritage and religion may gradually weaken. Instead, the identity of these communities may develop through finding their distinctive contribution to Australian society.

Within the awareness of the plurality of religions, young Australian people are increasingly thinking of religious faith not in terms of identity but as a range of resources on which they can draw. They see themselves drawing increasingly on the variety of religious resources from both East and West. They see themselves primarily as human beings who draw on various traditions and customs of life and practice.

As this new way of thinking about religion develops, so there is a greater appreciation of the common humanity of all peoples. Indeed, within the last decade, the ease of global communication has increased dramatically. The common needs and desires among human beings of all persuasions and commitments have become increasingly evident, as has the fact that all human beings are having an impact on our global environment.

The World Parliament of Religions, held in Melbourne in December 2009, affirmed the common need for human beings to recognise the spiritual issues of life. It also acknowledged the need to respond to the common challenges of the global inequality of wealth and poverty, and the challenges of climate change.

The diaspora communities are playing a role in allowing all Australians to be aware of their common humanity. In this way, they might also play a role in encouraging all people to draw on their diverse traditions, to contribute to the common needs of human life and society.

Appendix A

The Importance of Diasporas

Ninian Smart[1]

THE Jewish diaspora is the most important diffusion of people and ideas in the history of the world to date. There are however other diasporas that have hardly attracted the attention of students of religions, in spite of the fact that they are playing a more and more vital part in the revivification of their home religions. Thus there are diffusions of Hindus overseas from India, often substantial in number, in such places as Australia, Fiji, South Africa, Kenya, Guyana, North America and the UK. Also there are important groups of Sikhs and Tamils in Canada and the UK and elsewhere, who have had a financial and ideological role in stirrings in Punjab and Sri Lanka. Because of the oppression of Buddhist religion in Tibet, we have witnessed, in the last half of the century, the arrival of significant numbers of Tibetan refugees in India, Nepal, Britain, USA, Canada and elsewhere. In some places, the most likely form of Buddhism a Westerner is likely to encounter at home is Tibetan. There are, outside of the main Islamic territories, significant minority communities of Muslims, e.g. in parts of Europe, in other Western countries, in South Africa, East Africa and the Caribbean, and elsewhere. Chinese, Japanese, Korean and Vietnamese forms of Buddhism are widely dispersed in North America; Chinese religious culture is central in Singapore and important in Malaysia and Indonesia, etc.

In many of these diasporas, there is an element of exile. In some cases, it is the consequences of the harsh economic realities in which overseas communities have grown up (as in the case of the indentured labourers of the post-slavery British Empire). In other cases political persecution has driven folk abroad. But sometimes it is a more casual matter; people have migrated without extreme pressures. Thus many Algerians in France

[1] The chapter, published earlier as an article, was gifted by the author for this volume before his sudden death at his home in Birmingham, January 2001. The editors are grateful to Mrs Libushka Smart for permission to include the article in this volume.

and Turks in Germany have found it attractive to go to the host countries for reasons of economic opportunity. Likewise, Indian professionals have migrated in large numbers to the UK, USA and Australia. Migration has, for some, been a matter of opportunity, rather than life-or-death necessity. Even so, there remains a sense of exile when persons come out of their own culture and settle in among an alien majority in an adopted country.

These diasporas are important for us to study, and this for several reasons. The first is that it can provide a clue to patterns of religious transformations. One may find similar developments in different communities, which reflect parallel solutions to parallel problems. Such changes may also pinpoint problems in the religion which make its adaptation to a new environment difficult. So the first reason has to do with adaptation. Second, diasporas may themselves affect the home-based religion. Thus Sikh militancy is strong in Britain, and this helped to stoke the fires of passion in Punjab. Migrants often become wealthier than those left behind, and they may also be more exposed to education and foreign influences, and can export such influences back home. Third, the phenomenon of the diaspora is important, because of its great incidence in the modern world. In Los Angeles, California; in Birmingham, England; in Sydney, Australia; in Frankfurt, Germany and numerous other major cities of the world multi-ethnicity is now commonplace.

Incidentally, this diaspora phenomenon is also a great opportunity for students of religion. It is possible, up to a point, for students to do much of their fieldwork at home. You do not have, in many areas, to go far to meet Tibetans or Iranian Shi'is, or Japanese Pure Land Buddhists. This presence of other religions may help us, by the way, to be more realistic in appraising Western home-grown religions, that is Christianity and Judaism especially: we may be more open to seeing how they work on the ground, rather than just in the text. Generally speaking, in my opinion, Christianity and Judaism are the religions least well taught, because of seminary-type assumptions still guiding our curricula. And as for Hinduism, it is not even taught, because of the strident commitment to a secular curricula. A strong dose of sociology and anthropology, or history of religions on the ground, would inject colour and realism into religious studies in relation to these 'home-grown traditions'. In Australia we could follow the model adopted at the University of California Santa

Barbara, which instituted a programme called 'Religious Contours of California', funded substantially by the California Council for the Humanities. This later programme seeks to encourage the teaching of world religions by beginning with the forms of religion found in California itself: Hinduism, Buddhism, Catholicism, and so on, exemplified in various ways through the influx of Hindus, East Asians and Mexicans, as well as more traditional migrants into the state. This is a way of including diasporas as bridges to their native or classical manifestations. It has incidentally revealed extensive areas for research also. All this focuses on the diasporas, and does not take into account the way some religions have jumped their more traditional boundaries and taken root among new ethnic groups: Buddhism among Anglos or White people, Islam among American Blacks, and so on.

However, it is to the more theoretical aspects of the study of diasporas that I wish to draw attention to in the chapter. What are the kinds of religious changes one might expect? And what changes are found on the ground? Much obviously depends on the host societies. The migration of Christianity into India, in ancient times, and its survival in south India to the present time would imply some degree of adaptation to the most important structural feature of Indian society, that is to the caste system. In fact, this assumption seems to be borne out by experience. However, we may note in the modern period a special feature of the intercultural contact implied by the creation of diasporas — that because of European and American power during the colonial experience, certain powerful ingredients of Western life and values became a pervasive presence virtually throughout the world. Even countries such as Japan and Thailand, which did not fall under Western rule, had to absorb many Western values in order to retain their independence: China, though not formally conquered, was nevertheless greatly penetrated by Western economic and educational forces. So, when new diasporas were being created, either during or shortly after the colonial period, the people involved had already had some experience of the host societies before they migrated. Or else they migrated from one area of Western domination to another, as with Indian labourers going to the sugar plantations of Natal or Guyana. In any case, there was a powerful exposure to Western values, either directly in the colonising host countries or, at some remove, in Western-colonised countries.

In the last 25 years a different dynamic has also been important. Travel has become much easier, so even rather poor communities can maintain cultural contact with the homeland more easily. This has combined with other factors to encourage a kind of ecumenism. There is a sign of this, for instance, in the emergence of the paper *Hinduism Today* in the late 1990s, which styles itself as 'an international bimonthly newspaper fostering Hindu solidarity among 650 million members of a global religion'. Such a consciousness of belonging to a world community has grown considerably in recent times. Consequently, the divergences between diaspora and home communities are somewhat diminishing.

The need of other cultures to cope with Western values (or things perceived sometimes as Western, though in principle of universal scope, such as science and technology) meant that sometimes new religious movements from the homeland, also directed towards dealing with this problem, could flourish in the diaspora. Thus, in Fiji, Natal and elsewhere, the Arya Samaj has great vigour. Its 19th-century religious revivalism (back to the Vedas) gave it a conservative, even nationalist, attraction which served overseas communities well. Because of the peripheral character of exiles, they often feel the need to be more patriotic or traditional than the traditionalists. On the other hand, the simplification of Hinduism from a ritual perspective could be helpful in a situation of exile, where the maintenance of traditional rituals is difficult. It was difficult in the Hindu case for a number of reasons. First, indentured labourers were a relatively deprived group who nevertheless needed élite brahmins for the proper performance of public rites (and there were hardly any brahmins among the migrants). Second, the Hindu system is not one of much formal training. Customs and rituals are handed down from one generation to another by a kind of social osmosis. The rupture of this osmosis, implied by transportation overseas, proves to be a problem in Hindu education. Until recently, overseas Hindu groups were inadequately served for public rituals. Only in the last 25 years (what we may call the Global Period of world history) have provisions for ritual performance improved. Also, diasporic Hindus (*desis*) have begun building temples: *Hinduism Today*, in its 1 January 1986 issue, lists 47 temples in USA, but the list is very incomplete.[2] In a period of consolidation, then,

[2] Today it would be over 60. Australian Hindus started with two temples in the 1970s, they now boast around 46 temples (eds.).

there may be some revival of Hindu practice; but before the Global Period there was a long stretch when the survival of orthodox Hinduism was more problematic. Indeed, social changes — in Natal, for example, those brought about by a housing policy based on units suitable for accommodating the nuclear but not the extended family; and the growth of individualism, already favoured by capitalist and consumer values, and by urbanisation — have provoked a crisis for traditional Hinduism. There is an increasing proportion of ex-Hindu Indians who have become Pentecostal Christians in North America. This allows them to adapt *bhakti* religion to a more consciously individualistic religious pattern. We may also note that traditional Hinduism, in losing its old osmotic potential, has become somewhat unintelligible to a new class of young people growing up in a modern environment.

Nevertheless, we have seen the Arya Samaj has grown in vigour in these circumstances, as have other new movements, including the Ramakrishna Vedanta Math and Mission. So we may say that some of the pioneering movements of the 19th century, which involved reaction to Western values then present in India through the British occupation, have had an important role to play in helping the diasporic Hindus to adapt themselves to a new environment.

It might also be an interesting research project to see how far the various themes of the Hindu tradition are present in a non-Indian environment — themes such as caste, *yoga*, *bhakti*, pilgrimage, temple rituals, austerity (*tapasya*), wandering holy men, instruction in the scriptural traditions, regional variation, pundits, a strong sense of purity and impurity, household rituals, veneration of the cow, the practice of astrology, belief in reincarnation, the importance of acquiring merit, etc. These themes, which are woven together into the complicated fabric of Hinduism in India, do not all travel equally easily to new environments. The very act of going overseas implies something about purity and loss of caste, for instance. Though caste is not absent as a phenomenon in the diaspora, it is less rigidly observed (or, as an Indian sociologist told me wryly in Fiji: 'If a Fijian Indian tells you that there is no caste in Fiji, you can be sure that he will be of lower caste'). Cow veneration does not have the wide social outreach it has in India itself. Pilgrimage and wandering holy men are hardly in evidence. Temple rituals are, as we have seen, less easy to maintain, but are experiencing a revival. Regional variation at one time was more important overseas, because it implied a linguistic basis of division without the overarching presence of a brahmin superstructure; but in later generations this variation loses vitality because of the decay of the homeland languages. Most of the Hindu diaspora has to transact its communications in English. This already implies a certain sophistication, and the erosion of folk Hinduism. It is a further factor in the importance of the post-British Hindu movements, including some recent phenomena, such as ISKCON (Hare Krishna movement), which have a strong presence overseas; in effect, these movements reflect a second main wave of religious developments in overseas Hinduism. Such English-speaking movements have also led to a revival of interest in the practice of *yoga*. Generally, new revivals emphasise the importance of religious experience and thus of the *yoga–bhakti* polarity, even during a time of reconstruction of ritual Hinduism in an overseas context.

I remarked earlier that, during the Global Period, there is the tendency toward the consolidation of world religions, however dispersed. Thus we have the formation of such institutions as the World Fellowship of Buddhists and the Vishwa Hindu Parishad. This facilitates the evolution of a kind of ecumenical Buddhism, and is in part the consequence of a new feeling of identity, since Buddhism perceives itself as a world religion. The same goes for Global Hinduism. This concept is itself important, and I shall return to it below. The diasporas in the Global Period become somewhat more orthodox in tone. We have noted the case of Islam, and the convergence of Black Islam with Sunni orthodoxy. A similar evolution happened with the Bahai'i in the United States. But the case of Hinduism is itself peculiar: some scholars would deny that there is such a thing as Hinduism at all, or would argue that, even if we can speak of Hinduism, it does not have a single unitary set of beliefs or practices. This thesis of the non-existence or disunity of Hinduism has much to commend it, if we wish to represent realistically 'religion on the ground' in India; it is however no longer correct. For the fact is that Hindus have perforce had to define themselves over against a number of traditional rivals — the Buddhists (here the distinction between *astika* and *nastika* was important) then, more seriously, the Muslims, and, finally, European modes of Christianity. Important here is what may be called 'the modern Hindu ideology', pioneered by Vivekananda and developed by Radhakrishnan and others, affirming that Hinduism preaches the unity of religions and the unity in diversity of the Hindu tradition itself. Now, to some extent, this ideology, a powerful ingredient in the Indian nationalist movement, prepared the way for a pluralist state and, at the same time, provided a relatively convincing reply to criticisms launched at Hinduism by missionaries, social reformers and British administrators during the colonial period.

This modern neo-Vedantin kind of exposition of the nature of Hinduism has taken strong root among English-speaking Hindus, and though it neglects the tensions between differing forms of Hinduism on the ground (e.g. between Shaivism and Vaishnavism), it serves as an important platform for self-understanding, especially among diaspora Hindus. A more complex model could be espoused — viz. that there are four main movements among Hindus: Shaivism, Shaktism, Vaishnavism and Smarta Hinduism. The modern Hindu ideology, as I have called it, is largely a Smarta account. The more complex 'fourfold' understanding of the Hindu tradition, nevertheless, usually implies mutual toleration and a sense of unity among the branches of the religion, and so in practice comes to approximate the neo-Vedantin version. As a rule diasporic Hindus tend to be rather syncretic in their outlook; this is evidenced from the fact that major temples as such the Helensburgh Temple in Sydney and the Shiva–Vishnu Temple in Melbourne house a multitude of Hindu gods and goddesses.

From all this it may be observed that the diaspora itself contributes to the process of self-definition an ecumenical spirit and a kind of new orthodoxy. This is especially so in the Hindu case. So we may reply to those who say that there is no such thing as Hinduism: 'Maybe over much of its history there was no such clearly demarcated "-ism" as Hinduism; there is now'. In a sense Hinduism is a new religion, although its roots are of course very ancient.

The diasporic religions must exist, by their very nature, typically as minority groups (though sometimes, as in Fiji, they may come to constitute a majority). Those that are a 'minority at home' have no special difficulties, but there is a question as to how a faith which dominates its home environment, such as Islam with its concept of *dar al-islam* (homeland of faith) will work out its affairs in the overseas environment. This is in part because the home arrangements give the tradition unfettered opportunity to exercise its law. In a modern bureaucratic State there are further problems, such as regulations about the slaughter of animals and the conflicts between supposedly hygienic arrangements and the demands of traditional law. And in regards to Hindu cremation in the West there is prohibition on ritual lighting of the deceased body with the actual use of fire and sandalwood; instead a symbolic incense stick is lit and placed on the coffin lid and sent off into a pre-heated oven-like furnace (1200°F).

As there is a growing consciousness of the Global Period, it becomes apparent to every religion that globally it is, however dominant in a region, a minority. In this sense the diaspora manifestation of a dominant religion can provide experience which will, in due course, become relevant to the global situation.

Another interesting aspect of diasporic religion concerns the degree to which it may expand from an ethnic basis. While a diaspora group may originally have migrated for economic or political reasons, it may eventually acquire some degree of mission, if only at first osmotically. Thus Tibetan Buddhism, which at first was more concerned to preserve Tibetan traditions abroad — in India, the UK and elsewhere — has become an active presence; so that, like other Buddhist groups and institutions, it is attracting growing interest and converts among Anglos in the English-speaking Western countries. Similarly while much of Hinduism in South Africa is ethnic and disinclined to proselytise, the Ramakrishna Vedanta had a more outward-looking and missionary face. Hinduism there stands in an intermediate position between the more or less non-missionary minority religions, such as the Parsis, Sikhs, Jains and so on, and the more active and traditionally missionary groups such as the Buddhists, the Muslims and the Christians, and smaller groups such as the Bahai'i. But, as is well known, even Sikhism, which has been largely ethnic in basis, has gained some Anglo converts in the United States. So the distinction between missionary and non-missionary groups may gradually blur and fade away. At any rate, we can see that the impulse to spread and the need to present the teachings in a modern and clearly articulated manner will favour the adaptation, especially the linguistic adaptation, of the diasporic faiths.

There is a factor that the rather conservative minor religions have in practice to bear in mind; that the diaspora reinforces contact with major world cultural forces. This factor underlines the need for the faith to express itself in the face of universal religions and secular values. The same problem is faced by a limited ethnic religion (limited, say, to a tribal group) when it comes in contact with universal proselytising faiths. Each such religion needs to give a universal account of itself, and to articulate its teachings, perhaps under some general principle — e.g. that every group is entitled to its own cultural and religious traditions, and such traditions can, like the universal faiths, point to some aspect of the truth.

Admittedly such an argument gets away somewhat from tradition, which needed no defence. This new account of a religion's doctrines is an innovation. Maybe the ethnic group will fuse with others of a similar cultural affiliation, to produce some larger entity: thus it is common these days to talk about 'native American religion', as if there are common values distributed through the varieties of cultures that go to make up, and have gone to make up, the traditional small-scale mosaic which preceded European conquest in North America. Such Native American religion is now held to ally itself with certain universal values of the modern Western milieu, such as environmentalism.

The lesson seems to be that you can only deal with the universalist intruder by adopting a universal-type defence. It is thus a natural thing for diaspora religions, even if they have no great missionary pretensions, to evolve universal-type explanations of their teachings and practices. Often they may follow the lead of Western traditions and publish translations and editions of their scriptures, or adopt other external models of operation borrowed on the whole from the West. This degree of adaptation also makes their teachings accessible to the host community. Given that this is a Western style of community, and especially in the United States, attitudes to religion will be in general individualistic and privatised; and so it will not be unusual for religious searchers to hit upon a diaspora religious group and come to belong to it, whether that group is explicitly missionary or not. All this contributes to the cosmopolitan character of religion in major diaspora areas. Yet, at the same time, we have noted the tendency for diasporas in the Global Period to have a greater sense of self-definition because of increased communication, to and fro, between the homeland and the places of the diaspora.

All this represents the beginnings of blending. Apart from the adaptation of diasporas to host cultures, there are the possibilities, inherent in cultural interfaces, of new forms of 'betwixt and between', constituting religions in the making. Part of the Hindu diaspora are the migratory *gurus*, who have pioneered varying forms of religion which absorb elements from both East and West in new syntheses. We may differ as to their value or staying power, but it may well turn out that from among these various Eastern blends there will emerge a strong new religious tradition. Another factor in the life of diasporas is that members of a trans-ethnic religion will find new ways to work together, for mutual protection and the like.

Thus Cambodian, Vietnamese, Sri Lankan, Korean, Chinese, Japanese, Tibetan and other Buddhists are found in substantial numbers in southern California, and, through such organisations as the Sangha Council of southern California, they co-operate in various ways. Similar co-operative spirit prevails among the diverse groups that make up the Australian Buddhist community. So it may turn out that the diaspora situation will enhance ecumenism, even apart from the easier communications of the Global Period. There is, as we have seen, the analogous co-operation between Hindus of different languages in the Hindu diaspora, partly due to the decay of the linguistic heritage.

From time to time, I have touched on the phenomenon of the diaspora of sub-traditions. Here the classical case I have in mind is where an 'alien' sub-tradition of a dominant religion migrates into the area of that religion. In England, for instance, there are West Indian Christians, various kinds of Eastern Orthodoxy, largely ethnically based, etc. Gradually ecumenical tendencies soften the edges between such a group and the dominant kind or kinds of Christianity. This example leads us to wonder whether in a pluralistic society the diaspora religions themselves may not begin to belong to some kind of pan-religious ecumenism. It would be interesting to analyse the attitudes of believers in such societies. For instance, in Sri Lanka, despite the religious and cultural conflicts between Tamils and Sinhalese in recent times, there appears to be a tendency, especially among the Muslim leadership, to accept a world-view in which different religions have value if pursued with sincerity.

This is a world-view which encourages a pluralistic *modus vivendi*. It is an attitude of 'Islam within the wider framework of sincere religion'. That already is a modification of traditional Islam which, where it is dominant in a society, leaves only a limited place for alternative religions. There are signs in some diaspora societies of the desire for a world religion or world outlook. However, such a new development (finding echoes in neo-Vedanta and Islamic Sufism, etc.) can itself create a particularist backlash among the religions, and this in effect has already happened in Christianity, with works such as Kraemer's *The Christian Message in a Non-Christian World* (1938) and evangelical affirmations of the uniqueness of the Gospel. Liberal interpretations often come to be faced with conservative countermoves; and this, by the way, helps to increase the variety of types of religion.

These, then, are some thoughts about the study of diasporas, an area of research in religion which has been somewhat neglected. Some of the phenomena to which I have drawn attention in this essay have already been looked at by some scholars, including Zwi Werblowsky. It may be time for some worldwide systematic studies. This may also be a field which implicitly heralds important changes in world religions. We are entering, in the Global Period, a new era, not just of religious researches but of religious life. Not all the traditional religions, nor many scholars, have yet come to terms with these changes.

Ninian Smart

fig. B.1: Hawkers in South Australia: A wood engraving published by Alfred Martin Ebeworth, 11th March 1885. Obtained from the State Library of Victoria

Appendix B

'Afghan Cameleers', 'Indian Hawkers' and the Settlement of Australia

Race, Gender and the South Asian Colonial Diaspora

Richard Forster

Introduction

South Asian migration to the Australian colonies in the 19th century, although numerically relatively small, and diverse in character, constituted several important strands in the imperial webs of connection that were produced by and were constitutive of the British Empire (Metcalf 2007; Pearson 2003).[1] The contributions of 19th-century South Asian migrants to the establishment of a British presence in Australia have until recently been largely ignored and undervalued in popular and academic historiography. These contributions were practical and substantial as in the case of the so-called 'Afghan Cameleers' without whose skills and labour the arid interior of the Australian continent would have remained inaccessible to white colonists until the advent of motorised transport. Reactions to 19th-century South Asian migrants on the part of the 'white' majority also played a key role in the production of an Australian nationalism that ambivalently sought to distance itself from the prerogatives of the multi-ethnic British Empire. Although South Asian migrants were clearly not the beneficiaries of such nationalism, their experiences are a defining component of its history.

In providing a closer look at the experiences of South Asian migrants before the imposition of the White Australia policy via the Immigration Restriction Act, 1901, this chapter aims to make a modest contribution to the growing body of scholarship challenging the prevailing historical conception that 'British' settlement in Australia was homogeneously 'white.' Setting to one side the question of indigenous sovereignties and the problems they represent for such monochromatic visions of Australian

---

[1] See also Chapters 2, 6, 7 and 8 in this volume.

history, a growing body of scholarship has begun to demonstrate that from the arrival of the First Fleet in 1788, Australian society was much more diverse than conventional narratives are want to admit. Cassandra Pybus is particularly notable in this regard. Her work *Black Founders* reveals, for instance, that among the first shipments of convicts to Australia were a number of 'African-Americans', many of whom had probably fought in 'Ethiopian Regiments' on the side of the British during the American Revolution, before being convicted of various petty crimes in England and sentenced to transportation to New South Wales (Pybus 2006). As this chapter will discuss below, there were also small numbers of South Asian convicts transported to the Australian colonies from other parts of the British Empire, in addition to considerably larger numbers of South Asian servants and labourers who migrated as part of the households of free settlers.

Another related objective here is to survey and contextualise the experiences of South Asian migrants in terms of subtle shifts in prevailing discourses of 'race' across the 19th century and to recognise the role of such discourses in the production of Australian nationalism. As Andrew Markus has pointed out, 'skin colour was probably a less important basis for discrimination in the first half of the 19th century than in the last' (Markus 1994: 55). Inevitably, racialised discourses intersected with and were conditioned by prevailing notions of gender (Collins 1990; Allen 2008). For one thing, the 19th-century South Asian 'diaspora' in Australia, if that is the appropriate term, was almost entirely male, a fact that seems to have elicited shifting responses from the white majority during different periods. This chapter argues that during the early and mid-19th century, British settlers brought to Australia a racialised labour hierarchy in which South Asians were subordinated and effeminised via their relegation to domestic spaces as household servants, and in occupations such as shepherding which were deemed 'passive'.[2] This order was disrupted after the 1860s by the arrival of the 'Afghan' cameleers, a majority of whom as 'Pathans' and Panjabi Sikhs not only seem to have captured popular imagination in fulfilling the emerging British stereotype of a

[2] While I am responsible for any misapplication of the idea, this concept was initially suggested to me by Clare Anderson in an e-mail communication in April 2010.

'martial race', but in very real ways threatened the myth of superior white masculinity (Streets 2004; Sinha 1996; Allen 2012).

The greater independence and mobility of cameleers and hawkers in comparison to their counterparts in earlier periods seems to have been central to the negative reactions they endured. Moreover, European dependency upon the cameleers in their efforts to 'penetrate' the arid interior of Australia and establish viable mining and pastoral industries, and therefore to justify European claims to continental sovereignty, produced profound anxieties. Towards the end of the century increasingly bitter economic competition between Europeans, with their environmentally maladapted horse and bullock teams, and 'Afghans', with their more versatile and resilient camels, played a significant part in engendering impassioned calls for the exclusion of Asians and the reservation of Australia for the white man.

An examination of the rhetoric deployed in late 19th-century Australia to alienate South Asians suggests the confluence of various discourses concerning race. Although the xenophobia underlying nationalist aspirations was partially informed by the contemporary emergence of 'scientific racism' or 'social Darwinism', it also sprang from an imperialist tradition of a much earlier provenance. Sensationalist representations of 'Afghan Cameleers' and 'Indian Hawkers' in the late 19th century drew upon a morbid assemblage of tropes simultaneously casting them as passionate and irrational natives prone to 'running amok', whilst also portraying them as jealous and violent sexual predators, an alien threat to vulnerable and isolated white women and children. This rhetorical strategy drew on a long established tendency to feminise the native as irrational, while playing heavily upon white male fears of emasculation at the hands of the darker-skinned alien. Such racist tropes were used to especially pernicious effect when combined with more prosaic claims that South Asians, and Asians generally with their supposed willingness to work for low wages, posed a threat to the living standards of white working-class men and their families. Indeed, violence is a common thread running through many representations of South Asians in Australian press reports of the later 19th century. This unhappy association took a variety of forms. Whether they were represented as a threat to lonely white women, as prone to 'running amok', as perpetuating tribal blood feuds, or, as was all too common, as themselves the victims of violent 'crimes of opportunity', this association certainly appears to have contributed to the growing sense of xenophobia directed towards South Asians in Australia in the decade leading up to federation and the White Australia Policy. While opposition to South Asian migration was not unheard of in earlier periods, the presence of South Asians in the Australian colonies, contained as it was in domestic households and on remote pastoral stations, appears to have prompted far less anxiety of this sort. This shift reflects a broader change in which notions and categories delineating 'race' and 'class', and indeed what it meant to be 'British' became progressively less and less fluid over time.

Domestic Servants and Indentured Labourers

Indian migrants had been making their way to the Australian colonies from very early times. While it seems probable that some may have arrived independently in Australia as lascars (seamen) or merchants on the ships arriving from Indian ports, most Indian migrants in the earliest period of European settlement seem to have come primarily as the personal servants of free settlers, many of whom had spent time in the subcontinent before moving on to Australia. It is difficult to discern a clear picture of the earliest dates or the numbers of such arrivals. James Jupp writes of 'clear evidence of a handful of domestic servants in European households having left the port of Calcutta (Kolkata) to take up labouring work in Sydney in 1816' (Jupp 2001: 431). *The Sydney Morning Herald* reported in May1818 that some Indian servants had been robbed of 'a small Mahogany dressing case, a few articles of wearing apparel and two account book' while on the road from Sydney to Parramatta.[3] A reward of five pounds sterling was offered by a Mr Browne for information leading to the conviction of the offenders, and two pounds for the return of the account books. This must have been William Browne, a settler who had been granted 3,000 acres near Sydney Cove, and who had written to England two years earlier reporting that he had with him nine labourers that he had brought with him from India, and expressing hopes that an acquaintance due to arrive soon from India would be able to '. . . bring with her, besides

[3] *Sydney Morning Herald*, 9 May 1818.

domestic servants, some carpenters, blacksmiths, bricklayers and about twenty more labourers' (Westrip and Holrodye 2010: 122). In another letter Browne described the particular value of Indian labourers, as he saw it.

> Their mild and submissive manners, sobriety, honesty and docility, their abstemious habits where provisions are yet dear, and their low wage where labour is high, and not always procurable where wanted, made me desirous of having as many of them as I can induce to leave their homes. — ibid.: 123

Such favourable attitudes towards the pliable character of Indian servants and labourers appear to have been common among early European settlers, particularly those with connections to India. In her diary, composed in the 1820s and published in 1901, Mrs Elizabeth Fenton, who settled in Van Diemen's Land with her husband after he resigned a commission in the Bengal Army, mentions 'the boy I brought from India I have kept with the idea of training him for an inside servant' (Fenton 1901: 357). Joyce Westrip and Peggy Holroyde, in their recent, wide-ranging account of connections between Australia and India, have turned to oral histories in addition to written sources in recovering glimpses of the 'trickle' of Indian servants that accompanied British arrivals to 'several early settlements across the continent' (2010: 124). One of their informants, a descendant of Robert Campbell, a Scottish merchant who first arrived in Sydney from Calcutta in 1798 and would establish a profitable trade between the two port cities, recalled how 'Indians were taken to work on an isolated property called Brow at Bedalla', a property associated with the foundation of the dairying industry in New South Wales. In 1835, the Morley family arrived in Albany (in the extreme south-west of western Australia) with a complement of twelve Indian servants, most of whom appear to have had Tamil names. A few years later, in 1838, Thomas Lyell Symers returned to the same southern port with ten Indian servants, whose names, however, were not recorded (ibid.). The influential Prinsep family, among whose scions Charles Prinsep served as Advocate General to the East India Company in Calcutta (Kolkata) and held extensive Australian properties as an absentee landlord, also brought their own servants with them when they settled in Van Diemen's Land and the

Swan River Colony (now Perth) (ibid.: 254).[4] Prinsep, along with other members of the Calcutta elite including Dwarkanath Tagore, was a founding member of the Australian Association of Bengal, an organisation which sponsored trade between India and the Australian colonies. Among the 69 passengers on a vessel sponsored by this association in 1838 to sail from Calcutta to Adelaide were 'twelve coolies' and 'twelve native servants'. The return voyage carried the famous social worker Caroline Chisholm, her ailing husband and their three Indian servants (ibid.: 255).

Scattered examples abound throughout the early 19th century of the presence of Indian servants and labourers in the Australian colonies, indicating that domestic labour regimes familiar in other parts of the empire were also being replicated in the antipodes. Of course, as a tiny minority of the overall populations of these fledgling settlements, their presence marked something of an inversion of the racial composition of colonial South Asian society, where the white Sahebs were themselves a relatively rare sight. None the less, Indians in the Australian colonies may not have been quite as rare as all that in the early to mid-19th century. In 1838, Th. Walker gave evidence before the New South Wales Legislative Council's Immigration Committee to the effect that he knew of 1,203 Indian labourers in the colony who had been sent for by 111 settlers (Willard 1967: 7). Robert Scott reported to the same committee in 1841 that some landowners had as many as 40 Indians in their employment (ibid.).

While most South Asians arriving in Australia in the early and mid-19th century appear to have travelled as the employees of private individuals on a more or less ad hoc basis, attempts were made to arrange for large-scale importation of indentured Indian labour, with the approval and support of the appropriate colonial authorities. As early as 1836, John Mackay, who had formerly lived in India as a merchant and indigo planter, brought a formal proposal before the colonial government of New South Wales seeking a 'government bounty' for the importation of Indian labourers (ibid.: 3-4). The authorities refused to provide Mackay with any financial assistance, but a Select Committee appointed in 1837 did recommend that a few labourers might be brought out from India in order to ascertain their suitability in the event of future labour shortages.

---

[4] See also, 'Coolie Immigration', *The Inquirer*, Perth, 1 September 1847.

This was also considered expedient in light of plans for the eventual settlement of the tropical north where it was anticipated that there would be great demand for 'coolie labour' in the cotton, sugar, coffee and tobacco industries[5] (ibid.).

Although no official action was taken as a result of this recommendation, individual settlers continued to bring out small numbers of Indian labourers on their own initiative, even as questions regarding the suitability of South Asians for the Australian colonies began to be raised in public and official debates. W.C. Wentworth, prominent Australian-born explorer, journalist, politician and outspoken advocate of free settlement and the abolition of convict transportation, voiced his opposition to the importation of Indian labour before the 1837 Immigration Committee on grounds of 'racial purity' (ibid.). Later, however, he seems to have revised his opinion and taken part in a joint venture with one Captain Towns in obtaining Indian labourers. He also moved in the Legislative Council in 1852 that the Indian government ought to be informed of the need for labourers in New South Wales and of the desirable conditions awaiting potential immigrants (ibid.).

Despite such guarded expressions of official interest, circumstances conspired against any officially sanctioned schemes for the large-scale importation of Indian labour. During the 1830s, when demand for labour in Australia was high and proposals for recruitment from India were first considered, the discovery of abusive treatment of indentured labourers bound for Mauritius prompted the Indian government to temporarily halt further indentured immigration. By the time that the gold rushes of the 1850s again stimulated demand for labour in the Australian colonies, the Indian government had once more opened the way for overseas labour recruitment. But before any negotiations between the colonial governments could be finalised, however, demand for labour had waned, as large numbers of men drifted away from the gold fields in search of

5 Sporadic, small-scale private recruitment of indentured labour from South Asia (especially Punjabi Sikhs and Sri Lankans) did occur in the later 19th century during the establishment of the sugar and banana industries in northern Queensland. However, official support for expanding the scale of labour importation was lukewarm in the face of growing opposition to Asian immigration.

more reliable employment. Opposition to non-white immigration and its perceived threat to Anglo-Saxon 'racial purity' no doubt contributed to the quiet death that was the fate of proposals for large-scale recruitment of indentured Indian labour.

One vocal proponent of Indian labour was Phillip Friell, who had served the East India Company as Judicial Surveyor of the Ceded Districts and as a confidential *aide-de-camp* of the Nawab of Oude (Awadh), and was given the rank of colonel in his army.[6] After settling in New South Wales in 1844, Friell published a pamphlet in 1846 entitled, *The Advantages of Indian Labour in the Australasian Colonies* in which he argued that Hindus, especially 'Gurraree, Bheree Wallah and Gwallahs' from central India, were 'decidedly the best class' of labour available in the British empire for Australia's burgeoning pastoral industry, and indeed, being free of the vice of drunkenness, were generally superior to immigrants from Great Britain, at least for the purpose of shepherding.[7] Friell assured his readership that such men were to be 'readily procured', with thousands to be seen 'loitering around the Emigration offices in Calcutta, ready to ship on almost any terms' (ibid.).

Friell's own experiences with Indian labourers, however, indicate that the agreeability of such terms was in fact a serious point of contention. Friell had employed twenty Indian servants on his pastoral station at Tent Hill in New South Wales, and despite his protestations that they had come to the colony in full understanding of their contractual obligations and were content with their living and working conditions, appear to have walked off the job in protest against beatings, non-payment of wages, and deficient rations and clothing (Westrip and Holroyde 2010: 138). Friell vigorously defended himself in the press, insisting that any discontent among his Indian servants was due to the 'tampering' of vexatious 'magistrates and commissioners'.[8] Although he claimed to have satisfied the workers' complaints by increasing their rations and clothing allowances above the terms of their contract so that they enjoyed

6 'Domestic Intelligence: The Late Mr. Philip Friell, Esq.', *The Moreton Bay Courier*, Saturday, 4 February 1854.

7 See *The Morton Bay Courier*, Saturday, 26 December 1846 for extracts of the pamphlet, and Saturday, 4 February 1854.

8 'Coolies', *The Sydney Morning Herald*, 21 May 1847.

conditions better than that of European shepherds, it is telling that the same workers were also transferred to a remote property in an unsettled district beyond the prying eyes of the Attorney General's office and that of the Commissioner for Crown Lands (ibid.). Friell's explanations for the labour disputes in which he became embroiled seem unlikely to have had the intended effect of reassuring would-be proponents of Indian labour migration, but are also instructive as to the heights of condescension towards South Asians which were brought to Australia by British imperialists. While staggering in its own way, the racism espoused by Friell in support of Indian immigration differed substantively from that which would emerge in opposition to the same at the end of the century. Friell took great pains to point out to his Australian readers that,

> there never was a native of India from the Himalias to Cape Cormorin, who ever admitted that he had cause to be contented — nay, who would not rather assert that he had every reason to be discontented — and that he was the most wretched and oppressed being on the face of the earth.[9]

Indeed, in his pamphlet and his various protestations to the press, Friell contended that the success of any scheme of importation would be dependent upon the appointment of a competent government officer among whose responsibilities would be to 'disabuse the Indian native of the idea that he can tamper with agreements, and be a gainer by so doing, under the high rate of wages common here'.[10] Despite clearly believing that Indian labourers would be a great economic boon to individual pastoralists and the colonies as a whole, Friell rather pompously argued that such material benefits should be a secondary consideration. More importantly, the employment of Indian labour in Australia was a religious duty of loyal British subjects. Rather than be dissuaded by minor difficulties such as those that had presented themselves at Tent Hill, he implored of his fellow pastoralists:

> . . . let us rather buckle on the armour and meet these anomalous cases — if it be for the prosperity, not of this country only, but for these starving people. This is practical charity — the man who

---

9 'Coolies', *The Sydney Morning Herald*, 21 May 1847.

10 'Indian Labour', *The Moreton Bay Courier*, 19 December 1846.

> employs the greatest number of starving people is the best subject, but what are the real difficulties? almost nil. How are a handful of Englishmen governing one hundred and twenty millions of these very people? Not by oppression, God knows, but by that justice which is the glory of England, in striking from the negro his chains, and from the Briton his reproach, and this, I maintain, is the state of the British power contradistinguished to that of their former rulers; and what should prevent us here taking the trouble of understanding these people and adjudicating accordingly?[11]

Although Friell's calls for a programme of recruitment of indentured labour from India were ultimately unsuccessful, the relatively positive reception his writings received in the contemporary press are in marked contrast to the mood that would emerge towards Asian migration later in the century. Clearly, his paternalistic regard for Indian labour, however opportunistic, was informed (or at least rhetorically justified) by his sense of participation in the British Empire. This sense of participation in the empire would continue in the later part of the century but was increasingly subordinated to nationalist sentiments.

Convict Transportation: The Curious Case of Sheik and Swift

Another, lesser known, category of South Asian migration to the Australian colonies in the earlier part of the century was convict transportation. As noted above, a certain number of convicts with South Asian origins were transported from various British colonies in the Indian Ocean, such as Mauritius, to New South Wales and Van Diemen's Land during the 1840s (Jupp 2001: 593; Anderson 2004: 119).[12] While the lived experiences of those transported is a subject requiring further research, on preliminary

11 'Coolies', *The Sydney Morning Herald*, 21 May 1847.

12 Thirty-nine of the approximately 200 convicts transported to Australia from Mauritius were Indian-born, while others may have been descended from Indian-born parents. Others were former slaves and their descendants from places such as Madagascar, Mozambique and the isle of Bourbon (later Reunion). See Jupp, *The Australian People*, p. 593, and Clare Anderson, *Legible Bodies: Race, Criminality and Colonialism in South Asia*, Oxford, NY: Berg, 2004, p. 119.

examination it would seem that these men tended to be incorporated into a racialised labour hierarchy characteristic of the wider British Empire during this era. For instance, many of these convicts seem to have taken up positions in the households of free settlers as domestic servants.

One such example was Sheik Adam, a twice-transported convict originally from Bombay, who ended up in Van Diemen's Land in 1842 after a notorious career of 'convict marronage' on Mauritius which led British authorities to offer a princely sum of £ 50 in reward for his capture (Anderson 2000: 75-79). Ironically, after eventually being reconvicted on Mauritius for poisoning and robbing his victims, Sheik Adam was paroled and found employment in Van Diemen's Land as a cook in the service of the Campbell Town district police magistrate, Francis Henslowe.[13]

It was in Campbell Town in 1849 that Sheik Adam sought and received permission to marry fellow convict and 'house maid' Sarah Swift, who had been transported from Liverpool at the age of 19 in 1846.[14] That this cross-cultural, inter-racial marriage found official sanction in Van Diemen's Land in the middle of the 19th century the fluidity of notions of gender and race in the British Empire across the 19th century. As will be discussed in later sections of this chapter, marriages between South Asian men and white women were considered anathema by the end of the century in the Australian colonies and elsewhere. Indeed, even by mid-century inter-racial marriages between British and South Asians had largely fallen from favour in British India itself. According to William Dalrymple (2002: 60):

> The wills written by dying East India Company servants show that the practice of marrying or cohabiting with Indian bibis quickly began to decline: from turning up in one-in-three wills between 1780 and 1785, they are present in only one-in-four between 1805 and 1810. By 1830, it is one-in-six; by the middle of the century, they have all but disappeared.

If British men gradually stopped marrying and cohabiting with South Asian women as colonial power was consolidated, inter-racial marriages involving South Asian men and British women were undoubtedly fairly rare throughout the colonial era, but they certainly occurred. Dean

---

13 Tasmanian State Archives, CON37/1/1.

14 Tasmanian State Archives, CON52/1/3 (2); CON41/1/10.

Mahomed, for instance, believed to be the first proprietor of a curry house in the British Isles, married Jane Daly in Ireland in 1786 (Fisher 2004: 60). In the early 19th century several Indian men who travelled to Britain in order to teach Asian languages to E.I.C. recruits also married English women, as in the case of Addiscombe College's Meer Hassan Ali and Miss Biddy Timms (ibid.: 132). As Dalrymple (2004) notes, Biddy Timms's subsequent appointment as a milliner to the court of Princess Augusta suggests that her marriage to an Indian gentleman and a Muslim 'had not done any harm to her social position — on the contrary, it might even have enhanced it'. However, as Michael Fisher's account makes clear, British enthusiasm for bringing home native-speaking Indian *munshis* and their inter-racial marriages was relatively short-lived. According to Fisher, moves made in the 1820s to curb the practice of hiring native-speakers to teach in Britain reflected 'growing British imperialist and Anglicist attitudes' (Fisher 2004: 132).

This broader context makes the marriage of Sheik and Swift all the more interesting. One might surmise that the social acceptability of their union was a moot point given their already lowly convict status. Indeed, Swift's prior record of prostitution in Liverpool, and her conduct record in Van Diemen's Land, which lists offences such as 'being absent without leave', 'found in a public house', 'disturbing the peace', 'disorderly conduct' and 'larceny under the value of £ 5', not to mention 'talking in chapel', suggests that she was unlikely to have been regarded as a model of Victorian womanhood.[15] None the less, although sex ratios in the Australian colonies as a whole had begun to even out by the late 1840s, falling from 7:1 to 3.7 between 1841 and 1851, marriageable women remained a relatively scarce commodity in Van Diemen's Land at the time of Adam's marriage to Sarah Swift (Alford 1984: 15).

In such a demographic context, this marriage suggests that Sheik Adam's 'racial difference' was not, in the middle of the 19th century, perceived as constituting a threat to white masculinity in quite the way that it probably would have in later decades. As we shall see below, South Asian men came to be regarded as a particularly troublesome nuisance to white women in the Australian colonies towards the century's

---

15 Tasmanian State Archives, CON41/1/10.

close. The circuitous migration of Adam Sheik and his apparent acceptance in colonial society in Van Diemen's Land in the first half of the 19th century are illustrative of the imperial connections that existed prior to the consolidation of national boundaries within the empire by its end.

'Afghan Cameleers' and 'Indian Hawkers'

Another set of strands in this web of imperial connections brought the 'Afghans' to the Australian colonies in the latter half of the 19th century. Initially employed by European explorers in the 1860s, these South Asian camel handlers began to play an indispensable role in the expansion of pastoral and mining interests in interior regions from the 1870s.[16] Camels and their handlers were to prove essential in supplying remote settlements and in transporting commodities from the inland to coastal regions, just as they proved vital in the establishment of new forms of communications and transport such as the telegraph and railways. The economic importance of the camel gradually declined with the widespread adoption of the automobile in the early 20th century. During their 'period of usefulness', approximately 3,000–4,000 camel handlers are thought to have migrated from South Asia to the Australian colonies (Stevens 1989). Although many returned to the subcontinent after completing their contracts, others stayed on and, in spite of the spirit of the White Australia policy, married local women and started families, adapting to new ways of life (Brunato 1972).

This later 19th-century wave of South Asian migration differed from those of earlier periods in significant ways. Although the first generation of cameleers was brought out under contract to European entrepreneurs in what suggests a continuity with earlier labour hierarchies, a number of these migrants capitalised upon opportunities to establish their own camel-

---

[16] Several excellent works researching the Afghan Cameleers were published as Australia began to embrace multiculturalism during the 1970s and 1980s. See Madelaine Brunato (1972); Michael Cigler (1986); Pamela Rajkowski (1987); Christine Stevens (1989). See also, Philip Jones and Anna Kenny (2007); Tom L. McKnight (1969). More recently, Samia Khatun's insightful doctoral thesis, *Camels, Ships and Trains: Translation Across the 'Indian Archipelago', 1860–1930* (2012) has added considerably to our understandings of the lives and subjectivities of cameleers in Australia by utilising non-English primary sources and employing transnational framework.

carrying enterprises, undertaking for themselves the importation and breeding of further livestock and the recruitment of handlers. A handful of these South Asian entrepreneurs, most notably Abdul Wade and the brothers Faiz and Tagh Mahomet, became quite wealthy and acquired substantial prestige in their own and even in the wider European community (Stevens 1989: 156-58).

But even the experiences of the majority of more humble cameleers, who laboured under incredibly difficult desert conditions for relatively low wages, marked a new development in the history of South Asian migration. As we have seen, earlier generations of South Asian migrants had been predominantly employed as domestic servants in what was perceived as 'feminine' space, or as subordinate agricultural labourers and in 'passive' roles watching over flocks of sheep in isolated rural locales. While serving useful purposes, their presence was entirely contingent upon that of their European masters. The cameleers, by contrast, inverted this cross-cultural relationship by rendering the existence of European 'civilisation' in large parts of the continent entirely and vividly dependent on their skills and labour. While this labour continued be racialised in the European imagination, with only very few European Australians mastering the art of camel handling during the 19th century, it produced new anxieties which threatened the myth of white male superiority and contributed to virulently xenophobic strains of Australian nationalism (ibid.: 135).

Recent moves towards recognising the role of South Asian cameleers in Australian history have attempted to qualify the label 'Afghan' by noting that many of the cameleers came from parts of what is today Pakistan and even India. Philip Jones rightly points that this reductive nomenclature evinces the racist attitudes of the times. He quotes an 1893 letter to the editor of the Adelaide *Register* from a self-professed Afghan who insisted:

> . . . natives of Afghanistan are in very small numbers here. They might be easily counted on the tip of the fingers . . . the rest of the persons who are here and are hawking about or are employed as camel-drivers by Afghan masters of camels are all Berohees, Mekranees [*sic.*], Sindhees, Kutohees, Borees, Hindus, or natives

> of Bombay, Calcutta, or Punjab, who are, one and all, British subjects.
> —Jones and Kenny 2007: 21

While the majority of cameleers appear to have been Muslims from what is today Pakistan and Afghanistan, there were also a minority of Sikhs and Hindus among their number. However, according to Christine Stevens, although their ancestors may have settled in various parts of India during the preceding centuries of Islamic rule, the overwhelming majority of men recruited for the camel industry were indeed ethnic 'Afghans' from various Pashto or 'Pathan' tribes, whose ancestral lands had, in some cases, come under British rule as recently the so-called First Anglo-Afghan War of 1839-41 (Stevens 1989: 2).[17] Indeed, by the time of the Second Anglo-Afghan War of 1879-81, the camel carrying trade in Australia was well established and had already resulted in the recruitment of numerous men who identified the regions around the cities of Kabul and Kandahar as their places of origin. If several of these cameleering migrants, such as Ahmad Khan who worked on the Western Australian gold fields, or Morbine Perooz and Bye Khan who operated camel trains out of Bourke in western New South Wales, claimed to have fought under 'Lord Roberts of Kandahar' during his occupation of Afghanistan, or in skirmishes the North-West Frontier Provinces, many more were from tribes such as the Ghilzai, the Durrani and the Afridi, who had resolutely resisted the occupying British armies (ibid.).[18] Even the port city of Karachi, through which the majority of the camels and their handlers were disembarked for Australia, was formally part of the Afghan province of Baluchistan until the proclamation of the Durand Line in 1893, although it had effectively operated as British possession since the 1850s. To the generations of 'Afghan' men who utilised imperial connections in order to leave the subcontinent in search of their fortunes in the camel carrying

---

[17] In fact, as Cigler had pointed out even earlier, 'Even the name Afghan is not the national epithet but was given to them by the Iranians; its etymology and meaning is unknown. The national name with which the Afghans designate themselves, is Pakhtun (in eastern dialect) and Pashtun (in the south-east). From Pashtun or Pakhtun the Indian 'Pathan' was formed.' (Cigler 1986: 13.)

[18] This was one of the reasons cited by Gilbert Probyn Smith (see below), for the alleged disloyalty of many Afghan Cameleers in Australia.

companies of the southern continent, this constant shifting of sovereignties must have seemed like a natural feature of their world.

To be sure, towards the end of the 19th century Australian designations for South Asian migrants tended to be quite reductive, suggesting perhaps that as the young colonies slowly matured the presence and influence of settlers with histories of personal contact with British India was probably declining. One category or label of South Asian identity which was frequently employed towards the end of the century, 'the Indian Hawker', seems to have overlapped considerably with that of 'the Afghan', at least in the minds of many white Australians. As Stevens notes with reference to incoming camel handlers:

> there was little interest in the aliens; only their services as experienced camel attendants were wanted, never the men themselves. Bureaucrats paid scant attention to their native origins: Afghans, Pushtuns, North-West Frontier Province tribesmen, Baluchis. As long as they caused no trouble it was virtually the same to the colonial officials. — ibid.: 12

The conflation of the labels 'Afghan' and 'Indian Hawker' was perhaps always present to some degree, but seems to have increased as general resentment against non-whites sharpened at the century's end. As competition between strings of camels and bullock teams (operated by Asians and Europeans, respectively) descended into bitter hostilities in the 1890s, so too were Indian traders and merchants increasingly pushed out of coastal urban areas into more isolated inland and rural regions. While many Afghans and Indians gradually left Australian shores in the face of growing racism and official discrimination, for those who chose to remain, or had no choice but to remain, one of the few available livelihoods was that of hawking a variety of wares in the bush. Negative representations of 'the nuisance of the Indian Hawker problem' abound in the newspapers of this period, and are replete with intersecting discourses of race and gender that simultaneously construct itinerant South Asian men as un-Australian and effeminate, but also as troublesome sexual predators ready to take advantage of white women and children.

In 1947, Perth daily the *West Australian* published a nostalgic reminiscence of a childhood spent in a 'West Australian farming district' some 'half a century' earlier, simply entitled, 'The Afghan', which was accompanied by a line drawing depicting a bearded man wearing a large turban and riding a camel along the main street of a country town.[19] The writer described the isolation of growing up in a small farming community 'ten bumpy miles by old spring cart' from the nearest town, and faraway from the 'enchanted city' of Perth, before coming to her main subject.

> Into this rural quietness at fairly long intervals, perhaps twice a year, came the Afghan. Where he came from, his name, or his destination, we did not know. To us his tall figure, composed features, dark piercing eyes, his turban and his pack simply spelt the Afghan. Tumbling out from school on a summer afternoon, we would find his camel grazing near the school fence, while from a clump of trees in a near-by gully, a spiral of smoke signified his camp. When he came to the house, my mother allowed him to spread his pack on the big dining table. Its contents were to us symbols of the glittering world we had yet to see. There were rolls of bright cloth; shimmering scarves, silks and ribbons; shawls like fleecy clouds; 'pearl' necklaces, beads and ear-rings; and brooches sparkling with diamonds (we were sure!). There were moneyboxes, work-baskets, toys, and tins of sweets — strange and ambrosial to palates accustomed only to 'wholesome boiled lollies'. We pranced about the table, importunate in our desire for the gaudy trifles, while my mother carefully fingered the materials. The bargaining concluded, our round eyes gazed as the hawker produced small change from the folds of his turban. Reluctantly we watched him go to make the round of the few other houses, after which he strode back to his camp, there, as we imagined, to concoct some bizarre dish before he slept. Although curious, we did not venture near his twinkling fire. There was something aloof and forbidding about this itinerant, which discouraged a near approach. Even small boys, as far as I remember, refrained from cheekiness towards the somewhat different swaggie. Next morning as we went to school, no sign of him remained; but months later, as we came out from afternoon lessons, there once more would be the grazing camel, the spiral of smoke and the Afghan.[20]

---

19 'The Afghan', *The West Australian*, Perth, 27 November 1947.

20 Ibid.

What was it that seemed so 'aloof and forbidding' about 'this itinerant . . . Afghan' who clearly made a strong impression on the small child at the turn of the century in rural Western Australia? Perhaps the author had picked up on the fears and anxieties of some of the adults in her young life. The scene that she described 50 years later, of this strange turbaned man being invited by her mother into the house to display his wares, was a type of encounter that caused great consternation among many white Australian men towards the turn of the century.

In 1890, Mr Armytage, the member for South Grant rose in the Victorian Parliament to 'draw attention . . . to the practice of a large number of Indian hawkers going around the country and calling at farmers' houses in the absence of the male members of the family, and refusing to leave without extorting money from the women.'[21] Armytage objected to the 'excessive number of licences being granted to alien hawkers'. Such complaints were heard repeatedly throughout the decade in most of the colonies. The South Australian government, in 1893, for instance, responded to public outcries by instructing the Commissioner of Police not to issue any further hawker's licences to alien Asians (Rajkowski 1987: 155). Meanwhile, the North-Eastern Municipal Association of Victoria announced that it was 'resolved to enter an emphatic protest against the system of issuing hawker's licences in Melbourne to Syrians, Afghans, Hindus, and other coloured races' as

> the time had now arrived when the Indian hawker nuisance should be put a stop to as it was an increasing source of terror to women and children and a grave anxiety to the heads of families whose occupations took them away from their homes during the daytime.[22]

At this stage, the Attorney-General was reportedly of the opinion that rather than introducing new legislation, the most viable solution to the problem of 'Afghans and Indian hawkers . . . frightening unprotected women and children' simply rested with local Shire Councils refraining

---

21 'Victorian Parliament, Mr. Armytage Raises Some Pertinent Questions', *Barrier Miner* (Broken Hill), 29 July 1890.

22 'Coloured Hawkers in Victoria,' *South Australian Register* (Adelaide), 21 March 1893.

from issuing more licences than were thought necessary.[23] Deputations to the Victorian Premier 'in reference to the Indian hawker nuisance' were 'reassured that the government would do its best to stop a further influx of Asiatics' and the Premier's office issued instructions to the Licensing Court that it was in future to renew licences 'only to those hawkers who are conversant with the English language, and who seem desirable men to have them'.[24] The issue was also raised repeatedly in the NSW parliament in connection with the Coloured Races Restriction and Regulation Bill in 1896. In 1897, a meeting of the Harvey Agricultural Alliance (south of Perth in Western Australia) 'resolved to ask the government to take steps to stop the Indian hawker nuisance'.[25]

In 1891, the Adelaide *Advertiser* reported that 'the Indian hawkers have again been making themselves a terror', in a piece provocatively entitled, 'Turbaned Intruders'.[26] It was claimed that 'one of these turbaned plagues' had entered the bedroom of the daughter of a farmer near Horsham (Victoria), but that 'the Indian had disappeared through the window by which he had entered' when the girls' screams 'brought their father with a shot gun on the scene'. On the same night, the room of another farmer's daughter in the same district was also said to have been 'invaded', although once more the 'Indian hawker' somehow managed to escape. A few years later, in 1894, a Miss Beatrice Howell of Broadford (Victoria) was reported to have been slapped in the face by an Indian hawker after refusing to purchase his goods. The slap had supposedly rendered her unconscious and placed her in 'a critical state'.[27] The following year, an editorial piece in the *Australian Town and Country Journal* complained bitterly about 'that perpetual nuisance, the Indian hawker', who, it was claimed, 'haunts the suburbs of the great cities, and annoys the servants and frightens the children', just as he was to be seen to 'pervade the country districts, and beguile the weak minded, both young

---

23 'Indian Hawkers', *South Australian Register* (Adelaide), 2 April 1893.

24 See 'The Alien Hawker Nuisance' and 'Colonial Telegrams', *South Australian Register* (Adelaide), 18 and 23 September 1893.

25 'Harvey Agricultural Alliance', *The West Australian* (Perth), 20 October 1897.

26 'Turbaned Intruders', *The Advertiser* (Adelaide), 21 January 1891.

27 'Victoria', *Barrier Miner* (Broken Hill), 12 March 1894.

and old, into purchasing his tawdry wares'.[28]

The same editorial explicitly compared the Indian hawker with his Chinese counterpart, condemning the former as a parasite whose 'pedlar's pack' was nothing but 'an artful excuse for loafing about back premises on the off chance of picking up small articles which may in some other town be converted into cash'. While the 'Chinaman' was regarded as 'too numerous' he was at least 'diligent and honest' and above all, 'a producer'. By contrast, the Indian hawker, 'a nuisance that should be distinctly abolished' was said to produce nothing, and to take 'all his gains out of the country'. In 1897, the *Clarence and Richmond Examiner* of northern New South Wales, unfavourably compared Indian with European hawkers, who it claimed operated on a principle of barter which usefully provided the 'medium selector or farmer' with a handy means of disposing of surplus eggs and other farm products while procuring necessities without the need of journeying many miles. By contrast, the paper argued, the Indian hawker dealt 'solely in cash' and forced '. . . on the public descriptions of goods they would frequently be better without'.[29] Despite being 'not so useful a trader to the community generally as the European', it was evident to the *Examiner* that 'the countrymen of Ranji must be adept in the art of dealing'. After all, Indian hawkers made 'larger sums of money than many give them credit for . . . notwithstanding the professed all round antipathy towards them. . . .'[30]

Another related factor cited in the increasingly vocal opposition to 'alien hawkers' was the notion that this occupation was one that might provide 'a source of light employment for British men who were unable to get a living by physical labour'.[31] As Pamela Rajkowski puts it, hawking was deemed to have been a 'last resort for the unemployed' who now often 'ended up in asylums' because of the monopolisation over the trade by unwanted aliens (Rajkowski 1987: 154). Thus, the traditional British

---

28 'Indian Hawkers', *Australian Town and Country Journal* (NSW), 9 March 1895.

29 'Hawkers and Their Business', *Clarence and Richmond Examiner* (NSW), 18 December 1897.

30 Ibid.

31 *NSW Parliamentary Debates*, November 1896, p. 4969 cited in Rajkowski (1987: 154).

tendency to effeminise South Asians appears to have resurfaced in a kind of jealousy of Indian business acumen and displaced resentment against a perceived emasculation of the white race.

In addition to posing a threat to white masculinity in the ways described above, Indian hawkers were also at times regarded as a threat to public health more generally. As early as 1884, when an outbreak of small pox was discovered in Melbourne, the Chief Secretary of the Victorian government went on record in the Assembly to speculate that the 'introduction and dissemination of small pox was probably due to the importation and sale of Indian goods about Melbourne'.[32] Understandably, Indian traders were concerned that such negative publicity would diminish their business prospects. Abdul Musjid and Yacoob Ali wrote to the press 'on behalf of the Indian hawkers' to protest the statements they regarded as a 'cruel injustice'. Insisting that the goods they received from Calcutta had been thoroughly fumigated, they pointed out that they had been resident in the colony for over two years; long before the outbreak of small pox. They challenged their accusers to provide proof, and welcomed inspections of their goods, tenements and persons, reassuring the public that they all undergone the appropriate vaccinations. Significantly, they appealed to the English and Australian sense of justice and fair play, and pointed out that they were 'unoffending British subjects sojourning in a British colony' who had always endeavoured to do their best to 'conform to the practices of an English nation'.[33] The Indian traders were not without sympathisers. *The Argus* itself, in an editorial piece described the 'pet theory' of the Chief Secretary as 'mean', while Customs Agent, Thomas Young, also wrote to *The Argus* pointing out that no one from the customs department charged with examining Indian wares on their landing had subsequently succumbed to the small pox, and that the 'selfsame goods are carried to and from Brisbane, Sydney and Adelaide' where no manifestations of the disease had been reported. He concluded his letter by noting that the 'Hindoo traders' in his experience were 'cleanly, industrious and honest'.[34] Eventually, some months later the Central Board of Health

32 'The Hindoo Traders and the Small Pox', *The Argus* (Melbourne), 4 August 1884.

33 'The Indian Hawkers and Small-Pox', *The Argus* (Melbourne), 25 July 1884.

34 'The Hindoo Traders and the Small Pox', *The Argus* (Melbourne), 4 August 1884.

issued a statement to the effect that the Indian hawkers had not been the source of the infection.

Despite such occasional endorsements and this belated exoneration, many European men continued to be profoundly disturbed by the perceived threat posed by Indian hawkers to white women. By contrast, where their own perspectives have been represented, white women seem not to have viewed the infrequent visits made by Indian hawkers as frightening, but as eagerly anticipated events. Rajkowski, for example, basing her description on oral accounts she gathered from aged representatives of the last generations to witness 'Indian hawkers' in remote parts of regional Australia, wrote that 'the women and girls in particular would rush out to meet the hawker in anticipation of seeing the beautiful dress materials they were known to display' (Rajkowski 1987: 149-50).

As Rajkowski correctly points out, for all the anti-Asian sentiment reported in the newspapers and in parliamentary debates of the 1890s, 'it is more difficult to find such comments coming from the country people themselves' (ibid.: 154). None the less, Rajkowski also seems to underplay the extent to which physical violence featured in the lives of South Asians in the outback in the 1890s and early 20th century, and the extent to which this association contributed to their negative perception in and via print media.[35] She contends that in the newspapers of the 1890s there were no reports of 'ambushes, beating or fatal wounding of Asians *because they were hawkers*', and despite discussing the 1896 murder of Nazza Ali Khan in the Boggabri area of New South Wales by two teenage cousins, Frederick and William Dederer, reflects that 'the motive was never made clear' (ibid.). Rajkowski cleaves to this interpretation despite recognising that 'one Indian hawker was quoted as saying that there were a number of young men in the country, like the Dederers, who thought no more of killing Asians than of killing a dog and had not the discovery of the Indian hawker's body been made, a number of them would have been wiped out' (ibid.).

---

[35] Michael Cigler (1986 passim) also seems to have underestimated the extent to which South Asians became embroiled in violent conflicts, perhaps in part because of his concern to promote a positive image of multiculturalism and Australia's multicultural heritage.

The fact is that there were numerous instances in the late nineteenth and early 20th centuries of violence perpetrated upon Indian hawkers. At least a dozen such murders were reported in the press alone between 1885 and 1910.[36] It is, of course, impossible to know with certainty the extent to which these crimes were racially motivated, but it would surely be naïve to imagine that in a context of constant and widespread expressions of hostility towards the 'Indian hawker nuisance', racial prejudice played no significant part.

Certainly, the very itinerant nature of hawking, which involved often solitary travel over long-distances, made its exponents particularly vulnerable targets. Several of the incidents reported do appear to have been 'crimes of opportunity', as in one case in which an Indian hawker

> . . . was proceeding up the Belair Hill [South Australia], when he was overtaken by a man driving a horse in a cart, who offered to carry his bundle, which contained about £15 worth of jewellery, as well as other articles, up the hill. The Indian placed his bundle in the cart. Soon afterwards the vehicle got a little ahead, whereupon the driver whipped up his horse. The hawker gave chase, but was unable to catch the thief or find any trace of him.[37]

While this theft may have had little if anything to do with the race of the victim, it seems likely that the perpetrator knowingly took advantage of the social as well as the physical isolation of the hawker. Other crimes against Indian hawkers were more serious, with the victims being quite literally left for dead in out of the way locations, as in the Dederer case, or the murder of Kaiser Singh near Buchan (in Victoria) by John Conder in 1893,[38] or that of Merique Khan by Frank Ward at Eudunda (in South Australia) in 1899,[39] or of Booba Khan by Joseph Edmonds 20 miles from

---

36 For just a few examples, see: 'Police Intelligence', *The Argus* (Melbourne), 15 May 1885; 'Horrible Murder', *South Australian Register* (Adelaide), 28 November 1890; 'The Buchan Murder', *Traralgon Record* (Victoria), 28 July 1893; 'The Mount Mary Murder', *The Advertiser* (Adelaide), 25 February 1899; 'Miner's Rest Murder', *The Argus* (Melbourne), 30 March 1903.

37 'Robbery on Belair Road', *South Australian Register* (Adelaide), 19 July 1898.

38 'The Buchan Murder', *Traralgon Record* (Victoria), 28 July 1893.

39 'The Mount Mary Tragedy', *South Australian Register* (Adelaide), 25 February 1899.

Ingham (in North Queensland) in 1906,[40] all of which occurred in remote locations and appeared to have also involved the theft of the unfortunate hawker's wares.

In another infamous episode, two Afghan Cameleers, Noor and Jehan Mahomet were gunned down by teamster Thomas Brandon Knowles at a waterhole at Point Malcolm on the edge of the Western Australian gold fields in 1894 (Kabir 2005: 52-53). The altercation had apparently arisen over Knowles' objections to the cameleer's use of the precious water in their ritual ablutions, but no doubt reflected more general hostilities engendered by economic competition between teamsters and cameleers. Knowles' acquittal by jury in an Albany court house was greeted by 'loud applause and a rousing cheer from the enormous crowd both outside and inside the court'.[41]

By no means were all violent attacks on South Asians perpetrated by white Australians. Many of the more widely publicised incidents involved conflict between South Asian migrants. Reportage of such incidents often seized gleefully the opportunity to associate South Asians with the potential threat of violence. One prominent case involved Tagh Mahomet, who with his brother Faiz operated one of the most successful camel carrying enterprises with over 300 camels and a correspondingly large number of handlers. He was murdered by another Afghan in a dispute involving money and perhaps a long-standing and bitter tribal hostility (Stevens 1989: 97-100).

Often, sexual jealousy was cited as a motivating factor in conflicts between South Asian men. This was perhaps a fairly reasonable assumption given that almost all South Asians in the Australian colonies were male, and that marriages between Asian men and white women tended to be frowned upon by white society. As one letter to the editor of a Broken Hill newspaper complained:

> [T]hey come out here to stay for years; they bring none of their womenkind, and what is the result? Not only do they tend to low wages but they are ever on the hunt to satisfy their lustful cravings.[42]

---

40 'Alleged Murder', *Brisbane Courier* (Queensland), 24 November 1906.

41 'Trial of Thomas Knowles', *West Australian* (Perth), 7 January 1895.

42 W. Samoht, 'White Australia', *Barrier Truth* (Broken Hill), 27 March 1903, cited in Kabir (2005: 72).

fig. B.2 A 'Ghan hawker near Victoria downs, Northern Australia (photo: Donald Friend, obtained from the State Library of Victroria)

In one minor yet not atypical instance, Bootah Singh and Lily Yeaman were each fined £ 1in addition to court costs for assaulting another Indian hawker, Ottur Singh, in Mount Gambier (South Australia) in 1903.[43] According to *The Register*, 'it was said that the charms of Lily were the cause of the row'. *The Register* took a dryly sceptical approach to Yeaman's character. It noted that she was a white woman and, using scare quotes, identified her as Bootah Singh's 'housekeeper'. Casting doubt over her marital status, it observed that she had 'asserted' that she was a married woman. Nahid Kabir notes that Australian newspapers at the turn of the century generally tended to question the 'calibre' of white women who associated with Afghan men, dismissing them as 'generally poor and destitute' and 'apparently naïve about Islamic customs and beliefs, and somewhat emotionally or mentally unstable' (Kabir 2005: 71). While some white women married South Asian men, in the words of Christine Stevens, they tended to be 'European women living marginal lives themselves, as deserted wives or widows with dependent children, or prostitutes' (Stevens 1989: 220). The prospect of a white woman marrying a Muslim South Asian was unfathomable to federal Member of the House of Representatives, J.M. Fowler, who in 1909, wrote in the Western Australian *Sunday Times*:

---

43 'Magistrates Court, Mount Gambier,' *The Register* (Adelaide), 21 March 1903.

> Life as a Mohammedan wife will mean degradation and servitude. . . . Among Mohammedans women are regarded as a very inferior being. . . . Slavery is a mild term to describe the life of the average Mohammedan woman.[44]

South Asian men also married Aboriginal and 'half-caste' women, although there was also, at times, resistance to such alliances from Aboriginal society, and increasingly in the early 20th century from white officials in charge of Aboriginal 'protection' (Stevens 1989: 218).[45] In this context of social marginalisation, according to Christine Stevens, daughters of South Asian men came to be recognised as 'potential assets' (ibid.: 224). A system of bride-price came to be practised in which 'Afghan fathers took full advantage of their assets, often marrying off their very young daughters to very old men who had made a sum of money in the camel industry' (ibid.). In the case of Shamrose Khan, a cameleer based out of the 'Ghantown' at Broken Hill, the opportunity to marry came only when he was 'well into his sixties' and 'his friend's daughter became of marriageable age' (ibid.: 227). This bride-price system, at times, resulted in conflict, as in the case of the betrothal of Adelaide Moosha (née Khan) at Marree in South Australia in 1903. Adelaide's father Surwah Khan had accepted a deposit on a brideprice of £ 150 from Sher Khan, only to later accept a higher offer of £ 200 from another bidder, Moosha Khan. Embittered at having thus been usurped, Sher Khan lay in wait for his rival at the railway, shooting him nine times before fleeing the scene. Moosha Khan survived and later married Adelaide, while Sher Khan was found guilty of attempted murder and served a seven-year sentence in the Port Augusta prison (ibid.: 225-26). Several other 'crimes of passion' committed by South Asian men around the turn of the century were reported in the press in ways that contributed to the stereotyping of South Asian men as irrational and given to sudden bouts of enraged violence. In each of the cases discussed below, the perpetrator was deemed to have 'run amok'. Today this phrase has acquired a fairly innocuous, sometimes ironic colloquial meaning implying a loss of self-control and wild or erratic, or as in sense described by the *Oxford English Dictionary* as 'wild or wildly, headlong or

---

44 'A Piebald Australia', *Sunday Times* (Perth), 21 November 1909.

45 For a dramatic account of effects of the Aboriginal Act, 1905 upon the lives of one Afghan-Aboriginal couple, see Pamela Rajkowski (1995).

headlessly'.[46] At the turn of the century, this more general meaning was beginning to displace, but still drew heavily upon, popular recognition of a more specific connotation with a highly Orientalist genealogy. Originally, *amok* referred to what was believed to be a specifically Malay 'syndrome' in which the perpetrator, after experiencing some trauma or 'loss of public face' would commit suicide by indiscriminately attacking anyone he came upon in a public place, until he was in turn collectively restrained or, as often happened, he was killed by bystanders. This was, according to the Orientalist and later anthropological understandings, a kind of public ritual suicide with a somewhat collective dimension. During the 19th century, the term was employed fairly liberally by the British to explain (away) supposedly otherwise inexplicable acts of violence on the part of colonised people across South and South-East Asia.[47]

An incident that occurred on the main road of Ballarat (on the Victorian goldfields) in August 1893 is typical of the way in which the discourse of *amok* was often employed in descriptions of South Asian violence throughout the Australian colonies at this time. *The Advertiser* ran a report of the incident entitled 'A Hindoo Runs Amock', explaining that the police had had great difficulty in arresting the 'Hindoo' who 'armed with a pair of large tailor's scissors', threatened bystanders, hacked

---

46 *Oxford English Dictionary*, 'Amok, N. And Adv.' (Oxford University Press), http://www.oed.com/viewdictionaryentry/Entry/6512.

47 There are various theories regarding the origin of the term and concept of *amok*. The *Oxford English Dictionary* notes that it is first found in the Portuguese form of *Amouco* or *Amuco* in the 16th century, where it refers to a Javanese phenomenon of indiscriminate, suicidal mass killing. It has also been speculated that it has much earlier origins in ritualised martial acts of heroic resistance practised in southern India. More recent references recognise it as a peculiarly Malay 'syndrome', though one that is widespread throughout South-East Asia. The extent to which *amok* is in fact a colonial construction is the subject of some debate. For various points of view, see Robert L. Winzeler, 'Malayan Amok and Latah as "History Bound" Syndromes', in *The Underside of Malay History: Pullers, Prostitutes, Plantation Workers*, ed. Peter J. Rimmer and Lisa M. Allen, Singapore: Singapore University Press, 1990, pp. 214-29; John C. Spores, *Running Amok: An Historical Inquiry*, Athens, Ohio: Ohio Center for International Studies, Center for Southeast Asian Studies, 1988; Ronald C. Simons, ed., *The Culture-Bound Syndromes: Folk Illnesses of Psychiatric and Anthropological Interest*, Dordrecht: D. Reidel Publishing Company, 1985.

at the hands of one constable, and tried to stab another.[48] It also noted that he had previously been brought before the Police Court on a charge of lunacy but had been discharged as harmless. A slightly more detailed and somewhat contrasting account appearing in the *Barrier Miner* gave the man's name as 'Glomley Mahommet' and described him as

> an Indian hawker . . . who, it is said, is subject to outbursts of uncontrollable passion, under whose influence he has a craving to spill the blood of everybody he comes across.[49]

This supposed propensity for indiscriminate murder is strikingly reminiscent of clinical descriptions of the Malay 'syndrome', and yet was clearly at odds with the other account that suggested the offender had been recognised as mentally unstable but 'harmless'. The narrative of the more elaborate report continued in dramatic style.

> Seizing a pair of tailor's shears, he rushed up and down, chasing everybody he saw, shrieking wildly, smashing windows and threatening murder. The Chinese who were in the streets fled in terror, and most storekeepers closed and barred their doors.

In 1895, in the rural Queensland town of Warwick, another South Asian, an Indian hawker named 'Fuzzledean', was also widely reported to have 'run amuck' on the main street of town, this time armed with a revolver. While different newspaper accounts of the incident included varying levels of detail, they all tended to convey the impression that Fuzzledean was a 'maniac' who might easily have killed or wounded many more innocent bystanders than the two men whom he happened to shoot on that day. Almost all ascribed the cause of the tragedy to jealousy over a woman.

The most complete picture of events emerges from the report in Brisbane's *Queenslander*. In spite of itself, this account belies the general effort to depict Fuzzledean's 'murderous outrage' as evidence of the Asiatic propensity for irrational and uncontrolled behaviour on the order of the Malay 'amok'. Although clearly emotionally distressed and

---

48 'A Hindoo Runs Amuck', *The Advertiser* (Adelaide), 3 August 1893.

49 'An Indian Amuck', *Barrier Miner* (Broken Hill), 3 August 1893. The Muslim name 'Mahommet' suggests that *The Advertiser* used the common colonial appellation 'Hindoo' either erroneously or as a geographical referent rather than to denote religious persuasion.

overwrought, according to the *Queenslander*, Fuzzledean had quite deliberately waited outside a particular house until it was 'occupied by his wife and two other Indians', at which time he 'caught them unawares'. One of the men, 'Kummol', had recently arrived in Warwick from Dalby in order to take up employment in the service of Fuzzledean. Although Kummol was shot in the stomach, and later died on the way to hospital, Mrs. Fuzzledean stated that she believed that the bullet had been intended for her. According to the *Queenslander*, 'the second Indian, Meer Ahmed, grappled with the murderer, and he also was shot at, the bullet tearing his trousers. Fuzzledean then walked to the court house to give himself up.' The *Queenslander* carried the only report out of several appearing in newspapers throughout the colonies that chose to include this latter detail. On his way to the court house however, Fuzzledean was confronted by a Sergeant McNamara, who was visiting from the nearby town of Killarney. Perhaps feeling threatened, Fuzzeldean appears to have changed his mind about surrendering quietly. After a tense struggle in the busy street in which another policeman was shot in the foot, Fuzzledean was eventually taken into custody.

Most of the newspaper reports of this case seem mostly uninterested in the murder of Kummol and its apparently domestic context. The murder of the Indian was treated as a mere prelude to the brave action of the police in apprehending the crazed offender who 'ran down the main street brandishing a loaded revolver' in a 'perfectly frenzied state . . . quite oblivious of ultimate consequences.'[50] Describing Fuzzeldean as having 'run amok' was anything but innocent, despite the fact that the colloquialism was, by the 1890s, beginning to be freed of its original racial connotations and to refer more broadly to any type of wild or reckless behaviour, more or less similarly to the way in which it is often casually used today. The deployment of such language should be properly understood in terms of its earlier racialised portent and in the context of wider efforts to alienate South Asians in the Australian colonies of the British Empire.

The following year, in 1896, this fraught terminology appeared again

---

[50] 'Murder of an Indian: A Man Runs Amuck', *The Advertiser* (Adelaide), 16 October 1893, and 'Tragedy in Queensland', *Queanbeyan Age* (NSW), 19 October 1895.

in descriptions of an incident that occurred on the streets of Fremantle, the bustling port town of the Western Australian city of Perth. On this occasion an Afghan cameleer named Jumma Khan, who had been working in the colony for about two years, was said to have run amok with an axe, cleaving open the back of wharf labourer William Griffith's skull, before rushing up the High St 'in the middle of the thorough-fare' and, apparently randomly, felling a man named Thomas Henderson with a blow between the shoulders.[51]

At his trial, Jumma Khan entered a plea of not guilty on grounds of insanity, claiming in broken English and via an interpreter that he didn't know what he was doing at the time of his offence. Gilbert Probyn Smith, who claimed extensive 'experience of the race' to which Khan belonged and to have been witness to similar cases, and who would later give expert evidence before a Royal Commission to the effect that most Afghans were 'traitorously disposed to the country', volunteered his services to the prosecution as 'an interpreter of Oriental tongues'.[52] According to Probyn Smith, 'the tendency to run "amok" was to be compared to *delirium tremens* amongst Englishmen'.[53] He believed that the 'prisoner's brain was heated by continency [*sic.*], consequent upon being so long in the bush. Climatic conditions were often responsible for this murderous tendency'.[54] Despite the prosecution's witness thus seeming to support the insanity defence, the jury returned a guilty verdict and Khan was executed by hanging.

During the trial it emerged that Jumma Khan had worked for Faiz and Tagh Mahommet as a camel handler for two years, but had found the work difficult. On one occasion he had become lost in the bush for several days and had to be led back to the Mahomet camp by an Englishman. Lured to Australia by the promise of wealth, he had been contracted to Faiz and Tagh Mahommet for three years at 15 shillings per week. According to testimony from Mohammed Ameer, another employee

51 'A Fremantle Tragedy: An Insane Afghan Murders a Man in High Street and Wounds Another', *The Inquirer and Commercial News* (Perth), 11 December 1896.

52 'The Fremantle Tragedy', *The West Australian* (Perth), 4 March 1897.

53 Ibid.

54 Ibid.

of Faiz and Tagh Mahommet, Khan 'would not work properly . . . and was very bad tempered', frequently expressing his wish to leave Australia and return home. It was also said that he claimed to have been robbed of 20 pounds, was mistrustful of his fellow countrymen, and that on the day of his 'amok', he had attempted to buy a revolver in Fremantle with which he aimed to shoot a man on the goldfields. The *Albany Advertiser* noted that in contrast to the well-attended execution of another Afghan cameleer, Goulam Mahommet, several months earlier, Jumma Khan 'was entirely abandoned by his countrymen'.[55] Faiz Mahommet himself wrote to *The Inquirer* on behalf of 'the Afghan community of the colony' expressing deep regret for the death and injuries caused by Khan. In an effort to distance or absolve the Afghan community from the 'odium of the deed' committed by their countryman, Faiz offered to collect donations for the support of dependents of the victims.

Ultimately Faiz Mahommet's efforts to keep his community in the good graces of the white majority were to no avail. Relentless anti-Afghan propaganda did its work. The 1898 Royal Commission led to restrictions on mining rights for Afghans, while the federal Immigration Restriction Act, 1901 further reduced the status of South Asians in the colonies. When Faiz Mahomet, having resided in Australia for over 30 years and contributed in a major way to the development of several colonies, applied for naturalisation in the first decade after federation, he was turned down as a matter of policy (Stevens 1999: 148).

Conclusion

This chapter has provided some glimpses of the diverse range of migration by South Asians to the Australian colonies in the 19th century. On reflection it is hardly surprising that such migrations took place; after all, as is well known, South Asians dispersed widely throughout many parts of the British Empire, for a broad spectrum of reasons. What is interesting is the fact that their experiences have been largely elided from histories of Australian settlement, at least until the welcome arrival of a handful of corrective efforts in recent decades. One of the legacies of the 'White

[55] 'The Fremantle Tragedy: Execution of the Murderer', *Albany Advertiser* (Albany, WA), 1 April 1897. Goulam Mahomet was executed for the murder of Tagh Mahommet. See Stevens 1989: 158.

Australia policy' has been that this elision has all but subsumed popular memories of the ethnic diversity of 19th-century Australian history, such that the founding fathers' vision of the nation's future became successfully inscribed upon recollections of the past.

A particularly relevant irony is that Australian nationalism has frequently turned to the bush for its mythologies; the pioneering 'have-a-go' spirit and the ethos of 'mateship' thought to be so intrinsic to the Australian national character were, we are told, forged in the trying conditions of the rugged outback.[56] And yet, for those Australians who really did 'pioneer' the bush (many tens of thousands of years after the original inhabitants had done so, of course), South Asian migrants such as those we have briefly encountered in this chapter whether they were cameleers, hawkers and traders, shepherds, or labourers, although increasingly unwelcome, were anything but unfamiliar during the pioneering phase of settlement. Personal correspondences, journals and even shipping registers reveal that many early settlers, who were themselves 'old India hands' before voyaging further southward, brought with them a staff of domestic servants to recreate a kind of 'Raj down under'.[57] By the 1890s, however, to paraphrase David Walker, 'the practice of keeping any kind of servant was considered inappropriate by independently-minded Australians' (Walker 1999: 31). At the same time South Asian migrants, as cameleers and itinerant salesmen had themselves begun to exercise far greater independence and mobility than their earlier counterparts, a fact that accounts, partially at least, for the growth in hostility towards them.

That South Asians were a familiar presence in the Australian colonies at the turn of the century is attested to in numerous negative representations widely found in newspapers of the era.[58] Many of these representations depicted Indians and Afghans as at best a nuisance, and at worst as an alien and dangerous menace to white women and children,

56 Such mythology persists despite the fact that now more than ever, but even from very early times, a substantial majority of Australians were always urban residents.

57 This is the title of one of the chapters in Westrip and Holroyde 2010.

58 See Bilimoria and Gangopadhyay 1998b; Bilimoria 1989a, 1996, 1998, 2007: 308; and Chapter 1, p. 9, of this book.

prone to wild acts of random or sexual violence, in addition to undermining the economic prosperity of white men and the possibility of a more egalitarian future society. Herein resides perhaps the most compelling irony of Australian history with regards to its place in the British Empire. In rejecting the racial hierarchies and exploitation at play in other parts of the empire by exerting its sovereign right to exclude fellow British subjects based upon their race, Australian nationalism generated a particularly virulent form of xenophobia. But this did not always pass without acerbic challenges by South Asians — whether in residence, visiting as diplomats, or from their Indian nationalist base — in tandem with the revolutionary civil uprisings in South Africa (under Gandhi) and in North America (the Hindustan Ghadhar movement of California, staged by Sikh students, farm workers and secular Hindu professors). [59]

fig. B.3: Totaram Sanadhya (visited Australia 1914) (photo: Donald Friend, Obtained from the State Library of Victoria)

fig. B.4: Rt. Hon. V.S. Srinivasa Sastri and his secretary, G.S. Bajpai, in London en route Australia (1922)

[59] See Chapter 2, p. 67 with note 8, recounting observations of Totaram Sanadhya and Rt. Hon. Srinivasa Sastri during their 1914 and 1922 respective visits to Australia. See also, www.lib.berkeley.edu/SSEAL/SouthAsia/gadarcol.html

Contributors

A. About Contributing Authors and Editors

Each of the editors and all but two of the contributing authors have themselves experienced migration, in the case of the editors one from India, one of Indian descent originally from the Pacific, and one from the United Kingdom.

B. Contributing Authors

Surjeet Dhanji is a Ph.D. candidate at the School of Social and Political Sciences at the University of Melbourne, researching the social relations between the different groups of the growing Indian diaspora in Melbourne, Australia. She obtained her Masters in Development Studies at the University of Melbourne, having previously studied Bachelor of Science in Business Administration and International Finance at the University of San Diego, California, USA.

Focussing on her interests in forced and economic migration and ethnic minority groups, Surjeet has presented several papers in this area at post-graduate conferences. She has also published papers on the settlement of African refugees in Australia.

Salim Lakha has multidisciplinary qualifications in economics, urban studies, and anthropology. From 2001-09 he was the coordinator of the Development Studies Programme at The University of Melbourne. In 2011, he was a Visiting Senior Research Fellow at the Asia Research Institute, National University of Singapore. His research interests have included migration, transnational identities, and the international division of labour. His area of specialisation is India, and he has published extensively on industrialisation, labour relations, and the economic and cultural aspects of globalisation. In 2005 he completed a study that examined how transient Indian Information Technology professionals negotiated cultural difference in a transnational organisation in Australia. In 2009 Dr Lakha was a joint guest editor of a Special Issue of the journal *South Asia* titled 'Democracy, Civil Society and Governance: Contemporary Challenges in India'.

Heather Foster is an adjunct lecturer in the School of Education at the University of South Australia. After completing her undergraduate studies in anthropology and history at the University of Adelaide, she worked on various research projects at the University of Adelaide and the University of South Australia. She works mainly in the area of the Study of Religions, and Hindu communities in South Australia; she is currently vice-president of the Australian Association for the Study of Religions.

Richard Forster was born and raised in Brisbane, Australia, and currently resides in Maui while he is pursuing a Ph.D. in World History at the University of Hawaii at Manoa. His research interests are primarily in South Asia in world historical cross-cultural encounters. He examines the processes of identity formation such as communalism, religious, cultural and linguistic nationalisms, particularly in the context of British imperialism. He is also especially interested in transnational frameworks including world environmental history with their potential to 'rescue history from the nation'.

Margaret Kumar, Ph.D., completed a Bachelor of Arts; Graduate Certificate in Education; Master of Arts (Applied Linguistics); Master of Education (Language and Literacy Education). Dr Kumar is an academic and Higher Degree by Research Language and Learning Advisor who currently works at Deakin University. Previously she worked at the University of Melbourne. Through her work, Margaret has presented challenging perspectives on how teaching and learning practices for international students could be mediated. She has presented dialogic models on how international students from postcolonial backgrounds are represented. Presently, as Master of Education co-ordinator and Lecturer in Education at the Institute of Koorie Education at Deakin University, Dr Kumar is doing research on New Knowledge Systems and Aboriginal Education.

Selena Costa-Pinto is currently a staff at the Monash University, Clayton, Victoria. The research for her chapter grew out of her attempts at making sense of her own experiences, emotions and expectations as an Indian migrant living in Melbourne. The project was approved by Monash

University's Human Ethics Committee, and formed part of her Ph.D. thesis.

Manpreet Kaur Singh is best known as an SBS radio broadcaster in Australia. Her work covers across all platforms of journalism — newspapers, radio, magazines, television and online. She has made a significant contribution in the areas of social justice, cultural cohesion and multiculturalism, and has provided a strong platform for informed public debate on topical matters. Many of her articles have been published in newspapers, magazines and websites of international repute.

Michael Stevenson is Adjunct Research Associate with the Monash Asia Institute, Faculty of Arts, Monash University. His research interests focus on the comparative study of long-term social and cultural transformations and their impacts on individuals. He is also interested in issues connected with transnational migration and ethnic identities; and conflict and change with particular reference to contemporary India. Dr Stevenson lectured in anthropology at Monash University where he taught subjects related to development and globalisation, as well as the dynamics of prejudice and discrimination in industrial societies.

Carmen Voigt-Graf obtained a Ph.D. in Geography from the University of Sydney. Following a postdoctoral fellowship with the Australian Centre for Population Research at the Australian National University, she became a lecturer and later a senior lecturer at the University of the South Pacific in Fiji. During six years in Fiji, her research focused on development and migration issues in the Pacific Island region. She also held the position of Economic Adviser with the Office of the Chief Trade Adviser in Vanuatu, holding lead responsibility for the areas of investment and labour mobility. Voigt-Graf is currently a Fellow in the Development Policy Centre at the Australian National University. She has published numerous book chapters and journal articles in the area of migration, diaspora and transnationalism.

Editors (also authors)

Purushottama Bilimoria left his childhood country in the Pacific for New Zealand to pursue secondary and higher education in 1970, and after some years came to Melbourne to pursue his Ph.D. studies. Trained in philosophy with supplementary studies in jurisprudence, ethics, and religion he was always interested in the question of pluralism (vis-à-vis the spectre of 'relativism', of which most moral and analytical philosophers were apprehensive). After some years intermittently spent in India studying Sanskrit and Indian philosophy, and later completing a comparative work at All Souls' College, Oxford, he began to see how pluralism was not a threat. While teaching courses on 'World Religions', 'Asian Philosophy', 'Comparative Philosophy of Religion', and 'Cross-cultural Ethics', his appreciation of the possibilities within a pluralist structuration of social processes and worldviews increased. He is Editor-in-Chief (A) of *Sophia*, International Journal in Philosophy and Traditions, and also an Editor of the *International Journal of Dharma/Dharma Studies* (both published by Springer). While since 2000 he has been bi-located between the US and India (teaching at University of Stony Brook, and more recently University of California, Berkeley and Graduate Theological Union, as well as fellow with the Indian Institute of Advanced Studies in Shimla and Oxford Centre for Hindu Studies), he spends 3-4 months of the year as Honorary Fellow at University of Melbourne and Deakin University, pursuing his research work on Indian Ethics, Personal Law in India, the Indian Diaspora, History of Indian Dance in Australia, and the History of Comparative Philosophy in the Antipodes.

A little on his background: Around the late 1970s to mid-1980s, there was public debate rife in Australia on the desirability or otherwise of multiculturalism that had been heralded around the mid-1970s. Bilimoria was invited by the colourful Al Grassby — who was the Minister of Labour and Immigration in the Whitlam Government and initially given the responsibility of devising Australia's multiculturalism — to participate in one such forum. At the roundtable meeting that took place at La Trobe University, he was asked point-blank by Al Grassby: 'And what do the Indians think?' Frankly, he confessed, he had not investigated this matter as he had very little contact with the community, whereupon he received an impromptu lecture on the early history of Indians in Australia, as indentured labourers and camel-drivers, and the contributions they made to the development of the countryside. Grassby responded, 'You better study up this history and tell us what the Indians in this country today think about multiculturalism!' 'I'll think about it', the surprised scholar replied. Within a week, a package of material arrived in the post with old photos of turbaned cameleers, hawkers and pedlars, and 'Singhs' by camp-sides or on horse-carts.

The first book on *Indians in Australia: Sikhs of Woolgoolga*, by Maria de Leverpanche came out shortly afterwards, and that propelled more interest as well as providing resources for reading up extensively on this history; the book also suggested a framework for Bilimoria's own fieldwork among Indians in Victoria and Hindus in Australia. This is when more sustained work, intermittently between teaching and writing about philosophy and religion, on the South Asian diaspora began. In the years he increasingly spent in the United States, this interest expanded to incorporate immigrant experience of the Indian diaspora in the US (and his own too), and indeed more widely in the globalising world. Research on the Australian context and comparative observations allowed him to sift through the growing body of theoretical work on the phenomena of immigration and diaspora (in conversation with scholars such as Ninian Smart, Sneja Gunew, Fazal Rizvi and Arjun Appadurai) and resulted in a number of publications. The fruits of this work have been distilled with the recent shifts in immigration policy, which tilts towards favouring Indian immigrants and students, and in a major collaborative effort have given birth to this volume. So an innocent and somewhat naïve beginning ('stumbling upon multiculturalism') ends with a studied offering on diasporic/immigrant Indians.

Philip Hughes migrated with his parents, sisters and grandparents from the United Kingdom in the 1960s. While the cultures of the United Kingdom and Australia are more similar than India and Australia, he also has experienced some of the challenges in building a new life and a new community in a new land. The experience of migration probably contributed to his interest in culture and was one factor that led him to live in Asia for several years and study Asian cultures and religions. Over the last thirty years of his research, he has visited Asia many times and continued to study religious expression, particularly among young Buddhists, Muslims and Christians in Thailand. He believes that the basic cultural frameworks by which people operate are deeply embedded in us through our earliest experiences in life and through the acquisition of our first language. However, in our globalised world, it is of great importance to the development of world peace that we learn to understand each other and appreciate our different ways of thinking and living, particularly in relation to religion.

Hughes is an honorary research fellow at Edith Cowan University and at the Melbourne College of Divinity. An ordained minister in the Uniting Church of Australia, he works for the Christian Research Association through which he continues to be in dialogue with people of many faiths. He chairs the Council of Kingswood College, a Uniting Church school, through which he encourages an openness to people of all cultures and religious backgrounds. He is also the secretary for the Maroondah Interfaith Network, through which he seeks to encourage religious understanding and appreciation at the local council level.

Jayant Bhalchandra Bapat : From an Organic Chemist to a Hindu Academic and Community Priest: Transformation of an Early Settler. Jayant Bhalchandra Bapat embodies the themes in this book, for he has experienced migration from India to Australia. Over his years in Australia, he has become a leader and a priest for the community. He will continue to tell his story in his own words:

In January 1965, I was working as a research chemist in Alembic Chemical Works at Baroda in India on a salary of about four dollars per month. My wife and I had rented a one and half room apartment a long way from the factory and I bicycled to work. Then one day, a letter that was to change my entire life arrived in the mail from Monash University, Australia. They had offered me a postgraduate scholarship to undertake a doctoral degree in Chemistry. In spite of my wife being pregnant for the first time, we felt that I had to take up the offer. My wife would stay with her sister until the baby was born and then join me. I had no money for the ticket but thankfully a close relative lent it to me. When my superiors and colleagues at Alembic heard about this, they organised a farewell for me and suggested I learn German. They thought I was going to Austria! Few people in India knew Australia then; even fewer knew that the sixth continent had been inhabited for over 40,000 years by the Aborigines.

My uncle paid for the dark blue heavy woollen suit every overseas-going Indian wore, which was my very first suit. Travelling overseas was uncommon in those days and no one from our family had ever travelled abroad. I boarded an Alitalia flight one day in June. In addition to my wife who was quietly crying, there were over sixty relations who came to see me off at Bombay airport. Maybe they thought it would be the last time they would see me! Alitalia was the only airline that flew to Australia at that time, and that too only once a week! I did not at all enjoy the plane journey. First of all, I was quite scared. Second, as expected, my Indian English was difficult for the Italian flight attendants. Third, I had never had Western food, which I found totally bland. Finally, I did not drink alcohol at the time and when I asked for some water, I was given a sealed can. I did not drink it for the fear of incurring the wrath of the attendants if I did not finish it all! We arrived at Perth and I then had to catch two local flights to my destination: Perth to Sydney and Sydney to Melbourne.

There were only four Hindu families in Melbourne at that time, and I was the second person from the state of Maharashtra. The currency was the Australian pound and the country was predominantly an Anglo-Saxon nation, its culture a mix of Anglo-Celtic-Christian practices. The Greeks and Italians who had come earlier than the Indians, as assisted migrants, lived in their own enclaves. The few Egyptians and Lebanese who were also in Melbourne had done the same elsewhere in the metropolis. It was not at all easy for a person with 'dark' skin to come to Australia at the time; the unwritten 'White Australia' policy still reigned. I was able to come only because of the Monash University scholarship.

Thankfully, Monash had sent an Indian postgraduate student to receive me and I was to stay with an Indian family. It would have been around 35°C in Mumbai when I left; it was windy and less than 10°C in Melbourne. It took me quite some time to adjust to the cold windy weather, the broad Australian accent and a totally foreign culture. My wife joined me nine months later with our young baby girl. We started life in a two bedroom flat opposite Monash on my scholarship of the grand sum of Aus $ 2,000 per annum. My wife found it very hard initially, was depressed and would often cry. Our baby was found to suffer from a rare bronchial disorder. She was in and out of hospitals continually. We of course had no money for private health insurance and the only free hospital at the time was the now defunct Fairfield Infectious Diseases Hospital, over 26 km away. We had no car and our friends and my supervisor would take us once a week to see our baby. We took boarders to make ends meet. Life on the whole was very hard.

Apart from a few select spices that came from England such as Keen's curry powder, there were no spices, no Indian or Chinese vegetables and no Indian *dhal* or lentils. *Atta* (flour) that is used for making *chapatis* became available only in 1969, and that too had to be ordered from Swan Hill. We would often eat just rice, Keen-curry spiced potatoes, red lentils and cabbage.

A doctorate was a comparative rarity those days in Australia. Luckily I completed it within two and half years and took a lecturing job at the newly established Institute of Technology in the sleepy city of Bendigo.

Bendigo of the time had no Indians and an Indian with a doctorate was a novelty. I remember being called to a party at the Mayor's home within a matter of weeks. The town was even more Anglo-Saxon than Melbourne at that time. Only white bread was available. Rye bread came from Melbourne once a week in one shop only and had to be pre-ordered. Shops closed at 5 p.m. and were open on Saturdays only until 1 p.m. They were closed on Sundays. There were pubs all over the place but they closed at 6 p.m. and there was a rush on the publicans at 5.45 p.m. to get hold of 5 or 6 reserve beers before closing time. One could sit in the pub for quite a while, but selling alcohol after 6 p.m. was illegal. Most pubs were quite seedy and full of flies. Women were not allowed to enter the exclusive area of the bar, a male preserve. The Aborigines of course had no chance of entering the pub at all.

I came back to Melbourne in 1971 as a Senior Lecturer at the Caulfield Institute of Technology. Sometime later, this became Chisholm Institute, which was then absorbed by Monash University. I had thus completed the full circle, going back to my alma mater. I retired in 1998.

Both in Bendigo and in Melbourne, I was asked to talk about Hinduism at the local high schools. That was the first time I looked through reference books to find out what Hinduism was. However, at that time, I had no idea that one day I would be working for the Hindu community in Australia as a priest. For me, the catalyst for this major transformation was a telephone call in 1979 from a friend's wife in Sydney. She had been diagnosed with terminal cancer and given less than a few months to live. 'There is no Hindu priest in Sydney. You will have to do my last rites', she said. I felt I had no choice. In a great hurry, I got hold of some books on Hindu rituals from various sources. A close family friend who acted as a priest in his spare time gave me a lesson on conducting the Hindu funeral ritual. My knowledge of the Sanskrit language that I had learned at school came in handy. I conducted my friend's wife's funeral in Sydney within a few months of her phone call. Harrowing though it was, it was my first experience as a priest.

Since then, I have conducted over 800 rituals all over Australia. These have included several weddings, house blessings, funerals and various *pujas*. I have also become an authorised Hindu marriage celebrant. Initially, when the community was quite small, there was not much demand for these activities. In the past fifteen years or so, however, this has changed dramatically. The Indian community is the fastest growing community in Australia at present and this is reflected in the great need for rituals of all kinds. There are less than half a dozen lay priests in Melbourne and they conduct these rituals strictly as a community service. The honoraria they earn go to charities in Australia and India. Although this has earned us a lot of respect from the community, it has also become an onerous commitment for us all.

Through the rituals, I soon developed a basic knowledge of Hinduism. Because of the urgent need, I applied for authorisation for performing Hindu marriages. The application form for doing so was totally inappropriate for a religion other than Christianity; it dealt with church, denomination and congregation details. Finally one of the officers from the Attorney General's department in Canberra travelled to Melbourne to interview me. I was soon given the authorisation.

I then decided to embark upon research into Hinduism and was very fortunate that La Trobe University allowed me to do so in spite of the fact that I had no background in humanities. It took me ten years of part-time work to obtain a doctorate in religious studies. For the past twenty years, I have been an active researcher into Hinduism and 'things Indian'.

This then is the background of one of the first Hindus of the 1960s who came and settled in Australia. I have been very fortunate that the new country provided me the opportunities to better myself and even more fortunate that my work was recognised by the Australian Government through the award of an Order of Australia Medal (OAM) in 2011.

When I look back at the scenario 'then' in 1965 and compare it to 'now', it is difficult to believe my eyes and ears. With the rescinding of the 'White Australia' policy by the Whitlam Government in the early 1970s, things have changed dramatically. The population of Indian students is on the rise and almost all the taxi ranks in major cities are the preserve of Indians, most of them Sikhs. One can stroll through Foster Street, Dandenong in outer Melbourne, or the laneways in Parramatta in Sydney, and would find it difficult to believe that one is in a land that was exclusively white territory not long ago. The aromas of *chaat*, *samosa*s, *pakora*s and the like waft through the air and people queue to buy freshly made Indian sweets. One hears mostly Hindi and Punjabi spoken in these areas.

Marriages between Christians and Hindus are becoming more common. During the Hindu rituals, the non-Indian brides or grooms, dressed in expensive precious gem-studded *kurtas* and *pajamas* imported especially from India, are more than happy to repeat the Sanskrit chants when requested by the priest. In the reception that immediately follows, Bollywood dancing and drinking is the norm.

Temples and *gurdwaras* are springing up everywhere. There are now 46 Hindu temples and 31 Sikh *gurdwaras* in Australia and more are being built. Street processions such as that of the god Ganesh being taken to the waters for immersion, or a Hindu groom arriving on horseback to his wedding are not uncommon sights. The latest census shows that Hinduism and Sikhism are now the fastest growing religions in Australia.

Any diasporic experience produces major changes both in the receiving culture and the incoming culture of the diasporic group. A great deal of accommodation is required on both sides. Australia has seen its fair share of racial and cultural intolerance since the white settlement 150 years ago and it needs to be avoided at all costs. The incoming migrant on the other hand has to realise that one needs to make major changes to one's religious and cultural beliefs to fit into a different society. One has to learn the language, dialect, customs and manners at a late stage in life and start anew. This is often exceedingly difficult.

A number of questions come to the mind and need to be asked about the remarkable transformation that has occurred over a span of just 40 years.

Has this transformation produced the Australia that Whitlam and his government envisaged when they opened the gates? Are white Australians generally happy with this major change in the country's demography? Has this change produced race- and language-centred ghettos such as one sees in a number of Western countries? Is Australia likely to follow suit and declare in the near future, as some Western nations have recently done, that 'multiculturalism' is a failed experiment and so does not work? How is the Indian diaspora treated in this country? What kind of problems do they face, and are they able to tackle them successfully?

How do Indian migrant women fare? Do they face the same problems as their Australian counterparts, or do their problems have different dimensions? Do they face racial as well as sex discrimination? How do Indian students fare in their new educational environment? Do their learning backgrounds assist them or hinder their new learning? What are their job prospects in their chosen fields? Will they return to India or remain here? And who pays for the loss of talents ('brain-drain') back in India? Most importantly, how will this migration process develop in the future? Is it going to be the coveted cohesive multicultural mix that led to the dismantling of the 'White Australia' policy'?

The chapters in this volume discuss and attempt to answer some of the above questions; while the emphasis is on the Hindus and Sikhs, the topics included are applicable to all Indians. Additionally, we hope the book goes some way towards building bridges between the Indian diaspora and the receiving Australian culture.

Bibliography and References

Adam, E. and P. Hughes, 1996, *The Buddhists in Australia,* Melbourne: Multicultural and Population Research, Bureau of Immigration.

Al-Azmeh, Azia, 1993, *Islams and Modernities,* London/New York: Verso.

Alford, Katrina, 1984, *Production or Reproduction?: An Economic History of Women in Australia, 1788–1850,* Melbourne: Oxford University Press.

Allen, Margaret, 2005, 'The Chinaman Had no Fault Except that They Were Chinese: An Indian View of Australia in 1888', in S. Sareen (ed.) *Interconnections Identity, Representation and Belonging,* New Delhi: Mantra Press, pp. 202-17.

———, 2008, '"A Fine Type of Hindoo" Meets an "Australian Type": British Indians in Australia and Diverse Masculinities', in Desley Deacon, Penny Russell and Angela Woollacott (eds.) *Transnational Ties: Australian Lives in the World,* Canberra: ANU E-Press, pp. 41-58. @ http://epress.anu.edu.au/transnational_citation.html

———, 2009, 'Otim Singh in White Australia', in Susan Hosking et al. (eds.) *Something Rich and Strange: Sea Changes, Beaches and the Littoral in the Antipodes,* Adelaide: Wakefield Press, pp. 195-212.

———, 2012, '"Innocents Abroad" and "Prohibited Immigrants": Australians in India and Indians in Australia 1890-1910', in Ajaya K. Sahoo, Michiel Bass and Thomas Faist (eds.) *Indian Diaspora and Transnationalism,* New Delhi: Rawat Publications, pp. 350-65. (2006 version @ http://epress.anu.edu.au/cw/pdf/cw_part2.pdf, pp. 111-24.

Anderson, Clare, 2000, *Convicts in the Indian Ocean: Transportation from South Asia to Mauritius, 1815-53,* New York: Palgrave.

———, 2004, *Legible Bodies: Race, Criminality and Colonialism in South Asia,* Oxford/New York: Berg.

Anklesaria Aiyar, S., 2006, 'West's Discovery of India', *Times of India,* centrefold.

Appadurai, Arjun, 1991, 'Global Ethnoscapes: Notes and Queries for a Transnational Anthropology', in *Recapturing Anthropology,* ed. R. Fox, Santa Fe: School of American Research Press.

———, 1996, 1997, *Modernity at Large Cultural Dimensions of Globalization,* Minneapolis/London: University of Michigan Press. (Incorporates papers referred to as Appadurai (1990) and (1993a) and chapters therein.)

———, 2006, *Fear of Small Numbers: An Essay on the Geography of Anger*, Durham/Raleigh and London: Duke University Press.

Arguelles, Jose and Miriam Arguelles, 1972, *Mandala*, Berkeley/London: Shambala.

Bacchetta, Paola, 2004, *Gender in the Hindu National: RSS Women as Ideologues*, New Delhi: Women Unlimited.

Bacon, Jean, 1996, *Life Lines: Community, Family, and Assimilation Among Asian Indian Immigrants*, New York and Oxford: Oxford University Press.

Bahri, Deepika, 1998, 'With Kaleidoscope Eyes: The Potential (Dangers) of Identitarian Coalitions', in *A Part, Yet Apart*, ed. L.D. Shankar and R. Srikanth, Philadelphia: Temple University Press, pp. 25-48.

Ballard, B. and J. Clanchy, 1997, *Teaching International Students: A Brief Guide for Lecturers and Supervisors,* Canberra: IDP Education.

Ballard, R., 1994, "Introduction: The Emergence of *Desh Pardesh*", in Roger Ballard (ed.) *Desh Pardesh: The South Asian Presence in Britain,* London: Hurst and Company.

———, 2000, 'The South Asian Presence in Britain and Its Transnational Connections', paper presented at a conference on *Culture and Economy in the Indian Diaspora,* India International Centre, New Delhi, 8-10 April.

———, 2001, 'The Impact of Kinship on the Economic Dynamics of Transnational Networks: Reflections on Some South Asian Developments', paper presented at a workshop on *Transnational Migration,* Princeton University, Trenton, NJ, 29 June – 1 July.

Bapat, Jayant Bhalchandra, 1993, 'The Gurav Temple Priests of Maharashtra', *South Asia: Journal of South Asian Studies,* vol. 16, no. 10, pp. 70-100.

———, 2003, '"Gurava", "Kirtana", "Waghya-Murali", "Ganesha", "Holi", "Lalit", "Godhal"', in Margaret Mills, Peter Claus and Sarah Diamond (eds.) *South Asian Folk Culture: An Encyclopaedia,* New York and London: Routledge.

———, 2006, 'Hinduism', in Mary Touhy and Ray Elliott (eds.) *Ethics and Morality in a Multicultural Society,* Melbourne: Thomson Publishing.

———, 2008, 'The Lajjagauri: Mother, Wife or Yogini', in J. Bapat and I. Mabbett (eds.) *The Iconic Female: Goddesses of India, Nepal and Tibet,* Clayton: Monash University Press.

———, 2012a, '"Bhagavadgeeta", "Hinduism"', in *Cultural Sociology of the Middle East, Asia and Africa: An Encyclopaedia,* Thousand Oaks, CA: Sage Publications.

———, 2012b, 'Hinduism', in Mary Touhy, Ray Elliott, Paul Rule and Shaun Harper (eds.) *Religion and Ethics in a Pluralist Society,* Melbourne: Nelson-Cengage.

Bapat, Jayant Bhalchandra and Ian Mabbett, 2008 (eds.), *The Iconic Female: Goddesses of India, Nepal and Tibet*, Clayton, Vic.: Monash Asia Institute, Monash University Press; reissued in 2009, Somaiya Publications, Mumbai.

Bapat, Jayant Bhalchandra and Marika Vicziany, 2009, 'Mumbadevi and the Other Mother Goddesses in Mumbai', *Modern Asian Studies*, vol. 43, no. 2, pp. 511-41.

Bapat, Jayant Bhalchandra and P. Bilimoria, 1988, 'Hindus', in Ian Gillman (ed.) *Many Faiths One Nation: A Guide to Major Faiths and Denomination in Australia*, Sydney: Collins Australia, pp. 332-48.

———, 2009, in James Jupp (ed.) *The Encyclopaedia of Religion in Australia*, Melbourne: Cambridge University Press, pp. 329-40.

Barrier, Norman Gerald and Verne A. Dusenbery, 1989, *The Sikh Diaspora: Migration and the Experience beyond Punjab*, Delhi: Chanakya Publications.

Basingstoke, J., 2007 (ed.), *Religious Reconstruction in the South Asian Diasporas: From One Generation to Another*, Hampshire and New York: Palgrave Macmillan.

Bass, Michiel, 2006a, 'Cash Cows Milking Indian Students in Australia', *IIAS Newsletter*, vol. 42, no. 14, Autumn, Amsterdam: International Institute for Asian Studies.

———, 2006b, 'Students of Migration: Indian Overseas Students and the Question of Permanent Residency', *People and Place*, vol. 14, no. 1, pp. 8-23.

Batrouney, T. and J. Goldlust, 2005, *Unravelling Identity: Immigrants, Identity and Citizenship in Australia*, Altona, Vic.: Common Ground Publishing.

Baudrillard, J., 1983, *Simulations*, New York: Semiotext(e).

Bauman, Chad and Jennifer, Saunders, 2009, 'Out of India: Immigrant Hindus and the South Asian Hindus in the USA', Religion Compass, vol. 3, pp. 116-35.

Baumann, G., 1996, *Contesting Culture: Discourses of Identity in Multi-Ethnic London*. Cambridge: Cambridge University Press.

Baumann, Martin, 2000, 'Diaspora: Genealogies of Semantics and Transcultural Comparison', *Numen*, vol. 47, no. 3, pp. 313-37.

———, 2004, 'Becoming a Colour of the Rainbow: The Social Integration of Indian Hindus in Trinidad, Analysed along a Phase Model of Diaspora', in Knut Jacobsen, Pratap Kumar (eds.) *South Asians in the Diaspora: Histories and Religious Traditions*, Leiden: Brill, pp. 77-96.

———, 2008, *Global Hindu Diaspora Bibliography of Books and Main Articles* (pdf courtesy of author).

Beckford, James, 2007, *The Sage Handbook of the Sociology of Religion*, UK: Sage Publications.

Bellah Richard Madsen and Steve Tipton, 1991, *The Good Society*, New York: Alfred Knopf.

Bentor, Yael, 1996, *Consecration of Images and Stupas in Indo-Tibetan Tantric Buddhism*, Leiden: E.J. Brill.

Beyer, Peter F., 1994, *Religion and Globalisation*, London: Sage Publications.

———, 1998, 'The City and Beyond as Dialogue Negotiating Religious Authenticity in Global Society', in *Social Compass, International Society for the Sociology of Religion*, vol. 45, no. 1, pp. 67-80.

Bhabha, Homi K., 1994, *The Location of Culture*, London/NY: Routledge.

———, 1996, 'Culture's In-Between', in Stuart Hall and Paul Du Gay (eds.) *Questions of Cultural Identity*, London: Sage Publications.

Bharucha, Rustom, 1993, *Theatre of the World: Performance and the Politics of Culture*, London: Routledge.

———, 1998, 'The Shifting Sites of Secularism-Cultural Politics and Activism in India Today', *Economic and Political Weekly*, vol. 33, no. 4, 24-30 January, pp. 167-81.

Bhatt, C. and P. Mukta, 2000, 'Introduction: Hindutva in the West: Mapping the Antinomies of Nationalism', *Ethnic and Racial Studies*, vol. 23, no. 3, pp. 407-41.

Bhattacharjee, Annanya, 1997, 'The Public/Private Mirage: Mapping Homes and Undomesticating Violence Work in the South Asian Immigrant Community', in M.J. Alexander and C.T. Mohanty (eds.) *Feminist Genealogies, Colonial Legacies, Democratic Futures*, New York: Routledge, pp. 308-29.

Bhatti, R. and V.A. Dusenbery, 2001, 'From Settlers to Citizens', in R. Bhatti and V.A. Dusenbery (eds.) *A Punjabi Sikh Community in Australia: From Indian Sojourners to Australian Citizens*, Woolgoolga: Woolgoolga Neighbourhood Centre, pp. 115-222.

Bhogal, Balbinder Singh, 2012, 'Oak Creek Killings: The Denial of a Culture of Oppression', *Sophia*, vol. 51, no. 3, September, pp. 335-39.

Biggs, J., 1989, 'Approaches to the Enhancement of Tertiary Teaching', *Higher Education Research and Development*, vol. 8, no. 1, pp. 7-25.

———, 1991, 'Approaches to Learning in Secondary and Tertiary Students in Hong Kong: Some Comparative Studies', *Educational Research Journal*, vol. 6 (Summer), pp. 27-39.

———, 1999, 'Teaching International Students', in J. Biggs (ed.) *Teaching for Quality Learning in University*, Buckingham, UK: Society for Research into Higher Education & Open University Press, pp. 120-40.

Bilimoria, Purushottama, 1985, 'The Arya Samaj in Fiji: A Moment in Hindu Diaspora', *Religion* (Lancaster), April 1985, no. 15, pp. 103-30.

Bilimoria, Purushottama and Jayant Bapat, 1988, 'Hindus', in Ian Gillman (ed.) *Many Faiths One Nation: A Guide to Major Faiths and Denomination in Australia*, Sydney: Collins Australia, pp. 332-48.

Bilimoria, Purushottama and R. Ganguly-Scrase, 1988a, *Indians in Victoria (Australia)*, A Historical, Social and Demographic Profile of Indian Immigrants, East Melbourne and Geelong: Ethnic Affairs Commission of Victoria, and School of Humanities, Deakin University.

Bilimoria, Purushottama and R. Gangopadhayay, 1988b, 'Indians in Victoria', in *The Australian People*, (General Editor James Jupp), Sydney: Angus and Robertson, pp. 546-47.

Bilimoria, Purushottama, 1989a, *Hinduism in Australia: Mandala for the Gods*, Melbourne: Spectrum with Deakin University Press.

———, 1989b, *Yoga, Meditation and the Guru*, Melbourne: Indra Publishers.

———, 1991, 'A Problem for Radical (onto-theos) Pluralism', *Sophia*, vol. 30, no. 1, pp. 21-33; abridged version as, 'The Dismantling of Radical Religious Pluralism', Australian *Religious Studies* vol. 7, no. 2, pp. 69-77.

———, 1993, 'Temple Architecture: A Brief Overview and Its Symbolism', Bangla Samiti of Western Australia, October, pp. 23-31.

———, 1994a, 'Revelation without a Revealer', *Religious Understanding Revelation, Reasons and Belief*, Open Learning Rel 21 Text Book, Geelong: Deakin University and University of South Australia, pp. 69-91.

———, 1994b, 'Traditions and Transition in South Asian Performing Arts in Multicultural Australia', in Sneja Gunew and Fazal Rizvi (eds.) *Arts for Multicultural Australia;* Canberra/Sydney: Australia Council with Allen & Unwin, pp. 108-29.

———, 1994c, 'The Making of Hindu–Christian Dialogue in Australia', *Hindu–Christian Studies*, vol. 7, 1994, pp. 21-38.

Bilimoria, Purushottama and Rashmi Desai, 1995, 'What Might Tradition's Response be to the BJP's Hindu Rashtra Paritrayana Sadhunam', in Peter Reeves and John McGuire (eds.) *After Ayodhya: BJP and the Future of Indian Politics*, Western Australia: Curtin Centre for Indian Ocean and Peace Studies.

Bilimoria, Purushottama, 1996a, *The Hindus and Sikhs in Australia*, Religious Community Profiles, Bureau of Immigration, Multicultural and Population Research, Canberra, ACT: Australia Government Publishing Services.

———, 1996b, 'Hindus (in Australia)', in P. Hughes (ed.) *Australia's Religious Communities: A Multimedia Exploration*, 1st edn., Melbourne: Christian Research Association, 3rd edn. 2010.

———, 1996c, 'Review of Hafina Deen, *Caravanserai: Journey Among Australian Muslims* (Sydney: Allen and Unwin, 1995)', *Asian Studies Review*, vol. 19, no. 3, pp. 163-64.

———, 1997, 'The Australian South Asian Religious Diaspora', in John Hinnells (ed.) *A New Handbook of Living Religions*, Oxford/Cambridge, MA: Blackwell Publishers 1998, 1999, pp. 728-55.

———, 1999, 'The Making of the Hindu in Australia: A Diasporic Narrative', in T.S. Rukmani (ed.) *Hindu Diaspora, Global Perspectives*, New Delhi: Munshiram Manoharlal, pp. 3-34.

———, 2000, 'Testing "Delocalized Transnational Diasporia and PostColonial Hybridity" of South Asian Hindus in the Oceanic-Australia with Reference to America', Society for the Scientific Study of Religion Annual Conference, US (Published Abstract).

Bilimoria, Purushottama and C. Voigt-Graf, 2001, 'Indians in Eastern Australia', in James Jupp (ed.) *The Australian People: An Encyclopaedia of the Nation*, Melbourne: Cambridge University Press.

Bilimoria, Purushottama, 2002, 'Review of Steven Vertovec, *The Hindu Diaspora Comparative Patterns* (London/New York: Routledge 2000)', *South Asia*, vol. 25, no.2, pp. 290-92.

———, 2003, 'Indian Dance', in John Whiteoak and Aline Scott-Maxwell (gen. eds.) *Currency Companion to Music and Dance in Australia*, Sydney: Currency Press, pp. 330-31.

Bilimoria, Purushottama and Jayant Bapat, 2004, 2009, 2010 'Hinduism (in Australia)', in Philip Hughes (ed.) *Australia's Religious Communities: A Multimedia Exploration*, Melbourne: Christian Research Association, revised 3rd & professional editions, pp. 1-80.

Bilimoria, Purushottama, 2005, 'Hinduism', *Encyclopedia of Hinduism*, Melbourne: Cambridge University Press.

———, 2007, 'Transglobalism of Self-exiled Hindus: The Case of Australia', *Religion Compass*, 1/2 January, pp. 305-28. (Blackwell Publishing Doi: 10.111/j.1749-8171.2007.00020.x)

———, 2007a, 'Diaspora and Difference: Problems in Studying South Asian Religions in the Transnationalism and Diaspora Contexts', *Nidan, South African Journal of Hindu Studies*, vol. 19, pp. 1-22.

———, 2007b, '"September 11": Hindu and Asian Responses in Oceania', *Man in India: International Journal of Anthropology* (Special Issue on Indian Diaspora), vol. 87, nos. 1 & 2, January–June, pp. 83-102.

Bilimoria, Purushottama and Jayant Bapat, 2009, 'Hindu Beliefs, Practices and Life in Australia', in James Jupp (ed.) *The Encyclopaedia of Religion in Australia*, Melbourne: Cambridge University Press, pp. 329-40.

Bilimoria, Purushottama, 2009a, 'Hyperglobalization's Casualty: The Numerical Small', in Prakash Sarangi and Hans Logren (eds.) *Globalization and Politics: Indo-Australian Perspectives*, New Delhi: Social Sciences Press, pp. 77-96.

———, 2009b, 'The Relationship Between Hinduism and Hindutva' (written presentation), American Academy of Religion Panel on 'Who Speaks for Hinduism?' (Convenor Arvind Sharma, McGill University).

———, 2009c, 'Desi Performative Arts in Australia: From Lightfoot to Creative Indian-Australian Dance Movements (Illustrated)', paper presented at India Australia Studies Association Conference, Goa University, 18-21 January.

———, 2010, 'Dies of Culture and Religion: India and Australia, from Settlement to Post/modern Times', *Man in India: International Journal of Anthropology* (Special Issue on Transglobalism, Immigration, Adaptation and Ecology, ed. P. Bilimoria), (Issued for Australian Sanskrit Conference, 2011) vol. 90, nos. 1-2, pp. 163-82.

Bilimoria, Purushottama and Amy Reyner, 2010, 'Dying: An Approach to Care from Hindu and Buddhist Perspectives', in Elizabeth Mackinlay (ed.) *Ageing and Spirituality across Faiths and Cultures,* London: Jessica Publishers, pp. 138-51.

Bilimoria, Purushottama and E. Stansell, 2010, 'Suturing the Body Corporate (Divine and Human) in the Brahmanic Traditions', *Sophia,* vol. 49, no. 2, pp. 237-59.

Bilimoria, Purushottama, 2011, 'The Idea of Hindu Law', *Journal of the Oriental Society of Australia* (Issue for Australian Sanskrit Conference, 2011), Sydney, NSW: Oriental Society of Australia in the University of Sydney, vol. 43, pp. 103-31.

———, 2012a, 'Religion and Postcolonialism: Editorial Introduction', *Australian Religious Studies Review* (Special Issue Guest ed. P. Bilimoria), vol. 25, no. 2, pp. 97-101.

———, 2012b, 'Diasporic Borders: Of Deterritorialized Hindu–Sikh Transnationals: Australia, US, the Globe', Panel on *Being in Borderlands: The Negotiation of Boundaries in South Asian Religious Communities,* Dharma Academy of North American, American Academy of Religion Annual Meeting, Chicago (forthcoming in *International Journal of Dharma Studies,* 2015).

———, 2013a, 'The Politics of Secularization and its Moral Discontents/ Disenchantments', *Journal of Dharma,* vol. 38, no. 3 (July-September), pp. 231-52.

———, 2013b, 'Hindus in Australia and New Zealand', *Brill Encyclopedia of Hinduism,* Knut Jacobsen et al. (ed.) Leiden: E.J. Brill, pp. 193-205.

———, 2014, 'Spivak between Kant and Matilal', in Bilimoria & Al-Kassim, 2014, q.v. pp. 1-12.

Bilimoria, Purushottama and Al-Kassim, Dina, 2014a, *Critique of Postcolonial Reason: Deliberations on Gayatri Chakravorty Spivak's Thoughts,* New Delhi: Oxford University Press.

Bilimoria, Purushottama, 2014b, 'Disenchantment of Secularism: The West and India', in Matthew Sharpe and Dylan Nicholson (eds.) *Secularisations and Their Debates: Perspectives on the Return of Religion in Contemporary West* (Sophia Studies in Cross-cultural Philosophy of Traditions and Cultures), Dordrecht: Springer, pp. 21-38.

Bilimoria, Purushottama, 2015, 'Of Dance & Theory: History of Indian Dance in Australia, from Louise Lightfoot-Shivaram-Manipur dancers to Chandrabhanu', Australia India Institute Occasional Papers.

Bilimoria, Purushottama and Serena O'Meley, 2015, *The Silver Tongue of the Empire: Rt Hon Srinivasa Sastri's momentous visit to Australia, 1922,* (forthcoming).

Birch, David, 2000, 'Transnational Cultural Studies: What Price Globalisation?', *Social Semiotics,* vol. 10, no. 2, pp. 141-56.

Blainey, Geoffrey, 1983, *Tyranny of Distance,* Melbourne: The Sun Books.

Bouma, Gary D., 1993, 'Religious Identification in Australia: 1981-1991', *People and Place,* vol. 1, no. 2, pp. 13-17.

———, 1996 (ed.), *Many Religions, All Australian: Religious Settlement, Identity and Cultural Diversity,* Melbourne: Christian Research Association.

———, 2006, *Australian Soul Religion and Spirituality in the Twenty-first Century,* Melbourne: Cambridge University Press.

———, 2011, *Being Faithful in Diversity,* Adelaide: ATF Press.

Bouma, Gary D. and Jan Brace-Govan, 2000, 'Gender and Religious Settlement: Families, Hijabs and Identity', *Journal of Intercultural Studies,* vol. 21, no. 2, pp. 159-75.

Boyd, J.W. and F.M. Kotwal, 1981, 'The Indian Parsis in New Zealand', in Kapil N. Tiwari, *Indians in New Zealand Studies in a Sub-culture,* Price Milburn for The New Zealand Indian Central Association, Inc., pp. 163-82.

Bouma, Gary D. and Andrew Singleton, 2004, 'A Comparative Study of the Successful Management of Religious Diversity: Melbourne and Hong Kong', *International Sociology,* vol. 19, no. 1, pp. 5-24.

Brah, Avatar, 1996, *Cartographies of Diaspora: Contesting Identities,* London: Routledge.

Brennan, L. and Brij V. Lal, 1998 (eds.), 'Across the Kala Pani: Indian Overseas Migration and Settlement', *South Asia,* vol. 21 (special edition), pp. 1-237.

Brown, Judith M., 2006, *Global South Asians: Introducing the Modern Diaspora,* Cambridge, UK: Cambridge University Press.

Brown, Percy, 1940 (1971), *Indian Architecture: Buddhist and Hindu Periods,* 3rd edn., Bombay: DB Taraporevala Sons & Company.

Brunato, Madelaine, 1972, *Hanji Mahomet Allum: Afghan Camel-Driver, Herbalist, and Healer in Australia,* Adelaide: Investigator Press.

Calgar, A.S., 1997, 'Hyphenated Identities and the Limits of Culture', in Tariq Modood and Pnina Werbner (eds.) *The Politics of Multiculturalism in New Europe: Racism, Identity and Community*, London: Zed Books.

Caplan, Patricia, 1985, *Class and Gender in India: Women and Their Organisations in a South Indian City*, London: Tavistock Publications.

Chalmers, Don, 2001, *City of the Dead: A History of the Necropolis, Springvale*, Flemington, Vic: Hyland House Publishing Pty Ltd.

Chalmers, Don and S. Volet, 1997, 'Common Misconceptions about Students from South-East Asia Studying in Australia', *Higher Education Research and Development*, vol. 16, no. 1, pp. 87-98.

Chandrasekhar, S., 1986, *From India to America: A Brief History of Immigration, Problems and Prospects of Assimilation*, La Jolla, CA.: Population Review Books.

——— (ed.), 1992, *From India to Australia: A Brief History of Immigration, the Dismantling of the 'White Australia' Policy, Problems and Prospects of Assimilation*, La Jolla, CA.: Population Review Books.

Chapple, Christopher, 2008, *Yoga and the Luminous: Patañjali's Spiritual Path to Freedom*, Albany, NY: SUNY Press.

Charlesworth, Max, 1997, *Religious Inventions: Four Essays*, Melbourne: Cambridge University Press.

———, 1998, *Religious Business: Essays in Australian Aboriginal Spirituality*, Melbourne: Cambridge University Press.

Chatterjee, Partha, 1993, *The Nation and Its Fragments: Colonial and Postcolonial Histories*, Princeton: Princeton University Press.

Choudhary, S.K., 2008, 'Higher Education in India: A Socio-historical Journey from Ancient Period to 2006-07', *Journal of Educational Enquiry*, vol. 8, no. 1, pp. 50-72.

Chow, Rey, 1993, *Writing Diaspora Tactics of Intervention in Contemporary Cultural Studies*, Bloomington and Indiana: Indiana University Press.

Cigler, Michael, 1986, *The Afghans in Australia*, Australian Ethnic Heritage Series, Melbourne: Australasian Educa Press.

Clark, Manning, 1971, *A History of Australia*, vol. I, Melbourne: Melbourne University Press.

Clarke, C., C. Peach and S. Vertovec (eds.), 1990, *South Asians Overseas Migration, and Ethnicity*, Cambridge: Cambridge University Press.

Clifford, James, 1994, 'Diaporas', *Cultural Anthropology*, vol. 9, no. 3, pp. 302-38.

Clothey, F., 1983, *Rhythm and Intent: Ritual Studies from South India*, Madras: Blackie and Son.

Clothey, Fred W., 2006, *Ritualizing on the Boundaries: Continuity and Innovation in the Tamil Diaspora*, Columbia, S.C.: The University of South Carolina Press.

Cohen, Robin, 1997, *Global Diasporas: An Introduction*, London: UCL Press.

Cole, W. Owen and Piara Singh Sambhi, 1978, *The Sikhs: Their Religious Beliefs and Practices*, London/Boston: Routledge & Kegan Paul.

Conradson, David and Alan Latham, 2005, 'Friendship, Networks and Transnationality in a World City: Antipodean Transmigrants in London', *Journal of Ethnic and Migration Studies*, vol. 31, no. 2, pp. 287-305.

Coomaraswamy, Ananda K., 1977, 'An Indian Temple: The Kandarya Mahadeo' (written in 1947), reprinted in Coomaraswamy: *Selected Papers, Traditional Art and Symbolism* (General Editor Roger Lipsey, Bollingen Series LXXXIX), NJ: Princeton University Press.

Costa-Pinto, Selena, 2010, 'Making the Most of Technology: Indian Women Migrants in Australia', *International Migration*, 7 September (doi: 10.1111/j.1468-2435.2010.00640.x) [Wiley online library], pp. 1-29.

Craig, N., 2010, 'Students from Abroad Treated like Cash Cows', *The Sunday Age* (Melbourne), 23 May, p. 13, retrieved 3 October 2010, <http://newsstore.fairfax.com.au/apps/viewDocument.ac;jsessionid=6D2A3725C8974707F658715F36EA23F5?sy=afr&pb=all_ffx&dt=selectRange&dr=1month&so >.

Croucher, P., 1989, *A History of Buddhism in Australia 1848–1988*, Sydney: University of New South Wales Press.

Cummings, Cathleen A., 2014, *Decoding a Hindu Temple: Royalty and Religion in the Iconographic Program of the Virupaksha Temple, Pattadakal*, Los Angeles: South Asian Studies Association.

D'Cruz, J.V. and W. Steele, 2003, *Australia's Ambivalence Toward Asia*, (revised edn.) Clayton, Vic: Monash Asia Institute/Monash University Press.

D'Souza, Austin, 1976, *Anglo-Indian Education: A Study of Its Origins and Growth in Bengal up to 1960*, New Delhi: Oxford University Press.

Dalrymple, William, 2002, 'White Mischief', *The Guardian*, 8 December (accessed on 28 January 2012, http://www.guardian.co.uk/uk/2002/dec/09/britishidentity.india).

———, 2004, *White Mughals: Love and Betrayal in Eighteenth Century India*, London: Penguin.

———, 2007, 'How the East Was Won', *New Statesman*, 5 July (accessed on 11 February 2011. http://www.newstatesman.com/books/2007/07/british-marsh-india-colley).

Daniels, Roger, 1989, *History of Indian Immigration to the United States: An Interpretive Essay*, New York: The Asia Society.

Deakin, Alfred, 1893, *Temple and Tomb in India*, Melbourne: Melville, Mullen and Slade.

———, 1893, *Irrigated India: An Australian View of India and Ceylon, Their Irrigation and Agriculture*, London: W. Thacker.

Dempsey, Corinne G., 2006, *The Goddess Lives in Upstate New York: Breaking Convention and Making Home at a North American Hindu Temple*, Oxford and New York: Oxford University Press.

Devji, Fazal, 1992, 'Hindu/Muslim/India', *Public Culture*, 1992, vol. 5, no. 1.

Dhillon, Amrit, 2009, 'Countries Agree on Students', *The Age*, 3 September, retrieved 3 October 2010, <http://www.theage.com.au/national/education/countries-agree-on-students-20090902-f8g1.html>. See also http://www.deakin.edu.au/research/src/crefi/documents/international-graduates-employment.pdf

Dusenbery, V.A., 1995, 'A Sikh Diaspora? Contested Identities and Constructed Realities', in P. van der Veer (ed.) *Nation and Migration: The Politics of Space in the South Asian Diaspora*, Philadelphia: University of Pennsylvania Press, pp. 17-42.

———, 2008, 'Sikh Positionings in Australia and the Diaspora Concept', in Verne A Dusenbery, *Sikhs At Large: Religion, Culture, and Politics in Global Perspective*, New Delhi: Oxford University Press.

Eck, Diana L., 2000, 'Negotiating Hindu Identities in America', in *The South Asian Religious Diaspora in Britain, Canada, and the United States*, ed. H. Coward, J.R. Hinnells and R.B. Williams, Albany: State University of New York Press, pp. 219-237.

Evans, A., 2009, *The Australian Survey of Social Attitudes*, Australian Social Science Data Archives, Canberra: The Australian National University.

Featherstone, Mike, Scott Lash and Roland Robertson (eds.), 1997, *Global Modernities*, London: Sage Publications.

Fenton, Elizabeth, 1901, *The Journal of Mrs. Fenton: A Narrative of Her Life in India, the Isle of France (Mauritius), and Tasmania During the Years 1826-1830*, London: Edward Arnold.

Fenton, J., N. Hein, F. Reynolds, A. Miller, N. Nielsen Jr., G. Burford & R. Forman, 1993, *Religions of Asia*, New York: St. Martin's Press.

Fischer, K., 2010, 'In India Student-Recruiting Industry Ups the Ante for U.S. Colleges', *Chronicle of Higher Education*, vol. 56, no. 18, pp. A1-A22.

Fisher, Michael, 2004, *Counterflows to Colonialism: Indian Travellers and Settlers in Britain, 1600–1857*, New Delhi: Permanent Black, 2004.

Fleuret, Anne and Patrick Fleuret, 1980, 'Quantitative Methods and the Analysis of Social Change: A Case Study', *Journal of Anthropological Research*, vol. 36, no. 2, pp. 231-44.

Forsthoefel, Thomas A. and Cynthia Ann H. Humes (eds.), 2005, *Gurus in America*, Albany NY: SUNY Press.

Foster, Heather A., 1994, 'Hinduism in Nineteenth-Century South Australia', presented to the Concurrent National Conferences of Theology and the Study of Religions (Australian Association for the Study of Religions), Adelaide, 3-7 July.

———, 2002, *Accommodating Difference: The Cultural Construction of the Hindu Women of South Australia,* unpublished Ph.D. Thesis, University of South Australia.

———, 2007, 'Hinduism, Identity and Education', *Dialogue Australasia,* **17**: 34-36.

———, 2008, 'Religious Maintenance and Adaptation: An Example from the South Australia Hindu Diaspora', *Religion Compass,* vol. 2, no. 3, pp. 316-30.

———, 2010, 'The Development of Hinduism in South Australia', *Man in India,* vol. 90, nos. 1-2, pp. 223-34.

———, 2011, 'The First Indians: The Bruce and Gleeson Indentured Labourers in Nineteenth-Century South Australia', *The Historical Society of South Australia,* no. 39, pp. 21-30.

Freire, Paulo (1984) (1972), *Pedagogy of the Oppressed,* Middlesex: Penguin Books.

Gabay, A.J. (1984), 'The Séance in the Melbourne of the 1870s: Experience and Meanings', *Journal of Religious History,* vol. 13 no. 2, December, pp. 192-212.

Gabbi, R.S., 1998, *Sikhs in Australia,* Melbourne: Aristoc Press.

Gill, Gurdarshan Singh and Ranjit Kaur, 2010, 'Sikhism', in P. Hughes (ed.) *Australia's Religious Communities: A Multimedia Exploration,* 3rd edn. Melbourne: Christian Research Association.

Giddens, A., 1999, BBC Reith Lectures 1999: 1. Globalisation; 3. Tradition, Re-broadcast ABC Radio (Australia) 2000.

Goldberg, Ellen and Singleton, Mark (ed.), 2014, *Gurus of Modern Yoga,* New York: Oxford University Press.

Goldsworthy, David, 2001 (ed.), *Facing North: A Century of Australian Engagement with Asia,* vol. I: 1901 to 1970s, Melbourne: Melbourne University Press.

Gow, L., D. Kember, and J. McKay, 1996, 'Improving Student Learning through Action Research into Teaching', in D. Watkins and J. Biggs (eds.) *The Chinese Learner: Cultural Psychological and Contextual Influences,* Hong Kong: Centre for Comparative Research in Education; Camberwell, Victoria: Australian Council for Educational Research, pp. 245-65.

Grewal, J.S., 1990, *The Sikhs of Punjab,* Cambridge: Cambridge University Press.

Guha, R. and G.C. Spivak (eds.), 1988, *Selected Subaltern Studies,* New Delhi: Oxford University Press.

Guille, H., 1999, 'Globalisation and Labour Standards', paper cited in Jordan (2000) q.v.

Gunawardena, H., R. Wilson, S. Georgakis and N. Bagnall, 2010, 'Homogeneity Permanent Residency and Racism: Experiences of Indian Students at an Australian Sandstone University', *International Journal of Intercultural Information Management*, vol. 2, no. 2, pp. 164-77.

Gunew, Sneja, 1993, 'Multicultural Multiplicities: US, Canada, Australia', *Meanjin*, vol. 52, no.3, pp. 447-61.

Gupta, Himanee, 2003, 'Staking a Claim on American-ness: Hindu Temples in the United States', in *Revealing the Sacred in Asian and Pacific America*, ed. J.N. Iwamura and P. Spickard, New York: Routledge, pp. 193-208.

Hage, Ghassan, 1998, *White Nation: Fantasies of White Supremacy in a Multicultural Society*, Annandale, NSW: Pluto Press.

Hall, S., 1996, 'Introduction: Who Needs Identity?', in Stuart Hall and Paul du Gay (eds.) *Questions of Cultural Identity*, London: Sage Publications.

Hardy, Adam, 1995, *Indian Temple Architecture: Form and Transformation: The Karṇāṭa Draviḍa Tradition, 7th to 13th Centuries*, New Delhi: Abhinav Publications.

———, 2008, *The Temple Architecture of India*, New Delhi: Wiley.

Harlan, Lindsey, 2004, 'Reversing the Gaze in America: Parody in Divali Performance at Connecticut College', in *South Asians in the Diaspora: Histories and Religious Traditions*, ed. K.A. Jacobsen and P.P. Kumar, Boston: Brill, pp. 161-79.

Harris, J., 1990, *One Blood: 200 Years of Aboriginal Encounter with Christianity: A Story of Hope*, Sutherland, NSW: Albatross Books.

Harrison, D., P. Austin, P. Millar, 2010, 'Indian Student Visa Applications Fall by Half', *The Age* (National), 7 July, retrieved 3 October 2010, <http://www.theage.com.au/national/education/indian-student-visa-applications-fall-by-half-20100106-lubt.html >.

Harvey, David, 1973, *Social Justice and the City*, London: Edward Arnold.

———, 2005, *A Brief History of Neoliberalism*, New York: Oxford University Press.

Hawley, John Stratton, 2004, 'Global Hinduism in Gotham', in *Asian American Religions: The Making and Remaking of Borders and Boundaries*, ed. T. Carnes and F. Yang, New York: New York University Press, pp. 112-37.

Heidegger, Martin, 1971, 'The Origin of the Work of Art', *Poetry, Language, Thought*, New York: Harper & Row, pp. 17-87.

Helweg, A.W., 1992, 'Indians of the Professions in Australia: Some Theoretical and Methodological Considerations', in S. Chandrasekhar (ed.) *From India to Australia: A Brief History of Immigration; the Dismantling of the 'White*

Australia' Policy; Problems and Prospects of Assimilation, La Jolla, CA: Population Review Books.

Heredia, Rudolf C., 2007, *Changing Gods: Rethinking Conversion in India*, New Delhi: Penguin Books.

Hess, R.D. and M. Azuma, 1991, 'Cultural Support for Schooling: Contrasts between Japan and the United States', *Educational Researcher*, vol. 20, no. 9, pp. 2-10.

Hill Collins, Patricia, 1990, *Black Feminist Thought: Knowledge, Consciousness, and the Politics of Empowerment*, Boston: Unwin Hyman.

Hill, Ernstine, 1937, *The Great Australian Loneliness*, London: Jarrolds.

Hinnells, John R., 1994, 'South Asian Diaspora Communities and Their Religion: A Comparative Study of Parsi Experiences', *South Asia Research*, vol. 14, no. 1, Spring, pp. 62-108.

———, 1998, 'Comparative Reflections on South Asian Religion in International Migration', in John Hinnells (ed.) *The New Penguin Handbook of Living Religions* (2nd edn.) Oxford/Cambridge, MA: Blackwell Publishers; London: Penguin (1998, Paperback 1999), pp. 819-48.

———, 2000, 'Introduction: South Asian Religions in Migration', in *The South Asian Religious Diaspora in Britain, Canada, and the United States*, ed. H. Coward, J.R. Hinnells and R.B. Williams, Albany: State University of New York Press, pp. 1-11.

———, (ed.) 2007, *Religious Reconstruction in the South Asian Diasporas: From One Generation to Another*, UK: Palgrave McMillan.

Howe, R., 2003, 'A Movement of Influence: The Australian Student Christian Movement in the 1930s', in B. Howe and P. Hughes (eds.) *The Spirit of Australia II*, Adelaide: Australian Theological Forum.

Hughes, Philip, 1997, *Religion in Australia: Facts and Figures*, Melbourne: Christian Research Association.

———, 2007, *Putting Life Together: Findings from Australian Youth Spirituality Research*, Melbourne: Christian Research Association.

———, 2009, 'Religion and Occupation', *Pointers*, vol. 19, no. 1, March, pp. 12-16.

———, 2010a, 'Integrated Mission: Putting Welfare and Faith Together in The Salvation Army (Southern Territory – Australia)', *Australian Journal of Mission Studies*, vol. 4, no. 1, June, pp. 22-28.

———, 2010b, *Shaping Australia's Spirituality: A Review of Christian Ministry in the Australian Context*, Melbourne: Mosaic Press.

———, 2010c, 'Are Australians "Losing their Religion?"', *Pointers*, vol. 20, no. 2, pp. 1-6.

———, 2010d (ed.) *Australia's Religious Communities: A Multimedia Exploration* (CD-Rom), 3rd edn., Melbourne: Christian Research Association.

———, 2011, 'Values and Local Church Mission', *Australian Journal of Mission Studies*, vol. 5, no. 2, December, pp. 47-54.

———, 2012, 'The Impact of Recent Immigration on Religious Groups in Australia', *Pointers*, vol. 22, no. 4, December, pp. 1-8.

Hughes, Philip and E. Adam, 1996, *The Buddhists in Australia*, Bureau of Immigration, Melbourne: Multicultural and Population Research.

Humphrey, Michael, 1998, *Islam, Multiculturalism and Transnationalism from the Lebanese Diaspora*, Oxford, London, New York: Centre for Lebanese Studies and I B Tauris & Co.

Inglehart, R., 1977, *The Silent Revolution*, Princeton, NJ: Princeton University Press.

Irvine, Andrew, 2000, 'Cultural Participation and Post-Colonialism', *Sophia International* (Millennium Extra: Post-Colonial Critiques), vol. 39, no. 1 (March-April), pp. 171-207.

Jacobsen, Knut A. and Kristina Myrvold, 2011, *Sikhs in Europe: Migration, Identities and Representation*, Aldershot (UK): Ashgate Publishing Ltd.

Jacobsen, Knut A. and Pratap Kumar (eds.), 2004, *South Asians in the Diaspora: Histories and Religious Traditions*, Leiden: E.J. Brill.

Jaijee, I.S., 1999, *Politics of Genocide: Punjab 1984-1998*, Delhi: Ajanta Publications.

Jamrozik, Adam, Cathy Boland and Robert Urquhart, 1995, *Social Change and Cultural Transformation in Australia*, Melbourne: Cambridge University Press.

Jayaraman, R., 1988, 'Indians', in James Jupp (Gen. ed.) *The Australian People: An Encyclopedia of the Nation, Its People, and Their Origins*, Sydney: Angus Robertson, pp. 542-45.

Jayasuria, L., 1997, *Immigration and Multiculturalism in Australia: Selected Essays*, Nedlands: School of Social Work and Social Administration, The University of Western Australia.

Johanson, S., 2010, 'Why Buy East when You Can Mumbai West?', *The Age*, 11 September.

Johnson, Richard, 2010, 'Australia/India Trade Relations 1708–1808', *Man in India* (Special Issue on Globalism, Transnational, Gender and Ecological Engagement) vol. 90, nos. 1-2, pp. 147-68.

Johnson, Richard and Margaret Kumar, 2010, 'The Monsoon Wedding Phenomenon: Understanding Indian Students Studying in Australian Universities', *Higher Education Research & Development*, vol. 29, no. 3, pp. 215-27.

Jones, Philip and Anna Kenny, 2007, *Australian Muslim Cameleers: Pioneers of the Inland, 1860s–1930s*, Adelaide: Wakefield Press.

Jordan, Trevor, 2000, 'The Role of Religion in Globalising Civil Society', *Australian Religion Studies Review*, vol. 13, no. 1, Autumn, pp. 5-16.

Joshi, Vijay, 2000, *Indian Daughters Abroad: Growing Up in Australia,* New Delhi: Sterling Publishers Private Ltd.

Juergensmeyer, M., 1988, 'The Logic of Religious Violence: The Case of the Punjab', *Contributions to Indian Sociology,* vol. 22, no. 1, pp. 65-88.

Jupp, James (ed.) 1991, *Immigration,* Sydney: Sydney University Press, in association with Oxford University Press, Melbourne.

———(ed.), 2001, *The Australian People: An Encyclopedia of the Nation, Its People, and Their Origins*, Sydney: Angus Robertson; Cambridge: Cambridge University Press.

Kabir, Nadid Afrose, 2005, *Muslims in Australia: Immigration, Race Relations and Cultural History* (Studies in Anthropology, Economy and Society), London: Kegan Paul.

Kannabiran, Kalpana, 1998, 'Mapping Migration, Gender, Culture and Politics in the Indian Diaspora', *Economic and Political Weekly* (31 October), pp. WS-53-57.

Kehrberg, J.E., 2007, 'Public Opinion on Immigration in Western Europe: Economics, Tolerance and Exposure', *Comparative European Politics*, vol. 5, pp. 264-81.

Kelly, Peter, 2007, *Buddha in a Bookshop Harold Stewart and the Traditionalists,* North Fitzroy, Vic.: Ulysses Press.

Kember, D. and L. Gow, 1991, 'A Challenge to the Anecdotal Stereotype of the Asian Student', *Studies in Higher Education,* vol. 16, no. 2, pp. 117-28.

Khandelwal, M.S., 1995, 'Indian Immigrants in Queens, New York City: Patterns of Spatial Concentration and Distribution, 1965-1990', in Peter van der Veer (ed.) *Nation and Migration: The Politics of Space in the South Asian Diaspora,* Philadelphia: University of Pennsylvania Press, pp. 178-96.

Khandelwal, Madhulika S., 2002, *Becoming American, Being Indian: An Immigrant Community in New York City*, Ithaca: Cornell University Press.

Khatun, Samia, 2012, *Camels, Ships and Trains: Translation across the 'Indian Archipelago' 1880-1930*, unpublished Ph.D. Thesis, University of Sydney, Sydney.

Kim, Hanna H., 2005, 'Swaminarayan Movement'. In the *Encyclopedia of Religion,* ed. Lindsay Jones, vol. 13 2nd edn. Detroit: Macmillan, pp 8889-8893.

Knott, Kim, 1997, 'The Religions of the South Asian Communities in Britain', in John Hinnells (ed.) q.v., pp. 756-74.

Kramrisch, Stella, 1946, *The Hindu Temple,* Calcutta, 1946; repr., Delhi: Motilal Banarsidass, 1976, 1980.

Kull, Christian A. and Haripriya Rangan, 2012, 'Science, Sentiment and Territorial Chauvinism in the Acacia Name Change Debate', in S.G. Haberle and B. David (eds.) *Peopled Landscapes: Archaeological and Biogeographic Approaches to Landscapes, Terra Australis* 34, Canberra: ANU E-Press, pp. 197-219.

Kumar, M.K., 2004, *The Discursive Representation of International Undergraduate Students: A Case Study of a Higher Education Institutional Site*, unpublished Ph.D. thesis, Adelaide: University of South Australia.

Kumar, Margaret, 2011, *Discursivity, International Students and Representation*, Altona, Victoria: Common Ground Publishers.

Kumar, Margaret and S. Ang, 2008, 'Transitional Issues of Induction into Design Education for International Undergraduate Students: A Case Study Analysis of Architecture', *Journal for Education in the Built Environment*, vol. 3, no. 2, pp. 10-32.

Kumar, Pratap P., 2011, 'Editorial' Special Issue on 'Religion and the South Asian Diaspora', *South Asian Diaspora*, vol. 3, no. 2, March, pp. 1-3.

Kurien, Prema, 1998, 'Becoming American by becoming Hindu: Indian Americans Take Their Place at the Multicultural Table', in *Gatherings in Diaspora: Religious Communities and the New Immigration*, R.S. Warner and J.G. Wittner, Philadelphia: Temple University Press, pp. 37-70.

Lakha, S., 1992, 'The Internationalisation of Indian Computer Professionals', *South Asia: Journal of South Asian Studies*, New Series, vol. XV, no. 2, pp. 93-113.

Lal, Brij (ed.) 2006, *Encyclopedia of the Indian Diaspora*, Kuala Lampur, Paris: Editions Dider Millet.

Lal, Vinay, 2008, *The Other Indians: A Political and Cultural History of South Asians in America*, Los Angeles: UCLA Asian American Studies Center Press.

Langer, B., 1998, 'Globalisation and the Myth of Ethnic Community: Salvadoran Refugees in Multicultural States', in David Bennet (ed.) *Multicultural States: Rethinking Difference and Identity*, London: Routledge.

Leonard, Karen, 2007, 'The Second Generation: Questions and Answers', Keynote Address, International Conference on Globalization and Diaspora: 21st Century, University of Hyderabad.

Leonard, Karen et al. (eds.) 2004, *Immigrant Faiths: Transforming Religious Life in America*, New York: AltaMira Press.

de Lepervanche, Marie, 1984, *Indians in a White Australia: An Account of Race, Class and Indian Immigration in Eastern Australia*, Sydney: Allen & Unwin.

Lessinger, Johanna, 1999, 'Class, Race and Success: Indian-Americans Confront the American Dream', in Carla Petievich (ed.) *The Expanding Landscape: South Asians and the Diaspora*, New Delhi: Manohar.

Lewis, James R., 2002, 'Sikhism', in J.G. Melton and M. Baumann (eds.) *Religions of the World: A Comprehensive Encyclopedia of Beliefs and Practices*, Santa Barbara: ABC-Clio, pp. 1175-80.

Lewis, P., 1997, 'Arenas of Ethnic Negotiation: Cooperation and Conflict in Bradford', in Tariq Modood and Pnina Werbner (eds.) *The Politics of Multiculturalism in the New Europe: Racism, Identity and Community*, London: Zed Books.

Lowe, Lisa and David Lloyd (eds.) 1997, *The Politics of Culture in the Shadow of Capital*, Durham, NC: Duke University Press.

Ludden, David, 2006, 'History and Inequality', *IIAS Newsletter*, vol. 42, Autumn, pp. 28-29. Full text at http://www.iias.nl/wertheim/?q=nodes/5

Mabbett, Ian, 1983, 'The Symbolism of Mt. Meru', *History of Religions* (Chicago), vol. 23, no. 1, pp. 64-83.

MacKinlay, Shane, 2010, 'Heidegger's Temple: How Truth Happens When Nothing Is Portrayed', *Sophia*, vol. 49, no. 4 (Special Issue), pp. 499-507.

MacKinnon, Catherine, 1989, *Towards a Feminist Theory of the State*, Cambridge, MA: Harvard University Press.

Maddox, Marion, 1998, 'Religion and the Secular State Revisited', *Australian Religion Studies Review*, vol. 11, no. 2, Spring, pp. 98-113.

Magloff, Lisa, 2005, *Curriculum Visions*, Atlantic Europe Publishing (published in China).

Malpas, Jeff, 2006, *Heidegger's Topology: Being Place, World*, Cambridge, MA: MIT Press.

Mankekar, P., 1994, 'Reflections on Diasporic Identities: A Prolegomenon to an Analysis of Political Bifocality', *Diaspora*, vol. 3, no. 3, pp. 349-71.

Marginson, Simon, Chris Nyland, Erlenawati Sawir, and Helen Forbes-Mewett, 2010, *International Student Security*, Cambridge: Cambridge University Press.

Markus, Andrew, 1994, *Australian Race Relations: 1788–1993*, St. Leonards, NSW: Allen and Unwin.

Marton, F., G. Dall'Mba and L.K. Tse, 1996, 'Memorising and Understanding: The Keys to the Paradox?', in D. Watkins and J. Biggs (eds.) *The Chinese Learner: Cultural Psychological and Contextual Influences*, Centre for Comparative Research in Education, Hong Kong; Camberwell, Victoria: Australian Council for Educational Research, pp. 69-83.

Mason, G., 2010, 'Violence Against Indian Students in Australia: A Question of Dignity', *Current Issues Criminal Justice*, March 2010, pp. 461-65.

Masson, Jeffrey M., 1993, *My Father's Guru: A Journey through Spirituality and Disillusion*, Boston: Addison Wesley Publishers.

Matthew and Mir (see Mir, Ali)

Mazumdar, Sucheta, 1989, 'Racist Responses to Racism: The Aryan Myth and South Asians in the United States', *South Asia Bulletin*, vol. 9, no. 1, pp. 47-55.

McKnight, Tom L., 1969, *The Camel in Australia*, Melbourne: Melbourne University Press.

McLeod, W.H., 1968, *Guru Nanak and the Sikh Religion*, Oxford: Clarendon Press.

———, 1976, *The Evolution of the Sikh Community*, Oxford: Clarendon Press.

———, 1989, *Who Is a Sikh?: The Problem of Sikh Identity*, Oxford: Clarendon Press.

———, 1997, *Sikhism*, London: Penguin.

Meister, Michael W., 1983, *Encyclopaedia of Indian Temple Architecture*, ed. Michael W. Meister and M.A. Dhaky: American Institute of Indian Studies and University of Pennsylvania Press.

———, 2010, *Temples of the Indus: Studies in the Hindu Architecture of Ancient Pakistan*, Leiden: Brill.

Menon, Anusha, 2011, 'The Indian Link to Convict Australia', *Indian Link*, Melbourne, vol. 11, no. 5, April, p. 33.

Metcalf, Thomas R., 2007, *Imperial Connections: India in the Indian Ocean Arena, 1860–1920*, Berkeley: University of California Pres.

Michell, Georg, 1977, 'The Temple as a Link Between the Gods and Man', in G. Michell (ed.) *The Hindu Temple: An Introduction to Its Meaning and Form*, London: Elek Books; Delhi: B.I. Publications.

Mir, Ali, Biju Mathew and Raza Mir, 2000, 'The Codes of Migration: Contours of the Global Software Market', *Cultural Dynamics*, vol. 12, no. 1, March, pp. 5-33.

Mishra, Sudesh, 2006, *Diaspora Criticism*, Edinburgh: University of Edinburgh Press.

Mishra, Vijay, 2001, 'Diaspora and the Art of Impossible Mourning', in Makarand Paranjape (ed.) *In Diaspora: Theories, Histories, Texts*, New Delhi: Indialog, pp. 24-47.

———, 2007, *The Literature of Indian Diaspora: Theorising the Diasporic Imaginary*, London: Routledge.

Mitra, A., 2005, 'Creating Immigrant Identities in Cybernetic Space: Examples from a Non-resident Indian Website', *Media, Culture & Society*, vol. 27, no. 3, pp. 371-90.

Mullins, M., 2010, '"Hysterical" Indian Media Speak the Truth', *Eureka Street*, vol. 20, no. 1 (EurekaStreet.com.au).

Murphy, Una, 2008, 'Bhakti, Sankirtana and Gaudiya Vaisnavism: India to Australia — Foucaultian Analysis', Unpublished PhD Thesis, Geelong, Vic.: Deakin University.

Naidoo, Loshini, 2007, 'Re-negotiating Identity and Reconciling Cultural Ambiguity in the Indian Immigrant Community in Sydney, Australia' *Anthropologist* (Special Issue: A. Singh (ed.) *Indian Diaspora: The 21st Century*

– *migration, change and adaptation*, no. 2, pp. 53-66. (http://www.krepublishers.com/06-Special%20Volume-Journal/T-Anth-00-Special%20Volumes/Anth-SI-02-Indian%20Diaspora-Web/T-Anth-SI-02-05-053-066-Naidoo-L/T-Anth-SI-02-05-053-066-Naidoo-L-Tt.pdf) [accessed on 2 March 2011].

Nandy, Ashis, 1995-96, *Emergencies* 7/8, Special Issue: Plural Worlds, Ashis Nandy and the Post-Columbian Future Multiple Selves, ed. Vinay Lal, Los Angels: Group for Composite Studies, UCLA.

———, 2001, 'A Report on the Present State of Health of the Gods and Goddesses', *South Asia Postcolonial Studies,* vol. 4, no. 2, pp. 125-41.

Narayanan, Vasudha, 1992, 'Creating the South Indian 'Hindu' Experience in the United States', in *A Sacred Thread: Modern Transmission of Hindu Traditions in India and Abroad*, ed. R.B. Williams, Chambersburg, PA: Anima Publications, pp. 147-76.

Nimbark, Ashakant, 2004, 'Paradoxes of Media-reflected Religiosity among Hindu Indians', in *Asian American Religions: The Making and Remaking of Borders and Boundaries*, ed. T. Carnes and F. Yang, New York: New York University Press, pp. 98-111.

Nussbaum, Martha C., 2007, *The Clash Within: Democracy, Religious Violence, and India's Future,* Cambridge, MA: The Bellknap Press.

Padget, D., 1999, 'Review of Peter Beyer, *Religion and Globalisation*', http://www.indiana.edu/wanthro/beyer.htm, 2 September, source: Jordan (2000).

Palfreeman, A.C., 1965, *The Administration of the White Australia Policy*, Melbourne: Melbourne University Press.

Palmer, Norris W., 2006, 'Negotiating Hindu Identity in an American Landscape', in *Nova Religio: The Journal of Alternative and Emergent Religions* **10**(1): 96-108.

Paranjape, Makarand (ed.), 2009, *Sacred Australia Post-Secular Considerations*, Melbourne: Clouds of Magellan.

Parekh, Bhikhu, 1994, 'Some Reflections on Hindu Diaspora', *New Community*, vol. 20, no. 4, pp. 603-20.

Parker, Samuel K., 1992, 'Contemporary Temple Construction in South India: The Srirangam Rajagopuram', *RES*, vol. 21, Spring, pp. 110-23.

Parsons, Talcott, 1961, 'Culture and the Social System: Introduction', in T. Parsons et al. (eds.) *Theories of Society*, New York: Free Press, pp. 963-71, 984-88.

———, 1971, *The System of Modern Societies*, New Jersey (USA): Prentice-Hall.

Pearse, Meic, 2004, *Why the Rest Hates the West: Understanding the Roots of Global Rage*, Downers Grove, IL: InterVarsity Press.

Pearson, M.N., 2003, *The Indian Ocean* (Seas in History Series), London: Routledge.

Pieterse, Jan Nederveen, 1997, 'Globalization and Hybridization', in Featherstone, Lash and Robertson (eds.) *Global Modernities*, pp. 45-68.

Pippin, Lyrics from 'No Time at All', Pippin Soundtrack, Music and Lyrics by Stephen Schwartz.

Pybus, Cassandra, 2006, *Black Founders: The Unknown Story of Australia's First Black Settlers*, Sydney: University of New South Wales Press.

Radhakrishnan, Sarvepalli, 1960 (1927), *The Hindu View of Life*, London: George Allen & Unwin.

Rai, Amit S., 1995, "India on-line: Electronic Bulletin Boards and the Construction of a Diasporic Hindu Identity", *Diaspora* **4**(1): 31-57.

Rai, Rajesh (ed.), 2009, *The South Asian Diaspora: Transnational Networks and Changing Identities*, London/New York: Routledge.

Rai, Rajesh and Chitra Sankaran, 2011, 'Religion and South Asian Diaspora' (Introduction to Special Issue on 'Religion and the South Asian Diaspora') *South Asian Diaspora*, vol. 3, no. 2, March, pp. 5-13.

Rajkowski, Pamela, 1987, *In the Tracks of the Camelmen: Outback Australia's most Exotic Pioneers*, North Ryde, NSW/London: Angus & Robertson.

———, 1995, *Linden Girl: A Story of Outlawed Lives*, Perth: University of Western Australia Press.

Ram, Kalpana, 1996, 'Liberal Multiculturalisms NESB Women: A South Asian Post-colonial Feminist Perspective on the Liberal Impoverishment of Difference', in Ellie Vasta and Stephen Castles (eds.) *The Teeth Are Smiling: The Persistence of Racism in Multicultural Australia*, St Leonards, Sydney: Allen & Unwin, pp. 130-42.

———, 1999, 'Impossible Identifications: The University and Women of Difference', *Communal/Plural*, vol. 7, no. 2, pp. 213-30.

Rambachan, Anatanand, 2005, 'The Hindu Tree on America's Sacred Ground', in *Taking Religious Pluralism Seriously: Spiritual Politics on America's Sacred Ground*, ed. B.A. McGraw and J.R. Formicola, Waco, TX: Baylor University Press.

Rangan, Haripriya and Christian A. Kull, 2010, 'The Indian Ocean and the making of Outback Australia: An Ecocultural Odyssey', in Shanti Moorthy and Ashraf Jamal (eds.) *Indian Ocean Studies: Cultural, Social and Political Perspectives*, London: Routledge, pp. 45-72.

Ray, H.P., 2010, *Archaeology and Text: The Temple in South Asia*, Delhi: Oxford University Press.

Rees, Tomas James, 2009, 'Is Personal Insecurity a Cause of Cross-National Differences in the Intensity of Religious Belief?', *Journal of Religion and Society* 11. http://moses.creighton.edu/JRS/pdf/2009-17.pdf

Rizvi, F., 2005, 'International Education and the Production of Cosmopolitan Identities', paper presented at the Transnational Seminar Series at the University of Urbana-Champaign, 4 March.

Robertson, Roland, 1994, *Globalization Social Theory and Global Culture,* London: Sage Publications.

———, 1996, 'Globality, Globalization and Transdisciplinarity', *Theory, Culture and Society,* vol. 13, no. 4, p. 131.

———, 1997, 'Glocalization: Time–Space and Homogeneity–Heterogeneity', in Featherstone, Lash, and Robertson (eds.) *Global Modernities,* pp. 25-44.

———, 1998, 'Globalization and the Future of "Traditional Religion"' (paper presented at the Princeton Conference on *The Church and the World in a New Century: Faith and Responsibility in a Global Future*), p. 9.

Rukmani, T.S. (ed.) 1999, *Hindu Diaspora Global Perspectives,* Montreal: Concordia University; Delhi: Munshiram Manoharlal.

———, 2005, 'Women as Cultural Ambassadors in the Montreal Hindu Diaspora', *Nidan, International Journal for the Study of Hinduism,* vol. 17, December, pp. 53-63.

Samuelowicz, K., 1987, 'Learning Problems of Overseas Students: Two Sides of a Story', *Higher Education Research and Development,* vol. 6, no. 2, pp. 121-33.

Sanadhya, Totaram, 1919/1973, *Fiji Dwip Men Mere Ikkis Varsh* (My Twenty-One Years in Fiji) (in Hindi 1919, English translation 1973), Varanasi: Banarsidas Chaturvedi.

Saunders, Jennifer B., 2007, '"I don't eat meat": Discourse on Food Among Transnational Hindus', *Contributions to Indian Sociology* **41**(2): 203-23.

———, 2011, 'Mantras and Murtis: Fluidity in Contemporary Arya Samaj and Sanatan Dharm Practice', *Nova Religio: The Journal of Alternative and Emergent Religions* **15**(2): 50-69.

———, 2014, *Hinduism in America,* New York: Oxford University Press.

Scheifinger, Heinz, 2010, 'Om-line Hinduism: World Wide Gods on the Web', in *Australian Religion Studies Review,* vol. 23, no. 3, pp. 325-45.

Sen, Amartya, 2005, *The Argumentative Indian: Writings on Indian History, Culture and Identity,* New York: Farrar, Straus & Giroux.

———, 2006, *Identity and Violence: The Illusion of Destiny,* New York: W.W. Norton & Company.

Sharma, Arvind, 1994, *Women and Religion,* Albany: State University of New York Press.

Sharma, Renuka, 2013, 'Women Worshipping; Worshipping Women: Immanence and Transcendence in the Naya Yuga', in C. Chapple, Sunanda Shastri et al. (eds.) *World of Philosophy: A Harmony, Essays in Honour of Yagneshwar Shastri,* Delhi: Shanti Prakashan, pp. 132-54.

———, 2014, *Empathy Theory and Application in Psychotherapy,* Delhi: DK Print World (revised edition with new Introduction by Karin Brown).

Sherwood, Patricia, 2001, 'Buddhist Contribution to Social Welfare in Australia', *Journal of Buddhist Ethics*, vol. 8, pp. 61-74.

Sidhu, G.S., 1999, 'The Story of Sikhs Settling in the Sydney Area: Anecdotal and Personal Recollections', Souvenir of 12th Australian Sikhs Sports Carnival Sydney, pp. 11-13.

Simons, Ronald C. (ed.), 1985, *The Culture-Bound Syndromes: Folk Illnesses of Psychiatric and Anthropological Interest*, Dordrecht: D. Reidel Publishing Company.

Singer, Milton, 1972, *When a Great Tradition Modernizes,* Chicago: University of Chicago Press.

Singh, G., 1995, 'The Punjab Crisis since 1984: A Reassessment', *Ethnic and Racial Studies,* vol. 18, no. 3, pp. 476-93.

Singh, Kushwant, 1963, *A History of the Sikhs*, vol. 1: 1469–1839, Princeton: Princeton University Press; 2nd edn. 1991, Oxford: Oxford University Press.

———, 1966, *A History of the Sikhs,* vol. 2: 1839-1964, Princeton: Princeton University Press; 2nd edn. 1991, Oxford: Oxford University Press.

Singh, Nikky-Guninder Kaur, 1993, *The Feminine Principle in the Sikh Vision of the Transcendent,* Cambridge: Cambridge University Press.

Singh, P., 1999, *The Sikhs*, New York: Doubleday.

Singh, Pashaura, 2006, *Life and Work of Guru Arjan: History, Memory and Biography in the Sikh Tradition*, New Delhi: Oxford University Press.

Singh, Pashaura and Norman Gerald Barrier, 1996, *The Transmission of Sikh Diaspora in the Diasporsa*. Delhi: Manohar.

Singh, R., 2001, 'Sikh Community of Woolgoolga: A Comparative View', in R. Bhatti and V.A. Dusenbery (eds.) *A Punjabi Sikh Community in Australia: From Indian Sojourners to Australian Citizens*, Woolgoolga: Woolgoolga Neighbourhood Centre, pp. 230-41.

Singh, Supriya and Anuja Cabraal, 2010, 'Indian Student Migrants in Australia: Issues of Community Sustainability', *People and Place,* vol. 18, no. 1, pp. 19-30.

Sinha, Mrinalini, 1996, *Colonial Masculinity: The 'Manly Englishman' and the 'Effiminate Bengali' in the Late Nineteenth Century*, Manchester: Manchester University Press.

Sivaramamurti, C., 1971, *The Chola Temples*, Delhi: Archaeological Survey of India.

Śla çzka, Anna A., 2007, *Temple Consecration Rituals in Ancient India: Text and Archaeology*, Leiden: E.J. Brill.

Smart, Ninian, 1987, 'The Importance of Diasporas', in S. Shaked, D. Shulman and G.G. Stroumsa (eds.) *Gilgut*, Leiden: E.J. Brill, pp. 288-97.

———, 1989, *The World's Religions*, Cambridge: Cambridge University Press.

Smith, A.D., 1998, *Nationalism and Modernism: A Critical Survey of Recent Theories of Nations and Nationalism*, London: Routledge.

———, 1978, *The Smith Agama Collection: Sanskrit Books and Manuscripts Relating to Pancharatra Studies, a Descriptive Catalogue*, Foreign and Comparative Studies, South Asia Special Publication 2, Syracuse N.Y.: Syracuse University.

Smith, H. Daniel, 1981, 'Vahanas in the Cultic Art of South Indian in Temples', in *Proceedings of the Seminar on 'Temple Art & Architecture' Held in March 1980*, Bombay: Ananthacharya Indological Research Institute.

Smith, Michael P., 2005, 'Transnational Urbanism Revisited', *Journal of Ethnic and Migration Studies*, vol. 31, no. 2, pp. 235-44.

Snow, Jennifer, 2004, 'The Civilization of White Men: The Race of the Hindu in United States v. Bhagat Singh Thind', in *Race, Nation, and Religion in the Americas*, ed. H. Goldschmidt and E. McAlister, Oxford and New York: Oxford University Press, pp. 259-80.

Spinks, Harriet, 2010, 'Background Note: Australia's Migration Program', Department of Parliamentary Services, 8 October.

Spivak, Gayatri Chakravorty, 1988, 'Subaltern Studies: Deconstructing Historiography' in R. Guha and G.C. Spivak (eds.) *Selected Subaltern Studies*, New Delhi: Oxford University Press.

———, 1993, *Outside in the Teaching Machine*, New York; Routledge Classics.

———, 1999, *A Critique of Postcolonial Reason Toward a History of the Vanishing Present*, Cambridge, MA: Harvard University Press.

———, 2000, 'Diasporas Old and New: Women in the Transnational World', *Textual Practice*, vol. 10, no. 2, pp. 245-69.

Spores, John C., 1988, *Running Amok: An Historical Inquiry*, Athens, Ohio: Ohio Center for International Studies, Center for Southeast Asian Studies.

Spuler, Michelle, 2002, *Developments in Australian Buddhism: Facets of the Diamond*, Critical Studies in Buddhism 22, London: RoutledgeCurzon.

Sri Guru Granth Sahib (SGGS) (Sikh Holy Scripture, also called *Adi Granth, Granth Sahib*).

Srinivas, Mysore N., 1968, *Social Change in Modern India*, Berkeley: University of California Press.

Stratton, Jon, 1998, *Race Daze*, Annandale, NSW: Pluto Press.

Streets, Heather, 2004, *Martial Races: The Military, Race and Masculinity in British Imperial Culture, 1857–1914*, Manchester: Manchester University Press.

Srivastava, Sanjay, 1996, 'Postcoloniality, National Identity, Globalisation and the Simulcra of the Real', *The Australian Journal of Anthropology* (Special Issue 7, The National Artifice), vol. 7, no. 2, pp. 166-90.

Stevens, Christine, 1989, *Tin Mosques and Ghantowns: A History of Afghan Camel Drivers in Australia*, Melbourne: Oxford University Press.

Stevenson, H.W. and J.W. Stigler, 1992, *The Learning Cap: Why our Schools Are Failing and what We Can Learn from Japanese and Chinese Education*, New York: Summit Books.

Symons-Brown, Bonny, 2009, *Fed: International Students Need Protection: Educators, Students*, retrieved 3 October 2010, Australian Associated Press General News Pty Ltd.

Tambiah, Stanley, 2000, 'Transnational Movements, Diaspora, and Multiple Modernities', *Daedalus, Journal of the American Academy of Arts and Sciences*, 'Multiple Modernities' Issue, Winter 2000, pp. 163-98.

Tang, K.C.C., 1993, 'Spontaneous Collaborative Learning: A New Dimension in Student Learning Experience?', *Higher Education Research and Development*, vol. 12, no. 2, pp. 115-30.

Taylor, Charles, 2007, *The Secular Age*, Cambridge: Harvard University Press.

Taylor, Charles, A.K. Appiah, J. Habermas, S.C. Rockefeller, M. Walzer and S. Wolf, 1994, 'The Politics of Recognition', in Amy Gutmann (ed.) *Multiculturalism: Examining the Politics of Recognition*, Princeton, NJ: Princeton University Press.

Thapar, Romila, 1966, *A History of India*, vol. 1, Harmondsworth, UK: Penguin.

The Economist, 1998, 'India's New Government: Who's Afraid of the BJP?', 4 April, pp. 32-36.

Tinker, Hugh, 1977, *The Banyan Tree: Overseas Emigrants from India, Pakistan and Bangladesh*, Oxford: Oxford University Press.

Tölölyan, Khachig, 1991, 'The Nation-State and Its Other: In Lieu of a Preface', *Diaspora*, vol. 1, no. 1, pp. 3-7.

Tovey, J., A. Dhillon, J. Pearlman, and E. Jensen, 2009, 'Universities Release Plan for Student Security', *The Sydney Morning Herald*, 11 July, retrieved 3 October 2010, < http://www.smh.com.au/world/universities-release-plan-for-student-security-20090610-c3p2.html.

Tully, M. and S. Jacob, 1985, *Amritsar: Mrs Gandhi's Last Battle*, London: J. Cape.

Vasta, Ellie, 1991, 'Gender, Class and Ethnic Relations: The Domestic and Work Experiences of Italian Migrant Women in Australia', in G. Bottomley, M.M. de Lepervanche and J. Martin (eds.) *Intersexions: Gender, Class, Culture, Ethnicity*, Sydney: Allen & Unwin.

———, 1996, 'Dialectics of Domination: Racism and Multiculturalism', in Ellie Vasta and Stephen Castles (eds.) *The Teeth Are Smiling: The Persistence of Racism in Multicultural Australia*, St Leonards, Sydney: Allen & Unwin.

Vertovec, Steven, 1995, 'Hindus in Trinidad and Britain: Ethnic Religion, Reification, and the Politics of Public Space', in Peter van der Veer (ed.) *Nation and Migration: The Politics of Space in the South Asian Diaspora*, Philadelphia: University of Pennsylvania Press.

———, 2000, *The Hindu Diaspora Comparative Patterns*, London and New York: Routledge.

———, 2004, 'Religion and Diaspora', in Peter Antes, Armin W. Geertz, Randi R. Warne (eds.) *New Approaches to the Study of Religion: Regional, Critical, and Historical Approaches (Religion and Reason)*, Berlin, New York: Walter de Gruyter, pp. 275-303.

———, 2009, *Transnationalism*, New York: Routledge.

Voigt-Graf, Carmen, 1997, 'Migrant Experiences in Australia: Three Groups of Indians Compared', *Population Geography*, vol. 19, nos. 1 & 2, December, pp. 1-12.

———, 2000, 'Indians at Home in Australia: A Highly Diverse Transnational Community', Delhi: International Conference on Culture and Economy in the Indian Diaspora, 8-10 April (typescript).

———, 2001, 'Transnational Lives in Woolgoolga, Sydney and Punjab', in R. Bhatti and V. Dusenbery (eds.) *A Punjabi Sikh Community in Australia — from Indian Sojourners to Australian Citizens: Centenary of Federation Project*, Woolgoolga: Woolgoolga Neighbourhood Centre.

———, 2002, *The Construction of Transnational Spaces: Travelling between India, Fiji and Australia*, unpublished Ph.D. thesis, University of Sydney, Sydney.

———, 2003, 'Indians at Home in the Antipodes: Migrating with Ph.D.s, bytes or Kava in Their Bags', in B. Parekh, G. Singh and S. Vertovec (eds.) *Culture and Economy in the Indian Diaspora*, London and New York: Routledge, pp. 142-64.

———, 2004, 'Towards a Geography of Transnational Spaces: Indian Transnational Communities in Australia', *Global Networks*, vol. 4, no. 1, pp. 25-49.

———, 2008, 'Transnationalism and the Indo-Fijian Diaspora: The Relationship of Indo-Fijians and Its People', *Journal of Intercultural Studies*, vol. 29, no. 1 (Special Issue on Indian Diaspora in Transnational Contexts).

Volet, S. and J.P.P. Kee, 1993, 'Studying in Singapore–Studying in Australia: A Student Perspective', Occasional Paper No. 1, Perth, Australia: Murdoch University Teaching Excellence Committee.

Wade, M. and H. Gilmore, 2009, 'India is Losing Interest in our Universities, say Agents', *The Sydney Morning Herald*, 31 July, retrieved 3 October 2010, <http://www.smh.com.au/national/india-is-losing-interest-in-our-universities-say-agents-20090730-e32w.html>.

Waghorne, Joanne Punzo, 2004, *Diaspora of the Gods: Modern Hindu Temples in an Urban Middle-Class World*, Oxford and New York: Oxford University Press.

Walker, Allan, 1955, *Plan for a Christian Australia*, Melbourne: Methodist Church of Australia.

Walker, David, 1999, *Anxious Nation: Australia and the Rise of Asia, 1850–1939*, St Lucia: Queensland University Press.

Wallerstein, I., 1974a, *The Modern World System*, New York: Academic Press.

———, 1974b, 'The Rise and Future Demise of the World Capitalist System: Concepts for Comparative Analysis', *Comparative Studies in Society and History*, vol. 16, no. 4, pp. 387-415.

Ward, C., 2001, '*The Impact of International Students on Domestic Students and Host Institutions*', Report prepared for the New Zealand Ministry of Education, retrieved on 16 March; http://www.vuw.ac.nz/cacr/reports/docs/Ward-2001.pdf.

Warner, Stephen R., 1998, 'Religion and Migration in the United States', in *Social Compass, International Society for the Sociology of Religion*, vol. 45, no. 1, pp. 123-34.

Watkins, D., 1996, 'Hong Kong Secondary School Learners: A Developmental Perspective', in D. Watkins and J. Biggs (eds.) *The Chinese Learner: Cultural Psychological and Contextual Influences*, Centre for Comparative Research in Education, Hong Kong; Camberwell, Victoria: Australian Council for Educational Research, pp. 107-19.

Watson, J., 1997, 'A Peer Support Scheme in Quantitative Methods', paper presented at Biennial Conference, Professional Development Centre, University of New South Wales, Kensington, NSW, 20 November.

Weber, Max, 1946, 'Religious Rejections of the World and their Directions', in H.H. Gerth and C. Wright Mills, *From Max Weber: Essays in Sociology*, New York: Oxford University Press, Essay originally published in 1915.

Westrip, Joyce and Peggy Holroyde, 2010, *Colonial Cousins: A Surprising History of Connections Between India and Australia*, Adelaide: Wakefield Press.

Willard, Myra, 1967, *History of the White Australia Policy to 1920*, Melbourne: Melbourne University Press; 2nd edn., London: Frank Cass and Company.

Williams, Sir Raymond B., 1989, 'Costs and Benefits', in Sir B. Williams (ed.) *Overseas Students in Australia: Policy and Practice*, Canberra, Australia: International Development Program of Australian Universities and Colleges.

———, (ed.), 1992, *A Sacred Thread: Modern Transmission of Hindu Traditions in India and Abroad*, Chambersburg, PA: Anima Publications (repr. 1996, Columbia University Press, New York).

———, 1998, 'Training Religious Specialists for a Transnational Hinduism: A

Swaminarayan Sadhu Training Center', *Journal of the American Academy of Religion* **66**(4): 841-62.

———, 2004, *South Asian Religions and Immigration*, Hampshire and Burlington: Ashgate Publishing Ltd.

———, 2007, "Hindu Family in America", in *American Religions and the Family: How Faith Traditions Cope with Modernization and Democracy*, ed. D.S. Browning and D.A. Clairmont, New York: Columbia University Press, pp. 197-210.

Willis, Michael D., 2009, *The Archaeology of Hindu Ritual: Temples and the Establishment of the Gods*, Cambridge: Cambridge University Press.

Wood, Sally Percival, 2011, '"So, Where the Bloody Hell Are We?": The Search for Substance in Australia–India Relations', The Fearless Nadia Occasional Papers on India–Australia Relations, Winter, vol. 1, Melbourne: Australia–India Institute.

Yarwood, A.T., 1968, *Attitudes to Non-European Immigration Problems in Australian History*, Melbourne: Cassell, 1968.

Yuval-Davis, Nira and Anthias Floya (eds.), 1989, *Women-Nation-State*, London: Macmillan.

Zolberg, A.R., A. Suhrke and S. Aguayo, 1989, *Escape from Violence: Conflict and the Refugee Crisis in the Developing World*, New York: Oxford University Press.

Reports and Documents

7.30 Report, 2009, TV Program – 'Australia's International Education System under Review', Australian Broadcasting Corporation, 13 August.

Australian Bureau of Statistics (ABS), 1996, *Census of Population and Housing, Data for Indo-Fijians, Kannada-speakers and Punjabi-speakers*, Canberra: ABS.

———, 1996, *Census of Population and Housing*.

———, 2001, *Census of Population and Housing*. Available online at http://www.abs.gov.au/websitedbs/D3310114.nsf/home/Census+data

———, 2007, *2006 Census of Population and Housing. Melbourne (Statistical Division) – Victoria*, Commonwealth of Australia.

———, September 2009, *Australian Social Trends: Expanding Links with China and India*. (http://www.ausstats.abs.gov.au/ausstats/subscriber.nsf/LookupAttach/4102.0Publication24.09.092/$File/41020_ChinaIndia.pdf) [accessed on 16 September 2010]

———, 2009a, *A Picture of the Nation: The Statistician's Report on the 2006 Census*, ACT: Commonwealth of Australia.

Australian Government, Department of Immigration and Citizenship, 2009, *Report on Migration Program 2008-09. Financial year to 30 June 2009.* Retrieved on 17 September 2009 from http://www.immi.gov.au/media/statistics/pdf/report-on-migration-program-2008-09.pdf

Australian Government Education International, 2010, *International Student Data,* retrieved on 4 June 2010, <http://www.aei.gov.au/AEI/MIP/Statistics/StudentEnrolmentAndVisaStatistics/Default.htm>.

Australian Education International (AEI) Network, 2002, *Year 2002 Market Indicator Data,* retrieved on 4 June 2010, <http://www.aei.gov.au/AEI/MIP/Statistics/StudentEnrolmentAndVisaStatistics/2002/2002_Annual_Table_1_pdf.pdf>.

———, 2009, *2009 Annual International Student Statistics,* retrieved on 4 June 2010, <http://www.aei.gov.au/AEI/MIP/Statistics/StudentEnrolmentAndVisaStatistics/2009/2009_Annual.htm>.

Australia and India Trade from, 1788–1820 (Database) http://education.deakin.edu.au/try/ait/

Bureau of Immigration and Population Research Bulletin, 1993–2011.

BIMPR (Bureau of Immigration, Multiculturalism and Population Research), 1995, *Community Profiles, 1991 Census: India Born,* Canberra: AGPS

Census and Community Profiles, 1891-1991, 1996, 2001, 2006, 2011 Census, Bureau of Immigration, Multicultural and Population Research, Australian Government Publishing Service, Canberra.

1991 Census of Population and Housing, State Comparison Series Australian Bureau of Statistics Cat. No. 2731.0.

1991 Census Profile on Religion in Australia, Australian Bureau of Statistics Cat. No. 2510.0.

1996, 2001, 2006, 2011 Census Profile on Religion in Australia, Australian Bureau of Statistics.

1991 Census of India, State Profile.

Department of Education, Employment and Workplace Relations, 2010, Monthly Summary of International Student Enrolment Data, retrieved on 4 June 2010, http://www.aei.gov.au/AEI/MIP/Statistics/EnrolmentANDVisaStatistics/2010/2010Apr MonthlySummary pdf.pdf

DIAC (Department of Immigration and Citizenship), 2008, *The People of Australia. Statistics from 2006 Census,* ACT: Commonwealth of Australia (http://www.immi.gov.au/media/publications/research/_pdf/poa-2008.pdf) [accessed on 16 September 2010].

Indian Language, 2010, 'Indian Languages', retrieved on 4 June 2010, <http://encyclopedia.kids.net.au/page/in/Indian_language#Official_Languages> <http://encyclopedia.kids.net.au/page/in/Indian_language#Official_Languages>.

International Education and Development Services Program, 1995, *Curriculum Development for Internationalisation: OECD/CERI Study*, Department of Employment, Education and Training, Australia.

Other Significant Resources

Australian Broadcasting Commission (ABC) newsclips, Radio National, Radio Australia, ABC-TV.

PEW Research Center's Forum on Religion and Public Life, Global Religious Landscape, December 2012.

'South Asians in Australia: A Bibliography', South Asians in North America Collection, Bancroft Library, University of California, Berkeley (CA, USA); South/South East Asia Library, Doe Library, UC-Berkeley.

Special Broadcasting Service (SBS) Programs- http://apo.org.au/sites/default/files/AustraliasMigrationProgram.pdf [accessed on 7 December 2012], p. 11.

Srinivasa Shastri's Australian Visit, Australian National Library Archival Services.

http://www.iaasa.asn.au

http://uncommonlives.naa.gov/muslim-journeys/stories/cameleers-and-hawkers.aspx [accessed on 22 April 2011].

www.khalistan.com and www.khalistan.net

http://museumvictoria.com.au/collections/items/717941/notice-re-the-indian-hawker [accessed on 22 April 2011].

http://www.sbs.com.au/blog/119772/-Pooran-Singh-s-Ashes

www.sbs.com.au/punjabi (> photo galleries)

http://identities.asiaeducation.edu.au/resources/resource_page.html?resourceId=3030&pathwayId=0&showSectionId=1

http://www.hindustantimes.com/punjab/chandigarh/century-later-australia-to-acknowledge-sikh-generosity/article1-1211529.aspx Sikhchic.com

http://sikhchic.com/article-detail.php?id=4974&cat=12

http://www.lib.berkeley.edu/SSEAL/SouthAsia/gadarcol.html

Newspapers and Magazines

Adelaide Advertiser

Albany Advertiser

Australian News (1890s)

Australian Town and Country Journal

Barrier Miner (Broken Hill)

Barrier Truth (Broken Hill)

Brisbane Courier

Clarence and Richmond Examiner (NSW)

Hinduism Today

Hindustan Times

India Abroad

India West

Indian Link

Indian Voice

Literary topos 2013, 'Topos', retrieved on 2 July 2013, http://en.wikipedia.org/wiki/Literary_topos

Queanbeyan Age (NSW)

Queenslander

Sophia

The South Australian Register (Adelaide)

The Age (Melbourne)

The Argus

The Brisbane Courier

The Economist

The Guardian

The Illustrated Australian News

The Indian Weekly

The Inquirer, Perth

The Moreton Bay Courier

The New Statesman

The Sunday Times

The Sydney Morning Herald

Times of India

Traralgon Record (Victoria)

West Australian (Perth)

Archives

National Archives (National Library of Australia)

South Australian Gazette and Colonial Register (*SAGCR*)

State Records, South Australia

Tasmanian State Archives, Conduct Records

Victorian State Archives (La Trobe Library)

Community Publications

Bangla Samiti of Western Australia

Bhakti, Magazine of the Sri Mandir Society of Australia Inc. (Canberra-based)

Hindu Satsang Mandali of Victoria (Indo-Fijian)

Hindu Society of W.A. (Perth)

Hinduism Today (Global Hindu bi-monthly) from Hawaii.

Jagarani, Magazine of the Bengali Association of Western Australia

Newsletters of Federation of Indian Associations of Victoria (FIAV)

Panchavati, a newsletter of the Hindu Society of Victoria (Inc.)

Pittsburg Hindu Temple website and blog

Samachar, Newsletter of the Indian Society of Western Australia & Hindu Temple Assoc. of W.A.

Sanathana Sarathi Downunder (Sri Sathya Sai Organisation of Australia)

Saptagiri, a bi-monthly newsletter of Sri Venkateswara Temple Association, NSW; and also special occasion 'Souvenirs', archival material

Shanti, Newsletter of the Hindu Temple & Cultural Centre of ACT (Inc.)

The Hindu Foundation (Melbourne)

Turiya-Marga (Path of Consciousness), Newsletter of the Hindu Society of South Australia

Vakraduntha Vinagara Temple Association

Data Used in this Book

Evans, A., 2009, AuSSA_A_religiosity.sav (computer file), *The Australian Survey of Social Attitudes*, Australian Social Science Data Archives, Canberra: The Australian National University.

Source of the Wellbeing and Security Survey: This survey was conducted by Edith Cowan University, Deakin University, Anglicare (Sydney) and NCLS Research in 2002

Index